# Third Wave Feminism and Transgender

Feminism and transgender, as social factions or collective subjectivities, have historically evaded, vilified or negated each other's philosophy and subjectivities. In particular, separatist feminist theorists have portrayed the two 'sides' as consisting of mutually incompatible aims and subjectivities. These portrayals have worked to the detriment of both feminism and transgender.

*Third Wave Feminism and Transgender* considers what positive outcomes on society in general, and the law as it pertains to gender in particular, may emerge from the identification of and cooperation between third wave feminism and transgender. Challenging the 'internecine exclusion' between and within each faction, Davies shows that queer-inspired philosophical third wave feminism promises to be an inclusive social discourse providing a substantial challenge to mutual exclusion. Indeed, this book explores the span of maternal relations, including womanism, ethics of care and semiotic language and subsequently reveals how gender variant people can highlight the gendered operation of conventional ethics.

With a focus on Carol Gilligan and Julia Kristeva as key instigators of a philosophical third wave of feminism, this enlightening monograph will appeal to students and postdoctoral researchers interested in fields such as women's studies, transgender studies and gender law.

**Edward Burlton Davies** has undertaken research at Lancaster and Manchester Metropolitan Universities. His research interests focus on third wave feminism, womanism, gender variance and reconstruction of gender law.

# Routledge Advances in Feminist Studies and Intersectionality

*Routledge Advances in Feminist Studies and Intersectionality* is committed to the development of new feminist and pro-feminist perspectives on changing gender relations, with special attention to:

- Intersections between gender and power differentials based on age, class, dis/abilities, ethnicity, nationality, racialisation, sexuality, violence, and other social divisions.
- Intersections of societal dimensions and processes of continuity and change: culture, economy, generativity, polity, sexuality, science and technology;
- Embodiment: Intersections of discourse and materiality, and of sex and gender.
- Transdisciplinarity: intersections of humanities, social sciences, medical, technical and natural sciences.
- Intersections of different branches of feminist theorizing, including: historical materialist feminisms, postcolonial and anti-racist feminisms, radical feminisms, sexual difference feminisms, queer feminisms, cyber feminisms, post-human feminisms, critical studies on men and masculinities.
- A critical analysis of the travelling of ideas, theories and concepts.
- A politics of location, reflexivity and transnational contextualising that reflects the basis of the Series framed within European diversity and transnational power relations.

**Core editorial group**

Professor Jeff Hearn (managing editor; Örebro University, Sweden; Hanken School of Economics, Finland; University of Huddersfield, UK)
Dr Kathy Davis (Institute for History and Culture, Utrecht, The Netherlands)
Professor Anna G. Jónasdóttir (Örebro University, Sweden)
Professor Nina Lykke (managing editor; Linköping University, Sweden)
Professor Elżbieta H. Oleksy (University of Łódź, Poland)
Dr Andrea Petö (Central European University, Hungary)
Professor Ann Phoenix (Institute of Education, University of London, UK)
Professor Chandra Talpade Mohanty (Syracuse University, USA)

**Involving Men in Ending Violence against Women**
Development, Gender and VAW in Times of Conflict
*Joyce Wu*

**Third Wave Feminism and Transgender**
Strength through Diversity
*Edward Burlton Davies*

# Third Wave Feminism and Transgender
Strength through Diversity

**Edward Burlton Davies**

LONDON AND NEW YORK

First published 2018 by Routledge

2 Park Square, Milton Park, Abingdon, Oxfordshire OX14 4RN
52 Vanderbilt Avenue, New York, NY 10017

*Routledge is an imprint of the Taylor & Francis Group, an informa business*

First issued in paperback 2019

Copyright © 2018 Edward Burlton Davies

The right of Edward Burlton Davies to be identified as author of this work has been asserted by him in accordance with sections 77 and 78 of the Copyright, Designs and Patents Act 1988.

All rights reserved. No part of this book may be reprinted or reproduced or utilised in any form or by any electronic, mechanical, or other means, now known or hereafter invented, including photocopying and recording, or in any information storage or retrieval system, without permission in writing from the publishers.

Notice:
Product or corporate names may be trademarks or registered trademarks, and are used only for identification and explanation without intent to infringe.

*British Library Cataloguing in Publication Data*
A catalogue record for this book is available from the British Library

*Library of Congress Cataloging in Publication Data*
A catalog record has been requested for this book

ISBN: 978-1-138-09200-6 (hbk)
ISBN: 978-0-367-35509-8 (pbk)

Typeset in Times New Roman
by Taylor & Francis Books

**Valerie Dawes // Janette Keys Adamson Hamilton**

# Contents

1 Introduction: Potential for a transgender/third wave feminist coalition  1
2 Explaining trans lives: Silence and secrecy  19
3 The third wave: Career feminism or quiet revolution?  41
4 Legal review: The view from somewhere  67
5 Third wave philosophy: Dialogic negotiation  98
6 Identity essentialism to subjectivity-in-process: The whole trans person  132
7 Closed and static texts to open and evolving narratives: Articulation and openness  154
8 Exclusion to inclusion: Postdifference for 'Others'  181
9 Recommendations: Ghosts in the machine  207

*Appendix*  230
*Bibliography*  234
*Index*  252

# 1 Introduction
## Potential for a transgender/third wave feminist coalition

### 1.1 Investigating connections: potential for a coalition

This book addresses the problem of alienation between what might be called the factions of transgender and feminism by asking four key questions. First, the book asks whether these factions are inevitably mutually exclusive. Second, it asks if a quest for the root causes or 'aetiology' of gender variance could or should be pursued in order to explain any mutual exclusion. This is followed by a questioning of the usefulness of 'separatist' discourses pertaining to gender, discourses that are often constructed by sub-factions of transgender and feminism.

Discourses are conglomerations of ways of representing the world, influenced by a social theme, such as religion, the family, law or medicine. Separatist discourses exclude anyone from the discourse who doesn't fit into a preordained identity profile, a profile significantly maintained by the separatist discourse in question. 'Faction', in the context of this book, refers to the living embodiment of a smaller and organised discourse within the larger discourses of gender and feminism; specifically, the individuals and groups who put into play and embody the discourses of transgender and third wave feminism.

Discussion of the first three questions lead to answers to the fourth key question of whether there is potential for an inclusive trans and third wave feminist coalition that can escape from separatist discourses. These four key questions are discussed below.

*Question 1: Should we challenge internecine exclusion between transgender and feminism?*

'Internecine' (of or relating to conflict or struggle within a group) exclusion between and within factions and sub-factions of transgender and feminism needs to be challenged in order to assess any potential to turn negative reverse discourses into positive reconstructing discourses. Reverse discourses are taken to be a simple reversal of oppressive discourses that reverse the flow of oppressive power, for example an oppressive feminism may reverse the oppression of women to create oppression of men. Reconstructing discourses challenge reverse discourses without creating new oppressions as a result. The opportunity to reconstruct (what is for many) oppressive discourse, such as the discourse of heteronormativity, would come from the process of finding and exploiting chinks in its explanatory 'armour'.

Transgender and feminism might be described as movements, philosophies and/or collective identities or as all three coming together to form a faction or social discourse. Mutual hostility has occurred between the factions when the ideology of one is perceived as contrary to the interests of the other. This exclusion may operate because the factions are assumed by many to be only associated with certain sexual identities. For instance, feminist author Janice Raymond influentially argued that feminism belongs only to women,

> Women take on the self-definition of feminist and/or lesbian because that definition truly proceeds from not only the chromosomal fact of being born XX, but also from the whole history of what being born with those chromosomes means in this society.
>
> (1979:116)

Both Sheila Jeffreys (1997) and, later, Germaine Greer (2000) reinforced a divide between feminism and transgender when claiming that gender transition is a conservative gender-role reinforcing procedure, based upon bodily mutilation and, according to sociologist Sally Hines, '... *in 1997, Sheila Jeffreys offered explicit support for Raymond's position in her article "Transgender: A Lesbian Feminist Perspective," which refueled the feminist attack on transgender*' (Hines, 2005:60).

The editor of *Trans/Forming Feminisms*, Krista Scott-Dixon, described how responses in a 2001 Canadian feminist magazine article were hostile to the notion of trans people's involvement with feminism,

> Trans was positioned as something antithetical or irrelevant to or at least outside of feminism, and the notion that trans people could be feminists, feminists could be trans allies or that there could even be something called transfeminism has been poorly considered.
>
> (Scott-Dixon, 2006:23)

Hines also noted how, '*second wave feminism has been largely hostile to transgender practices*' (2005:57), perhaps referring to what we can now identify as a philosophically, rather than chronologically, based second wave of feminism as not all feminists who were active in the time of the second wave would have held this opinion and some contemporary feminists will hold this opinion.

Conversely, trans people have often displayed hostility to feminism. For instance, Monica, a participant from the author's online discussion site, the *Transstudy*, described all feminists as political fanatics who only criticise, and who will bend the truth to suit their own cause (Mar 18, 2005). She narrated a particular dislike for trans-unfriendly feminists,

> ... There is only one capacity in which I should wish to serve transphobic feminists, namely as their taxidermist. ... Nothing would give me more satisfaction than to leave the lot of them tastefully arranged in a glass case, all stuffed and mounted.
> (Monica Mar 9, 2006, in <Transpregnancy>)[1]

Hostility to feminism from trans people and their supporters can derive from conflating all feminisms with feminism. For instance, in the following quote Tina Vasquez seems to be referring to separatist feminism, rather than all feminism,

> It has been said that feminism has failed the transgender community. It's hard to disagree. Trans women have been weathering a storm of hate and abuse in the name of feminism for decades now and for the most part, cisgender feminists have failed to speak out about it or push against it.
> (20 May 2016)

However, she later states that, '*our feminism loves and supports trans women and that we will fight against transphobia*', indicating her recognition of trans-friendly feminisms.

Hines noted common feelings of exclusion post-transition trans men and women gained from philosophical second wave feminists, while those who may be identified as philosophically third wave feminists, with a notable queer influence, were generally perceived as more inclusive, '*In particular, both [trans men and women] draw on experiences of rejection from second wave feminism, while more positive stories are told about relationships with contemporary feminism as informed by queer ideology*' (Hines, 2005:75)

Exclusion has also occurred between sub-factions within each faction, hindering the possibility of forming a cohesive subjectivity ('subjectivity' is taken by the author to mean identity as an evolving phenomenon) based movement. For instance, '*Queer theorists have shown how traditional lesbian and gay theory and politics have been (and often remain) exclusive towards those whose identities fall outside of that which is deemed to be "correct" or "fitting" ...*' (Hines, 2005:61),

> They [lesbian and gay friends] laughingly talked about my dating Alexie and asked me if I knew that she was "really a man" who was clearly confused because she took hormones, lived as a woman ... . I lost my words and felt like the freakish object they were making her out to be.
> (Johnson, 2013:55)

This kind of in-group internecine exclusion is examined in Chapter 6, in relation to the situation of transitioning people on one hand and what some transitioning people have labelled as 'transgenderists' on the other. Such in-group exclusion, this time within the group known as 'women', also applied heavily in the lives of black women in the USA and UK who felt excluded from what they saw as the elitist discourse of second wave feminism in the 1960s and 70s.

Internecine exclusion may severely hinder the development of transgender and feminism since excluding large portions of the population from either faction will profoundly limit their potential for social change. Both transgender and third wave feminism have been challenged as not being real movements or factions just as feminists and trans people have often been challenged as not being real women and men, sometimes, as we have seen in the above quotations, by those hailing from the other faction. The author seeks to present the realness of each faction partly by challenging the 'realness' of discourses such as separatist feminism and heteronormativity.

## *Question 2: Should we just accept gendered subjectivites rather than s earch for their aetiology?*

The author presents the factions and related subjectivities of transgender and third wave feminism as 'real' because they exist as evolving phenomena, rather than being identifiable by fixed definitions. The author questions the quest for the aetiology or precise definition of the essence of gender and, following (those construed by the author to be) third wave philosophers such as Judith Butler, Carol Gilligan, Julia Kristeva, Susan Stryker, Sandy Stone and Stephen Whittle, proposes that it is a more fruitful and positive goal to concentrate on ways of accepting gender variance, rather than defining it.

Jennifer Harding stated that the kind of gender variance known as transsexualism was pathologised by the imposed voice of many medical and psycho-analytical practitioners in the early twentieth century and was then described in the late twentieth century as 'Gender Dysphoria' at the expense of encouraging self-representations from trans people themselves (1998). In the 1950s to 1970s, treatment for gender transitioning trans people moved from the area of intersex medicine to being a sub-interest of psychiatry and many trans people accepted their classification into a mental health condition. This enabled access to hormonal treatment and surgery via the consent of psychiatrists and general practitioners, but also came about because some psychiatrists thought this classification to be true. The label 'transsexualism', as a mental health disorder, first applied in the DSM III (1980), was later changed to 'Gender Identity Disorder' in DSM IV[2] (1994). Both gave the impression of trans subjectivity as a failing of identity caused by the individual's psychological being, or as a phenomenon induced by family upbringing. All these imposed definitions led to denied choice for trans people wishing to articulate what they themselves felt about their gendered being.

The personal life story provided by transsexual patients to their transition specialists, adapted to help ensure smooth access to medical reassignment as noted by Sandy Stone, became informally known as the 'plausible personal history', informed by 'The Obligatory Transsexual File' (1991). This was a life story informed by a carefully collected scrapbook of article clippings by each transitioning person, often collected over a lifetime of personal gendered behaviour. As Stone discovered, reassignment specialists eventually realised that potential gender transitioners matched criteria to be accepted for medical transition because they were constructing such files and were reading sexologist Harry Benjamin's (1966) definitional criteria for 'transsexualism' in order to construct an acceptable story of gender dysphoria.

Developed narratives of gender variance emerging since the 1990s encouraged people to reinterpret trans subjectivity as healthy and functional, rather than pathological. This mode of narrative seems to have been notably influenced by Michel Foucault who, in the 1970s, proposed that personal subjectivity, including sexual subjectivity, was negotiated in reciprocal relationships of power rather than being an essential element of the subject (1998[1978]), an idea later backed up a growing number of researchers such as Tracey Lee (2001). Lee suggested that, as at 2001, the medical profession retained the sway of power in relationships with transitioning people but also suggested that trans men had found chinks in the power relationship in which they could provide their own input. Foucault argued that power is never absolute since there is always the potential for its critics or those it oppresses to find and exploit its Achilles heel or chinks in its discourse armour (Prado, 2000). In this way, new or newly revealed subjectivities can surface from social suppression once a concerted move is made to narrate and negotiate them into discourse. Even those silenced by oppressive discourse can locate and exploit these chinks, '...*silencing is rarely complete as individuals and groups find creative ways to expose unequal power relations and unjust social arrangements*' (Yep and Shimanoff, 2013:140).

Similarly to Foucault, Judith Butler theorised that social and self-definitions of sexual subjectivity could lead to actual subjectivity. Butler's argument was a challenge to conventional accounts of sexual subjectivity which maintained that this subjectivity is entirely located and developed within the individual, and, that sex, gender and sexuality all cause each other in a biologically and developmentally fixed manner,

> ... "the body" is itself a construction ... Bodies cannot be said to have a signifiable existence prior to the mark of their gender ... Some feminist theorists claim that gender is "a relation," indeed a set of relations, and not an individual attribute.
> (Butler, 1999[1990]:13)

Butler's theory, and other social constructionist accounts of gender formation, can be used as a challenge to images of gendered aetiology that have been overtly and covertly provided by medical and legal discourses over the last few centuries.

A contribution by *Transstudy* participant Clarette follows Butler's theory by suggesting that people actually follow gendered scripts, meaning socially shared accounts of the essence of gender, in order to construct what is usually taken to be biologically given gender. However, Clarette thought that these scripts are not easily identifiable,

> My point is more that scripts have not been immediately available even for those who do not wish to be known as trans people. Of course, large aspects of their developing scripts may be rather less available to those who steer clear of established social scripts, for whatever reason, but that should not be regarded as indicating that it is somehow easy to just adopt "the other script" in the course of transitioning – or following transition.
> (Clarette Jun 17th, 2006, in <The Paper>)

In this quote, Clarette suggests that the process of changing one's own gendered script is not easy but she acknowledges the existence of these scripts and the fact that they may be subverted through chinks in the armour of discourse. In Chapter 8 thought is given to how scripts that produce essentialised gendered identities may be circumnavigated by those who do not fit into conventional gendered discourse.

In 1967, Harold Garfinkel discovered that those who contravene taken-for-granted social behaviour and appearance, given in social scripts, can reveal how social customs guide and shape our lives. These customs are otherwise socially invisible because of their apparent normality and 'common sense' nature. Other social scientists followed Garfinkel's lead in order to *'uncover the unwritten rules by which all social actors guide their lives'* (Namaste, 1996: 24). Ki Namaste described how social scientists, influenced by the Birmingham Centre for Cultural Studies, for instance in the work of Stuart Hall, investigated relationships between lived experience and representation to show more fully how subjectivity is socially constructed from real-life interaction (1996).

In addressing a particular instance of the social construction of sexual subjectivity, Namaste criticised Butler's earlier work for providing interpretations of trans subjectivity and society not related to the actual lived conditions of trans people's lives (Butler later provided much support for trans subjectivity in her book *Undoing Gender*). Namaste argued that Butler overlooked the context of gender drag performance in favour of imposing her own theoretical definitions of how drag performativity stood as a challenge to gender stereotyping. Namaste also criticised Marjorie Garber for reading trans lives at an academic distance (1996). For instance, Garber's interpretation of 'transvestite' as merely a metaphor for crisis of gender category shows how 'transvestite' is not discussed as a real-life subjectivity. In this way, Namaste and other progressive gender theorists have highlighted a need for open and evolving discourse that includes accounts from the social subjectivities in question.

Contrasting with humanities-based queer theory and feminist research that has philosophised at a distance from trans lives, the disciplines of transgender theory and third wave feminist theory have often drawn from narrative produced by a range of subjectivities in order to reveal how personal and cultural constructions of subjectivity are negotiated across gender, ethnic and class lines. For instance, Chilla Bulbeck revealed how these constructions form differently in other cultures through kin connections rather than via the nuclear family (1998).[3] Development of such negotiated constructions was boosted by the creation of forums for self-expression for gender variant people to discuss their ideas of subjectivity, and by feminist consciousness-raising groups in the second wave. In the case of trans people using the internet since the 1980s, these developments have been characterised by Stephen Whittle as '*The Trans-Cyberian Mail Way*' (1998). While the individual's own body will always affect an individual's perceptions of themselves and others, Whittle claimed that people could avoid this influence to some extent by using online forums to discuss their perceptions of gendered essence. People's feelings of gender variance often have to be concealed in non-online life. The strategic concealing and revealing of their inner gendered essence, often to protect themselves and others from abuse, regularly forms gender variant people into expert gender performers and negotiators. This performing and negotiating has now been used to reveal and then challenge rigid portrayals of gender in social discourses such as medicine and law.

A growing number of texts, including contributions to anthologies, written by gender variant people since the 1970s have been autobiographies. This move towards 'narrative visibility' is what Jennifer Harding (1998:33–34) and other gender theorists advocated as a requirement for the establishment of subjectivity politics, or politics showing identity as a process, providing the space for personal reinterpretation of gendered existence. In this way, subjectivity politics in the industrial West has become a means for oppressed groups such as people of colour, women, gay people and then trans people, to have subjectivity, and subjectivity oppression, recognised. However, a side effect occurred for trans people from the 1980s onwards, when oppressed people were pigeon-holed into identity because of its very visibility. Nevertheless, subjectivity politics paved the way for oppressed people's recognition in discourses of medicine, law and, perhaps most crucially, in social life.

All the above examples of gender variant people and theorists of gender variance providing insights into the essence of gender challenge the acceptance of definitions of gendered aetiology provided by researchers distanced from their research subjects. The value of accepting narratives of gender from gender variant people, rather than imposed aetiologies, is investigated in Chapters 6 to 8.

## *Question 3: Should we reveal separatist discourses?*

The third research question involved the quest to determine whether transgender or feminism are or were separatist discourses, or whether it is the case that certain kinds of transgender and feminism are or have been separatist, and the importance of revealing any such exclusionary discourse. Separatism is a type of discourse claiming that only those having clearly defined identities can be a part of the discourse in question. Separatist discourses may be found in many different cultural and social locations, and may feature in law, medicine, transgender or feminism.

Trans people's move towards narrative visibility seemed to find support from philosophical third wave feminism's apparent ethos of inclusion for various social standpoints. This ethos of inclusion was notably inspired by the efforts of women of colours to have their experiences and lives acknowledged by second wave feminists. As bell hooks (small initials) noted, feminist waves one and two were/are significantly focussed on women forming identity based feminist groups to focus on single functional issues of (apparently) common oppression (1984). [H]ooks suggested that 'solidarity' replace this 'support' since for her solidarity meant progress through radically critical, but non-competitive, engagement with a panorama of feminist issues and feminist-friendly subjectivities rather than being a kind of victim support only for those perceived to be proper feminist subjects (63, 64).[4] Backing up this sentiment is a statement on 'qwe'reness' by Julia Johnson whose take on queerness is, '*a reflexive practice of solidarity built on radically intersectional relations that address our distinctions and separations as a basis for seeking commonality*' (2013:52), envisioning strength through diversity.

As described above, and unlike an inclusive third wave ethos or solidarity, some feminist commentary has been openly exclusionary towards trans subjectivities and transgender philosophy. For instance, in the 1970s Janice Raymond claimed that 'transsexuals' colluded with medical experts to produce accounts of 'sex changing' that bolstered the patriarchal gender divide by confusing biological sex with cultural portrayals of gender,

> "The Transsexual Empire" is ultimately a medical empire, based on a patriarchal medical model. This medical model has provided a "sacred canopy" of legitimations for transsexual treatment and surgery. In the name of therapy, it has medicalised moral and social questions of sex-role oppression, thereby erasing their deepest meaning.
> 
> (1979:119)

> ... it might seem that what men really envy is women's biological ability to procreate. Transsexuals illustrate one way in which men do this, by acquiring the artefacts of female biology. Even though they cannot give birth, they acquire the organs that are representative of this female power.
> 
> (107)

However, Raymond's theory didn't thoroughly investigate trans people's motives for working in conjunction with medical experts to produce scripts of transitioning subjectivity, described by Sandy Stone as the 'The Obligatory

Transsexual File' (1991). Raymond accused male-to-female trans people of touring the 'Otherness'[5] of womanhood since she believed that they did not give up their masculinist privilege when living as a woman. With a small initial letter 'other' simply means 'different'. Feminists, such as Simone de Beauvoir and bell hooks, adopted 'Other' with a capital 'O' to indicate oppressed subjectivities that serve merely to emphasise an advantaged subjectivity's apparent superiority (de Beauvoir, 1949). A classic example of oppressed Other is the gender of 'woman', which has served to emphasise the apparently superior Subject gender of 'man'.

As well as being 'Othered' by men, Raymond theorised that women would also be the 'Others' of male-to-female trans people when they infiltrated all levels of women's society in order to obtain dominant positions, like cuckoo chicks being placed in nests (1979:104). Ironically, because of its anti-trans stance, Raymond's *Transsexual Empire* inspired many trans people to initiate the process of writing themselves into theory and practice (Stryker and Whittle, 2006:131). Raymond did not accept that there is scope for people to find chinks in the armour of gender-based socialisation. She claimed that everyone, including intersexed people, is soon brought into one or other of the gender folds and cannot escape the effects of their gender-based rearing (1979).

A number of trans philosophers such as Carol Riddell, Sandy Stone, Gordene Mackenzie, Judith Halberstam, Jacob Hale, Susan Stryker, Kate Bornstein and Stephen Whittle seem to have contradicted the dualistic operation of conventional gender-based rearing by, consciously or unconsciously, espousing or supporting a third wave philosophy of inclusivity towards varied gender subjectivities. They did so, and do so, by providing living embodiment of, cerebral passion for and activism in the name of respect and inclusion for all gendered subjectivities.

A critical reading of trans subjectivity was provided by Bernice Hausman, but one that was more constructive for the transgender cause than Raymond's. When reviewing transgender autobiographies of the 1930s to early 1980s, Hausman noticed the influence of medical models, and heteronormative discourses, of trans subjectivity, '*What I find latent in these texts is not the possibility of an "authentic" account of the transsexual, nor a particularly subversive story about sexuality, but the idea of the transsexual subject as an engineered subject*' (Hausman, 1995:147).

Hausman's theory concurred with Sandy Stone's 'Posttranssexual Manifesto' by suggesting that these narratives were largely guided by a medical model of heteronormative reassignment (1995:143). Stone described how trans people would reinforce the model by colluding with physicians,

> ... candidates for surgery were evaluated on the basis of their performance in the gender of choice. The criteria constituted a fully acculturated, consensual definition of gender, and at the site of their enactment we can locate an actual instance of the apparatus of production of gender.
>
> (Stone, 1991:291)

10  *Introduction*

Hausman saw this model of transition as a closure of discussion, relegating subversive readings of transgender to the margins of gender discourse. This may be seen as the revealing of a medical separatist discourse, where only those who fit into the heteronormative script will be accepted for transition treatments. Like Stone, Hausman wondered whether there were more valid transgender narratives to be found than the medical transition-friendly personal accounts and formal texts.

Other feminists ventured interpretations of trans subjectivity, but again usually at an empirical distance from trans people themselves, thereby risking the production of, or support for, separatist accounts. For instance, according to feminist academic Sarah Ahmed (1998:106, 107), the transvestite's use of items such as feminine clothes, makeup and games, are more likely to promote a conservative gender role than to challenge gender stereotyping. Ahmed felt able to say this despite (several years earlier) Annie Woodhouse (1989) and Marjorie Garber (1997[1992]) having argued that, although transvestism displays stereotyped gender signs, it can also be construed as a disruption of gender referents because of its transgendering essence. Woodhouse experienced a considerable advantage over many humanities-based feminists and queer theorists in that she was actively researching and socialising with a group of transvestites for over a year.

Identifying philosophy that bolsters social separatism and that which challenges it, such as that described above, became essential to the research project that led to this book, in order to reveal barriers to a feminist/transgender alliance.

### *Question 4: Should we assess the potential for a transgender/third wave feminist coalition?*

Following on from the first three research questions, the author considers what positive outcomes on society and the law may emerge from cooperation between the factions of transgender and third wave feminism. Ethics of care, as described later in this section and which the author found to be theoretically connectable to both factions, showed potential to challenge the 'Othering' that can result from separatist discourse by identifying similarities rather than essentialised differences between the factions. Essentialised differences deriving from imposed aetiologies can be revealed by examining the historical social construction of gendered subjectivities.

As argued in the discussion of question 3, accounts that essentialise or provide fixed perspectives of gendered difference and those written at a subjective distance from real lives, need to be challenged. This challenge can come in the form of interpretations of sexual subjectivity emerging from a philosophical third wave feminist perspective, following on from philosophically queer and third wave insights into gender construction provided by inclusive theorists such as Foucault, Butler, Kristeva and Gilligan. These insights now include gender interpretations from (for instance) Anna Marie Cox et al.

(1997), Jeannine Delombard (1995), Emi Koyama (2003), Andrew Shail (2004), Alison Stone (2004) and Greg Tate (1995).

In challenging feminist essentialisation of womanly identity, Emi Koyama claimed that there are '... *as many ways of being a woman as there are women ...*' (2003), rallying against the idea of feminists as a kind of reverse Stepford Wives, all having to follow the same separatist agenda and code of appearance. Koyama mentioned that the trans woman's experience of 'Othering' gave her the potential for empathy with other women subtly excluded from the category 'woman' (249). This is particularly pertinent to discourses of femininity, society and law that exclude, and therefore cast as different,[6] people from the category 'woman', for instance feminists, lesbians, financially poor women, sex workers, trans women and 'third world' women.

In order to avoid the problem of essentialising womanhood, feminist philosopher Alison Stone conceived of women as a 'genealogy', adapting a concept generated by Foucault (1991 [1971]) to the situation of women, and mentioning that, '... *all cultural constructions of femininity re-interpret pre-existing constructions and thereby compose a history of overlapping chains of interpretation, within which all women are situated*' (2004).

This statement hints at the way language within discourse moulds gender representations over time. Genealogy is defined by shared experience rather than shared identity, and derives from experiences of subjectivity in the past while moulding itself from these experiences in the present. Third wave feminist theorists characteristically perceive identity as 'subjectivity' or identity-in-process, in the sense of genealogy. They understand that subjectivities are nothing if not paradoxical and contradictory as evidenced by changes in definitions of subjectivity over time and between cultures. Nevertheless, these theorists typically consider that subjectivities are real at any one point in time and that this has real consequences for the way they are received by wider society, and that these consequences necessitate the resource of subjectivity-based politics as a way of protecting by identifying both the subjectivities and the oppressions.

Feminists' and trans people's interactions with the law have often been problematic because of essentialised notions of who is properly a man or a woman, and because of the various rights and duties that are assumed to accompany each gender. These interactions have also characteristically taken considerable time to bear fruit, '... *law is notoriously slow to make change and is known to be well behind social change in general*' (Holmes, 2006:112).

Ethics of care have been applied by gender variant people (including feminists and trans people) wishing to challenge heteronormative law in order to show how natal (those born in the body of) females and males can have gender that contradicts what is expected from their original appearance, but that this is not detrimental to society. That the character of both transitioning and gender variant subjectivities has been given consideration in these challenges is supported by Namaste's claim that, '*Once we acknowledge the energies transsexuals have invested in repealing legislation which enforces a compulsory sex/gender system, it is impossible to reduce transsexual identities to those which enact an "uncritical miming of the hegemonic"'* (Namaste, 1996:189).

Ethics of care contrast with traditional Western industrial ethical operation by standing as a challenge to universal standards, rules, and the apparent impartiality administered by an ethic of justice, or what Foucault called 'the code',

> ... we should not be surprised to find that in certain moralities the main emphasis is placed on the code, on its systematicity, its richness, its capacity to adjust to every possible case and to embrace every area of behaviour. With moralities of this type, the important thing is to focus on the instances of authority that enforce the code ... .
> 
> (Foucault, 1986[1984])

Ethics of care is seen by the author as plural and ethic of justice as singular. This is because ethics of care are implemented in a tailor-made way to each ethical question or case whereas the ethic of justice applies pre-determined ethical codes to each question or case.

Ethics of care also queries the need to 'pass'. 'Passing' means doing what one can to assimilate into the codes of appearance and behaviour required by a gender with a related gender script approved by society in general. Instead, these ethics rely on closer examination of personal and community relationships in order to examine the particular case of the individual. Ethics of care are useful to the investigation of the circumstances of trans people and feminists since their individual gendering and its effect on their legal interactions is often far from being a straightforward matter.

Carol Gilligan linked ethics of care with women's inter-relationships but did not maintain that it was only women who could employ, or benefit from, this kind of ethical interaction,

> ... it is hardly convincing that Gilligan thought that the styles of moral reasoning she identified in her research and the preferences of women to reason more frequently in one style rather than in another reflected some ontological and universal essence called "femaleness". The problem of gender difference is much more complicated in her work, and ultimately rests with the ahistoricity of the cognitive-developmental framework within which Gilligan – at least initially – set out her research.
> 
> (Benhabib, 1995: 194)

Inclusively, third wave thinking like Gilligan's is, theoretically at least, open to input from and consideration of all ethnic, sexual and social subjectivities[7] so can, in theory, be particularly associated with ethics of care. In a similarly inclusive mode, Whittle supported the investigation of, and inclusion for, a wide range of trans subjectivities and interests instead of calling for a narrow focus on the claim for all trans people to be reassigned surgically and hormonally into heteronormative identity (2002a). A similarly socially inclusive philosophy was espoused in the narratives of some *Transstudy* participants, for example from Raelene, '*Each and everyone of us is a unique individual, and should be treated as such. There is no one size that fits all*' (Nov 11th, 2005, in <What advice to a Newbie>).

Such inclusive philosophies may initiate a move from representations of trans people as medically defined stereotypes and feminists as biologically defined stereotypes towards their recognition as fully individual people who are often noticeably able to respect the individuality of others in turn. This kind of inclusive philosophy bodes well for a coalition between trans and third wave factions.

## 1.2 Building connections: how to form a coalition

> A feminist ethic of care begins with connection, theorized as primary and seen as fundamental in human life. People live in connection with one another; human lives are interwoven in a myriad of subtle and not so subtle ways.
> (Gilligan, 1995:122)

As mentioned in the above section, of some humanities-based queer theory and feminist research, there has been too much study of trans subjectivity as a theoretical phenomenon at the expense of research into the lived experience of trans people. Harry Benjamin, as early as 1966, noticed that many commentators theorised trans subjectivity 'from without', seemingly referring to theorising by non-trans (as in his own case) or non-trans-friendly people, '*(Virginia) Prince has made valuable contributions "from within", while most other writers on the subject (including the present one), decidedly approach the subject "from without"*' (Benjamin, 1966:36).

This book attempts to add to efforts to redress this omission by drawing upon interactive research such as the 'looking with' the trans subject recommended by Namaste (1996). A way of 'looking with' the trans subject is to empathise with and gain inside knowledge of his, her or hir social world. Martha Cooper and Caroline Blair (2002) noticed how Foucault recommended a kind of self-reflexive standpoint epistemology as the optimum means to investigate personal narratives, '*Foucault suggested that it should be those most closely involved in a domain of practice or inquiry who address the problems of truth, power, and conduct in that arena*' (2002:527).

This seems to be an ethics of investigation aligning closely with ethics of care, '*Clearly despising those communicative postures that are aimed at winning, eliminating an opponent, or even defining an interlocutor as an opponent, Foucault propounded a communicative stance that respects the Other ...*' (527).

Perhaps those 'most closely involved' can include those empathic with a research community or those with significant knowledge of this community, as well as those with similar sexual subjectivities. If so, Foucault's ethical philosophy could enable those who are not conventionally seen as trans to investigate trans subjectivity and theory, just as it could involve male-embodied subjects with feminist research. The author is not sure whether he holds a legitimate trans or feminist subjectivity. It is perhaps his empathy with trans and feminist subjectivities that enable this trans/feminist investigation.

The possession of a passionate or personally political stance in order to undertake research should not be read as a negative hindrance to objective research. It can act as a spur to engender in-depth, creative and relevant research and can reveal the effects of someone's subjectivity on the research. The author aimed to provide a reflexive account of his social/academic standpoint to *Transstudy* participants and aim to present the same to readers of this book, in order to avoid presenting the research as a completely objective 'view from nowhere'. The term 'view from nowhere' was devised by Thomas Nagel in 1986 and was given a feminist application by Sandra Harding in 1991, '*It is necessary to avoid the "view from nowhere" stance of conventional Western epistemology while refusing to embrace the exhalation of the spontaneous consciousness of our experiences ...*'[8] (1991:311).

Thomas Kuhn (1962) described the spirit of the term as often coming in the form of the traditional operation of conventional scientific method where the attainment, and presentation, of detached objectivity with regard to the subject matter of one's research is recommended as desirable and achievable. However, such a 'tabula rasa' of personal input into research is in fact impossible to possess and implement, and can easily lead to false objectivity because that very objectivity is not under scrutiny.

Gilligan described what she perceived as a patriarchal view or 'voice' from nowhere compared with a relational voice from somewhere,

> Hearing the difference between a patriarchal voice and a relational voice means hearing separations which have sounded natural or beneficial as disconnections which are psychologically and politically harmful. Within a relational framework, the separate self sounds like an artefact of an outmoded order: a disembodied voice speaking as if from nowhere.
> 
> (Spring, 1995)

To obtain involvement with the research community in order to investigate their 'view' or 'voice', the main data collection source for the research became a body of narratives submitted by trans people: the *Transstudy*. Analysis of the narratives involved examining them through a feminist-inspired critical discourse analysis. The critical discourse analyst views language not as a mirror of experience, but as more of a distorting mirror, which produces a 'reflection' of discourse that changes slightly every time it is used. Whittle pointed out that discourse analysis does not involve reliance on a fixed analytic method since it is by nature a self-reflexively evolving phenomenon,

> To discuss discourse is to set out on a voyage of discovery, as 'there is no analytic method'. 'Doing' discourse analysis and justifying it as scientific

method all too often presents one with the dawning realisation that 'each step rests on a bedrock of "intuition" and "presentation"' (Potter and Wetherall, in Parker, 1992) and it becomes important to recognise the limitations of what it is possible to accomplish.

(2002a:42)

So, one should attempt to recognise the limits of any discourse that one might inadvertently produce in the wake of criticising another discourse.

## 1.3 Conclusion

This introduction highlights how problems emerge when feminism and transgender, as social factions or collective subjectivities, sometimes evade, vilify or negate each other's philosophy and subjectivities. Particularly, it was seen how separatist feminist theorists have portrayed the factions as consisting of mutually incompatible aims and subjectivities. This portrayal has worked to the detriment of both factions because literature reviews and data analysis suggest that trans people's and feminists' shared knowledge deriving from gender oppression can bolster one another's causes.

Analysis of the first research question identified the need to form a challenge to internecine exclusion between and within each faction by reconstructing the discourses associated with both. Exclusion deriving from each faction seemed to be associated with their link to certain sexual subjectivities, perceived to be identities by separatist mentalities. Both factions have been portrayed as unreal by elements of the other faction and by other hostile groups.

The second research question on 'acceptance versus aetiology' revealed the need to portray transgender and third wave feminist factions and subjectivities as real in a sociological, rather than biological interpretation. Social constructionists, following on from Foucault, introduced perspectives of subjectivity as negotiated, even by those in apparently weak positions in power relationships. These perspectives eventually enabled challenges to medical and legal aetiologies of sexual subjectivity. Narrating gender variance into visibility can lead to oppression if it becomes more visible but the alternative is to be discussed into or out of existence by others.

The third research question asked if transgender and feminism are by nature 'separatist discourses', or whether certain sub-factions within them are separatist. [B]ell hooks' feminist model of social relations, 'solidarity', promises to replace separatism, which might also be called essentialist exclusivity in order to facilitate understanding between gender variant people. Philosophical third wave feminists' stated identification with those 'Othered' from heteronormativity promises to bolster this kind of solidarity.[9] Feminist separatist theory maintaining that trans people follow a heteronormative script has been contradicted by such people coming 'out' as gender variant and by espousing inclusion for a range of gender variant subjectivities.

Discussion of the fourth research question found that philosophical third wave feminism expanded upon the queer project to challenge the essentialisation of sexual and philosophical subjectivities. The notion of genealogical similarities encourages empathy between those 'Othered' from apparently disparate discourses. These similarities derive from a perspective of individual essence as 'subjectivity', a continually forming construction formed in negotiations with the society within which the individual finds him, her or hirself. Carol Gilligan identified ethics of care as the optimum way to reduce stereotypes and to support silenced subjectivities. Using these ethics, genealogical overlaps between sexual subjectivities can be revealed, clearing the pathway for potential coalitional union.

The second part of this chapter suggested that much theorising of trans subjectivity has, historically, been applied from 'without', whether at a physical, social or subjective distance from gender variant people. It seems clear that someone with empathy for a social community can research that community, particularly if subjectivity is accepted to derive from, and to connect via, socially formed genealogy. Any such empathic alliance can be revealed via inclusive research so that the 'view from somewhere' can be revealed for its influence on the research and as a positive way of facilitating the voices of gender variant people.

In Chapters 2 to 4, a series of literature reviews investigates key themes that have shaped discourses of trans subjectivity, third wave philosophy and the law as it relates to gender. The analysis in Chapters 6 to 8 is formed from themes initiated by the literature reviews and by participant narratives from the *Transstudy*. Chapter 9 is formed from three ultimate themes of recommendation deriving from the literature review and analysis chapters.

## Terminology

In this book 'gender variant' is used as an umbrella term for the main subjects of this study because it is generally taken to include all those who voluntarily or involuntarily transgress heteronormative codes of sexual identity. It is a term introduced by Press for Change in their negotiations with the Equality Bill Committee, as a potential replacement for 'gender reassignment'. 'Gender oppressed' is intended to mean those whose preferred or realised gendering has been a target for heteronormative abuse.

'Trans woman' and 'trans man' are used to describe the transitioned gender of those previously known (in science) as 'transsexual men' and 'transsexual women'. For instance, a person previously known as a transsexual woman is now referred to as a trans man, recognising their correct gendered essence.[10] 'Trans' is taken to mean those people involved in the gender transition process. In this book 'transgender' generally refers to trans philosophy or non-transitioning trans subjectivity. Whittle linked 'transgender' to trans subjectivity that doesn't necessarily involve medical reassignment, '*Transsexualism is currently being redefined to come under an umbrella term transgenderism, a larger group which is no longer medically defined...*' (Whittle, 1998b:46)

'Heteronormativity' refers to the idea that there are only two possible genders, that these are 'man' and 'woman' and that these are developed in the womb and cannot be transitioned later.

'Sexual subjectivity' is taken to mean the combination of an individual's:

- natal birth sex, e.g. whether they are born with testes or ovaries, or alternatively an intersex condition,
- gender, meaning the way that a person's sexually subjective behaviour, appearance and language manifest as an outwardly recognisable type of sexual being,
- sexuality, or how a person thinks of themselves with regard to the process of having sex, and
- sexual orientation, i.e. attraction to a person or people who maintain certain gender performance(s).

'Identity' is taken to mean apparently fixed biological or personality traits while 'subjectivity' is taken to mean identity-in-process. 'Preferred gender' refers to the gender the trans person wishes to manifest in social life. 'Realised gender' is intended to refer to gender that is achieved by the individual in a process of transition. 'Transition' is taken to mean the whole social, legal and/or medical route to gender realisation and 'reassignment' is taken to refer just to the medical aspects of transition.

The pronouns of 'ze' and 'hir' have been used to refer to those who do not identify as man or woman.

## Format of *Transstudy* quotes

All quotes from the *Transstudy* have been quoted verbatim in this book with no spelling or grammar amendments, therefore '(sic)' is not deployed in *Transstudy* quotes. This was done to preserve the character of each participant's narratives. The author sometimes inserts explanatory notes in square brackets into a *Transstudy* quote. Titles of *Transstudy* topics accompanying *Transstudy* quotes are put inside chevrons. *Transstudy* references are ordered with name of participant first, date that the narrative was posted, and topic title, e.g. (Monica Mar 11th, 2005, in <respected in your workplace>). Sometimes, reference is made to 'TransEquality' legal cases. This refers to legal cases with which Press for Change has been involved. Pseudonyms have been allocated to all *Transstudy* participants and individuals from TransEquality cases.

## Notes

1 Please see the end of this Introduction for an explanation of the format of *Transstudy* quotes.

2 The full title of DSM V is: *Diagnostic and Statistical Manual of Mental Disorders V* (2013). It is the latest such manual designed to identify mental illnesses as discreet phenomena and is used worldwide. Transsexualism was removed from DSM IV, meaning it is no longer officially classed as a mental disorder. However, it was replaced by the category of 'gender identity disorder', continuing the subtle pathologisation of this subjectivity.
3 Narratives of gendered negotiation have also been discussed by Michel Foucault (Barbin and Foucault, 1980), Sandy Stone (1991), Leslie Feinberg (1996), Jay Prosser (1998), Harriette Andreadis, (1999) and Tracey Lee (2001).
4 White middle class feminist academics had appropriated feminism to focus on issues of relevance to their own interests such as sexual liberation, lesbian identities, and anti-male critiques, overlooking the lot of poor women of colour – hence the formation of Southall Black Sisters in London.
5 'Tourist of Otherness' is a term adapted from bell hooks' critique of part-time voyeurs of social ethnicities, as hooks thought Western subjects were when visiting exotic people and locations, '*..the longing of whites to inhabit, if only for a time, the world of the Other*' (1992:28).
6 The concept of gendered difference is addressed in Chapters 3, 5, 6, 8 and 9. There is an important difference between separatist difference (exclusion of difference) and inclusive difference (inclusion of difference).
7 As theorised by Heywood and Drake (1997).
8 The last part of this rather elaborate quote seems to mean refusing to submit to the eradication of the consciousness of our experiences.
9 For instance, by feminist or feminist-friendly writers such as Julia Kristeva (1993), Gloria Anzaldúa (1983), bell hooks (1984), Judith Butler (2004), Rebecca Walker (1995), Leslie Heywood and Jennifer Drake (1997), and Alison Stone (2004).
10 The terms 'trans people', 'trans man' and 'trans woman' were coined in 1996 by Christine Burns and Stephen Whittle, when asked by the MPs Lynn Jones and Evan Harris, for simple words to describe the community of trans people in a simple way.

# 2 Explaining trans lives
## Silence and secrecy

**Introduction**

Theory ventured by sexologists and psychoanalysts, built up in the late nineteenth and early twentieth centuries, was eventually found lacking as an explanation of gender variant subjectivity by many gender variant people themselves, whereas autobiography offered to provide perspectives from real gender variant lives. Jay Prosser described the feeling of unnameable identity encountered by many gender variant people, before the period when they began to be asked for first person accounts of their own gender variant experience. Like Sandy Stone, Prosser suggested that narrating gender variant subjectivity is a necessary precursor to its full realisation in social and bodily form (1998:5). As described in Chapter 1, Janice Raymond and Bernice Hausman portrayed trans people as products and perpetrators of medical discourse,

> What we witness in the transsexual context is a number of medical specialities combining to create transsexuals – urologists, gynecologists, endocrinologists, plastic surgeons, and the like.
> (Raymond, 1979:xv)

> ... transsexuals' investment in the idea that identity resides in the body's tissues, regardless of the fact that the official medical story of transsexualism treats the body as contingent to the mind's identifications ... is, of course, made manifest in the demand for "sex change," since demanding to be made into the other sex suggests that "being" at the level of the mind (gender) is not enough.
> (Hausman, 2006:341)

As a result of the increasing production of personal narratives, trans people are not any longer, and perhaps never totally were, these kinds of products and perpetrators. Personal narratives, in the form of published biographies and autobiographies, have been drawn upon to inform this chapter and some of the content of following chapters. References to the main autobiographers or biographical subjects in this chapter often refer to their first names as their books dealt with sensitive issues of a personal nature, just as do the contributions of *Transstudy* participants.

Niels Hoyer's *Man into Woman* (1933) was probably the first published account of a particular individual's reassignment. The book provides insight into the life of its protagonist, Lili Elbe, formerly the Danish artist known as Einar Mogens Wegener (Hirschfeld, 1926). In *But for the Grace* (1954), Robert Allen, who claimed his physical transition from female to male in his late 30s and early 40s was due to natural bodily processes, provided a moving tale of the battle for psychological survival when all around him seemed to be fundamentally different. *Christine Jorgensen: A Personal Autobiography* (1967) describes how, in 1950, after finding clues to the 'real her' in endocrinological reports and literature, Christine embarked for Denmark on the quest for the physical realisation of her true self, via the newly emerging phenomenon of reassignment surgery. This sea crossing became a personal metaphor for crossing the borders of gender, bringing escape from what she called the 'half-life' of her earlier days (1967:101). Georgina Turtle, who said that she never self-identified as trans, claimed that she was born intersexed in 1923 but was raised as a boy and spent her early adult life as a man (1963). In her mid-30s, she began a complex process of transition to womanhood. Turtle wrote a study of people she claimed were 50 'O-men' and 'O-women' (gender variant women and men respectively in contemporary phraseology) in 1963, though the taxonomic system she used was one of her own invention that has not been supported by evidence.

The set of later autobiographies reviewed in this chapter includes *Conundrum*, opening with Jan Morris recalling the feeling, at three to four years old, of being born into the wrong body (1974). This feeling prevailed throughout her young life, notably in 1953 in the company of a group of men undertaking the then very masculine endeavour of conquering Everest. Jan felt that, *'Once more on Everest I was the outsider'* (81), despite her possession of a very healthy functional male body. In *April Ashley's Odyssey* (1982), April recounted how she underwent risky reassignment surgery in Casablanca while leading a colourful life as a cabaret performer. Her life story involved being subject to a legal precedent in the English courts that would shroud trans people's lives, not just in the UK but in many other countries, for the next 30 years. The decision in the case of *Corbett v Corbett/Ashley* [1970], a divorce case which, instead, became the annulment of April's marriage to Arthur Corbett as if it never had existed, 'cleansed' trans subjectivity from society, resulting in many trans people wondering about the legitimacy of their gender.[1] In *Dear Sir or Madam*, Mark Rees provided his self-definition of gendered being, another instance of increasing opportunity for trans people to provide narratives that expand their notions of gendered subjectivity, '... *I regarded myself as male, cursed with a female body ... I didn't want to be seen as a woman, either feminine or butch*' (1996:14).

Mark's battle to gain recognition for his preferred gender culminated in a hearing at the European Court of Human Rights. Although this meant threats to his efforts to pass as male, it ultimately gave him the opportunity to fight for trans people's right to pass as themselves in a gendered sense.

Still more recent autobiographies provide alternative reflections on gender transition. For example, in *The Testosterone Files* (2006), Max Wolf Valerio relates how he seemed to have generally had a good time in his early life, a quantum shift away from the experiences of Mark Rees and Robert Allen. However, when entering puberty, Max's feelings of difference to girls caused him confusion when he could not use his body as would a boy of his age. In *Both Sides Now* (2006), Dhillon Khosla described how growing up into manhood from a girl-based childhood provided him with insights into both gendered positions, allowing him to find himself as a healthily rounded gendered being.

The following chapter content is organised into three themes that emerged from reviews of the above autobiographies, from *Transstudy* narratives, from a selection of literature addressing the phenomenon of trans subjectivity, and from links to feminist issues. These themes link to issues of difference, real lives and 'looking with' introduced in Chapter 1, and to aspects pertinent to philosophical third wave feminism and gender law discussed in Chapters 3 to 9.

## 2.1 Silence and secrecy

A barrier to gender variant people's 'finding of themselves'[2] through narrative and discourse can be extrapolated from a theme to be found in *The Will to Knowledge* by Michel Foucault. Foucault described how, following the 'age of repression' that commenced in the seventeenth century, the Victorian era imposed 'taboo, non-existence and silence' on sexualities and gendered behaviours classed as deviant (Foucault, 1998[1978]). However, Foucault theorised that what was to be silenced (alternative sexualities and genders) had first to be named in order for them then to be identified for silencing, and that such naming paradoxically led to the flourishing of sexual discourses within a culture of heteronormative repression.[3]

Foucault traced the development of the age of sexual and gender discourses from early monastic settings, to a burgeoning in the eighteenth century, reaching its apotheosis in the Victorian era. As the new outpatient clinics of 'modern' psychiatry became a new type of 'confessional', a new age of confessional sexuality and gender seems to have erupted in the eighteenth to nineteenth century, manifesting in what Foucault observed rather dismissively as, '*the only civilisation in which officials are paid to listen to all and sundry impart the secrets of their sex*' (7). Modern confessional media took up the baton of defining sexualities that deviate from the norm, silencing the voices of individuals beneath the stereotypes,

> ... much of our savoir, our knowledge, is, has always been, in some way, mediated, derived not from direct acquaintance with facts or with events but from hearsay, from friends, from books, from magazines, from

newspapers, from the radio, from films, from television, from CDs, from the internet ... Thus reality can be interpreted through the media: patients' expectations of (and disappointments about) their therapy were partly based on media representations ...

(Solange, 2005:35)

The Victorian vehicle of gender and sexuality repression metamorphosised into scientific discourse, operated via *political, economic and technical incitement* and was informed by medicine, then psychiatry and sexology (Foucault, 1998[1978]:23). Foucault's interpretation of 'discourse' could include language, body language, living spaces, dress codes and any number of cultural conventions. Scientific discourse introduced the new ideology of rationality and started to supersede religion, which was losing its power as what Marxist philosopher Louis Althusser might have identified as 'ideological state apparatus' (1971),[4] or what Foucault identified as a power relationship, power being for Foucault that which reaches beyond the state and its apparatus (Prado, 2000). The result was gender prescribed by the establishment rather than originated by the individual. One could only have only one gender from the two on offer, and that one gender was to define one's being.

It should be noted that Foucault's notion of power was not purely or even majorly the application of conscious and deliberate domination. As Carlos Prado has pointed out, power as theorised by Foucault is produced from a long history of interconnected events and relationships and is therefore effectively impersonal in its accumulated form (2000:65).

Between the lines of the new scientific discourse were ethereal essences that Foucault deduced to be 'silences'. These were the flip side of things actually said, manifesting in language designed to conceal (1998[1978]:24). Closely delineated conditions, under which sexuality, gender and alternatives to heteronormativity were discussed, in order to channel sexual practice into reproduction and gender into societal institutions such as the family unit, gave rise to the second part of what Foucault revealed as the culture of sexual and gender taboo, namely 'secrecy' (34). Foucault proposed that secrecy operated to allure people into discussing what was silenced as a result of its prohibited essence. Sexuality and gender was something that needed to be identified as dark and dangerous so that adults would feel the need to gossip about it, in order that its deviant manifestations could be socially shunned via alienation within discourse.

Examples of the iron grasp of silence and secrecy can be found in literature. We can deduce that homosexuality was still not an esteemed attribute in the late 1950s from Richard Hauser's account of the fear of stigma experienced by gay men and lesbian women, which in turn derived from the 'secrets' surrounding their sexual subjectivity. Hauser castigated this as a, '... *stupid cloak of secrecy* ...' (1962), preventing those who were homosexuals from discussing the possibility of a homosexual existence for themselves. The cloak of secrecy could also be kept in place by female spouses of gay men who tried their hardest to protect their family and lifestyle from the onslaught of prejudice.

Hauser attempted to remove the 'cloak' to some extent by giving narrative voice to select homosexual subjects. Unfortunately, he lessened the possibility of subjectivity for transvestites, drag artists and cross-dressers by labelling them and their sexual subjectivity as, 'false transvestist' (78–79). He considered these people likely to be childlike exhibitionists who wished to be women, contributing to the infantilisation of trans-like subjectivities as discussed in the next section of this chapter.

In 'Theorising Early Modern Lesbianisms' (1999), Harriette Andreadis propounded the theory that in the sixteenth and seventeenth centuries the boundaries between female heterosexuality and what we now call lesbian identity had not been demarcated. This led to a different kind of silence and secrecy that was actually carried out by those discussed, producing a social space where women's same-sex erotics could flourish covertly. Andreadis theorised that the deliberate hiding of lesbian erotics by those involved was a strategy to evade drawing attention to their desires. Her term for the silence and secrecy surrounding and pervading same-sex erotics was, '*an erotics of unnaming*' (125). She claimed that such erotics were evident in some women's literature of the time, and argued that these works evidenced a kind of underground subversive reworking of patriarchal literary conventions.[5] However, she considered that female same-sex relations later became easier to suppress at a time when increasingly revealing narratives of gender brought them out into the open, in the dawn of the Enlightenment era. Although it seems that the erotics of unnaming allowed a peaceful existence for its subjects, the author contends that it disallowed the possibility of proudly leaving the closet and declaring one's sexual subjectivity as personally political.

Andreadis cited Michael McKeon's (1995) proposition that the compartmentalisation of human identity and gendered contribution culminated in the patriarchy of the eighteenth and nineteenth centuries. Areas of work were allocated to each sex and normative discourses of gender roles ensured that everyone was prominently segregated to one half of the gendered divide. In this new age of bipolar gendering, only those genders and sexualities given a name came to be accepted as legitimate (1999:140). As argued by Foucault, it appears that what might be called a 'politics of naming' in the eighteenth and nineteenth centuries developed to create control through labelling and pathologisation of what were deemed to be undesirable identities. An example can be found in the form of Case 99 in Krafft-Ebing's *Psychopathia Sexualis*, named as a case of '*acquired homo-sexuality*' following from the subject's self-description,

> General Feeling: I feel like a woman in man's form; and even though I often am sensible of the man's form, yet it is always in a feminine sense. ... And all that means one alone can know who feels or has felt so. But the skin all over my body feels feminine; it receives all impressions,

whether of touch, of warmth, or whether unfriendly, as feminine, and I have the sensations of a woman.

(1893:209)

Krafft-Ebing's Case 131, named by him as an instance of 'gynandry', concerned Count Sandor Vey, a person we might now describe as a trans man. Krafft-Ebing noted of Sandor Vey that, '*S's characteristic expressions – "God put love in my heart. If he created me so, and not otherwise, am I, then, guilty; or is it the eternal, incomprehensible way of fate?" – are really justified*' (317).

The love mentioned was love for those seen to be of the same physical sex to Sandor Vey. These were the first medial accounts of what was to become the classic story of trans people as 'trapped' in wrongly sexed bodies and with gendered interests that contradicted their sexed embodiment, a trope identified and investigated by Sandy Stone in 'A Posttranssexual Manifesto' (1991). Redirecting patients' sexual subjectivity into heteronormativity was expected by Krafft-Ebing to resolve the 'problems' of people such as Case 99 and Sandor Vey.

'Passing', also referred to as 'living in stealth' in trans circles, is perceived by some as trans people deferring to oppressive 'politics of naming' but by many such people as an attempt to avoid being the victim of silent and secret discourse. Trans activist Leslie Feinberg considered that passing facilitated culturally imposed self-denial designed to ensure that the subject fits in with the dictates of establishment culture, '*Passing means having to hide your identity in fear, in order to live. Being forced to pass is a recent historical development. It is passing that is a product of oppression*' (1996:89).

Critical literary theorist Marjorie Garber thought that a masculinist operation of silence and secrecy attempted to impose passing by the diffusion into culture of a deviant subjectivity, '*The "longing" for self-effacement and reabsorption is a domesticated and, I would suggest, finally once again a patriarchal or masculinist longing, which is transferred onto the figure of the transvestite in a gesture of denial or fending off*' (1997[1992]:75).

Garber argued that instead of succumbing to the bonds of heteronormativity through passing, the transvestite acts as a figure for desire, desire being that which escapes definition and disperses everywhere (75). In Shakespeare's *A Midsummer Night's Dream*, Garber ascertained a correlation between the changeling and transvestite in their temporary and silent manifestation. She then associated changeling and transvestite with the idea of the boy. The boy is ambiguously gendered, subject to impending change and the target for domination by those who have mastered the patriarchal order (88, 89, 90). Boys are therefore society's accepted 'transvestites' and he who continues to be dragged screaming into 'grown-up' society will be designated as 'boy' in order to socially eradicate him from manhood. This is an inspired reading of an operation of silence and secrecy but, however, does not deal very well with the day to day reality of life of someone labelled 'transvestite'.

Despite the pernicious operation of silence and secrecy, some trans narratives reveal how trans people began to 'find themselves' by reading, and later producing, accounts of trans subjectivity. For instance, Lili Elbe seemed to find herself partly through reviewing scientific literature, rather like Christine Jorgensen did in the *New York Public Library*, as the fictional Stephen Gordon did in Sir Philip's private library in *The Well of Loneliness*, and as did Stephen Whittle at age 11 in a Manchester Library,

> From eleven I got permission [to go to the adult section of the library] and would sit in the medicine and psychology section, frantically reading everything I could ... I spent so much time reading books and thinking, Somebody must have been born a girl and grown up to be a man.
>
> (Self and Gamble, 2000)

In 1951, when flying back to New York to meet her family after her gender reassignment with her endocrinologist, Christine Jorgensen 'found herself' when reflecting that there were other 'Others', like herself, in the spectrum of sexual subjectivity (1967:170). Her quiet contemplation of the transition from GI to woman was the 'calm before the storm' of publicity awaiting her on the tarmac of New York International Airport. Despite her narrated feelings of horror and bewilderment at such public pandemonium, she later related a feeling that her newfound fame had contributed somewhat to liberating others to feel that they could produce their own narratives of transition. The silent and secret editing of trans narratives had been contravened in such instances, and would start to lose its iron grip on the representation of trans subjectivity.

However, silence and secrecy were and are still evident in dominant narratives forming closed and static texts that continue in a loop of exclusion. Carol Gilligan noticed one such narrative as prevalent in accounts of psychological development by theorists such as Freud, Piaget and Kohlberg,

> ... the silence of women in the narrative of adult development distorts the conception of its stages and sequence.
>
> (1982:156)

Gilligan challenged this exclusion by including the voices of women into a formation of a new perspective on the nature of morality and ethical procedure.

In 'Queering Theory', Larry Cata Backer identified how the perfection of silent and secret domination of gender minorities serves to maintain dominant gender discourse as 'common-sense' and essential, and therefore as apparently 'not-discourse',

> Our dominant heterosexualist culture has so refined the techniques of annexing the 'oppositional' discourse of its sexual minorities that it passes virtually unnoticed and unopposed (Brown, 1996). Such discourse is, 'in

every instance a function or extension of history, convention, and local practice' (Fish, 1984–5, p.439).

(1998:189)

Sandy Stone issued a clarion call for trans people to rise up and be heard rather than be discussed into false existence by others. As discussed above, this silence and secrecy was and is still frequently maintained when a trans person feels obliged to merge into the established gender order and to resist knowledge of their pre-transition history. As mentioned in Chapter 1, Stone revealed how in the 1950s–70s narratives of transsexualism worked effectively to obscure narratives of gender variance, '*Besides the obvious complicity of these accounts in a Western, white male definition of performative gender, they also reinforce a binary, oppositional mode of gender identification. ... There is no territory between*' (1991:286).

Stone argued effectively that a notable number of trans people are just that, *trans* people and that, rather than hiding through passing as 'normal' man or woman, these individuals should be proud to proclaim the fact of their non-heteronormative trans subjectivity. Such a reclamation of subjectivity seems to mirror that urged by second wave feminist Simone de Beauvoir when calling for women to reassign their sexual subjectivity from object (losing oneself) to subject (finding oneself),

> Indeed, along with the ethical urge of each individual to affirm his subjective existence, there is also the temptation to forgo liberty and become a thing. This is an auspicious road, for he who takes it – passive, lost, ruined – becomes henceforth the creature of another's will ...

(1949:21)

## 2.2 Infantilisation and the 'refusal to grow up'

> As with males theorizing about women from the beginning of time, theorists of gender have seen transsexuals as possessing something less than agency. As with "genetic" women, transsexuals are infantilized, considered too illogical or irresponsible to achieve true subjectivity ...

(Stone, 1991:294)

Deploying an authoritative voice, which would inspire further silent and secret discussion of gender and sexuality, Freudian psychoanalysts considered that the client's conscious narrative was not a reliable indicator of experience. In the period from 1890 to 1905 Sigmund Freud constructed his manifesto on the psychosocial development of human sexuality, interpreting any gender variance as properly a temporary psychological step towards heteronormative sexuality. He construed ongoing gender variance as a failure to participate in the full process of sexual conditioning from infancy to adulthood. Neurosis resulted, he theorised, marked by an immature state of mind from failing to bridge the span from adolescence to mature heterosexuality (Foster, 1985 [1956]:151).

In 1966 Harry Benjamin, Magnus Hirschfeld's protégée and the first doctor to open up a gender transition clinic in the USA, added transvestism to this state of infancy by suggesting that it may derive from, '*An immature or an infantile sexual constitution (fostered by a faulty upbringing) ...*' (1966:37–38). It can be said that the infantilisation of gender variant people was thereby incorporated into developmental theory with a concomitant loss of their social 'voice'. 'Voice' is used here in the sense of Gilligan's idea of differently gendered access to social communication.

In 1979 Janice Raymond further shored up this interpretation of trans people as failed gendered selves, as people too sick and immature to make responsible decisions about their own gendered existences. Whittle, when later critiquing Raymond and commenting on the position of trans women, noted how separatist feminist theory contributed to the idea that development into anything but a woman or man, similar to the heteronormative model of gender development, was a sign of immaturity,

> A failure of history means one is always a child, never a woman, a failure of performance means that the individual does not make the grade as a woman, and finally a failure of biology means that the individual is a man.
> (Whittle, 2005:159)

In the first section above it was suggested that Western culture has associated transvestism with the image of the boy; something transient, not fully formed and not capable of involvement in grown-up discussion, an association that can work to oust gender variant people from 'grown-up' discourse. Marjorie Garber identified J M Barrie's Peter Pan as a boy who never changed. Almost without exception, the pantomime and some film versions of *Peter Pan* required performance by women actors. Garber speculates that women have been seen by some as equivalent in status to boys since, like changelings and (male) transvestites, they are often portrayed to be too feminine and/or innocent to join the grown-up masculinist order (Garber, 1997[1992]:168).

Similarly, Carol Gilligan speculated that women would always be viewed as immature when viewed through the prism of masculinism,

> ... as long as the categories by which development is assessed are derived from research on men, divergence from the masculine standard can only be seen as a failure of development. As a result, the thinking of women is often classified with that of children.
> (1982:69–70)

Also, when reviewing Janet Lever's research on children's games, Gilligan suggested that maturity, at least in the industrial West, was and is assumed to be a masculine feature,

> Lever implies that, given the realities of adult life, if a girl does not want to be left dependent on men, she will have to learn to play like a boy.
>
> (1982:10)

In a later work, when commenting upon the custodial appropriation of women by masculinity, Gilligan noted that,

> The neurobiologist Antonio Damasio tells us that we register our experience from moment to moment. In our bodies and our emotions, we pick up the music or "the feeling of what happens". When we fail to record these signals in our minds and thoughts, our thoughts become divorced from our experience and we can readily fall under the sway of false authority.
>
> (2011:33)

> The traumatised person, experiencing his or her own voice as ineffective, as powerless, adopts the voice that carries power and authority.
>
> (2011:88)

It seems that women and gender variant people have been expected to be seen and not heard in patriarchal culture. Like women, many gender variant people's moral development will also be seen as a divergence from the masculinist standard since it often evidences the kind of bi-gendered 'view from somewhere' as described in Chapter 1.

The lived condition of some men's refusal to join the masculinist order was pathologised into a condition called the 'Peter Pan Syndrome' (PPS) by Psychologist Dr Dan Kiley, something he theorised that he had suffered from himself. Kiley delineated six symptoms of 'PPS': '*Irresponsibility, Anxiety, Loneliness, Sex Role Conflict, Narcissism, and Chauvinism*' (1983, cited in Garber, 1997[1992]:182). Although related to delinquent men refusing to take on adult roles, these symptoms reflect those suggested in the 1970s by Leslie Lothstein as a way of identifying the characteristics of transsexuals,

> Lothstein concluded that his ageing male transsexual patients were depressed, isolated, withdrawn, schizoid individuals with profound dependency conflicts. Furthermore, they were immature, narcisstic, egocentric and potentially 'explosive' ...
>
> (Walters and Ross, 1986:58)

These portrayals of immaturity worked to construct an image of trans subjectivity as unreal and infantile, and often trans people's parents have been held to blame for this apparent route to immaturity. Dr Kiley followed *The Peter Pan Syndrome* with *The Wendy Dilemma* which hypothesized that many women, the 'Wendys' who mother the men in their lives, can initiate and sustain PPS in their male partners. Some women resisted this interpretation because it attributed blame for PPS purely to women (Thomas, 27 February 1996).

Contrasting with the pantomime representation of Peter Pan, the female-to-male cross-dresser with a depthless character and (different to Kiley's interpretation) spotless morals (Peter Ackroyd in Garber, 1997[1992]:176), is the effeminate Captain Hook who resembles pantomime dames (read male-to-female cross-dresser). Lack of complexity represented by the female-to-male pantomime transvestite mirrors Garber's portrayal of the lack of complexity in the image of 'the boy' as negated individuality ripe to be recruited into masculinity. On the other hand, Hook can be taken to manifest both the loss of innocence and the immature sexuality associated with male transvestism. Garber highlighted Jacqueline Rose's insight that rather than being feminine, Peter Pan is bereft of sexuality and gender, a clean slate (Garber, 1997 [1992]:177–178). Both characterizations are portrayed as outside the world of grown-up heteronormative gendering. In such representations, it seems that both types of trans subjectivity have to be assigned to the inferior (feminine) half of the heteronormative divide, rather than standing as a legitimate and grown-up 'whole' genderings of their own.

Turning to the autobiographies and texts reviewed for this literature review, we can detect narrative portrayals of infantilisation endured by the trans authors. Robert Allen, the autobiographer whose transition to manhood was officially recognised in 1944, related an account of prejudice being mercilessly dished out to him for most of his young life, deriving from what his oppressors saw as a an individual not growing into the correct gender. Exclusion started early in his life when experiencing the 'freemasonry' of the playground (1954:31) and the '... *wound of knowing that I was absolutely alone* ...' (33). Describing the cruelty of children to those perceived to be different, Robert applied descriptive passages such as, '... *whipping a shroud from a terrifying corpse* ...' and '... *a dog trying to get away from a swarm of wasps*' (41). It seems that Robert was excluded from growing up with the other children by being demonised and banished from their activities.

If one's gendered feelings are stigmatised by society then Georgina Turtle, who transitioned to womanhood after self-diagnosing as intersexed, believed that the 'O-sexual' (gender variant) individual would impose a self-curfew on relations with others and that this would result in an inability to mature (1963:49). This move to immaturity seemed certain to badly affect libidinal life-force, leading to a kind of emotional castration. Turtle apparently found indications of a refusal to grow up in the tendency of some 'O-sexual' subjects not to marry, and in efforts to seek careers if 'O-women' (female-to-males or trans men). Despite Turtle's efforts to present the term 'immaturity' as a scientific term, this term still comes across as pejorative in her work. Perhaps what Turtle saw as trans people's 'refusal to grow up' might have been deliberate and healthy alternative life-styles rather than pathological dysfunction.

On page 60 of *Over the Sex Border*, Turtle pointed to the pressure imposed upon male-to-females in their early lives to demonstrate masculinity in the years before accepting, or being able to accept, their trans selves. Despite their best efforts, many of these young 'O-men' experienced what would become a lifelong experience of lack of esteem and recognition in spheres of social endeavour from family to school to the world of work. The school system developed a personality of self-blame within the young 'O-boy' as he failed to match the exploits of his peers. With the development of puberty, many 'O-boys' and 'O-girls' would endeavour to stay inside to hide away what for them were abhorrent sexual bodily developments and/or to avoid gender oppression (1963:63). This, Turtle says, continued into adult life where there was a, 'suppression of the normal social life' (82) and an isolation developing from the O-person's feelings of being misunderstood (56). George Brown's later theory of the 'Flight into Masculinity' suggested that, conversely, an appropriation of extreme gendered behaviour can be displayed early in their lives by male-embodied people who later seek transition to womanhood. Such individuals can seek to prove their manhood in overt, open and extreme ways before acknowledging their wish to adopt the 'opposite' gendering (2006[1998]).

Despite some informative insights, Turtle brandished the sweeping, and infantilising, statement that, *'Perhaps the greatest single difficulty in any attempt to assist transexualists and O-sexualists with their problem lies in their inability to accept facts'* (1963:142).

She declared this even though recognising that facts and theory are subject to change (158–9). We could ask whose facts it was that Turtle wanted trans people to accept. Feminists have criticised the wielding of facts as if they are written in stone and are part of the 'common sense' founded status quo, for instance Sandra Harding's work challenged traditional scientific assumptions that objectivity and truth are not influenced by the subjectivity of the researcher,

> Objectivism results only in semi-science when it turns away from the task of critically identifying all those broad, historical social desires, interests, and the values that have shaped the agendas, contents, and results of the sciences as much as they shape the rest of human affairs.
>
> (1991:143)

> To insist that no judgments at all of cognitive adequacy can legitimately be made amounts to the same thing as to insist that knowledge can be produced only from "no place at all": that is, by someone who can be every place at once.
>
> (153)

The facts and logic available at Turtle's time were of their time and largely followed the contemporary medical model and can be seen to represent an imposition of representational 'voice' upon trans people.

Mark Rees, the trans autobiographer from Tunbridge Wells who 'came out' to fight for recognition of transitioned subjectivity, didn't realise that he would lose his freedom for gender expression when entering puberty, a time when society expects the young person to start fulfilling their ascribed gender role (1996:6). Isolation proved to be his reward for not fulfilling the sexual scripts that were supposed to accompany adolescence. Mark noted how there was no recognition of body dysphoria or trans subjectivity in children and adolescents when he was growing up. He stated how, '*I was boyish because of being unconvinced of my physical sex*' (35). In a similar way, the young Stephen Whittle displayed a reluctance to enter conventional and natal-based heteronormativity as a child,

> I felt that I was trapped in childhood, I was trapped but I didn't want to go forward, but that also felt like a trap, because, y'know, whether I liked it or not I was going to go forward ...
>
> (Self and Gamble, 2000)

Mark found that being forced into self-centredness, from lack of opportunities to relate with others, meant that he could not grow up and that others would direct the blame back at him for not being grown-up. Despite all this, Mark's trans subjectivity was consistent through childhood, adolescence and adulthood, challenging ideas of trans subjectivity as deriving from teenage role confusion. He eventually found a description of something like his particular trans subjectivity in the form of a *Times* newspaper report at the 1969 London Gender Symposium,[6] an epiphany-like instance of 'finding himself' (75).

Judith/Jack Halberstam's own personal performance of female masculinity and her/his writing of the self through the academic narrative in *Female Masculinity* was operated by '*refusing to engage*' with male masculinity, via the agency of his/her own self-definition, '*Such affirmations begin by not subverting masculine power or taking up a position against masculine power but by turning a blind eye to conventional masculinities and refusing to engage*' (1998:9).

A '*refusing to engage*' cut short by murder was something Jacob Hale detected in the real life, rather than the life story appropriated by transgender activists, of Brandon Teena,

> Three young people's self-determination and agency were ended by the murders John Lotter and Marvin Thomas Nissen committed. ... The function of naming as solidifying insertion into the social fabric is what drives transgender activists ... to insist that "Brandon Teena" and masculine pronouns as markers of transsexual or transgender configurations of this young person's identity are the only correct modes of representation.
>
> (1998:313, 317)

Hale considered that the real-life Brandon's 'refusing to engage' with gender markers inevitably led to exclusion and to life in a gendered '*border zone*',

Border zone inhabitants infer reasonably that their lack of fixed location within categories is prohibited by the more firmly located, that such absence will be used as grounds for subjecting them to multiple indiscriminate erasures ... Indiscriminate erasure of a living border dweller's multiple complexities, ambiguities, inconsistencies, ambivalences, and border zone status hinders that subject's ability to build a self through which to live.

(1998:319)

Addressing filmic narrative rebellion against dominant masculinity, Halberstam asked, '... what's the point of being a rebel boy if you are going to grow up to be a man?' (1998:5) Rebellion is not an easy thing, however, and Halberstam noted the general idea that, '... female gender deviance is much more tolerated than male gender deviance' (5), the former being understood as a healthy identification with powerful masculinity. However, Halberstam noted that girls' rebellion is dramatically challenged when they enter adolescence, noted above as being the case for Mark Rees when entering puberty. Masculinity when displayed by the adolescent female is characteristically viewed as immaturity, or resistance to adulthood, despite being viewed as maturity in males. It seems, as Halberstam points out, that tomboyism must be temporary to be acceptable, just like transvestism is portrayed as only healthy when temporary, when it is seen as fun, or as Garber termed it, as a 'progress narrative'.

A progress narrative is described by Garber as interpretation of identity or subjectivity as a temporary response to circumstances, for instance a reading of trans subjectivity as temporary gender variance to pass as one gender in order to avoid detection as another (Garber, 1997[1992]:8, 69, 70). The progress narrative interprets trans subjectivity as a temporary response to circumstances that will either be terminated by a return to the original gender or will involve a 'change' into the opposite gender.

Sean Mattio describes progress narratives in the following way,

> When applied to the "narrative" of history or society, the progress narrative refers to a story skewed to emphasize the idea of progress from the past to the present. It aims to create a unified forward movement. But when applied to fiction, the progress narrative refers to a strategy that appears to move the character forward, but really keeps them in the same place.
>
> (2010)

Mattio describes how the progress narrative characteristically avoids serious consideration of sexual subjectivity by framing gender variance as a humorous performance by a character trying to evade the negative consequences of revealing their 'true' gender. The progress narrative has also been applied to the real lives of gender variant people, such as jazz musician Billy Tipton, but presents their gendering as a simple performance, rather than as the performativity of gender theorised by Judith Butler. Butler theorised that self-representations of gender, whether consciously personally political or not, can change actual gender if they are reinforced significantly through many repetitions, and that this is what constitutes the process of performativity. The social agent becomes, 'an object rather than the subject of constitutive acts' (Butler, 1988:519).

The discourse of heteronormativity was applied by trans-unfriendly critics to the life of Billy Tipton to make his male gendering seem less than whole. In *Vested Interests* Garber attempted a personal reading of Tipton's life in order to establish his real sexual subjectivity. Tipton was always male for his wife and son but became subject to imposed definitions of identity (1997 [1992]:8, 69, 70). Garber read between the lines of Tipton's official biographies to reveal a progress narrative imposed from without. The progress narrative applied the concept of 'passing' to Tipton's life as a man when, like many trans people, all his passing seems to really have been done before his gender transition when he had to pass as the gender he was not.

Progress narratives are narratives imposed onto the subject by others and take no account of the subject's own view of their subjective development. In this way they obstruct the open and evolving narratives presented by gender variant 'voices from the margins'. A voice from the margins will not automatically present an open and evolving narrative of subjective development but, and when encouraged by the bloom of other gender variant narratives, characteristically often will. Subjective development is the process of being built up, and building up and finding oneself, as a gendered person.

As noted in the introduction to this chapter, autobiographer Max Wolf Valerio seemed to have generally had a good time in his early life, unlike Mark Rees and Robert Allen. However, when moving through adolescence, he discovered that something akin to tomboyism would not be a temporary affair in his life, unlike it had been for his mother and aunt, and not as it was expected to be in society's view of tomboyism as a progress narrative. He contrasted his feelings to the tomboys he grew up with by claiming that,

> I know without being able to articulate it that my feelings are different in dimension, in texture, in meaning. I know, somehow, deep down, that I will never grow out of it, and furthermore, I don't want to.
>
> (2006:42)

This caused him much frustration until he experienced an 'epiphany moment' of self-realisation when accidentally coming across a book on the subject of female-to-male reassignment. This was not a gloriously comforting and warm epiphany but was at least a sowing of the seeds of realising his real self. He became worried that 'women' who want to be men are 'unevolved', bringing to mind the type of criticisms of gender variant people as immature and sexually undeveloped discussed earlier in this section,

> ... *confused women who want to be men, women so maligned and self-hating, so unevolved as to think they are men. Unsophisticated, not exposed to feminism. Poor, old-fashioned, twisted-up bull daggers from some small town in pigfart nowhere who can't face the fact that they're actually dykes* [Author's italics].
>
> (2006:78)

In later adulthood he underwent a belated process of growing up into his new manly body, when given the chance to adjust to all its startling new vagaries,

> The energy I felt initially, so overwhelming, has quietened. I've grown into it. With time, as you become larger, more muscular, the energy begins to fill a space appropriate to its circumference. In other words, you grow up.
>
> (2006:328)

In narratives provided by *Transstudy* participants, a distancing from identification with the heteronormative growing up process and a perception of this process as an act, rather than a natural process, was sometimes in evidence,

> In later years I found it difficult to conceive of myself as either an adult (because adults seem to come in two types ;-) or as having/being a definite gender. I was in hiding, to an extent. I did notice other people of my own age adopting gender-stratified roles. I have never felt able to completely do this, even as an act. I have generally suspected people of putting on a better act than me, rather than being the things they say they are.
>
> (Clarette Jan 4th, 2006, in <Min and Max Transition Ages?>)

Participant Monica looked to the future to see a time when the shackles of the heteronormative script for maturity, at least in the way that it precludes those who transition, might be unlocked,

> I envisage a time, far into the future, when transsexual boys will be identified in childhood and then brought up from that moment as girls in the anticipation that they will grow up to be women and in the normal course of events become wives/partners and mothers.
>
> (Monica Feb 21st, 2006, in <Transpregnancy>)

Many trans people have emphasised the possibility of alternative maturities by embodying and espousing the complementarity of gendered positions different to the purely heteronormative in healthily functional relationships.

## 2.3 Which trans identities are real?

Feelings of non-identification with what is generally taken to be growing up into 'real' gender often make the gender variant person feel less a person than those who 'do' gender in what is taken to be the correct fashion. As well as trans people, women and feminists have been portrayed as child-like, causing them to question their own subjective validity. This might explain the trans/third wave feminist empathy for others who have sometimes been designated as being outside the realms of 'real' humanity/adulthood such as gay people, disabled people and oppressed ethnic groups. Examples of gender variant people's doubting their own gendered legitimacy are to be found throughout literary fiction, fact and gender variant narratives. For instance, believing that the validity of gendered identity lay in the matching of gender and anatomy with lifestyle, Venus Xtravaganza in the film *Paris is Burning* (1990) wanted to become a 'real' woman by gaining a vagina and middle-class security (Prosser, 1998:48). In *The Well of Loneliness,* the childhood Stephen Gordon almost felt less real than her dolls because they fitted in with accepted gendering whereas she did not (Prosser, 1998:162).

Notions of gender reality in the Industrial West largely derive from the work of those nineteenth-century sexologists who extrapolated from the dualised differences they detected in male and female anatomy and physiology. This prompted a new 'discourse of feeling' making genders seem inherent. Seeing came to equate with believing in the new Western scientific paradigm and led to genitalia materialising as the prime indicator of sexual subjectivity, just as later, Lord Justice Ormrod used this prime indicator in the case of *Corbett*, '*Ormrod devised a test based only on three factors; the chromosomal, the gonadal, and the genital features at the time of the birth of the individual concerned*' (Whittle, 2007a:39).

This meant that those who transgressed conventional notions of sex, gendering and/or sexuality became unreal gendered beings. This new sex and gender bipolarity influenced pre-operative trans people in the 1950s who adopted Karl Heinrich Ulrichs' 1860s notion of man or woman 'trapped in the wrong body' in order to be accepted to convert to the 'opposite' sex. Such self-representations certainly worked to obscure the possible realness of what is now (and previous to sexology) recognised by some as sexual subjectivity different to the heteronormative.

As well as for those working from medical, sexological or legal perspectives, trans people have typically held illegitimate identities according to some feminist factions, who have contributed to imposing 'voice' upon trans people and transgender theory. For Bernice Hausman, as discussed in Chapter 1, transsexuals only achieved existence through medical discourse directed by medical practitioners, '*Hausman rejects the notion that we can read gender as an ideology without also considering it as a product of technological relations*' (Halberstam, 1998:160). This was a perception of gender transition forwarded by a trans-sceptical feminist but one that has some grounding in the way that trans subjectivity has been presented in the past. As also discussed in Chapter 1, according to Janice Raymond, trans people colluded with medical experts to produce a medical narrative of crossing sex boundaries, rather than a narrative of realising their inner gender, whatever that may be. In *The Transsexual*

*Empire* she portrayed trans women as patriarchal infiltrators of women's spaces (1979:104), gaining access to these sacred sites in the form of what might be called a Trojan Woman. Sheila Jeffreys differed from this perspective by seeing 'transsexual' surgery as the patriarchal control of otherwise deviant identity, rather than 'transsexuals' actively having a hand in maintaining the patriarchal order, *'When such surgery became available in the 1950s, stories of having a woman's soul in a male body were interpreted as the criteria for diagnosing a new breed of person constructed by medical science, the transsexual'* (2005:51).

Trans people have regularly been relegated to one 'half' of heteronormative gender by separatist feminists like Jeffreys and Raymond, invariably to the wrong half for those trans people who do identify as heteronormative. When identifying what she saw as the *'transsexually constructed lesbian-feminist'*, Raymond stated, *'It is he [sic] who recognises that if female spirit, mind, creativity, and sexuality exist anywhere in a powerful way, it is here, among lesbian-feminists'* (1979:108).

Raymond realised that this could be read as a compliment to trans women who identified with or as lesbian-feminists but seems to have intended it as indication of a desire to dominate lesbian-feminism. Raymond overlooked feminine trans people who didn't wish for medical reassignment treatments in her reading of trans subjectivity, perhaps because then almost nobody could imagine a 'sex change' without the 'change of sex'. Raymond stated that,

> Women take on the self-definition of feminist and/or lesbian because that definition truly proceeds from not only the chromosomal fact of being born XX, but also from the whole history of what being born with those chromosomes means in this society.
>
> (1979:116)

However, it is evident that natal women can become patriarchs fully imbued into oppressive masculinism, defying this hypothesised influence of their XX chromosomes. This can happen when a woman perceives that she is better off actively promoting, and/or believes in, and/or has little choice but to join, a patriarchal community or society. This has been the case for many women but notable examples include the Sworn Virgins in Albania (National Geographic, 2011) and Margaret Thatcher in the UK. The reality of aligning the ideology of feminism strictly with one biological sex comes under question in such instances. Raymond's essentialist alignment of a certain ideology with the female is something quite different to the chosen and developed gendered relations of genre and genealogy.

Some other feminist readings of trans subjectivity have been fundamentally different to those outlined above but are nonetheless problematic for trans people. As discussed above, Marjorie Garber conflated transvestism with a queerly postmodern kind of metaphoric essence, evoking a 'third term' in the form of the transvestite (1997[1992]:11, 12, 17). Garber's reading of transvestism was a useful challenge to the ghettoisation of gender. However, in the case of trans subjectivity, trans people often reject the idea that it is a purely metaphorical/ethereal essence since this presentation of their sexual subjectivity does not match their feelings and does not present this subjectivity as something substantial in the eyes of society, medicine and the law.

In 'The Empire Strikes Back: A Posttranssexual Manifesto' Sandy Stone portrays trans subjectivity as subjectivity based in the gender borderlands rather than as a fixed part of human nature. Nevertheless, for Stone, trans subjectivity was identifiable and valid, and not necessarily just a temporary stage of transition from one sex to another. Stone addressed the question; which came first, trans identity or the sex reassignment operation? The accounts of transition given by male-to-female trans people such as Lili Elbe (1933), Hedy Jo Star (1955) and Jan Morris (1974) can give the impression that it was the latter by providing romantic fairy-story narratives where a newly gendered person seems to emerge as a butterfly from the cocoon after reassignment. These accounts of the 'newly born' trans woman tended to offer the image of a 'Stepford Wives' representation of 1950s Western womanhood suddenly manifesting out of thin air, '*They go from being unambiguous men, albeit unhappy men, to unambiguous women. There is no territory between. Further, each constructs a specific narrative moment when their personal sexual identification changes from male to female*' (Stone, 1991:286).

However, contradicting Stone's criticism of Jan Morris's account of reassignment as magical transition, Jan herself described how she did not undergo a sudden transformation of body, '*The process was infinitely slow and subtle ...*' (1974:117). When she writes that she, '*... went to say goodbye to myself in the mirror*', it was perhaps for dramatic effect, rather than thinking she was actually going to experience a complete change of self. Jan's feelings of mysticism and the promise of magical transformation in the aura of Casablanca are therefore perhaps narrative embellishment from a well-known descriptive writer, rather than an account of real experience.

Challenges to the notion of trans subjectivity as a pathological condition, that could be rectified by bringing the subject in line with heteronormativity via magical medical transformation, appeared in the 1980s. According to Stone, Marie Mehl found that the trans person was no more susceptible to mental illness than members of the general population (1991:292–3). Reports such as Mehl's engendered a revolution in trans people's self-representations by opening up the opportunity for pre-operative trans people to venture less pathological and more personal narratives of sexual subjectivity. In an argument that human existence should be recognised as complex and subject to progressive change, rather than as fixed or subject to magical transformation, Stone cited Donna Haraway's idea of the spiritual Native American 'Coyote' (295). This was Haraway's metaphor for a healthy life that interacts with its environment. A trans person adopting the Coyote spirit would acknowledge their connection to the past and their connection to both the masculine and feminine, allowing room for gendered contradiction and 'wholeness' of gendered being.

In contrast to the views of Raymond, Hausman and Jeffreys, Stone saw the possibility for the trans person to engender, 'new and unpredictable dissonances which implicate entire spectra of desire' (1991:296), suggesting that trans subjectivity had something to add to the state of heteronormativity. In contrast to Prosser's grounding of trans subjectivity in bodily makeup, and Garber's transvestism as ethereal dispersal, Stone's trans person became a 'genre'. By 'genre' Stone meant a category of belonging with no set borders of definition but nevertheless 'embodied' as a kind of living text,

> I suggest constituting transsexuals not as a class or problematic "third gender", but rather as a *genre* – a set of embodied texts whose potential for *productive* disruption of structured sexualities and spectra of desire has yet to be explored.
>
> (1991:296)

Various interpretations or aetiological constructions of the reality of trans subjectivity can be gleaned from the autobiographies and texts assessed for the purposes of this chapter. Drawing from the dualised science of the time, Michael Dillon, the first female-to-male transitioning person in the UK to obtain treatment (in the 1940s), stated that, '... *either the body must be made to fit the mind, as we have said, or the mind be made to fit the body ...*' (1946:65). In attempting to account for the fact that some of what he called '*pseudo-hermaphroditic*' individuals sought reassignment, and that some did not, he forwarded a social constructionist, if genetically based, aetiological explanation by speculating that, '*Certain cells contain certain genes; certain genes will make for certain tendencies, but environment may have the final decision as to whether the tendencies become actual or not*' (1946:71).

Contrasting to such a genetically determining account, according to Christine Jorgensen, Dr Hamburger (her endocrinologist) claimed that there was no such thing as 'normal' male and femaleness and that most people are located somewhere on a continuum between these sexed polarities (1967:159). As well as believing in such a continuum, Christine revealed her support for self-definition of sexual subjectivity, mentioning that, '*It seemed to me that the selection of sex determination should lie with the individual in an effort to live freely, so long as it was to no one else's disadvantage*' (196). However, In Denmark, Christine's reassignment doctors imposed their own views on her sexual subjectivity by relating her feelings of womanliness to her feminine hormonal activity and this kind of aetiology is now thought by some to explain trans subjectivity.[7] In a letter to her family she remarked that, '... *the real me, not the physical one, has not changed*', in order to reassure her family that she was still who she had always been, suggesting she thought that it is the body that is processed in reassignment, rather than the self.

When commencing visits to a trans men's support group in adulthood, autobiographer Dhillon Khosla noticed that the visitors presented a range of gendered and sexual dispositions, unlike any uniformity that might be expected from stereotypes of trans men. He observed of one visitor that, *'Both his vocal pitch and his mannerisms were extremely effeminate, and he made some allusion to his sexual interest in men'* (2006:8). It is now generally accepted by the trans community and by a number of transition specialists that trans people as a whole evidence a spectrum of personalities, genders and sexualities and yet can still all express a genuine desire for bodily reassignment. Dhillon himself inwardly rebelled at the idea of having to pass as stereotypically male in order to satisfy the demands of the Real Life Experience (34). He experienced perceptual shifts with the 'shifting boundaries' that accompanied his change in gender role, providing him with potential to provide insights into both conventional gender roles.

## 2.4 Conclusion

As described in section one, Foucault theorised that, in its efforts to identify those sexual subjectivities to be hidden and silenced, the Victorian era ironically engendered a flourishing of discourse around sexual subjectivity. However, discussion of such subjectivity was channelled into certain closely delineated narrative forms. The resulting 'silence and secrecy' did nothing to open and evolve discourse but imposed stereotypes from a distance instead of allowing its targets to find themselves through mutual communication.

Scientific discourse took over the reins of gender definition and it took a long time before trans people acquired the agency to begin reclaiming their own sexual subjectivities from gatekeepers of the new scientific metanarrative. When they did, they would contribute to the formation of their subjectivities via shared and evolving narrative. These contributions would allow gender variant people to influence the 'politics of naming' genders that began to burgeon with positive and negative consequences for the subjects of vociferous and open (as opposed to silent and secret) discourse.

In the second section it was found that theory or culture ascribed onto gender variant subjectivity (imposed 'voice') has often resorted to 'infantilisation' of the gender variant person. This has had the effect of denying gender variant people's contribution to 'grown-up' theory and society. Psychoanalysis, sexology and separatist feminism all contributed to the equating of trans subjectivity and gender variance with immature development where gender variant people were expected to be seen (researched) and not heard (philosophising). However, with increasing narrative access, gender variant people have narrated experiences of exclusion in contexts of family, school, work and leisure and how they have then been blamed for not maturing as expected when dealing with this exclusion. A 'refusal to grow up' would be attributed to trans subjects when society was blind to the trans subject's own particular gendered growing.

The third section, examining 'real' subjectivity, suggested that expulsion from the heteronormative gender order resulted in gender variant people gaining a fuller view of gender by looking at it from the outside in, with a more panoramic 'view from somewhere'. This often came after long periods of questioning their gendered legitimacy when so much cultural convention was shored up against them. However, trans-unfriendly feminist commentators, amongst others, had various theories of aetiology to impose upon trans subjectivity from a distance. Narratives, theoretical and autobiographical, produced by trans people in the 80s began to reclaim the definition of trans subjectivity by portraying medical intervention as a way of aligning the body with inner gender rather than simply facilitating a transformation of biological sex. Sandy Stone's vision of trans subjectivity as 'genre' suggested that such narratives could extract trans subjectivity from the schema of heteronormativity.

Chapter 3 is influenced by the themes of silence/secrecy, maturity and gendered/philosophical realness, in order to pick up on the cross-over between third wave and transgender perspectives of subjectivity, contradiction, narrative sharing and ownership of the means of definition.

**Notes**

1 Such feelings of legitimacy were addressed by Whittle (2006c) and are discussed in Chapter 6 as well.
2 A term used throughout the thesis to mean people's discovery of their own inner subjectivity.
3 From the sumptuary laws of King Edward III, through seventeenth century raids on Molly Houses (Norton, 1992), defining 'normality' is still often the aim of those in positions of definitional power, for instance in Ken Zucker and Susan Bradley's work with young trans people (1996).
4 ISAs include the family, media, religion and education. The structure of these social institutions engenders the individual's self-image, values and identifications.
5 In mainstream literature of the time, female same-sex relations were imagined as safely external to conventional culture by attributing them to the classical world or to mythical and far away countries (1999:127–8).
6 Precursor to the World Professional Association for Transgender Health (WPATH) International Symposiums on Transgender Health.
7 As suggested by Havelock Ellis (1928:82), Harry Benjamin (1953:86–7), Melissa Hines (January 2004), Whittle (2002a:48) and *Transstudy* participant Monica (Monica Apr 3rd, 2005, in <Christian Institute vs the GRB>).

# 3 The third wave
## Career feminism or quiet revolution?

**Introduction**

This chapter investigates published narrative discussion of third wave feminism. It theorises connections between a third feminist wave and transgender philosophy. The way that third wave feminism is named and presented follows on from the analysis of a 'politics of naming' in Chapter 2, to argue for and against the naming of such a wave. The formation of the reality of third wave feminism can be compared with the analysis of the reality of gender variant subjectivity and its connection to, and possible formation by, genre and genealogy. The third wave of feminism seems to align with the third phase of feminism identified by Julia Kristeva in *New Maladies of the Soul*, where differences in subjectivity are respected and included rather than held in suspicion and excluded, '... *the other is neither an evil being foreign to me nor a scapegoat from the outside, that is, of another sex, class, race, or nation*' (1993:223).

Kristeva theorised that the fixing of the identity 'woman' in the first feminist wave was necessary since it brought about a clear identification of women's exploitation in legal and material matters. Her notion of a second phase resembles the second wave of feminism, which began to identify differences inherent in the identity 'woman'. Her idea of a third phase includes the recommendation that any differences identified should not be assimilated into dominant subjectivities like 'feminist', 'women' or 'heteronormative' or be rejected on the basis of 'identity',

> I am not simply alluding to bisexuality, which most often reveals a desire for totality, a desire for the eradication of difference. I am thinking more specifically of subduing the "fight to the finish" between rival groups, not in hopes of reconciliation ... and not through a rejection of the other.
> (1993:222)

Support for Kristeva's difference inclusive third phase/wave comes from those who may be labelled as third wave feminists such as Alison Stone (2004), Seyla Benhabib (1992) and Rebecca Walker (1995), as well as from philosophical third wave feminists from other chronologically based waves.

Difference inclusion may be identified as the prominent feature of a philosophical third wave but the chronological third wave (early 1990s to present) is affected by social and cultural events not pertaining in the previous two waves (Friedlin, 2002; Jouve, 2004:199; Chakraborty, 2004:211). Globalisation, a different kind of gulf between rich and poor, environmental issues, the internet and new social subjectivities all call for a feminism that considers who are the real victims of organised masculinist exploitation on a larger scale and with a different organisational basis. The third wave considers these effects of modern life while drawing from developments made in other feminist waves to form what is arguably an identifiably new feminism. However, it can be contended that third wave feminism shouldn't necessarily have to present itself as different to the first two waves just for the sake of innovation or novelty. This contention mirrors the way that some contemporary trans narrators have endeavoured to understand the effects of trans subjectivity rather than pursue a quest for its aetiology and definition.[1] Nevertheless, as Rebecca Walker speculated of the new generation of feminist writers, '*They change the face of feminism as each new generation will, bringing a different set of experiences to draw from, an entirely different set of reference points, and a whole new set of questions*' (1995:xxxiv).

Whether these new writers are 'third wave' is an area for speculation, partly because few feminists seem to self-describe as 'third wave feminist'. This may be because feminists prefer to investigate rather than administer labels and are still investigating the nature and validity of the label, 'third wave feminism'. Below are four suggested areas that appear to suggest the nature of third wave philosophy, a philosophy-in-process that relates to, and holds potential to empower, gender variant subjectivities and transgender and feminist theories in their interactions with the law.

### 3.1 'Personally political postmodern identity'

During the 1960s and 70s, or what might be called the chronological second wave, feminism was very much influenced by social construction theory. This opened up the nature/nurture debate with regard to the development and essence of gender and later became of importance to trans people searching for explanations of their trans subjectivity. However, social construction theory, the theory that subjectivity is developed from influences other than, or as well as, inherent features (Burr, 2003), was a double-edged sword when adopted as an explanation of gender development. For instance, some people read this explanation as an argument that people should or could be socialised into or out of what were deemed to be unacceptable subjectivities, providing an image of gender variance and trans subjectivity as temporary or curable, with heteronormativity as the acceptable norm.

Identity is, for social constructionists, more accurately described as 'subjectivity' or identity-in-process. Foucault conceived of subjectivity as deriving very significantly from power, knowledge and other social influences,

... we believe that there is a strong account [in Foucault's thought] of the self in relation to *practices* and thus *culture* that emphasises both active and passive elements of the shaping of subjectivity – both self-constitution and cultural/discursive shaping of individuals as two aspects of the making of subjects.

(Belsey and Peters, 2007:176)

Social constructionists suggest that subjectivity is affected by, '*The particular representations of selfhood, the particular ways of accounting for ourselves, that are available to us in our culture*' (Burr, 2003:139).

In a passage of text indicating the emergence, in theoretical developments from psychoanalysis to postmodernism, of the notion of the subject as subject-in-process, Sara Ahmed stated that, '... *the psychoanalytic dis-placement of the Cartesian subject through the articulation of a concept of the unconscious provided the condition of possibility for a postmodern understanding of the subject and sexual difference as radically indeterminate and unstable*' (1995:17).

This statement challenges the notion, developed from sexology and early psychoanalysis, that we can pin down the aetiology and predict the development of sexual subjectivity. Similar to Marjorie Garber, Jean Baudrillard proposed that the 'transvestite' or 'transsexual' challenges this pinning down by uprooting sexual signs and signified objects and phenomena that are supposed to apply to one gender only (1993[1990]). Ahmed also posited that a transfer of signifiers occurs but saw the transvestist subject adopting all the stereotyped signs/signifieds of the feminine subject under patriarchy, reproducing such signs uncritically. Transvestism free of any personal politics, or social critique, is perhaps a 'postmodern identity' because it transgresses boundaries of gender and yet is perhaps identifiable as a type of gendering. However, as Ahmed suggests, it is not necessarily a personally *politically* postmodern identity, an identity based upon personally political beliefs.

Watson and Whittle provide a similar argument to Ahmed by considering that, '*As such, dissident genders are not of themselves subversive but recreate norms through the repetition of them*' (2005:201). The gender norms that Ahmed saw the transvestite recreating can only be subverted if transvestism is visible in society, whether in the form of unconventional gender appearance or visible in narrative accounts of transvestism and its relation to heteronormativity. This book argues that third wave theorists would not wish for people to possess postmodern non-identity (as opposed to a more identifiable 'subjectivity'), free from personal politics, and also would not expect people to have to uncritically belong to gender ascribed to them at birth.

Rita Felski claims that Derrida, Deleuze and Baudrillard all wished to challenge automatic ascribing of gender, an ascription that starts at birth, and describes how, '... *feminists are in turn increasingly appealing to metaphors of transvestism to describe the mutability and plasticity of the sexed body*'. Despite the openness of some feminists to such 'postmodern identity', otherwise identifiable as 'identity-in-process' or 'subjectivity', Felski highlighted the fact that, '… *transgenderism remains a necessarily ambiguous figure for feminist theorists*' (1994:572). The notion of multiple and shifting identities is also often vigorously questioned by trans people opposed to the concepts of identity-in-process and/or the possibility of gender created from political stance.

Ahmed discussed Arthur Kroker and David Cook's perspective on the potential anomie engendered by postmodern non-identity (1995:20). Kroker and Cook argued that dualistic gender might well be challenged by the gender androgyny to be found in much postmodern capitalist ideology but it is done so in a way that works just to emphasise gender as a manufactured and superficial item. In a similar way, it can be seen that third wave feminism is sometimes conflated with postfeminism because of its links with apparently manufactured capitalist ventures such as popular culture, 'cyberidentity' and girl power. What is meant to be an empowering way of challenging ascribed gender through the micro-politics of everyday representations becomes confused with a postfeminist reinforcement of artificial, aggressive, acquisitive or overly feminine identity. This book argues that third wave feminism combines and empathises with inclusive and different 'voices', such as those from other feminist waves, trans people and ethnic minorities, in order to challenge this errant conflation.

Rather than non-identity, *politically* postmodern identity represents a concept of identity that can be chosen or moulded to some extent, turning it into 'subjectivity'. Subjectivity promises to be a means to evade the barriers to inclusion that stymied second wave attempts to make feminism difference friendly. For instance, it would address how women of colour felt particularly disinherited from the second wave of feminism because they didn't seem to fit the 'identity' required of feminism,

> In 1989 Angela Davis, interviewed for *Feminist Review*, concluded that the overwhelming majority of black women had felt no connection with the 1970s feminist movement. … the 'double jeopardy' of black women was masked within a feminist 'sisterhood' articulated largely by white, middle class, heterosexual women.
>
> (Gamble, 2001:32 and 33)

In order to address the conundrum of differences in subjectivity to be found within 'women' and 'trans people' as social groupings, some feminist and transgender theorists tried to interpret subjectivity in a different way. This was to involve retaining subjectivity for the purposes of subjective politics but would evade criticism of essentialising people from very different backgrounds under one homogenizing banner. Theorists involved in undertaking this examination of subjectivity through a third wave focus include Kristeva, hooks, Butler, Haraway, Stone, Whittle, Stryker and Feinberg.

Such difference-friendly feminists and trans theorists attempted to combat the effects of identity essentialism, while allowing a definable subjective space for subjectivity politics, by applying the concepts of what might be called 'genre and genealogy'. It has been seen that Sandy Stone envisioned trans people as a 'genre' in order to rehabilitate them from medical pathology imposed by reassignment specialists. Preceding this was Foucault's notion of genealogy, briefly introduced by the author in a *Transstudy* posting,

> The idea of genealogy has been construed by Michel Foucault as an alternative way of looking at history. He said that what we perceive as history is a patchwork of recordings that may or may not involve the truth. Identities are to a large extent man-made, and sometimes even woman-made, as we negotiate their meaning through history. So Foucault might admit that he himself was a genealogy, an identity made up of what has been discussed and written about him over his life-span.
> (The Researcher May 5th, 2007, in <Being Un-PC oops>)

According to Foucault himself, '*The purpose of history, guided by genealogy, is not to discover the roots of our identity but to commit itself to its dissipation*' (Foucault, 1977:162).

Similar attempts to revise identity as subjectivity came from Stephen Whittle (2002a) and third wave theorist Alison Stone (2004) who revised trans people as a 'genre' and women as a 'genealogy' respectively, and from Susan Stryker who visualised trans subjectivity as subjectivity-in-process formed from abject exclusion,

> Transgender rage is the subjective experience of being compelled to transgress what Judith Butler has referred to as the highly gendered regulatory schemata that determine the viability of bodies, of being compelled to enter a "domain of abjected bodies, a field of deformation" that in its unlivability encompasses and constitutes the realm of legitimate subjectivity. ... Transgender rage furnishes a means for disidentification with compulsorily assigned subject positions.
> (2006[1994]:253)

In a similar way, and quoting the work of Hart (1992), Carl Stychin described the shared 'Otherness' that can evolve from rage to produce a new kindred of the oppressed,

> Furthermore, the urgency and anger felt by many around HIV and Aids also fuelled the rise of a more radical, uncompromising politics: '... rage rather than mere acceptance, rejection of a flawed tolerance rather than demands for integration ... (Hart, 1992).'
> (Stychin, 1995:144)

Whittle claimed that a trans community had emerged from shared experiences of oppression and that it classed itself as a genre in the way described by Sandy Stone (2002a:82). He observed how, in 'The Empire Strikes Back'

(1991) Stone interpreted trans people as 'embodied texts' who could challenge fixed texts delineating sexual identity. Whittle stated that, '*Arguably essentialist, trans-theory does not, however, avoid social construction in that it recognises the artefacts of gender and sex that render them specific to any given social situation*' (2002a:82). These concepts of gender opened a space for gender variant and/or trans people to choose to realise their preferred gendered subjectivity without having to rely on biological evidence available at the time.

Developing Butler's notion of performativity, Alison Stone conceived of women as a social rather than biological group, realising that women as a category have been subject to '*overlapping chains of interpretation*' that sometimes suggested '*fictitious commonalities*' such as those that blighted the second wave (2004:86, 89). Such fictitious commonalities were also identified by Ednie Kaeh Garrison, '*... the "second wave" when feminism became synonymous with "women's issues". Chandra Mohanty has called this slippage the "feminist osmosis thesis" – the assumption that women are feminists by virtue of their experiences as women*' (2005:241).

Stone's remedy for fictitious commonalities was to conceive of women as a coalitional group, related by, '*overlaps and indirect connections within women's historical and cultural experience*' (2004:90) and '*infinitely varying while entangled together historically*' (92). Genealogy therefore seems to be third wave in operation for Stone, drawing meanings from pre-existing forms (or waves) in order to reconstruct present ones when, '*... each appropriation of existing standards concerning femininity effects a more or less subtle modification of their meaning with reference to changing contexts, power relationships, and histories*' (91).

Using genre and genealogy, trans people and women can be classifiable, for the purpose of subjectivity politics, but in a different way to traditionally ascribed categorization that has been used (whether deliberately or not) to keep trans people and women in 'their place'. This place has worked to the long-term detriment of trans people and women since it is a place mostly determined by patriarchs operating from strong positions of definitional power in politics, law, medicine and the family. However, philosophically second wave feminism itself inadvertently used the essentialisation of identity to exclude women of certain social ethnicities and more deliberately used it to send trans people back to their natal sexes, for instance by Raymond, Greer, Hausman, Jeffreys and Millot. Hopefully, the (theoretically at least) positively difference-inclusive project of third wave feminism will avoid what *Transstudy* participant Monica saw as a dysfunctional progression of feminist waves,

> What concerns me about Feminism, Ed, is this. ... First wave feminism seemed to consider us M2Fs as their 'sisters'. ... Second wave feminism regarded us as fakes and 'pantomime dames'. ... Third Wave Feminism thinks we should be poured into their melting pot and stirred. ... For all one knows, Fourth Wave Feminism will probably want us

to be some kind of third and fourth sexes and Fifth Wave Feminism might want us to be burned at the stake.
(Monica Jun 18th, 2006, in <Trans and Feminist Theories>)

Although Monica is right to be wary (amongst other things) of a postmodernist gender 'melting pot', this is not the stated project of third wave feminism. It is rather a commitment to freedom of expression, movement, speech and social connections that can engender an energetic allegiance to the feminist cause where feminism becomes a politically postmodern identity of its own, rather than a collection of people related by biological embodiment or social status.

It is the allegiance to feminism and a range of 'in-process' but identifiable subjectivities that makes third wave feminism a cohesive alternative to the threat of the anomie that might emerge from postmodernist feminism. Third wave philosophy (feminist or transgender) is theory ready to incorporate change and promises to expand the feminist propensity for the absorption of philosophical perspectives in an eclectically magpie-like endeavour.

## 3.2 Contradiction

The concept of 'postmodern identity' seems to be a contradictory pairing of terms but indicates the phenomenon of 'subjectivity' when examined closely. Leslie L Heywood and Jennifer Drake (1997) emphasised how the increasingly complex history of feminism has led third wave feminists to accept contradiction, or what appears to be contradiction, as an inherent feature of a third wave perspective. They view this feminism as a complex hybrid born from other waves and a multitude of subjectivities, leading to a more rounded or whole feminist subjectivity. They describe how this hybridity can act as a healthy adaption to the various complex oppressions facing feminists today. They also see how no feminist is free from susceptibility to become an oppressor themselves because of the Russian doll-like nature of oppressions within oppressions, portrayed as 'internecine conflict' in Chapter 1, that can develop from the slightest lapse into self-assurance. Identifying this kind of oppression is the first step towards eliminating it, and this is what third wave feminists attempt to do through inclusive communication.

Heywood and Drake placed American rock musician Courtney Love and American singer-songwriter Me'Shell NdegéOcello as contradictory characters, hypothesizing them as progeny of third wave feminist 'parentage' (1997:4–6). Love and NdegéOcello seem to be more down-to-earth characters than convention following 'conservative feminists', a feature that seems to match the characteristic 'in-touch-with-the-real-world' tendency of many trans activists and theoreticians. Heywood and Drake refer to this characteristic as 'lived messiness' and this type of living is no doubt familiar to those alienated by the apparent social 'cleanliness' of conservative-functionalist discourse. Another third wave anthology editorial pairing, Rory Dicker and Alison

Piepmeier, also detected the third wave's focus on and embodiment of gendered complexity,

> One way that the third wave distinguishes itself from the second wave is through its emphasis on paradox, conflict, multiplicity, and messiness. This generation's feminism is often informed by postmodern, poststructuralist theories of identity; as a result, we are able to see the constructed nature of identity as well as the way in which gender may be a performance that can be manipulated and politically altered as it is performed.
> (Dicker and Piepmeier, 2003:16)

Hopefully, third wave feminists perceive parallels between complex womanly subjectivity and those subjectivities we have come to describe as gender variant and trans, through a perceptive lens informed by 'genre' and 'genealogy'. Gender variant subjectivities serve to highlight sexual subjectivity as contradictory since these subjectivities deny the essential connection of anatomy and possibly physiology to gender and sexuality. As previously noted, this interpretation of sexual subjectivity has been strongly contested by feminists such as Raymond, Hausman and Millet who only see contradiction as revealing the non-reality of trans subjectivities.

In third wave anthology *To Be Real*, Jeannine Delombard described how, circa 1985, the 'lesbian sex wars' revealed the lived messiness of sexual subjectivity in dealing with efforts to define the essence of lesbianism (1995:24, 27–29). Lesbians seemed to be asking themselves, '*Should one operate erotics of the same and/or erotics of the Other*'? In 1995 the lesbian community experienced a butch-femme renaissance, which called into question the actual interpretation of 'butch' and 'femme', as notably assessed by Judith Halberstam (1998). Some lesbians stood fast in the face of resurrecting gender dualisms, something they saw as a heteronormative enterprise. However, like Halberstam, Delombard claimed that butch-femme actually flouted the constricting dualisms of heteronormativity by complicating straight masculinity and femininity. Delombard claimed that, '*Far from simplifying our relationship, butch-femme layers it with a tantalizing intricacy and a highly erotic contradictoriness*' (1995:31).

Alternative gendering such as butch/femme may not so easily create oppressed 'Other' genders as has occurred in heteronormative society because of the complexity they bring to the apparent obviousness of gender. In allowing for subjectivities like butch-femme and vanilla lesbianisms to coexist side by side, Stacy Gillis and Rebecca Munford (2004:168) declared that, '… *as will be shown, third wave feminist politics allow for both equality and difference*'. This positive, inclusive and understanding approach to difference is presented as 'postdifference' later in this book.

The lived messiness of the third wave may manifest in the way that it is theorised by some to exist without 'boundaries', unlike most metanarratives of gender and social relations,

> Often what we accept as a sign of "purity" is the ability to mark out boundaries ... Since I believe in impurity (pollution, mixtures, mestizas), working to make the boundaries of third wave feminism clear and distinct is particularly unsatisfying.
>
> (Garrison, 2005:253)

If third wave feminists cannot completely escape metanarratives, they can at least be aware of their proliferation, and refer instead to 'theoretical narratives that are not one', to paraphrase a phrase by Luce Irigaray (1985), [2] in order to announce theories' spread and their complex essence. Metanarratives are always contingent for third wave feminists, meaning that, as Foucault speculated, truth can never be arrived at once and for all but we can probably gain brief glimpses of some of its aspects through inclusive debate. Lived messiness inevitably involves, but accurately describes, the untidy nature of theories and human conditions despite being sometimes uncomfortably unfixed as Leon from the *Transstudy* considered, '*Yeah ... they [feminist and trans academics] keep changing their collective academic/medical minds ... its all very annoying*' (Leon Jun 15th, 2006, in <Trans and Feminist Theories>)

Challenging my alignment of feminism with transgender, Leon was not keen to associate feminism with trans subjectivity and transgender philosophy, describing the two as incompatible or contradictory,

> She [Germaine Greer] is like the Scottish weather..just wait 5 minutes and she will chnage her mind..just like all so called feminists !..its an evolving thing, as women chnage their goal posts. .a very female thing *laughing*... Trans people dont change their goal posts they just exist and have tried to simply BE. with the wonderful Press for change guys always pushing for our rights to exist....its SO COMPLETLEY DIFFERENT ...feminism isnt at all linked to being trans...belive me Ed I know I AM TRANS.
>
> (Leon Jun 26th, 2006, in <Trans and Feminist Theories>)

However, Leon was perhaps unaware of the rigidity of much philosophical second wave ethos, notably espoused by Greer herself in her dismissal of trans subjectivity as unreal. Feminism, just like any other human philosophy or discourse, involves people from different philosophical and personally political backgrounds and so cannot be accurately stereotyped as a metanarrative, or alternatively as postmodern, without invoking confusing contradictions. Philosophical third wave feminists/transgenderists perhaps wish to be part of a feminism-in-progress rather than a feminism-in-stasis characteristic of some philosophically second wave ideology.

Feminist theory and philosophy has been classed as inferior to positivistic and (so called) objective research because of its reliance on reflexivity.[3] In a comment upon the way that Gilligan's research challenged that produced by a positivistic approach, Carol Smart pointed out how the impact of Gilligan's work, '... *has been felt very widely inside and outside the USA because of its power to validate the 'feminine' and to give meaning to that which is constantly dismissed as irrational, illogical, and inconsistent*' (1989:72).

Gilligan notably described how male theorists have been blind to the way that women introduce apparently contradictory complexity to gendered experience, '*The failure to see the different reality of women's lives and to hear the differences in their voices stems in part from the assumption that there is a single mode of social experience and interpretation*' (Gilligan, 1982:173).

She also described how the morality of responsibility, characteristically displayed by women, introduced the confusion of complexity into the masculine moral world, '*At the same time, it becomes clear why, from a male perspective, a morality of responsibility appears inconclusive and diffuse, given its insistent contextual relativism*' (Gilligan, 1982:22).

Gender variant people can be seen to add even more gendered complexity, but this can be interpreted as providing useful insights into the constructed essence of gendered experience. Many gender variant people view their own sexual subjectivity from within and heteronormativity from without, providing an important inversion of many people's perspective on such subjectivity.

## 3.3 Inter-wave philosophy and maternal relations

An element of the postmodern affects the way that many third wavers perceive feminism as identifiable in 'waves'. These are not fixedly identifiable waves but, as described by Delombard (1995), they 'trans' the normal concept of waves as separate movements, contradicting the expectation that they are discreet. These waves are sometimes chronologically related to feminist movements but can alternatively be described as philosophies that can span all of feminist history and can be linked to feminists from or between any chronological wave. Ednie Kaeh Garrison likened the waves of feminism to radio waves where such waves, '... *can be used to communicate information in the form of ideas, words, narrative, consciousness, knowledge*' (Garrison, 2005:243).

Garrison also compared the ebb and flow of feminist waves to tidal waves, theorising that feminist waves return to previous chronological waves in order to manifest as hybrid forces composed of these previous ambulations. [B]ell hooks seemed to align with this inclusive wave metaphor when perceiving feminism to be formed from a potpourri of social and theoretical inclusion (Gamble, 2006[1998]).

The 'lived messiness' of combining elements of all feminist waves makes for more of a whole feminist experience that can sit comfortably with social subjectivities not usually associated with feminism. Third wave feminism appears to embrace such social and theoretical inclusiveness while not rejecting previous feminist philosophy and figureheads.[4] Methodological procedure in more inclusive feminisms has involved researchers communing closely with the real lives of those living in the research community, for example in the ethnographic work of Anne Oakley in 1975.

For Heywood and Drake, third wave feminism appears to be a community-orientated wave, in a similar vein to the feminism promoted by Delombard (1995), Garrison (2005) and hooks (1997). The communal combining of feminisms suggested by these theorists might be described as a kind of inter-wave philosophy. An inclusive community, self-critical and personally political with a 'view from somewhere', might stem from third wave feminism and could act to include 'Othered' subjectivities and those portrayed as gendered 'immigrants and refugees' in the sense that they are seen by many as new to the gender that they adopt. Heywood and Drake proposed that, '*Communities today have to be imagined on different bases than that of the separatism of identity politics, bases such as what hooks called a "commonality of feeling"*' (1997:17).

Some feminists have examined inter-wave philosophy and community orientation by applying what the author identifies as the metaphor of 'maternal relations'. From a psychoanalytical perspective, Julia Kristeva theorised that maternal relations are psychologically buried in human development in early childhood developmental stages. Such ties are repressed in the name of forming structured hierarchies that provide security in the form of separate identity formation and subject positioning within one's native society. The potential for a perhaps more feminine networking of kinship relations is lost in community development directed by the resulting symbolic communication. However, ghostly traces of the maternal relationship usually remain in the psyche and cause us to yearn for the deep understanding gained from this primary bond, '... *the psyche represents the bond between the speaking being and the other, a bond that endows it with a therapeutic and moral value*' (1993 [1979]:4).

If the concept of maternal relations can be transposed to the reality of maternal relations between feminist generations, this reality sometimes seems different to the utopian vision provided by philosophical third wave theorists. Gillian Howie and Ashley Tauchert addressed inter-wave relations between feminists and remarked that, '*Unfortunately, because patriarchy is built upon the symbolic and real severance of productive matrilinear relations, the generational transitions within the feminist tradition are inherently fraught and conflict is aggravated by increasingly competitive conditions within, and without, the academy*' (2004:45).

Any of the metaphorical mother/daughter feminist conflicts investigated by Astrid Henry in *Not My Mother's Sister* (2004) may derive from confusion imposed by such patriarchal manoeuvres. Feminists try to compete in a masculinist and patriarchal environment while attempting to maintain links with less hierarchical feminist networks that span generations and/or personal politics. For instance, some second wavers have identified what they see as, '... *the transition from a movement based on the "we" to today's sea of disparate "I"'s*' (Friedlin, 2002), in revealing what they see as a kind of postfeminist 'I want it all and I'm going to get it' corporate ladder-climbing kind of feminism. Phyllis Chesler interpreted the instigators of the second wave as a band of 'sisters' rather than daughters, arguing that 'sisterhood' helped free second wavers from the fetters of metaphorical first wave motherhood in order to form their own agency in expression (Henry, 2004:9). However, this seems different to the 'sisterhood' envisaged by hooks where women are metaphorical sisters with women from other ethnicities and feminist waves (1984:43–65).

In 'Genealogies and Generations', Gillis, Howie and Munford (2004) suggest that third wave feminism might be reinforcing a 'generational account of feminism', seeming to conflate it with the exclusionary operation of post-feminism. The chronological third wave may provide this account whereas the philosophical third wave, in theory, does not. Third wave feminists consider that, though many of them do exist in a different generational period, they can have their own theoretical spaces while not needing to sever connections with feminist 'mothers' or 'older sisters'. They recognise that philosophical third wavers have often lived and worked before, in and between chronological first, second and third wave periods. Progressive feminists can empathise with the spirit of each wave, accepting that each previous chronological wave was functional in its time and that feminism needs to move with the times. Feminists of any chronological or philosophical wave, and any sexual subjectivity, would then not be automatically essentialised out of any other wave membership, a situation compared to a 'third generation' by Kristeva,

> The meaning I am attributing to the word "generation" suggests less a chronology than a signifying space, a mental space that is at once corporeal and desirous. ... For this third generation, which I strongly support (which I am imagining?) the dichotomy between man and women as an opposition of two rival entities is *a problem for metaphysics.*
> (1993:222)

The handing down of knowledge from feminist generation to feminist generation is a way of avoiding reinventing the wheel,of having to rediscover all previous feminist insights anew. Zita stated that, '*To me the most pressing task for the feminisms of our time, both inside and outside academe, is this cross-generational moment ...*' (Summer, 1997:1), outlining the necessity for cross-generational relations. Cross-generational relations can ensure, as Felski thought, that many histories written by women and postcolonial peoples which, '*... seek to contest and transform our view of the past by discovering its exclusions, oppressions, and hidden triumphs, to rewrite and extend, rather than to negate, history*' (1994:571), are not buried in a dusty library.

If trans people can benefit from and contribute to maternal relations, for instance through the medium of shared narratives, then they may escape their position as passive receivers of scientific discourse handed down to them from psycho-medical experts, legislation handed down by the legal fraternity, and stereotyping representations handed down by separatist 'heteronormatives'. This has occurred to some extent with the emergence of theory, philosophy, narratives and legal activism produced by trans people who may be 'third wave' in a way similar to the third wave feminists mentioned so far. Narrative through maternal relations may unite all those who belong to the 'kindred' of those who do not fit, in the sense ventured in Gloria Anzaldúa's (1983[1981]) description of those on the 'Other' side of borders separating privilege from oppression.

## 3.4 Womanism: excluded but inclusive

Feminists including Heywood and Drake attribute the initiation of the third wave to the community-orientated efforts of women of colour in the 1980s. Like much of third wave feminism past and present because of its apparently contradictory nature, women of colour feminism could be described as invisiblised[5] and therefore 'unnamed' and unrecognised until the 1990s. Heywood and Drake described how feminism of colour brought to our attention the coloured neutrality of whiteness where a 'community of no community'[6] exists, just as has often been the case with regard to capitalism and masculinism, which often appear to be natural and functional social discourses. The 'community of no community' needs to hide its true nature since in reality it operates as a community of domination. This is a different kind of invisiblisation to that experience by women of colour feminists in that it works to the advantage of those invisiblised.

Rebecca Clark Mane warns that, '*As a discursive formation, whiteness has the special quality of lacking specific fixed content in itself*', forming invisible discourse and maintaining an unnamed quality, '*the problem of how whiteness refuses to name itself, how it always likes to remain "hidden"…*' (2012:73–74). She recommends that, '*locating whiteness requires reading absences, following traces and ghosts, and privileging syntax (how something is said) over content (what is said)*' (74), bringing to mind the mode of semiotic or pre-symbolic language theorised by Kristeva. White discourse still often masquerades under a mass-schema of common-sense and taken for granted discourse.

In this way social subjectivities and communities can be invisiblised by powerful discourse in order to keep them subdued, as Astrid Henry has detected about the hidden community of racial feminist struggle where,

> The struggle for gender equality is not independent from the struggle for racial equality; race isn't merely some earlier, and thus disposable, concern which helps to launch feminism. Rather, race is intrinsic to feminism, always there when it begins, always essential to whatever shape feminism takes.
>
> (2004:164)

'Womanism' has come to be a way of naming, and therefore revealing, the unacknowledged efforts and influence of women of colour's feminist ethos and lifestyles over the decades. This ethos and collection of lifestyles appears to have operated via the kind of 'erotics of the unnaming' mentioned in

Chapter 2, rather than emanating from a 'politics of the named' or overt political stances. Alice Walker used the term 'womanist' in *In Search of Our Mothers' Gardens* to refer to a mother of female children and to indicate a woman who loves other women and who is a proponent and exponent of women's culture. The womanist is dedicated to the survival of both men and women and her feminism concerns the welfare of both, in the way that bell hooks believes womanists should be inclusive of men's liberation and that men are also harmed by gender roles. The womanist communicates via lived experience as much as through academic theory.

Astrid Henry highlights how the pioneering work of women and feminists of colour led to the formation of the third wave. Examples of this work can be found in contributions to *The Third Wave: Feminist Perspectives on Racism*. This anthology might be described as a 'ghostly anthology', since according to Garrison, *'Although this book never materialized, the desire for it is such that people do speak as though it exists'* (2005:249). In this anthology, which was of fundamental influence to the third wave even though unpublished, Lisa Albrecht described how third wavers did not assign women from different generations to different feminist waves but drew from their particular experiences to highlight feminism's need to concentrate on including wrongfully excluded others into its philosophy and movements. Henry described this anti-exclusionary operation by womanist writers/activists in the following way,

> [T]he contradictory character of the third wave emerged not from the generational divides between second wavers and their daughters, but from critiques by Cherrie Moraga, Gloria Anzaldúa, bell hooks, Chela Sandoval, Audre Lorde, Maxine Hong Kingston and many other feminists of colour who called for a "new subjectivity" in what was, up to that point, white, middle class, first world feminism. These are the discourses that shaped, and must continue to shape, third wave agendas in the years to come.
>
> (2004:32)

Womanism, with its situation in tailor made, non-hierarchical[7] relations and non-'Othering' (Moraga 1983), and adaptation to the socio-political environment,[8] aligns with the mores of ethics of care. It is not an opposing doctrine to feminism, according to bell hooks (1989:181), and actually may embody the original form of third wave feminism, which may have existed from the dawn of humanity, and in an unnamed fashion, long before the other two waves which have been based in what might be termed as modern and postmodern (industrial) society respectively. Although not a collective wave in the modern sense, this wave would have formed collective relations through extended feminist 'families'. It has derived from the real-life struggle of oppressed women's lives,

> True feminism springs from an actual experience of oppression, a lack of socially-prescribed means of ensuring one's well-being. ...

> Above all, true feminism is impossible without intensive involvement with production. All over the African diaspora, but particularly on the Continent, the black woman's role in this regard is paramount. It can, therefore, be stated with much justification that the black woman is to a large extent the original feminist.
>
> (Steady, 1985:36)

Helen Charles criticises Filomina Steady for appropriating feminism as a black phenomenon but Steady just seems to be acknowledging the historical development of the phenomenon and not implying that black women own feminism. Charles also criticises Walker for imposing the term womanism onto black women, saying that they should have the choice whether to take up the term and should consider whether it distances black women from white, just like the term 'feminism' distanced white women from black (1990:18). She warns that it may act as an uncritical blanket term as did 'feminism' in second wave feminism (1997:282) and that, for Walker, it is too focused upon maternal and spiritual matters to be a political stance (1997:284).

In addressing the need for a separate term to indicate women of colour's feminism, Clark Mane claims that, '*Many foundational third-wave texts suggest that race and racial justice are foregrounded in third-wave theorizing, yet women-of-color feminists and their antiracist allies have challenged this inclusive claim*' (2012).

Perhaps inclusion is theorised and recommended in third wave theory, rather than being a real feature of third wave lives and activism. Clark Mane detected '*a set of structuring grammars of whiteness*' (72) in key third wave texts operating via, '*… postrace historical narrative, the postmodern abstraction of women-of-color theories, the flattening and proliferation of difference through a long list of interchangeable elements, and irreconcilable contradiction*' (2012:72).

She warns that, '*… inclusion alone is insufficient. What matters is not the token inclusion of chapters and voices but how difference is theorized, navigated, and understood and the effect it has on the core project of feminism*' (2012:83–84).

Here she makes us investigate the actual term 'inclusion' to realise that the token placing of theory and women of colour theorists in proximity to white feminism is not real inclusion but just strategic placing. However, it could be argued that including texts and theorists in academic forums at least draws attention to them. But Clark Mane maintains that only a 'decolonial analysis' can address the cultural factors that name, define and revise third wave feminism. She seems to believe it is possible to empathise with subjective differences, in order to build a feminist coalition, rather than leaving them alone when they seem too contradictory. This will work to counter what hooks saw as the 'commodification of Otherness' where the exotic and unknown Other is a stereotype to be explored and consumed by the subject wishing to undergo an adventure in order to attain the impression of transforming their own subjectivity, '... *whatever difference the Other inhabits is eradicated, via exchange, by a consumer cannibalism that not only displaces the Other but denies the significance of that Other's history through a process of decontextualization*' (1992:31).

Here the Other has no political subjectivity and is not seen as a real person. This kind of stranger fetishism that replaced stranger oppression was also detected by Anzaldúa in the situation of women of colour after the second wave of feminism (1983:204, 206). It also seems to apply to the current situation of gender variant people subject to the commodifying interest of the media and consumer culture.

Despite the many instances of oppression and stranger fetishism from white culture, Anzaldúa, in identifying the need to seek out kindred spirits, does not exclude whites from the list of people she loves (1983:206). She seeks coalition with anyone who needs to find a space to exist when excluded from all mainstream culture,

> I build my own universe, El Mundo Zurdo. I belong to myself and not to any one people.
> I walk the tightrope with ease and grace. I span abysses. Blindfolded in the blue air. The sword between my thighs, the blade warm with my flesh. I walk the rope – an acrobat in equipoise, expert at the balancing act.
> The rational, the patriarchal, and the heterosexual have held sway and legal tender for too long. Third world women, lesbians, feminists, and feminist-orientated men of all colors are banding and bonding together to right that balance. Only together can we be a force. I see us as a kind of network of kindred spirits, a kind of family.
>
> (1983:209)

Feminists now generally accept that many social and psychological differences exist between women, and this was recognised by hooks in 1984 who suggested that solidarity of 'sisterhood' was needed because, '*There can be no mass-based feminist movement to end sexist oppression without a united front* ...' (1984:44). [H]ooks contrasted sisterhood to the idea of '*shared victimization*' emphasised by bourgeois second wavers. Shared victimization came to resemble the exclusionary operation of patriarchy, with the creation of what might be viewed as 'women's clubs' rather than 'old boys' networks. Privileged feminists came to resemble beneficent Victorian colonial philanthropists who would tolerate token inputs from women of colour if they did not threaten to compromise the relatively comfortable position of their white middle-class enclaves. The result was a kind of social cleansing of women who didn't fit in with bourgeois subjectivity. When women of colour became fashionable, Anzaldúa noticed how the 'pseudo-liberal ones' would take on a, '*missionary role. She attempts to talk for us – what a presumption!*' (1983:206).

Astrid Henry (2004:15) points out how the chronological second wave mother figure is seen as white, and, the author suggests, as an activist academic lesbian. There are many more types of feminist 'mother' and maternal relationships and women of colour have yielded many examples of these. These relationships have helped women to avoid reinventing a 'square wheel' by making the same mistakes again, where they, 'end up repeating a white second-wave inattention to the intersectionality of identity' (97). Conversely, Carol Siegal argues that ignorance can lead to new developments unfettered by links to the past and then new 'wheels' can be constructed (2000:108). Henry points out that this sentiment is echoed by Joan Morgan who believes that young women have to escape the apron strings of maternal relations in order to form their own feminist voice (1999:156).

For Rebecca Walker, access to the mother figure was a rather suffocating experience where she felt trapped in a feminist 'ghetto' (1995:xxix). The contradictions involved in the difference between her feminist life and the lives of her feminist foremothers were felt by young feminists 'Othered' from second wave feminism because of a feeling of not being real feminists. 'Mother' suggests a non-sexual relationship with 'daughters', where the mother will be rejected, according to Henry (2004:125). Maternal relations, as used in this book, is a metaphor for womanly communication where the mother is not confined to another generation/wave and so does not have to be rejected in this way and doesn't have to be feared as an all-powerful and pervasive maternal figure.

When the author cites woman of colour feminists as associated with maternal relations, he does not automatically disassociate anyone else from the maternal, just as neither Gilligan or Kristeva did in their theories of maternal relations. The author believes that women of colour can be proud of any association of maternal relations and that if they are not then this is likely because all things feminine seem to be devalued in industrial societies. This is a controversial viewpoint and will not be held by some feminists and women of colour. The author does not suggest that all women of colour display maternal relations.

Maternal relations can be linked to the idea of communion, explained further in Chapter 5 and focussed upon by Dan P McAdams, expanding the definition provided by David Bakan (1966). This interpretation of communion is more about communicative bonding than establishing the self, as is the case for communion's counterpart, 'agency'. Communion seems to be inherent to the discourse of womanism, as articulated poetically by Alice Walker with reference to communion between generations, '*And so our mothers and grandmothers have, more often than not anonymously, handed on the creative spark, the seed of the flower they themselves never hoped to see: or like a sealed letter they could not plainly read*' (1983[1976]:240).

Communion should also take place between women and men for Walker and is not a separatist agenda (1983[1976]:xi). Despite difficulties in intergenerational bonding for some young feminists, it is also evident in the work of younger women of colour writers such as Pragna Patel who suggested alliances to combat oppression of women and that subjective differences lead to strengths,

> Women Against Fundamentalism, with its heterogenous composition of women from a variety of religious backgrounds, is an example of the new direction in which coalition feminist politics is developing. In WAF recognizing our differences gives us strength, and a better understanding of the complexities involved in resisting racism, sexism and fundamentalism.
> 
> (Patel, 1997:267)

While not wishing to take on the label 'third wave', Kimberley Springer (2002) perceived young women of colour's communion-like relations as relations building and as a link with feminist foremothers. Womanism is characterised as a non-hierarchical, organic and non-separatist way of communicating that works to give voice to hidden societal subjectivity, including that of the woman of colour and other multiply oppressed subjectivities (Moraga, 1983; Lorde, 1984). In this way, it is a very communion-based social discourse.

The activities that womanists have engaged in, in order to share their experiences and make their silences speak, in the spirit of communion, form a kind of multi-issue activism, in contrast to large social issue theorising, that brings to mind the way that Gill Frith used 'quilting' as a metaphor for such communication,

> Since its inception, Black feminist criticism has questioned the distinction between 'high' and 'low' forms of art. Alice Walker (1984) echoes and extends Barbara Smith's emphasis on communal activity, to argue that the Black female creative tradition includes quilting, gardening and singing the blues .... Charlotte Pierce-Baker (1990) takes up the quilting metaphor and applies it to the literary curriculum. Demonstrating the connections between Jane Eyre and Harriet Jacobs' slave narrative, *Incidents in the Life of a Slave Girl* (1861; reprinted 1988), she argues that studying two rebellious, 'confessional' texts together creates a 'quilting of voices' which highlights the similarities and differences between two women from very different backgrounds.
> 
> (Frith, 1993:169)

As well as being a metaphor for micro-politics/issues and creative traditions, the notion of quilting seems to tie in with the meaning of Foucault's version of history and subjectivity as mosaics of genealogies, and with Bornstein's perception of gender variance as a patchwork of subjectivities (Whittle, 1998:48). To describe history in 'Nietzche, Genealogy, History' (1971), Foucault uses terms such as, '... *singularity of events*' (76) '... *numberless beginnings*' (81) '... *series of interpretations*' (86) '... *countless lost events*' (89). Here history is a quilted patchwork rather than linear continuum.

Metaphorical quilting of the idea of identity is suggested by Clark Mane as a way to challenge identity stereotypes,

> ... when Carrillo Rowe explicitly named white women and women of color in her article "Locating Feminism's Subject" (2000), respondent Patrice Buzzanell resisted this naming because, she argued, "[Carrillo Rowe's] use of binary categories misrepresents the varied experiences and shifting identities of White women and women of color and divides all women into two seemingly impenetrable camps. When she juxtaposes Whites and people of color, she eliminates the shifting, socially constructed, and negotiable nature of social membership as well as the kind of language that can bring women together in their fight against the consequences of White privilege" (Buzzanell 2000, 83).
>
> (2012:75)

Here we see a requirement for a perspective similar to Anzaldúa's border subjectivities via recognition of how the quilting of social construction takes place to produce subjectivity, rather than ready-made identities existing from birth. This perspective is gained from the 'view from somewhere' of marginalised subjectivities. As Clark Mane says, womanist texts such as Anzaldúa's have highlighted the existence of contradiction in subjectivity as a way of challenging common-sense normative discourse, while attempting to make positive use of the contradiction. She sees academic third wave theorists, such as Heywood and Drake, merely acknowledging contradiction rather than trying to work it into something positive. She believes that certain feminist anthologies form an effective quilting of, rather than token inclusion of, women of colour contributions where editors work with authors to form a 'collective and collaborative process' that challenges the modus operandi of conventional academic feminist anthologies (2012).

These contributions are not subsumed in the whole or sectioned off on their own so as not to deny individual input or to segregate subjectivities. If women of colour have contributed with highly socially beneficial inputs like this then shouldn't they be acknowledged for doing so, without labelling them as belonging to a certain social identity? This acknowledgment is different to saying that all women of colour *are* maternal, emotional, earthy, non-academic, family-orientated etc. An example of how such acknowledgment can be made is provided by Ann Russo who says how women of colour, *'felt more accountable to their broader communities in terms of expanding opportunities'* (2013:41) in the scenario of university alliance formations, without saying they are always more accountable.

Helen Charles warns of the danger when women of colour are segregated into association with micro-issues and micro-politics. The same danger can emanate from associating them with traditional crafts, like quilting. It can lead to absence from the main scene of feminism and apathy about ability to effect major change (1997:288). The 'unnaming' involved in being under the political radar can lead to invisibility for those oppressed for being different and will deny them their collective movement. Nevertheless, it seems that 'womanism', and its threads of communication, at least work as ways to acknowledge how women of colour have contributed to, have formed the idea of, and how they need, feminism.

## 3.5 The third wave: an open and evolving discourse?

Howie and Tauchert (2004) described how academic feminism emerging in higher education of the late 1960s in the USA and Britain roped feminists into following a new schema of feminism to satisfy the demands of a livelihood in academia. This became a kind of career feminism that initiated taboos against deviation from the bourgeois feminist script. Such a constrictive script deterred a potentially feminist-friendly Kristina Sheryl Wong (2003) from associating with feminism in early adult life, and initially subdued the young Rebecca Walker by asking her to live up to forebodingly high standards. Wong is a third generation Chinese/English theatre performer who has addressed the situation of Asian/American Women. Walker, daughter of Alice Walker, author of *The Color Purple*, is a feminist writer who worked to create empowerment through activism for young women and is said to have been a founder of the concept of a third wave of feminism. Wong noticed how academic feminism was additionally deterring since much of it applied so much convoluted jargon that it effectively excluded those from outside of the humanities based academic fold. Heywood and Drake (1997) referred to Walker's theorising in third wave anthology *To Be Real* in order to describe how, for Walker, third wave feminism seemed to flout the feminist academic schema in being forgiving of transgressions against the new academic feminist 'law'. Here was a chance of redemption for those who erred from the bourgeois academic feminist path by having the wrong type of social subjectivity (1995:xxxvii).

Howie and Tauchert (2004) saw a link between 'commercial logic' and what might be described as the academic theory production mill where a constant search for theoretical novelty must be married to the neat insertion of research into academic formula. This paralleled the way that products in postmodern capitalist society must fit a formula while appearing to be novel, from the three-minute pop single to a new brand of motor-car as the latest variant of tinned 'freedom'. In consequence, academic feminism has partly become a clique for those with insider knowledge, who can theorise in the right way in order to perpetuate the clique, '... *as Gayatri Spivak suggests, feminist criticism too, like all forms of critique, "is complicitous with the institution within which it seeks its space," and must recognise this to be a force for change*' (Edelstein, 1993:198).

However, criticism of chronological third wave feminism as the latest form of a self-perpetuating clique may overlook the fact that feminists in the 1980s and 90s were under pressure to produce feminist work as scholarly endeavour in order to justify the existence of Women's Studies departments when faced with institutionalised academic elitism and scepticism. Battling such elitism was again a burden for feminist academics in the late 2000s and is undoubtedly so in the 2010s where academic cut-backs have blighted their progress.

The 'academisation' of Women's Studies led to accusations of second and third wavers being career, rather than ideological, feminists (Howie and Tauchert, 2004). However, many philosophical third wavers, and notably women of colour, were responsible for highlighting the failing of career feminism when it is operated in the interests of the privileged elite. Howie and Tauchert described how awareness of the potential exclusion of 'Other' voices, emerging in the late 1970s within feminist minorities, kindled an interest in alternative narratives of feminism.

The third wave may take this opportunity to run with the baton of inclusive feminism, passed over from ethnic and social feminist minorities. The aim is a re-radicalisation of feminism, as opposed to the de-radicalisation that sometimes accompanied feminism's acceptance into the academy. Calls for re-radicalisation are evident in a number of philosophical third wave narratives (which sometimes include contributions from trans authors), where controversial topics are addressed and/or language is accessible and down-to-earth and not full of theoretical 'gymnastics'. Re-radicalisation also seems to have been called for by Kristeva as a way of initiating social change, '*I agree with Kristeva that changing artistic and representational practices can enable as well as reflect sociopolitical changes. Without speaking – and hearing – differently, we cannot be differently*' (Edelstein, 1993:204).

Henry (2004:31) noticed the proliferation of representatives, or 'voices from somewhere', from various social demographics, such as age, ethnicity and class, in third wave feminist anthologies such as *Listen Up* (1995), edited by Barbara Findlen and *To Be Real* (1995), edited by Rebecca Walker. The same could be said of the more recent *Colonize This!* (2002), edited by Daisy Hernandez and Bushra Rehman. Philosophical third wavers attempting to widen the target congregation for feminism have been, from the mid-1990s onwards, reintroducing an actively political element to feminism by including criticism from those of various social standpoints. This kind of inclusive critical analysis also features to some extent in *Catching a Wave* (2003), edited by Rory Dicker and Alison Piepmeier, and *Third Wave Agenda* (1997), edited by Heywood and Drake. Philosophically, third wave emphasis on inclusive writing also featured in chronologically second wave anthologies/collective writings addressing the phenomenon of the second wave, such as *This Bridge Called My Back* (1983), edited by Cherrie Moraga and Gloria Anzaldúa, and 'The Combahee River Collective Statement' (1986). Paula Austin, coming from a disadvantaged background, described a feeling of inclusion into the ethos of *This Bridge*,

> ... I was a poor Black girl, living in someone else's apartment in an all-white neighborhood, where my family was seen as "the help". ... It [This

Bridge Called My Back] was the first time I saw in print something I could identify with, the intersection of history, culture, oppression and identity.

(Austin, 2002:161)

*Sisterhood Is Powerful* (1970), the renowned radical anthology edited by Robin Morgan, concentrated mainly on chronologically second wave developments but did address women of colour's issues and prostitution, making for a more inclusive read. Anthologies *Third Wave Feminism* (2004), *Different Wavelengths* (2005) and *No Permanent Waves* (2010) are collections of contributions mainly provided by the academic elite who critically address the phenomenon of the third wave. However, *No Permanent Waves* also includes discussion of hip-hop feminism and sex work, which are not so characteristic of academic anthologies.

With regard to trans anthologies that may stand as open and evolving, *Reclaiming Genders* (1999), edited by Kate More and Stephen Whittle challenges the traditional gender dualism and features input from writers of different backgrounds with different approaches to the concept of trans subjectivity. *Trans/Forming Feminisms* (2006), edited by Krista Scott-Dixon has an inclusive slant for gender variance and challenges the validity of gender heteronormativity as common-sense discourse. Emphasis on points of view from a broad range of social and philosophical backgrounds and perspectives features in trans anthology *The Transgender Studies Reader* edited by Susan Stryker and Stephen Whittle (2006).

Unfortunately, re-radicalisation and accessible narratives may contribute to less funding and support for feminist-based study from academic institutions, if seen to flout a conventional academic schema. The 1980s and 90s brought in introduction of market forces into public services, including Higher Education, ... expansion [of] not students from [the] working class but expanding middle class families ... and ... new measures of control, through financial resources and fiscal management. (David, 2004:111)

These measures meant that,

Feminism has been indoctrinated into the academy through the discipline of women's studies. It has moved out of the social and political spaces from where it emerged. Women's studies have collapsed the diversity that was part of the feminist movement into a discipline that has become a homogenous generality. For women in the third wave then, one needs to have the academic training of women's studies to be an "accredited feminist".

(Hurdis, 2002:288)

Adding to fears about the mainstreaming of academic feminism, Professor Laura Hebert commented that, '*Frustration has been voiced by some feminists that the poststructuralist deconstruction of the subject undermined the potential for political action*' (March 2007:34). This deconstruction, philosophised about in academic humanities departments and perhaps taken up in the theory and subjectivity of individual queer-inspired academics, brings to mind an 'erotics of unnaming' but with no positive results for its broader subjective community. However, networking between those from various oppressed social, ethnic and gendered subjectivities is perhaps leading to reconstruction of mainstream feminism's 'Others' (those with negatively dualised difference) to 'others' (those with empowered difference).

How are philosophical third wavers reconstructing the discourse of feminism? The third wave, as it currently stands, appears not to be political in the same way as the second wave in the 1960s and the first wave at the beginning of the last century. There is little mass demonstration but there is perhaps rather a quiet revolution working on many fronts simultaneously, or focussing on multi-issues and direct action, as described and listed by Jennifer L Pozner (2003:37–44). These include women as war correspondents, the ethics of global trade, demonisation of mothers on benefits and continuing threats to women's reproductive rights. This multi-issue activism is reminiscent of neighbourhood/community politics and 'micro-politics' focussing on local issues which nevertheless can affect women in different locations. Women's activism has characteristically been quieter than men's as Irene Diamond and Lee Quinby point out,

> Because so much of women's political activity occurs at the local level and stems from their involvement in the sustenance of life, they often manifest an ethic of activism that confronts domination without the smashing and terror so characteristic of masculinist revolutionary action.
> (1988:xvii)

Is the quiet revolution of third wave feminism different to other revolutions because of its multi-issue and multi-subjective approach and/or because of its quietness? If so, is this because it is not attempting to replace one hegemony or metanarrative with another? This replacement of metanarratives is something that Larry Cata Backer warns is the tendency to occur when 'revolution-speak' takes over an up and coming faction's rhetoric. Backer describes how the very act of essentialising a group identity can work to make the new group identity as much an essentialising phenomenon as the dominant identity has already been (1998:193). This may well have operated in the development of separatist gender philosophies. Queer, and queer-friendly philosophies such as third wave feminism, theoretically work to at least indicate that this essentialising can occur.

However, the quietness of the third wave may be, as Henry argued, because today's young women are typically much more cynical about their prospects of gaining the power to effect social change, or are much more complacent and comfortable about their social positions, than were their second wave sisters in the 1960s (2004:37). There is a feeling that there is little chance of inspiring the kind of organised and cohesive feminist activism prevalent in the earlier period. Henry also pointed out how Kate Roiphe identified an apathy inspired by confusion in identifying what is now the 'enemy' for feminism (2004:38,39). This enemy, as suggested in the third section regarding bourgeois feminism, can perhaps sometimes be found within feminism itself as well as more obviously located in oppressive masculinism.

## 3.6 Conclusion

The first section of this chapter addressed the connection of philosophical third wave feminism to 'postmodern identity', which differs to both modernist fixed identity and postmodern non-identity. It derives from the theory that subjectivities will be subject to social construction over the lifetime of the subject but that discreet subjectivity can be identified at any one time, enabling the possibility of subjectivity politics. Postmodern identity or 'subjectivity' equates with genre and geneaology which, when combined with a personal politics can allow discoursal arenas such as medicine and the law to understand that those who passionately fulfil a gender role, rather than just being ascribed to a certain gender at birth, should be accepted into that gender for all social and legal purposes.

In the second section, it was suggested that the third wave is particularly geared to recognise 'contradictions' inherent in subjectivities, particularly the subjectivities of feminism and gender variance. These subjectivities have conventionally been determined through metanarratives such as separatist feminism, biology and/or psychoanalysis. Recognition of contradiction can reveal the complexity or 'lived messiness' of sexual/social subjectivity and can lead to empathy with those from different sexually and ethnically subjective locations, engendering a subjective 'view from somewhere'. 'Lived messiness' addresses the intricacy of gendered existence and works to include those from variant genders that are otherwise taken to be unreal. It follows that an understanding of subjectivity can only be approached by an analysis of the individual and how they have been formed by their psychological make-up and social construction, rather than from a psychoanalytical or social identity blueprint.

The third section suggested that the feminist waves are not discreet entities but are infused with the spirit and developments of preceding waves. This vision of how the complexity of 'lived messiness' forms waves can be compared to the formation of subjectivities such as mother and daughter. The mother may be a 'wave' helping to form another wave in the form of the daughter. However, communication deriving from the earliest mother-child bond has been identified as overridden in the world of language by Kristeva but is alluded to notably in many women of colour's poetic writings.

The fourth section opened with consideration of how women of colour have unveiled the white patriarchal and/or gender separatist 'community of no community' in order to highlight philosophical third wave feminists' and gender variant people's need for 'maternal relations' where knowledge can be handed down and around between feminist waves. Womanism is an ethos and collection of lifestyles that acknowledges such 'unnamed' efforts and influence of women of colour on the third wave. It aligns with the ethics of care, is not an opposing doctrine to feminism and is not intended to be owned by one ethnic grouping. Womanist writers have presented and investigated the mother/daughter relationship as a metaphor for inter-wave relations, identifying the influence of the mother, the problems of living up to what the mother has done and challenging the authority of the mother. Womanists have also used 'communion' in order to recognise the contributions, characteristics and strengths of the other and to negotiate these into the best possible use. The building up of subsequent alliances is described as 'quilting' to describe how the connecting of voices doesn't subsume one into another but connects them closely by threading that creates a patchwork of equity.

In the fifth section it was found that contradictory views of the third wave as conservative and career-based on one hand, and as radical and evolving on the other, can be gained from reviewing different accounts about and by third wave feminists. A measure of increase in access to academic narrative for people of varied class, gender and ethnicity has meant that voices from diverse subjectivities with diverse means of narrative presentation are now sometimes included into feminist discussion. The reformation of feminism itself is perhaps most passionately being informed by previously excluded 'Others' and by those choosing to reform or question their own bodily and social subjectivities. Third wave feminism is, at least theoretically, about respecting past struggles for 'voice' in order to form a discourse developed through genealogical research and empathy.

In Chapter four the idea of philosophical waves is applied to the development of law as it pertains to gender in Western industrial society. These philosophical waves relate to the social and philosophical subjectivities formed by and informing the waves, rather than to chronological, biological and status related identities. The chapter examines how the 'lived messiness' of gendered subjectivity can be addressed by postconventional ethics, maternal relations, and by looking at agency and communion in communication. Recognition of this will lead to inclusion into legal discourse for gender variant people in order to allow them some measure of ownership of, and involvement with, this discourse.

## Notes

1 Attempts by theorists and trans people to find the holy grail of trans aetiology were highlighted in Chapter 2.
2 Irigaray presented the female gender as, *'this sex which is not one'* (1985).
3 Reflexivity has been described in this way, *'To be reflexive, in terms of a work of anthropology, is to insist that anthropologists systematically and rigorously reveal their methodology and themselves as the instrument of data generation'* (From: www.california.com/~rathbone/lexicon.htm).

4 However, the concept of having famous names in feminism is treated with caution by third wave feminists since this can emulate conventional academic reification of certain human beings.
5 This is one of the terms, including 'infantilisation', deployed by Neil Thompson to describe the application of debilitating social treatment of oppressed subjectivity groups (1998:82–83).
6 Providing a falsely objective 'view from nowhere', as described in Chapter 1.
7 The womanists that Alice Walker grew up with were not concerned with making a name for themselves although being very gifted (Walker, 1983[1976]:231–331). Patel applied a 'womanist' perspective to hierarchical oppression in the family (1997:262).
8 For instance when the *Southall Black Sisters* and *Brent Asian Women's Refuge* provided respite from violence and persecution (1997:256).

# 4 Legal review

## The view from somewhere

**Introduction**

This chapter focuses on how gender variant people, including women,[1] feminists and trans people, have been shaped by, but also how they have been inspired to shape, the law as social discourse. The author suggests that the law pertaining to gender in Western industrial society has developed through three philosophical waves of its own, which parallel the philosophical feminist waves and manifest as a more inclusive discourse in the form of a philosophical third wave. The concept of postconventional ethics is discussed in order to link it with the idea of a philosophical third wave of gender legislation. It will be seen how Gilligan's (1982) concept of postconventional ethics involves allying ethics of care (recognition that, and respect for the idea that, subjectivities are individually formed), with an ethic of justice (recognition and protection of subjective categories).

This chapter, as a 'view from somewhere', is intended to bring to mind the reflexive contemplation of subjectivity notable as a feature of the philosophical third wave. This is a view of society from the outside in, gained by the oppressed societal 'Other'. This idea might also be seen as an extension of psychoanalyst Jacques Lacan's 'mirror stage' of human development, first introduced in 1936, but developed by him in the 1950s and 1960s, as a social, more than psychological, phenomenon. In the 1950s and 60s Lacan theorised that, rather than gaining an image of self from an actual mirror, infants grow up developing different images of themselves derived from impressions about, and then mimicry of, the people, community and the environment with which they interact (Nobus, 1999:119,120). Trans people's own self-images are, by definition, notably complex and therefore contradict many of the perceptions applied to them by people who have only seen gender in the heteronormative 'mirror'. These self-images also challenge notions of psychoanalytical development that predict gendered development deriving only from one's natal sex, a challenge also taken up by Julia Kristeva who, like Lacan, reconstructed the idea of psychoanalytic development as more of a socially-based process.

Marilyn Edelstein noted the importance of subjective development to the development of society, '*I agree with Kristeva "that there can be no socio-political transformation without a transformation of subjects: in other words, in our relationship to social constraints, to pleasure, and more deeply, to language"'* (1993:202).

Law has characteristically developed in a discoursal bubble to cater for an apparently bi-gendered world. However, transgender theory and philosophical third wave feminism have shown gendered subjectivity to be a complex and varied issue. Only if legal discourse is aware of itself as in-process will it better be able to accommodate gender as in-process too. It will consequently be able to reform those parts of 'black letter law', whether in the UK or elsewhere, where principles of law are taken to be well defined and free from doubt, alteration or challenge in relation to two, and only two, genders.

## 4.1 Radical struggles for single functional issue legislation

Early gender legislation and rights were hard fought for and these fights were necessarily based upon identity group cohesion because it was these identities that were originally chosen by oppressors for suppression. Women (and later gays, lesbians and trans people) had to struggle hard to gain a collective voice before they could begin to articulate ideas about addressing the deep roots of social oppression. What first wave feminists were doing was very radical at the time even though, when their activism is perceived in isolation from the on-going feminist movement, it seems that these women were ultimately attempting to fit in with patriarchal society. Imelda Whelehan warned that combating prejudice in a purely identity related based way would not ultimately work when, '*an "ideology of gender" is constantly perpetuating the "reality" and "naturalness" of inequitable sexual and racial divisions*' (1995:60). Even so, as Whelehan said of liberal feminism, the feminist first wave's, '*... fight for equality created the conditions whereby dissenting feminist stances could emerge*' (1995:42).

The first gender legislation might be construed as the culmination of a gender legislatory 'first wave' because it was focused upon single functional issues from the early nineteenth century such as: divorce, women's property, women's right not to be beaten by their husbands, and by the early twentieth century: the right to suffrage. These foci had the effect of promoting gender equality through assimilation, rather than providing any attempt to value genders for their differences. Chronological second wave legal milestones involving pay, employment, education and services were also of a philosophically first wave nature because they dealt with single functional issues, rather than involving an examination of deep rooted socio-legal discourse. This is an issue picked up by Carol Smart when addressing the effectiveness of attempting to instigate change through legal means only,

> ... [Catherine] MacKinnon concedes a great deal to law. She argues that it is law that can legitimize women's aims, without which they remain unrecognized. Yet I doubt that law does this. ... There are other ways of

challenging popular consciousness other than through law, even though law may on occasions provide a catalyst. But it is also mistaken to imply that once legitimized by law, women's claims will not be de-legitimised by law at a later stage.

(Smart, 1989:81)

In Britain chronological first and second wave feminists' activism and lobbying led to two key acts that would pave the way for further gender equality legislation. The Equal Pay Act 1970 forbade unequal allocation of pay and conditions to men and women for undertaking the same or similar work. However, this Act did not provide for those wishing to claim for equal pay with someone of their own legal sex, as a transitioning person may wish to do. Second wave feminists in the UK were instrumental in the development of The Sex Discrimination Act 1975 (SDA), which became the major sex and gender discrimination legislation for a period of over 35 years. Later, it would be repeatedly amended, but initially the Act also just dealt with the protected categories of men and women. In their original form, neither Act provided special recognition or protection for trans subjectivity or gender variance. Only after amendment by the Sex Discrimination (Gender Reassignment) Regulations 1999, did the SDA formally protect people who '*intended to undergo, or who are undergoing or who have undergone gender reassignment*'[2] from discrimination on the grounds of gender.

Although gains first had to be made by lobbying and protesting for single functional issue matters, the acts could not address social life in a comprehensive way. These Acts were still largely based on a masculinist perception of equality with the result that being equal to others could sometimes mean being equally dysfunctional or equally miserable. For instance, the SDA was held to be working if, for example, an employer who dismissed a trans woman also said they would dismiss a trans man, i.e. genders of transition were being treated equally, but in effect equally badly.

The limitation of the ability of equality to solve societal disparities was suggested by a participant in Gilligan's college student study, '*People have real emotional needs to be attached to something, and equality doesn't give you attachment. Equality fractures society and places on every person the burden of standing on his own two feet*' (1982:167).

Gilligan hinted how the ethics of care can act to investigate exactly whose equality it is that is promoted by what has been called the 'ethic of justice' or 'morality of rights', '*The morality of rights is predicated on equality and centered on the understanding of fairness, while the ethic of responsibility relies on the concept of equity, the recognition of differences in need*' (Gilligan, 1982:164).

The reflection in law of the structural dominance of masculinism, operating with a morality of rights not focussed upon investigating sexual subjectivities, was notably observed by Susan Atkins and Brenda Hale in *Women and the Law* (1984). Their book theorised that gender was a deep-rooted division in society and that this division was reflected in the law, '*If the way in which society is structured pre-empts women's equal participation in the law-making process and in the distribution of benefits in society, they are not being accorded equal citizenship*' (Atkins and Hale, 1984:183).

After the Sex Discrimination (Gender Reassignment) Regulations 1999, Whittle et al. (2006) noticed that the updated SDA defined 'transsexual' and 'gender reassignment' in restricted ways that did not include all the gender variant people who needed this Act's protection. Only those trans people involved with the (physical) reassignment process were offered recognition and protection. Other gender variant people and those who transitioned by social means only (through choice or lack of opportunity) were therefore excluded. Much more socially inclusive legislation was required for these people. Atkins and Hogget remark that, '*Since 1970 we have seen radical changes in the laws affecting the separate spheres of men and women*' (1984:4). The next section considers to what extent this was successful in addressing the social roots of gender oppression.

## 4.2 Any gender you want as long as it's heteronormative

What might be identified as the second wave of gender legislation resulted from the findings that there were differences inherent in the identity 'woman' and that transitioning people were different to their birth-attributed gender. However, genders for many feminists and legal specialists were still identity, rather than subjectivity, based so there was no recognition of gender as genre and genealogy. As noted earlier, Alison Stone (2004) considers that gender as inherent identity led to the perception of 'fictitious commonalities' and Sandy Stone considers that, '*Under the binary phallocratic founding myth by which Western bodies and subjects are authorized, only one body per gendered subject is "right"*' (Stone, 1991:297).

The possibility of bodily sex as a personal choice or as a developed phenomenon, rather than an essential attribute, is not a new concept. For instance, it was a theory prevalent in the days of Pliny the Elder (c.23AD–79AD) and, in his society, was based upon the sexual activity of the individual concerned. According to Whittle and Turner (2007), the legal assignment of people to one sex or the other derived from the introduction of property laws in the industrial West and the definition of sex for the purposes of law has been a legal morass ever since, in the rare instances when it has been addressed. More and more indicators and aetiologies of biological sex have been proposed and have added to the confusion over how to properly define sex, gender and/or sexuality.

In the legal case of *John A C Forbes-Sempill v The Hon Ewan Forbes-Sempill* (1967),[3] one can see the dualism of sex was enforced and no ground was given to the idea that sex and gender are irrelevant to relationships. However, the judge, Lord Hunter, recognized that sex was a 'spectrum', that Ewan was phenotypically male (could penetrate his wife) and that overwhelming evidence revealed Ewan as psychologically male (Whittle and Turner, 2007:4.4). This case was contrary to all others, up until 2003, in allowing the latter two ways of determining sexual subjectivity.

However, *Forbes-Sempill* preceded the landmark case of *Corbett* in supporting the idea that biological evidence could and should establish to which side of the sexed divide a person belongs. Such biological determination would lead to Lord Justice Ormrod presenting trans woman April Ashley primarily as the member of a sex, the male sex, rather than as a gendered woman and/or as an individual with individually developed gender. When British law did come round to providing recognition for a person's own, but legally sanctioned, interpretation of their gender, with the implementation of the Gender Recognition Act 2004 (GRA 2004) and Equality Act 2010 (EA 2010), again, this recognition only extended as far as the two conventional genders.

In the legal case of *Corbett v Corbett [1970]*,[4] April Ashley, a cabaret performer in the1950s, underwent gender reassignment in 1960 in Casablanca under Dr Georges Burou. She married the Hon Arthur Corbett in 1963 but the marriage was annulled in 1970 on the grounds that April had been born male, in a landmark legal case. Ormrod, who had a medical background, considered that sex was determinable by limited medical testing of the body, testing that was not actually undertaken on April. April's gender and/or psychological sex and her interpretation of these, were not considered relevant to the definition of her sexual subjectivity, even though Ormrod used gender, rather than sex, terms in referring to marriage as '... *essentially a relationship between man and woman*' (Whittle, 2002a:8).[5] This assumption ensured that a heteronormative and biologically based sex dualism determined sexual subjectivity.

*Corbett* had the effect of bringing in universal case law prohibiting the marriage of those people that selected medical experts considered to be of the same sex. While portraying April as male for the purposes of *Corbett*, her case actually went on to have the effect of marking trans people as different to either male or female by forcing them to reveal any history of transition when producing documents such as their birth certificate. Trans people were consequently denied the ongoing possibility of passing as their preferred gender.

Echoing the earlier experience of Herculine Barbin, as related by Foucault (Barbin and Foucault, 1980), it seems that April Ashley did not have much of a say in, or input into, the determination of her own sexual subjectivity. She had not called for the divorce and there was no organisation like Press for Change to provide her with practical and moral support at the time. If it was accepted that trans people undergo 'gender confirmation treatment', a phrase that Whittle (2002a:7) followed Harry Benjamin in adopting in preference to 'sex change', then April's self-representation of gendering would have stood much more chance of being accepted as authentic.

Despite Psychiatrist Martin Roth being involved in the determination of April's sexual subjectivity, Ormrod dismissed the importance of psychological sex in *Corbett* (Fallowell and Ashley, 1982). April's case revealed that there was no precedent in English law to determine how an individual's sex should be defined. She speculated that the case worked to create a third sex, the representatives of which were excluded from marriage altogether, whether this be marriage to women or men (227). She also ventured that, '... *marriage is not a biological relationship*' (229), expanding this sentiment to state that, '*I do not see that it makes sense to treat marriage as something entirely separate from the currents of social life of which in fact it is one of the key components*' (229). The court ruling ensured that the axe fell on any determination of sex and gender by psychological or social criteria for many decades. The personal effect on April was an annihilation of her self-worth; something that shattered her concentration by challenging her thought process (222).

When addressing the general process of the law, April related a feeling that, '... *because it is so cold and impersonal a force, out of fear one catches at anything which will give it some human aspect*' (210). She seemed to provide a narrative desire for ethics of care to replace a distant and essentialising ethic of justice. She also suggested that, '*If we were always and only to refer back to first causes, then civilization could never happen at all*' (228), seeming to criticise the law's overlooking of the effects of the social construction of gender. No one (still) knows exactly what of sexual subjectivity is natal and what can develop with time, but awareness of this subjectivity as a process seems to provide much more comprehensive insight into individual gendering. As well as portraying the gendered individual as a subject-in-process, April suggested that the legal concept of 'transsexualism' was similarly 'in-process', '*As Christine Jorgensen's lawyer, Robert Sherman said: "The legal entity of changing sex is only now evolving. It will take twenty years before it is established"*' (230).

A step towards acceptance of trans subjectivities as legally valid was made in judgments of the New Zealand case of *Attorney-General v Otahuhu Family Court*,[6] but still not in relation to the context of marriage (Sharpe, 2006). In this case Judge Ellis emphasised the recognition of social and psychological subjectivity in the definition of sexual subjectivity and the lack of socially adverse effects that transitioned gender has for society in general. However, Andrew Sharpe deduced that Judge Ellis's focus on social and psychological subjectivity involved an expectation that such subjectivity be congruent with heterosexual relations. Sharpe argued that latent homophobia in the law was here made transparent since rulings in previous cases had masked such homophobia by referring to the importance of bodies that function together sexually, a legal focus identified by Sharpe as 'functionality', rather than implying that certain bodies are sexually compatible by gender alone. Nevertheless, the case helped initiate the move to including (albeit heteronormative) transitioned subjectivity into society, a move later bolstered by cases like *Goodwin*, '*I*' and *L v Lithuania*.

Even when the concept of determination of gender by sex assigned at birth was addressed by the law, it still generally strove to portray both as essential or unchanging features that cannot evolve or be different to heteronormative. Sharon Cowan highlighted the roots of this essentialising operation deriving from something akin to Sharpe's concept of the law's homophobia, '*Because post-operative transsexual people are, literally "made to fit" within existing sex and gender structures, they are no longer a threat to the heteronormative order*' (2005:72). Did the introduction of the GRA 2004 in Britain change this gender essentialising legal perspective of sexual subjectivity?

Some 35 years after the ruling in *Corbett*, the GRA 2004 in Britain allowed trans people full legal recognition of their preferred gender. To some extent, this Act recognised gender as linked to self-perception. When enough documentary support for the preferred gender is deemed to have been submitted, the Act provides recognition of preferred gendered status, and takes this to have existed from birth. The Act does not require that applicants for Gender Recognition Certificates undergo or promise to undergo reassignment surgery. However, applicants do still have to convince the Gender Recognition Panel that they are or have been subject to bodily dysphoria and many still have to live in a heteronormative gender role for two years (the Real Life Experience) and convince the Panel that they will continue to do so indefinitely. The requirement is to self-represent as man or woman, rather than as gender variant.

Another drawback of the GRA 2004 for some trans people, harking back to the heteronormative appropriation of marriage emphasised by *Corbett*, was, before the Marriage (Same Sex Couples) Act 2013 (M(SSC) 2013), its requirement that an already married partner should divorce before gaining a Gender Recognition Certificate. This meant that marriage was still gender related in Britain and one could only choose a marriage partner from the opposite heteronormative gendering. The situation in the USA was much the same, for instance *Transstudy* participant Kimana had to reveal and pass as her natal sex for the purpose of marriage to her female partner. Kimana commented, '*It just proves that our government doesn't understand that people fall in love with people, NOT specific genders or sexes*' (Dec 9th, 2005, in <Trans Marriage>). This requirement that a trans person divorce after what might be many years of marriage may have dissolved, or at least interrupted and re-defined, entirely functional relationships.

Whittle and Turner (2007:8.2) described how, in *House of Lords* debates on the content of the GRA 2004, Lord Winston pointed out the infinite complexity of defining biological sex, ultimately interpreting the enterprise as a futile endeavour. Whittle and Turner (2007) argued that such inputs to the GRA 2004, and its reinterpretation of biological sex as being the same as gender, rather than observably determining gender, meant that the Act 'performed' sexual subjectivity, in the sense of the on-going negotiation and production of gender theorised by Judith Butler.

However, as discussed in 'That Woman is a Woman' (2004), Cowan saw the heteronormativity of UK law continuing in the Bellinger case and beyond and proposed that legal operation still operated covertly to maintain the sex/gender distinction. This occurred despite recent legislation, including the GRA 2004, which purported the view that gender determines sex, and despite advances in gender recognition made in Goodwin, '... *it remains the case that legal reasoning does nothing to challenge the distinction between sex and gender or the biological and therefore "natural" basis of that distinction*' (Cowan, 2005:73).

Although the GRA 2004 eliminated the demand that transition can only be possible with surgery, the GR Panel still demanded the attendance of a legal and a medical expert who may well be personally guided by traditional and conservative discourses in assessment of gendered subjectivity. Cowan suggested that the GRA 2004 was designed to accept gender, leaving sex as unchallenged, supporting the view of sex as essential, as a common-sense feature that everybody understands. In effect, the heteronormative order prevails as transitioning people are expected to assimilate into heteronormativity (with a defined and reassigned sexed embodiment) for the purposes of gender recognition, with little opportunity to articulate their own views about the matter.

Cowan described how, differing to legal debate in the UK, recent Canadian law has investigated the construction of gender as a result of discussing law in discrimination contexts (2005:69). Reviewing the Canadian legal situation from the 1990s onwards, Cowan believed that more exploration of gender issues occurs in discrimination cases than in marriage cases because, '... *there is less at stake, heteronormatively speaking*' (81 – footnote). For instance, instead of determining aetiology of sex in *Mamela v Vancouver Lesbian Connection*, the court treated Mamela as belonging to the wider category of transsexual (83). In such instances, Cowan argued that,

> The court thereby accepts self-identity and avoids messy debates over sex/gender criteria. It does not however provide clear guidelines as to what exactly is a transsexual person, and whether it is or should be completely a matter of self-definition.
>
> (84)

In a less positive case for gender variant people, Cowan described how, in the case of *Nixon v Vancouver Rape Relief Society*, VRRS saw no possibility for an individual to escape the influence of perceived gender via 'social and lived experience' (85). The VRRS argument was based on gender rather than essential sex but was so deterministic of gender, states Cowan, that gender was completely essentialised (86). Cowan concluded that, for the law, reality of gender depends on the situation. She noted how the feminist concept of rape has tended to work from a separatist discourse of sexual subjectivity, hence the difficulty for trans people to be accepted to provide or gain support at women's refuges (89).

It seems that sensitive negotiations of womanhood such as those addressed in *NvVRRS* are best informed by sensitive claims to inclusion by transitioning women, as it would be detrimental to come across as forthrightly masculine, '... *even when one is pronounced legally a woman, there may be situations where living as, working as and being a woman is also dependent on careful negotiations with the surrounding community*' (90).

Sensitive negotiations of the essence of gendered subjectivity, between law-makers and gender variant people, were still not a major part of the formation of the GRA 2004.

Before the M(SSC) 2013, British trans people who wished to reengage in a formal relationship with their original partner after transition were afforded this opportunity via the Civil Partnership Act 2004. However, as pointed out by Pierre de Vos, civil partnerships suffer in comparison to marriage because marriage is based largely on its 'symbolic impact' (2007:47). Marriage is still recognised as being 'the real thing' by many, significantly because many people have grown up being imbued with romantic ideas of this social union. Marriage also often provides superior partnering benefits to those afforded by civil partnership. Gay/lesbian/same-sex people, in most nations, have found themselves 'cleansed' from marriage for no socially functional reason other than maintenance of the heteronormative status quo.

De Vos concluded that marriage and civil unions in South Africa came to resemble apartheid segregation, while draft legislation pronounced, in rather *Animal Farm*-like manner, the recognition of same-sex relationships as 'separate but equal' (de Vos, 2007:45). This was, according to de Vos, a covert attempt to segregate homosexuals into civil partnerships, in order to placate those who could not bear the thought of non-heterosexual marriage. People were again being stereotyped as genders and sexualities rather than being classed as individuals with individual desires. Under pressure from LGBTI activists, the South African Constitutional Court eventually implemented the *Civil Union Act* that allowed people a choice of civil union or marriage. However, de Vos considered that access to marriage for same-sex people in South Africa is still restricted in subtle ways, even if it may now appear to be open to all.

This comparison of partnership segregation with apartheid is also made by legal queer theorists Tucker Culbertson and Jack Jackson, who take up Andrew Sullivan's observation that, on the surface, same-sex marriage in San Francisco and Massachusetts challenged the social exclusion of gays and lesbians, '... *prohibitions against, or facial differentiations of, same-sex marriage create the unjust "sense of being 'separate but equal'"* (*Sullivan, 2004:A21*). *It [same-sex marriage] is thus the death of homosexual apartheid in the United States ...*' (2009:140).

However, these authors interpreted the inclusion of gays and lesbians into marriage as a hailing into heteronormativity, an assimilation and integration producing equality rather than equity (fairness and impartiality) between genders. This apparent equalising didn't really address the social roots of oppression, the underlying homophobia. Inequality continues with the implementation of the M(SSC) 2013 since, according to section 1 of the Act, Canon Law of the Church of England states that marriage is between opposite-sex couples only. Same-sex marriages are thus called 'same-sex marriages' and not 'marriages'.

## 4.3 'Othering'

From the discussion in the previous section it can be seen that some gender variant people have been more 'Other' to heteronormativity in the law than people who undertake a fully heteronormative gender transition. However, it can be seen that heteronormatively transitioning people have also remained significantly 'Other' in this way. Whittle noticed how 'Othering' had for a long time occurred to women in the eyes of the law; they became 'Other' to men or 'not-men' in the heteronormative structure of sexual subjectivity (2002a:13). 'Woman' was not a stand-alone 'whole' gendering in this hegemonic[7] set-up but relied upon the gender of man for its own definition, as notably argued by Simone de Beauvoir.

As seen in the cases of *Corbett* and *Wilkinson v Kitzinger*, 'Othering' has been carried out by the law applying categories while not actually defining those categories. People are perceived to belong to the categories of either man or woman so that the law can discriminate indirectly against those who do not. An instance of such discrimination was identified by Stychin where, in the US case of *Bowes v Hardwick*, the seemingly category free law against sodomy really targeted gay relations (1995:149). Sodomy and gay relations are associated by most so the effect was a curfew on such relations. This kind of 'definitional incoherence' marked a negative use of the avoidance of categorisation so that the law could avoid being seen to discriminate against a certain gender variant subjectivity.

In 'Foucault's Monsters, the Abnormal Individual and the Challenge of English Law' (2007) Sharpe dealt with the metaphor of 'monster' as a way of identifying how some people have been identified as 'Other' in French and English law. He found that the 'monster' was that which contravened common-sense ideas of subjectivity such as those found in discourses of law, medicine and heteronormativity. Although the term 'monster' is not used in Western industrial society to identify anyone but serious criminals any more, the concept still underlies the effect of some stated and unstated categorisations and the process of silent and secret negotiation works to reproduce such categorisations. Georges Canguilhem, according to Sharpe, theorised that the most feared kind of monster was that which is formed from living flesh,

> Indeed, for Canguilhem, "[t]he qualification of monster must be reserved for organic beings." The term monster is another name for hybridity or "otherness within sameness," and typically refers to a creature that is both, and simultaneously, human and non-human.
>
> (Sharpe, 2007:385)

Sharpe described how, for Canguilhem, that which transgresses the law is also monstrous but that science helped reduce superstitious views of irregular bodies as monstrous,

Canguilhem is led to the conclusion that today "life is poor in monsters." For with the development of science a view of body irregularities as having a monstrous cause could no longer be sustained.

While deformity or disability "may well be something that upsets the natural order" it does not lead to the designation monster because "it has a place in civil or canon law ...".

(386)

This may be because disability is often visible difference and the formal and informal search for aetiology characteristically relies on visibility. For Foucault, the monster confounded legal classification and aetiology. This confusion of classification can be seen in the case of *Corbett* and many legal trans cases that followed around the world. Sharpe noted that Foucault drew from Canguilhem's theory to posit that the abnormal individual in modern society has *invisible* difference, as opposed to an irregular body,

> ... the monstrosity of the abnormal individual lies in interiority or psyche. ... Foucault's genealogy of the abnormal individual serves to foreground a shift from the body to the soul as the object of legal concern. ... the abnormal individual's monstrosity is of an invisible kind.
> (388)

Foucault's move to conceive of the monster as deriving from invisible difference seems to tie in with the modern situation of gender variant people. In most cases, gender variant and/or pre-operative trans people seem to have no observable different biology. Foucault also demonstrated how genealogy created categories from previous categories, whether in French or English law (390). Therefore, 'monsters' were developed through genealogy, rather than defined from biological analysis, albeit in different ways in French and English law.

Since the concept of gender transition was developed, gender variant and trans people have been legally perceived as 'Other', and therefore as monstrous in an unstated way, to heteronormativity. This is reduced to some extent if they seek to assimilate fully into heteronormativity. However, they are often still socially *perceived* as 'Other', even with full transition and reassignment. In addressing this challenge to trans acceptance, the EA 2010 introduced a legal concept of 'perception', to identify individual and group readings of gender difference based on the appearance of another person. Perception in this context is designed to combat oppression based upon whether the oppressor thinks the victim is gender reassigned, rather than if the victim is actually gender reassigned.

Recuperation into heteronormativity has been imposed upon trans people for much of history and in many cultures. This was famously the case for Herculine Barbin, a hermaphrodite living in nineteenth century France, who was forced to choose one heteronormative sex or the other, rather than the socially unacceptable subjectivity of being something other to the two. Michel Foucault noted how, in Herculine's time,

> ... hermaphrodites were free to decide for themselves if they wished to go on being of the sex which had been assigned to them, or if they preferred the other. The only imperative was that they should not change it again but keep the sex they had then declared until the end of their lives ...
> (Barbin and Foucault, 1980:viii)

> It was [later] no longer up to the individual to decide which sex he wished to belong to, juridically or socially. Rather, it was up to the expert to say which sex nature had chosen for him and to which society must consequently ask him to adhere.
> (Barbin and Foucault, 1980:ix)

Looking at hir case retrospectively, and by imposing our own reading of hir subjectivity, we can perhaps deduce that Herculine was intersex or hermaphrodite. However, the French legal system required hir to be one gender and one corresponding sex only. As Herculine was in love with a woman, sie agreed to become a man despite hir misgivings. As Hercule, sie left hir home town and went to Paris where shortly afterwards sie committed suicide when sie could not form a consistent image of hirself as a gendered being, largely because of the inappropriateness of hir gendered upbringing (Barbin and Foucault, 1980:xi, Whittle and Turner, 2007 3.7).

Gender variant people can still often find themselves identified as 'Other' to heteronormativity without being protected by any legal status as 'Other'. 'Othering' more often happens when people decide for themselves that a person is gender variant or trans, a process identified by gender variant people as 'reading' or as a failure to 'pass' and, identified in the EA 2010 as 'perception'.

Those who have gendering that seems to fall outside of accepted heteronormativity will be targets for abuse from many sections of the community, sometimes even including the subtle complicity of public authorities, although the latter have recently had to officially align with the requirements of the EA 2010's Public Sector Equality Duty. This abuse can be covertly socially sanctioned for years until perpetrators get bored or victims are forced to move from jobs, homes and/or families. Although the EA 2010 affords protection for those who can demonstrate that they have been perceived to be 'Other', this can often come too late for the harassed trans person.

In the legal cases of *Goodwin* and *T* (2002)[8] the European Court of Human Rights (ECtHR) recognised that transition is a far from easy process for the transitioning subject and considered that the aetiology of trans subjectivity could not be fully determined. Therefore, this court proposed that trans people's gendered subjectivity should be recognised before and during transition, and not just afterwards, in order to respect people's genuine efforts to transition and to support inclusion for transitioning subjectivity rather than to pursue a so far futile quest for its aetiology. Because of trans people's concerted efforts to realise their preferred gender, the ECtHR determined that trans people should not be treated as inferior 'Others' to heteronormativity and that their preferred gendering should be given full recognition in law. The ECtHR also determined that, in the case of *Goodwin*, that transitioning people held real gendering for the purposes of marriage, even if this gendering did not consist of proven biological difference to others with the same natal sex, and even if a marriage partner could not procreate.

However, those who are deemed not to fit a heteronormative schema, despite making their best efforts to act as responsible citizens, still often succumb to social 'Othering'. For instance, Sarah Beresford dealt with the issue of to what extent lesbians are perceived to hold real gendering for the purposes of being accepted as mothers. She argued that lesbians should be perceived as grown up by the law and very able to take on the mantle of parental responsibility. Moran et al. describe how Beresford provided an ethics of care like investigation of the legal and actual category of 'woman', '... *her detailed analysis of case law and the reality of law in practice serves to reveal a divergence, or 'gap', between the constructions, expressions and representations of women's self-identity and those that are imposed upon them by law*' (1998:4).

Beresford noted that, '... *the law's concept of lesbian identity cannot be easily reconciled with the diversity of women's experiences and sexual identities. Lesbian mothers are forced to inhabit a 'legal body' not of their own making and construction*' (1998:57).

This legal body is simply that of the 'woman', where woman is again expected to be the stereotyped 'Other' of man and derives from a history of woman as property of the husband with no legal voice in marriage. It is a body with a history of being expected to be seen (as heteronormatively attractive) and not heard, leading to consequences such as lesbianism remaining 'unnamed',

> Lesbian identities and experiences, have a long cultural history, although much of that history remains undocumented, concealed or invisible ...
> (59)

> For the lesbian to be a 'mother', she has to 'mimic' the construction of 'woman' as heterosexual. As 'motherhood' is understood in terms of heterocentric normativity, the sexuality of motherhood is rendered invisible.
> (60)

The heteronormative monopoly of motherhood engenders a heteronormative monopoly in care, because heteronormative mothers are seen to be society's main carers. This subsequently creates a cultural barrier to potential inclusion into, and involvement with familial positions of care for those with other sexual subjectivities. In a similar argument to the one put forward in the legal case of *X, Y and Z* by Whittle, Beresford asked why a parent cannot be primarily defined as such by their relationship to their children; by what they do rather than what they are,

> As a mother, a woman is further constructed according to the distinction 'married' or 'unmarried', which in turn are made to signify respectively 'good mother' and 'bad mother'. Here we have categories of mother which are defined not in terms of the relationship between the child and the mother, but by reference to the marital status of the mother ...
>
> (61)

> What is important is not necessarily what sexual identity is 'better' than another, but the quality of parenting.
>
> (64)

We can deduce from Beresford's arguments that lesbians are better off, at least as part of a short-term strategy, appearing and behaving in a heteronormative way, just as has been the case for transitioning people who have felt compelled to pass into heteronormativity. We are all taken to intuitively know how to behave in such a way; we are all expected to be 'in' on the heteronormative schema. Just like gender variant people, including trans people and the intersexes, lesbians were, and to some extent still are, expected to pass and not be political; not to have a voice. As Beresford indicates, those in positions of high discoursal power allocate the terms on which gender variant people can enter society, an administration of authority that Whittle identified as, '... *the hegemonic processes of government that continue to set the boundaries within which normalisation and absorption into society are allowed for "outsiders"*' (1998:42).

In 'Gemeinschaftsfremden' Whittle addressed how compulsory pre-operative sterilisation 'socially cleansed' trans people from biological parenthood and from ownership of their bodies in some societies (1998b). This was an extreme incidence of the 'Othering' of trans people from heteronormativity. If a society couldn't prevent trans parenting for trans people by such biological means, then it seems that it would attempt to prevent it by social means, as in the legal case of *X, Y & Z*. Until trans-authored texts like *Respect and Equality* started to emerge, few who were subject to discourses of heteronormativity and gender transition had sufficient voice and support to stand a chance of modifying these discourses.

Morgan Holmes identified a more positive allocation of terms in which gender variant people can enter society than those described by Beresford and Whittle. Holmes described how, on the surface at least, the 1999 ruling of the Constitutional Court in Bogotá addressing the gendered position of an intersexed child, provided recognition of intersex as a sexual subjectivity of its own and did not follow this with a demand for rehabilitation into heteronormativity for the child concerned (2006:102). This court decision followed legal developments identified by Holmes where children who could articulate themselves could gain some measure of agency in self-definition of gender.

The Bogotá court determined that children are not born with the autonomy needed for an ability to choose how to represent their gender, but can develop this ability in time.

However, Holmes theorised that, in contemporary industrial, including legal, culture, one cannot be viewed as a real person without falling in line with the heterogendered dualism of complimentary 'Subject'/'Other',

> For Marianne Valverde, the heterosexism of everyday assumption appears quite clearly in the cliché that "opposites attract." The essentialist notion that sexual pairing through opposition is the only appropriate mode has enormous practical and ideological consequences.
> (Holmes, 2006:110)

Single people, homosexuals, bisexuals and gender variant people are often under suspicion and perceived to be inferior because of their flouting of this dualism.

The Bogotá court at least moved towards more of a focus on the well-being of the child and less on the upholding of institutionalised gender dualism. Like Foucault, Holmes noted that for Herculine Barbin in seventeenth-century France allocation of gender was the preserve of the legal establishment. In the Bogotá case, the court debated whether, if the child wishes to define itself as 'other' in gender variant or intersexed senses, it had the right to do so. Nevertheless, this right to self-definition would remain subject to certain family circumstances, and reassignment treatments could still sometimes be applied to a new born infant who could obviously not provide their consent.

In assessing the Bogotá case, Holmes called for a focus on valuing difference, or otherness (small 'o'), rather than searching for aetiology, '... *it is worth asking why so many conditions are medicalised and why we seek to "normalise" them when we might just as easily seek to value them*' (2006:118).

This and the previous chapter sections demonstrate how a philosophical or gender normative second wave of case law and gender legislation eventually implemented advances in the recognition of trans people's preferred gender, but only for heteronormative identity, rather than for non-transitioning gender variant subjectivity. From *Corbett* until the implementation of legislation such as the GRA 2004 and the M(SSC) 2013, transitioning people had been 'Othered' from marriage, parenting and social life by having a legal definition of sexual subjectivity supposedly based upon biological sex imposed upon them. The next two sections describe the move towards legal self-definition for trans people, if not gender variant people as a whole, mirroring the third wave emphasis on articulation of subjective difference.

### 4.4 Agency and communion

Chapter 5 introduces 'agency' and 'communion' as components of the critical discourse analysis tailor-made for the research that led to this book. Since the mid-1970s trans people have liaised with one another in order to increase both for trans people facing the complexity of the law. For instance, after working with organisations such as The Gender Trust and the Beaumont Society, Whittle coordinated the FTM Network from 1989 until 2007. In 1992 he founded Press for Change with Mark Rees, Myka Scott and Krystyna Sheffield. This section introduces key legal cases that, often in conjunction with the trans help groups such as FTM Network and PFC, engendered trans people's active involvement with the legal definition of, and protection for, trans subjectivity, thereby reducing their status as 'Other' in society and to the law.

In 1996 the transgender lobby group Press for Change played a key part in supporting activist 'P' against her former manager, 'S', and employers Cornwall County Council in the legal case *P v S and Cornwall County Council [1996]* (*P v S & CCC*).[9] Employers could henceforth not dismiss an employee in Britain simply because the employee underwent gender transition. As mentioned in Press for Change case notes, '*Trans people might still have no job security today had a training manager from Cornwall ['P'] not responded to her dismissal by taking her employers all the way to the European Court of Justice in 1995*'.[10]

Workplace discrimination against trans people was commonplace until *P v S & CCC*, and some employers discriminated equally (badly) against trans men and trans women. *P v S & CCC* was based on the definition of gender, not sex, and several discrimination cases influenced by *P v S & CCC* have consequently not relied on the biological and/or surgical status of the trans individual as evidence of their sexual subjectivity (Whittle and Turner, 2007:7.3). The GRA 2004 has formalised this ruling by eliminating physical reassignment as a necessary condition of belonging to one's 'acquired' gender.

Both because of the individualised focus by Press for Change, and the interpretation of gender gained from 'P' herself, trans activists and legal participants had begun imbuing legal processes with the notion that an individual-orientated approach is needed in addressing the issue of personal sexual subjectivity.

Sometimes a trans person could find themselves as both lobbyer for anti-discriminatory law and the subject of supposedly anti-discriminatory law. This was the case for 'X' (Stephen Whittle), in the legal case of *X, Y and Z v UK [1997]*, when even a cursory glance at the family life of petitioners 'X,Y & Z' revealed a happily functional family. 'X' fulfilled every interpretation of the definition of fatherhood except for the then societally and legally required one that he should be of the correct medically defined sex. In a later interview 'X' asked,

> What is a father? ... In law we do not have a definition of a man, only a series of ascribed roles. Every other male parent of a child by donor insemination is allowed to register himself as the father of the child.
>
> (Grice, 22 March 1997)

In the case of *X, Y & Z*,[11] people disputing the right of 'X' to be a father cited danger to the family being of primary concern.[12] What they really seem to have meant is danger to the concept of the 'nuclear family', a concept identified by George Murdock in 1947 to describe a family where parents are uncomplicatedly heterosexual. As evidenced by the discussion of marriage in the second section of this chapter, legal definitions of gender have been linked to the protection of the idea of the nuclear family. For instance, in Great Britain before 2014, one could transition gender but one had to transition into a heteronormative sexual subjectivity in order to enter the realm of marriage and one still has to do so in order to be recognised as a father.

The court could have facilitated 'X's' legal recognition as father by referring to Article 8 of the European Convention of Human Rights which states that, '*Everyone has a right to respect for his private and family life, his home and his correspondence …*'. However, the ECtHR argued that the failure of UK law to recognise the relationship between 'X and Y' as that of husband and wife did not constitute a failure to respect family life. This left out any consideration of X's right to define his own subjectivity, and his long established and accepted social role as father.

Dissenting Judges Casadevall, Russo and Makarczyk seemed to acknowledge the hard work that 'X and Y' had put into creating the optimum conditions for their family to flourish. Judge Vilhjalmsson reasoned that the issue was not about the biological connection of 'X' to the child but was rather about his classification as a male and a man since other non-biologically related men had been classified as fathers to their family's children. Judge Foighal emphasised the European government's agreement to implement a duty to take special care of oppressed individuals and Judge Gotchev considered the case from the point of view of the child involved, rather than from that of those who have a stereotypical view of a family. All these dissenting judges' opinions promised hope that trans people might have their personal circumstances taken into account in similar future cases, in the manner of investigative ethics of care, rather than simply by means of examining their attributed social identity.

*Transstudy* participants Monica and Sadie addressed the <Trans Parenting> topic question of, 'What sexual subjectivity is the best one to present to one's children?' by suggesting that the optimum such subjectivity would be the most genuine one, whether it fitted in with the requirements of the nuclear family or not. Here, we find narrative support from the voice of trans people for the consideration of the individual's interpretation of their own sexual subjectivity and parenting status, and the actuality of a parent's relationship with their children.

The nuclear family is not inherently functional or dysfunctional, but parents should have the choice of whether to form such a family or to choose a different family structure. Supporting the option for choice of family structure, Imelda Whelehan explained how family was an important locus of social cohesion for black feminists even though radical and socialist feminists had severely criticised the social institution of the nuclear family, '... *black feminists were faced with the reality that the family forms they experienced were more often than not the only cushion against systematic racism in the public sphere ...*' (1995:114).

Whittle extended the wish to eliminate gender stereotyping of families and parenting to a desire to eliminate gender stereotyping of child development. He visualised the evolution of child development, and its interaction with parent development, as a reconstructive, or politically and socially progressive, project,

> The International Bill of Gender Rights promotes a vision of the world in which child-bearing and child-rearing are by and about the development of people rather than by and about the development of men and women. This vision is symbolic of the reconstructive project of the new trans community; going beyond the deconstructive enterprise of modernity.
>
> (1998b:53)

Adam P Romero detected a similarly reconstructive project in the way that Martha Fineman wished to establish the concept of a queer family structure,

> Fineman would cast aside the current concentration on marriage and, more generally, the sexual connection as the core familial relationship. Instead, Fineman would completely re-orient society's concern for family so as to revolve around the caretaker-dependent relationship, regardless of who is the caretaker and who is the dependent.
>
> (Romero, 2009:194)

In a similar way to Whittle, Fineman, and Beresford (1998:61), Flynn addressed the question of whether parenthood should be defined by what one does rather than what one is taken to be, mentioning that, '... *the depth and intensity of a parent's bond in no way depend on a person's route to parenthood ...*' (Flynn, 2006:42).

In a US legal case involving Suzanne Daly, Flynn noted how the Nevada Supreme Court ruled that Daly had terminated her status of parenthood simply through undertaking gender transition. However, if it is taken that she terminated fatherhood it doesn't logically follow that she had terminated parenthood. This case demonstrated that the discourse of parenting was still very gendered, just like the discourse of marriage.

The Florida Court of Appeal provided a more empathic response to the situation of Michael in the legal case *Kantaras*. Even though it invalidated Michael's marriage because of his gender transition, the court admitted that it had not considered the parent–child bond and the best interests of the child involved. A few US courts have moved on to recognise the concept of functional or de facto parenthood and this has sometimes been applied to trans parents' situation in a limited way, '*Some courts have used the doctrine of functional parenthood, also known as "de facto" parenthood, to grant varying degrees of continuing contact with a child to persons who have established a parentlike relationship with the child ...'* (46).

In the case of *Bellinger v Bellinger [2003]*, [13] the link between sexual subjectivity and familial position, in this case marriage, was again deployed by the court involved. Mr Justice Johnson refused the application made by Elizabeth Bellinger to gain recognition that her marriage was valid on the basis that the Attorney-General decided that she had never been legally female. Judge Johnson ruled that no definition of female had been provided by parliament but this factor was used against Mrs Bellinger, rather than in her favour. As in the situation of 'X', Bellinger's definition of her own sexual subjectivity was not accepted as relevant. In the final ruling, no account was taken of the effect of feminising hormones on her psychological sex, or of the recent discovery that the three indicators of sex relied upon in *Corbett* could change to some extent after physical reassignment.

In 'That Woman is a Woman' (2004), Cowan pointed out that the *Goodwin* judgment marked a departure from the legal attempt to define transsexuality via biological aetiology (2004:80). However, the House of Lords in *Bellinger* seemed to cling to gender distinctions between male and female because the issue of marriage was at stake (81), as theorised to be the case in *Attorney-General v Otahuhu Family Court* by Sharpe. This connection of law with heteronormativity continued in the production of the GRA 2004 and EA 2010 in the form of providing 'gender reassignment' as a protected category,

> The Gender Recognition Bill, while reforming some of the worst aspects of UK law on transsexuality, seems nevertheless to perpetuate the fear of contamination of (heterosexual) marriage. It also relies on medical (though non-surgical) determinations of 'successful' reassignment.
> (90)

Biology was still used as the common-sense indicator of real sexual subjectivity in *Bellinger* with sex being perceived as more real than gender (83). Cowan describes how the law continued in this way its efforts to determine the aetiology of sexual subjectivity, *'The Law Lords in Bellinger continue the legal quest for the Holy Grail – the truth of sex'* (83). Heteronormative discourse again emphasised essentialised differences and so protracted the idea of separate spheres for men and women, and this discourse was, as we have seen, a very carefully protected bastion in the case of marriage.

Ruling in the case of *Bellinger*, Lord Hope saw no possibility of anyone contravening the ascribed barrier of biological sex, mentioning that, '... *A complete change of sex, is, strictly speaking, unachievable*' (84). No one knows how to effect a complete change of sex to this day but even gender transition cannot be effected if trans sympathisers, who try to make inroads for acceptance of self-description and for the formation of aetiologies-in-process, rather than concentrating on the search for aetiology, are not involved in discourses of gender variance, feminism, medicine and the law.

The concept of choice of gendered essence was not considered viable in this legal case and consequently no truck was given to the concept that choice might eventually engender real sexual subjectivity, or might reveal sexual subjectivity hidden from our current paradigm of knowledge,

> ... much reference is made throughout the case to biology and reproduction, with Lord Nicholls following in a similar vein by stating clearly that one cannot chose one's sex: "... self-definition is not acceptable. That would make nonsense of the underlying biological basis of the distinction".
>
> (84–85)

Also, resistance to the concept of in-process subjectivity, as opposed to fixed identity, could be detected in the decisions deriving from *Bellinger*. According to Cowan,

> The judges felt compelled to come to a definite conclusion about Mrs Bellinger's sex for the purposes of marriage and decided that she is not a woman. This result demonstrates a fear of unclear boundaries, especially in the area of sex, and mirrors a similar kind of resistance to intermediate categories and unclear sex boundaries in Goodwin.
>
> (85–86)

Nevertheless, Cowan noted an increasing potential for the voice of the gender variant subject to be heard in the discourse of law, '... *recent cases such as Goodwin and W v W have at least recognised the importance of gender and self-perception rather than relying on birth bodies as the basis for determining sexual identity*' (86). However, this has still only been within the scope of a heteronormative paradigm, '*The trouble is that, as Sandland (2003) has suggested, recognising gender rather than emphasising sex does not necessarily involve eschewing binary and inflexible ideas about what it is to be male/ female*' (86).

In *Bellinger*, Lord Hope suggested same-sex marriage as a way of allowing trans people to marry. However, Cowan believed, this treated Mrs Bellinger as a homosexual masquerading as the other gender. Mrs Bellinger retained a position as an unstated monstrous 'Other' needing to be repelled from sacred heteronormative institutions.

More positively for trans people, in reviewing *Bellinger* in 2003, Lord Nicholls added significant new determinants of sex to those ventured by Ormrod. These four became: '... *the internal sex organs other than the gonads, hormonal patterns and secondary sexual characteristics, style of upbringing and living, and self perception*' (Whittle, 2007:40). The latter two determinants are of crucial importance to this book since they relate to the idea of subjectivity as identity-in-process. These two factors draw from an individual's life experience and relate to Foucault's idea of subjectivity formed from interaction[14] (1998 [1978]) or McAdams' ideas of 'agency' and 'communion' (2001).

Mr and Mrs Bellinger actually lost their case significantly because, '... *it would have been legally reprehensible to recognise the marriage of someone who had technically committed perjury at its time in order to obtain it*' (Whittle, 2007:40). The House of Lords decided that in other circumstances a parliamentary process should determine sex for the purposes of marriage while referring to a new seven-point determinant guide, rendering the sex-determinant decision in *Corbett* obsolete. In this instance, the law was 'in-process' in recognising new interpretations of sexual subjectivity, even though it tended to present such subjectivity as a constant.

## 4.5 Postconventional ethics?

Drawing from Gilligan's developmental theory (1982), it seems that morality can manifest in different ways by different genders. Morality emanating from men has so far derived largely from agency and morality deriving from women has derived more so from communion. Nevertheless, according to social constructionist perspectives such as that provided by Gilligan, genders and their accompanying moral outlooks are significantly socially created, rather than deriving straight from biological sex,

> No claims are made about the origins of the [gendered] differences described or their distribution in a wider population, across cultures, or through time. Clearly, these differences arise in a social context where factors of social status and power combine with reproductive biology to shape the experience of males and females and the relations between the sexes.
>
> (Gilligan, 1982:2)

The evolution of gender law into an inclusive law-in-process could lessen the propensity to covertly segregate gender by associating a gender with one type of moral judgment and ethics, thereby reducing the propensity to create self-fulfilling prophesies in the form of people with gender-dictated moral development. This section expands upon Chapter 1's introduction to Gilligan's concept of ethics of care, to discuss how she tried to broaden its ethical efficacy by imagining an ethics drawing from gendered moralities traditionally displayed differently by men and women.

Ethics of care seem particularly relevant to the social situation of trans people when relying upon the law, as is evident in the legal cases and legislation reviewed in sections 2 and 3 above. The cases demonstrate that in order to gain accurate insight into trans people's sexual subjectivity and its effects, one must investigate the individual's self-definition and the way that their gender manifests in real life.

The law may perceive gender but it must realise that gender also perceives the law, especially when deploying a 'view from somewhere' gained from gender exclusion. For instance, Lady Brenda Hale and Mavis Maclean, '... *were working mothers in the 70s, when they were among a group of academics who looked at law for the first time in the context of society and how the laws impacted on women's lives*' (Dyer, 9 January 2004).

The womanly gendering of Hale and Maclean seems to have played a significant part in how they perceived the law. Hale didn't call for women to become equal to men but to become full citizens in their own right. Also, she seemed to embody Gilligan's ethics of care in the way that she could empathise with a legal client as an individual and not as a stereotype. Hale provided the leading judgment in the case of *A v West Yorkshire Police* [15] in the House of Lords, 2004. In effect, she rewrote the Sex Discrimination (Gender Reassignment) Regulations 1999, by removing restrictions on body searching, with the effect of opening up the policing profession for people who have transitioned gender.

How do the ethics of care theorised by Gilligan and (for example) put into practice by Hale relate to third wave feminism? Jacqueline Zita attributed to third wave feminists, '... *our ever persistent call for freedom and social justice*' (Summer 1997:6). This seems different to freedom *from* care for others and the belief that everyone should fend for themselves. It resembles Foucault's call for an ethics opposed to dictatorial power, whether emanating from '*religion, science, or political oppression*' (Diamond and Quinby, 1988:xv). Foucault thought that ethics evolved from a non-deliberate but plural endeavour,[16] involving the input of different people and theories/ideologies, and revealed how this had worked when ethics were focused on issues of sexuality, definitions of illness and relations of authority.[17]

Despite this insight into the evolution of ethics, Foucault neglected to address the effect of gender on ethics, overlooking the full importance of how gender 'genealogy' could challenge gender hegemony. In answer to this, an ethical focus on gender was developed by feminists, and notable among these was Carol Gilligan. Like Kristeva in *Women's Time* (1993), Gilligan revealed how language is subject to gendered influence and exposed how women have been side-lined from participation in the construction of influential social narrative, losing their social voice when socially constructed as having infantile moral codes (1982:68–70),

> The developmental ordering of these two points of view [masculine/feminine] has been to consider the masculine as more adequate than the feminine and thus as replacing the feminine when the individual moves towards maturity.
>
> (Gilligan, 1982:69)

> At the interior of this psychosymbolic structure [Western Christian civilization], women feel rejected from language and the social bond, in

which they discover neither the effects nor the meanings of the relationships they enjoy with nature, their bodies, their children's bodies, another woman, or a man. The accompanying frustration, which is also experienced by some men, is the quintessence of the new feminist ideology.
(Kristeva, 1993:213)

If feminist waves are more than chronological, (generationally based) it is arguable that we can associate Gilligan's perspective on ethics of care with the third wave. Gilligan theorised that genuine freedom and social justice could only be achieved through a case-by-case consideration of individual circumstances, matching the third wave and womanist call for consideration of the special subjective situation of the individual and the idea that maternal relations should involve relationships that are mutually beneficial and where the social backgrounds of all parties are given respect and attention. While criticised for providing the image of an essentialist connection between gender and ethical perception, Gilligan actually theorised that each individual's ethical procedure is likely to be determined by the way that social discourse has shaped their gender, rather than from the influence of gender apparently given at birth. Her perspective is convergent with third wave support for the idea of socially constructed subjectivity that is constructed but nonetheless valid and real at any point in time; gender as genre and genealogy rather than as fixed essence,

Listening to women's voices clarified the ethic of care, not because care is essentially associated with women or part of women's nature, but because women for a combination of psychological and political reasons voiced relational qualities that were otherwise unspoken or dismissed as inconsequential.
(Gilligan, Spring 1995:123)

Cressida J Heyes, a self-identified third wave feminist, dismissed the notion that Gilligan provided an essentialist connection between women and ethics of care, especially in her work following *In a Different Voice* (Heyes, Summer 1997). This connection is also disputed by Seyla Benhabib (1992) who maintained that although Gilligan did not explain the social construction of gender, she did point out that she perceived gender to be significantly socially constructed. A social constructionist would not say that ethics of care are an essential feature of trans women rather than trans men, just as Gilligan didn't theorise that ethics of care was inherent to women, but he/she could say that trans people generally may have an enhanced insight into how gender can affect one's relationship to moral issues.

This enhanced insight was suggested by Whittle in relation to several areas of life, work and leisure (8 July 2007). Many trans people will have lived in both gendered roles so they will have special insight into their effects. Some transitioned people, like Leon in the *Transstudy*, have argued that they have only ever actually been one gender but they will still often have initially had to conform to the wrong gender, and will probably have picked up insights into how the 'other' gender thinks. For instance, Leon's narrative below echoes some of the insights into gendered thinking elicited in *In a Different Voice*,

> Re how women and men think, well yes its VERY different, I can vouch for that, and thats why I know I am a man....although I would say that I also know that men are more sensitive than women, who THINK they are, as women are more emotional, but not sensitive. With men life is very direct, women its thought about more on an emotional level, its far more complex.
> (Leon Jul 11th, 2006, in <How do you believe you will you age?>)

In arguing that Gilligan's moral developmental theory does not suggest transparently connected gendered identities and moralities, Benhabib mentioned that, '*We do not have to think of "coherent identities" along the lines of the sameness of physical objects. We can think of coherence as a narrative unity*' (1992:198).

So, Gillian's theory was a developmental theory with a difference, being a theory that allows for divergence of development from any psychological or social developmental script. This was a concept of negotiated subjectivity and morality similar to Alison Stone's interpretation of women as a 'genealogy' (2004). Benhabib called ethics of care a, 'dialogic model of ethics' (1992:197), meaning that ethics are always in-process (for the individual and society) and that they are dependent on genders-in-process. The dialogic model recognises the input of both inquirer and subject of inquiry, seeing that the latter has some, if limited, opportunity to present their image of self. Dialogic negotiation can be detected in accounts of trans support groups guiding and interacting trans people involved with the law through legal mazes and precedents, as discussed in the fourth section.

Conversely, Law makers have generally depended upon an image of impartiality or neutrality in order to administer an apparently neutral ethic of justice,

> Where [Catherine] MacKinnon is most persuasive in her work on feminist jurisprudence is in her critique of law as a universal, objective system of adjudication. It is here that she comes closest to Gilligan in the recognition that law's neutrality is in fact the expression of gendered interests.
> (Smart, 1989:80)

This apparent neutrality mirrors the contemporary Western social construction of manhood, the immovable pillar not to be bothered by the emotionally and communally based moral procedure characteristically applied by women. Gilligan sought to uncover this hiding of gender influence under neutrality by recommending women champion ethics of care, where women can consider society's 'Others' as subjects with agency and legitimate 'voice' while, just as crucially, considering themselves in the same way. Gilligan revealed how this kind of self-agency was characteristically alien to women at the time of her abortion study,[18]

> While her [research participant Judy's] judgment clearly exists, it is not expressed, at least not in public.
> (1982:80)

> [research participant Denise] sees the issue as one of "strength," and she struggles to free herself from the powerlessness of her own dependence ...
> (1982:81)

Although critical of what passed as a gender-neutral ethic of justice, in later work Gilligan developed a belief in a possible and necessary complementarity of the ethics of care and an ethic of justice,

> Raelene's response of Nov 11th, 2005, where she posits that each individual case for SRS needs individual care, seems to mirror Carol Gilligan's notion of a 'responsibility orientation' to morality where there the moral focus is on caring for others. However, Gilligan suggests a final stage in moral development called the 'postconventional stage' where those guided by the responsibility orientation acknowledge the impact of unequal treatment, the effects of which are combatted by a 'justice orientation', similar to that for which Monica seems to call. It is the combination of these two bipolarised orientations that form a hybrid postconventional ethics.
> (The Researcher Nov 13th, 2005, in <What advice to a Newbie>)

Benhabib speculated that Gilligan's postconventional project was not intended to wholly replace the ethic of justice with ethics of care,

> Many of her formulations rather suggest that she would like to see the ethics of justice complemented by an ethical orientation to care.
> (1992:180)

> Questions of care are moral issues and can also be dealt with from within a universalist standpoint. Such a universalism supplies the constraints within which the morality of care must operate.
> (187)

The ethic of justice can put a safeguard in place to prevent ethics of care descending into the anarchy of total favouritism for in-groups or family, something Benhabib pointed out as characteristic of Mafia law.

Despite their recommendation of an involvement of the ethic of justice, it seems that neither Gilligan nor Benhabib would agree with Jürgen Habermas, who deemed that ethics of care issues should be located on the margins of ethical theory with an ethic of justice located firmly in the centre. Benhabib countered this view by arguing that,

> ... the moral issues which preoccupy us most and which touch us most deeply derive not from problems of justice in the economy and the polity, but precisely from the quality of our relations with others in the "spheres of kinship, love, friendship, and sex".
>
> (184)

Such moral issues can be detected in the description of legal cases in this chapter, and as issues prominent in second wave philosophy, such as abortion and personal politics.

In a move that aligns with the project of postconventional ethics, Selma Sevenhuijsen called for a reconstruction of justice in order to make it part of ethics of care. Sevenhuijsen believed that justice can be adapted in order to take account of '*situations and consequences*' and can be construed of as a process rather than fixed rules (Edwards and Mauthner, 2002:23).

It can be deduced that Gilligan's postconventional ethics is designed to involve ethics of care as one side of a coin backed with the ethic of justice, comparable to identity politics informed by identity-in-process (subjectivity), as discussed in Chapter 3. Both of these moral constructs would satisfy the third wave call for appreciation of inclusion for recognised difference and subjectivity as a process. Nevertheless, the input of ethics of care is vital in revealing what is arguably a particularly feminist ethos, '*... namely that we are children before we are adults, and that the nurture, care and responsibility of others is essential for us to develop into morally competent, self-sufficient individuals*' (Benhabib, 1992:188–189).

Gilligan argued that the compromise position of postconventional ethics completes this move to moral maturity,

> While an ethic of justice proceeds from the premise of equality – that everyone should be treated the same – an ethic of care rests on the premise of nonviolence – that no one should be hurt. In the representation of maturity, both perspectives converge in the realisation that just as inequality adversely affects both parties in an unequal relationship, so too violence is destructive for everyone involved. This dialogue between fairness and care not only provides a better understanding of relations between the sexes but also gives rise to a more comprehensive portrayal of adult work and family relationships.
>
> (Gilligan, 1982:174)

Just as ethics of care should not be an equally oppressive mode of ethics to the worst instances of the ethic of justice, it should also not be the ethic of justices' unequal 'Other'. Postconventional ethics may reduce these risks by balancing one mode of ethics against the other and may also be a genuinely mature way of ensuring that ethics of care are integrated into mainstream ethical practice.

## The Equality Act 2010

What kind of legislation could satisfy the seemingly contradictory coupling of ethics of care with the ethic of justice? Does the EA 2010 move towards this utopian state of affairs? The EA 2010 was partly designed to revise the Equality Act 2006 (EA 2006) in order to replace most previous British gender legislation by simplifying it, standardising much of its content and updating its scope, according to the Government Equalities Office (2011). The Act was to bring all aspects of the UK's anti-discrimination law and equality law under one roof, alongside the UK's European obligations under the Equality Directives. It was proposed that the Act be presented in easily accessible language, for instance the government considered what definition of 'gender reassignment' would be most accurate and understandable (Dean, 8 July 2008). The EA 2010 resembled the EU Commission's proposal of a single anti-discriminatory directive that would recognise and protect seven separate strands or protected categories including 'gender reassignment'.

The Act re-introduced the Public Sector Gender Equality Duty, which requires public-sector and public-funded bodies and their employees to implement an onus of care in the way that their policies, programmes and services affect people belonging to the seven strands, promising a significant move towards addressing direct and indirect discrimination.[19] It was intended that this Duty should not be implemented in too bureaucratic (incomprehensible and complex) a manner, again offering the promise of access to the law for non-legal people, whether implementing, or affected by, the Duty.

The EA 2010 does seem to represent a leap in the evolutionary scale of legal ethics pertaining to oppressed subjectivities by requiring proactive provision for equality and increased access to areas of public life for previously excluded 'Others'. However, like the GRA 2004, the Act retains a definition of trans subjectivity that seems to exclude those not transitioning into a heteronormative gender. According to the Act itself, one has to be, 'intending to undergo, undergoing or having undergone gender reassignment', to be included into the category of 'gender reassignment', which means a transition from one heteronormative gender to another even though not necessarily involving medical reassignment,

> [The Act] mentions individuals who have proposed, commenced or completed gender reassignment as a group which falls within the remit of the new Commission for Equality and Human Rights … . Again there is no express mention of transgender or gender variant people other than those individuals who fit the statutory legal definition, which clearly is intended

to only afford protection to the small sub group of transsexual people who seek medical supervision for gender reassignment.

(Whittle, Turner and Al-Alami, 20 December 2006:34)

Only after extensive protest from Press for Change and other activist groups was there included, in Part 1 Chapter 2 S. 7 of the explanatory notes to the EA 2010 on its parliamentary website,[20] a description of 'gender reassignment' as something other than a medical process. This section changes the definition of 'gender reassignment' to be found in the amended SDA 1975 by, *'no longer requiring a person to be under medical supervision to come within the section'*. Even so, this protected category is still called 'gender reassignment', suggesting an interpretation of the subjectivity as a transfer from one heteronormative sexual subjectivity to another. Paragraph 41 of these explanatory notes even refers to *'a process to change his or her sex'* and *'a transsexual person'* as pertaining to those with the protected characteristic, portraying gender transition as a change of sexual subjectivity rather than a confirmation of such subjectivity.

Returning to the claim by the Government Equalities Office that the EA 2010 will be more accessible (non-exclusionary through using clear language) than previous gender legislation, employers and the British Chamber of Commerce have expressed concerns about the increasing burden of paperwork and management that the Act will entail. The government has countered this by stating that the legislation will make the law clearer for organisations and that there will be a greater opportunity for the inclusion of those from diverse subjectivities who can add experience and talent to these organisations (Kornacki, 1 Oct 2010). It seems that employers will have to be proactive in establishing fair opportunities and access for employees and clients but that this will increase benefits deriving from inclusion such as a wider pool of expertise and knowledge of gender variance.

However, a client of Press for Change's TransEquality advice service presented a challenge to the potential inclusiveness of the EA 2010,

> ... we are now worse off with the so called single Equality Law (with all its excemptions on single sex facilities, services and jobs) than we were without it as the SDA and GRA had made our rights quite clear. Whilst the GRA wasn't perfect, this was as a result of the ban on gay marriage, but it did lay down our rights, but the SEA has reversed many.
>
> (Anonymous Quote)

This seems to be an exaggeration since the EA 2010 has generally opened up social inclusion for trans people. However, exemptions to provision of access to separate and single sex services (SSEs) to those who have transitioned do exist and such backtracks to inclusion may be shrouded by an obfuscation of trans people's rights through wording that provides inadequate clarity on who is protected and in which circumstances.

Ensuring that either the ethics of care or the ethic of justice do not become the inferior 'Other' of the other can only occur if the new onus of care brought in by the EA 2010 really does work to eliminate direct and indirect discrimination by addressing the social roots of difference-phobias, rather than just to recognise subjective difference. This onus of care must be able to recognise previously invisiblised difference such as gender variance as well as provide 'umbrella' standardization of equality protection via the ethic of justice.

## 4.6 Conclusion

In the first section the advances made in 'single functional issue legislation' and gender equality, suggested to be a philosophical first wave of gender legislation, were seen to have been radical and progressive in their time and to have engendered subsequent advances in gender law. However, it was argued that a new approach to the formation of gender law was needed in order to create a gender inclusive society, otherwise the heteronormative hegemony would continue indefinitely. This required replacing the emphasis on gender equality and single-issue lobbying with a focus on gender equity, or recognition of and respect for difference, and investigation of the social roots of difference-phobias.

In the second section it was found that what might be called a 'philosophical second wave of gender legislation' culminated in the recognition of difference in the achievement of gender, for instance the trans person's different route to gender, but still only provided recognition of gendered heteronormativity as the end result and only for transition from one heteronormative gender to another. Legislation subsequent to *Corbett* marked a slow progress towards recognition of transitioned gender but genders falling outside the remit of heteronormativity were invisiblised by medicine and the law, with the subtly coerced cooperation of trans people themselves (Stone, 1991). This meant that social expectations attached to each gender remained intact and that, for instance, it was still hard to conceive of a natal female-bodied person becoming a father.

The third section described how the law has 'Othered' gender variant people from categories of man and woman while not defining these categories. Sharpe theorised that anything that defied common-sense social scripts, and that which was 'otherness within sameness', or human yet non-human, was portrayed as 'monstrous' in English and French legal discourse. In both discourses, a genealogical evolution of discourse modified what was perceived as 'monster' over time. This unstated genealogical evolution of subjectivity was hidden under the guises of 'common sense' and ahistorical discourse. The concept, and consequent revealing, of genealogy provides hope that categories can be reconstructed by gender variant people in order to produce categories influenced by gender variant people themselves so that they may attain human rights and social voice in modern society.

the fourth section described how the involvement of gender variant people with their own legal cases and those of others has eased the introduction of what might be called a third wave of gender legislation, where difference can be respected and recognised rather than automatically assimilated into the norm. Beginning with *P v S & CCC*, trans people's involvement with case law allowed them to present trans people as individuals whose 'view from somewhere' presented a valid account of gender variance. Like Whittle, Beresford and Fineman, Flynn discovered that the discourse of parenting was still highly gendered, just like the legal discourse of marriage. Like Whittle, Flynn believed that a parent should be defined by what they do, rather than by their ascribed identity. The case of *Bellinger* stands as an exemplar of how trans legal activists contributed to the slow transformation of trans people from 'Others' of heteronormativity to empowered 'others' whose difference could be valued or, for those who wish to be accepted as men and women, whose choice of similarity can be respected.

In the fifth section it was noted how there has been a shift in transgender philosophy from a focus on certain defined issues and identity (first wave philosophy) to inclusion of a broad range of issues and subjectivities pertaining to trans people's claims to legal protection (Whittle, 2002a:81). However, Whittle warned that, '*The lesson that must be learnt is that legal recognition of a "sex change" will not automatically provide protection in the workplace (or other parts of life, for that matter)*' (2002a:106). A third wave of gender law might address oppressive discourse with a 'postconventional ethical' approach that provides gender variant people with rights to equality protection, while involving a focus on the individual that allows appreciation of their particular social circumstances. It may combine traditionally gendered moralities in order to evolve them into a moral maturity.

The Equality Act 2010 was assessed to determine how far it might embody a move towards postconventional ethics. The Act does provide for specific protected strands and ways of investigating individual cases of oppression (ethics of care) within universalizing equality legislation (ethic of justice). The Act is intended by the government to increase inclusion for trans people by using accessible language. However, simplification of language may actually create social exclusion through not describing exactly which trans people are protected, and in what ways. Crucially, the schema of heteronormativity is upheld by referring to trans people's protected characteristic as 'gender reassignment', thereby excluding many gender variant people from special protection and recognition.

Before the analysis of themes identified in Chapters 2 to 4 and the formation of reconstructed themes (themes drawn from gender variant narratives and research, intended to advance the rights of gender variant people) is undertaken in Chapters 6 to 8, Chapter 5 summarises how the *Transstudy* methodology was formulated and points out the importance of narratives to this book. This methodology derived from key components of a third wave (trans, feminist and legal) philosophy, as identified in Chapters 2 to 4. These components might be summarised as voice, alternative maturity, alternative reality (from Chapter 2), subjectivity, contradiction, maternal relations, accessible discourse (from Chapter 3) and difference inclusion from sections three and four of this chapter.

## Notes

1. Many women have held and many hold gender that is variant to masculine and/or heteronormative gendering, which has traditionally secured a place in Western industrial society as the superior or neutral/default type of gendering.
2. Following the attorney General's advice in the case of P v S and Cornwall County Council, [1996] European Court of Justice, Case C-13/94, [1996] IRLR 347.
3. John Forbes-Sempill v The Hon Ewan Forbes-Sempill (1967) unreported, Scottish Court of Administration.
4. Corbett v Corbett [1970] 2 All ER 33.
5. Such a view of marriage as only possible between man and woman was also taken by Sir Mark Potter in his ruling in *Wilkinson v Kitsinger*, as described in the next section.
6. New Zealand Attorney-General v Family Court at Otahuhu [1995] NZ Fam LR 57.
7. Gramsci believed that hegemony notably manifested as skewed symbiotic social relations unbalanced in favour of dominant groups and ideologies such as the bourgeoisie, capitalism, the integral state, civil society or the ruling class (Bocock, 1986).
8. Goodwin, Christine v UK Government, Application No. 28957/95 (1995) ECHR; I v UK Government, Application No 25608/94 (1994) ECHR.
9. P v S and Cornwall County Council, Case C-13/94 [1996] IRLR 347, ECJ.
10. From: http://www.Press for Change.org.uk/node/1025.
11. X, Y and Z v UK (1997) 24 EHRR 143, ECHR.
12. For instance, see Don Horrocks' challenge put to Whittle in the BBC television debate programme, 'Newsnight' (2002) (see Friday, 12 July, 2002, 16:04 GMT 17:04 UK, http://news.bbc.co.uk). Horrocks neglected to mention the small incidence of families splitting up because of the gender reassignment of one partner compared with the number of families splitting up because of other reasons.
13. Bellinger v Bellinger [2003] UKHL 21, [2003] All ER (D) 178 (Apr).
14. Known by Foucault as 'reciprocal elucidation' (Diamond and Quinby, 1988:xi).
15. A v Chief Constable of West Yorkshire Police [2004] UKHL 21.
16. As described by Diamond and Quinby (1988:xv).
17. See Prado (2000:53–84) with reference to Foucault (1975) *Discipline and Punish*.
18. Referred to as 'selflessness' in a later article by Gilligan.
19. It was noted in the second part of this chapter that the SDA did not adequately address the roots of discrimination, something which an 'onus of care' may move towards doing.
20. These can be seen at http://www.legislation.gov.uk/ukpga/2010/15/notes/division/2/2/1/4.

# 5 Third wave philosophy
## Dialogic negotiation

**Introduction**

The primary resource for the research leading to this book came in the form of personal narratives of trans subjectivity elicited by members of the *Transstudy*. Published narratives produced by those involved with third wave feminism, as introduced in Chapter 3, formed a basis for comparison with *Transstudy* narratives. The research was based on the author's desire to investigate how feminist and trans factions might combine to reduce stigma attached to oppressed sexual subjectivities, so that they may gain access, agency and voice in social discourses such as culture, medicine and the law. This research was intended to be driven by a non-separatist or difference inclusive feminist ethos and was structured by a critical discourse analysis framework, informed by themes developed in Chapters 2 to 4. This ethos and methodology was thought to be appropriate in view of the subject of study (gender and discourse) and the author's personally political standpoint (inclusive feminist).

## 5.1 Ethical framework: setting up and maintaining the *Transstudy*

### *Ethical approach – qualitative research*

Blaxter et al. considered that, '... *those with social justice concerns will include the very topic of the research as part of their ethical framework*' (2001:161). The research questions, dealing with issues of cooperation between transgender and feminist factions, aetiology of gender variance, utility of separatist discourse and potential for an inclusive trans/third wave feminist coalition, were intended to be ones that addressed ethical issues while employing qualitative research to allow in depth investigation of social justice concerns.

The author considered that his university's ethical policy was required for the protection of all parties concerned but was aware, and in tune with, the notion of ethics as an ongoing process. In a similar way, Clandinin and Connelly identified a methodological ethics-in-process with regard to the span of the research process,

They [ethics] are not dealt with once and for all, as might seem to happen, when ethical review forms are filled out and university approval is sought for our inquiries. Ethical matters shift and change as we move through an inquiry.

(2000:170)

However, these authors also warn that ethics-in-process are subject to any official initial stipulations of ethical approval and this may restrict any negotiations of ethics during the research process (170). In explaining ethics-in-process, Edwards and Mauthner provide the example of Benhabib's recommended ethical methodology,

> She argues that ethics is about concrete rather than generalised situations, in which relations of care belong at the centre rather than the margins. What is moral and ethical is arrived at through an active and situationally contingent exchange of experiences, perspectives and ideas across differences ...
>
> (2002:25)

It could be said that the research for this book employed ethics of care (in-process) based on the use of an informal format and narrative basis in order to establish connections and communication between participants, the author considering himself to be one such participant, rather than distant observer. Stanley and Wise outlined a feminist ethic for researcher relations with participants in *Breaking out Again*,

> ... insistence that the 'objects' of research are also subjects in their own right as much as researchers are subjects of theirs (and objects of other people's); acceptance that the researcher is on the same critical plane as those she researches and not somehow intellectually superior; and, most fundamental of all, no opinion, belief or other construction of events and persons, no matter from whom this derives, should be taken as a representation of 'reality' ...
>
> (1993:200)

In Stanley and Wise's research paradigm participants turn from objects to subjects and have a voice to contribute to the actual operation of the research. The author involved himself as a fellow participant in the *Transstudy* in order to strive for such a paradigm. In efforts to address issues of 'Othering' within the research, the author, for instance, commented upon spiritual knowledge ventured by participant Kimana and participants addressed issues of exclusion in the <Hidden trans men> and <Black Trans> topic thread contributions.

Researchers adopting an inclusive research methodology need to remain sensitive to differences but not to avoid them when they are identified as this avoidance ensures that 'separate spheres' established by essentialising discourses will always remain in place. Such spheres can lock their subjects into conclaves of research not investigated by or involving other subjectivities.

### Recruitment to the **Transstudy**

Participants were introduced to the *Transstudy* when contacted by the research supervisor. The supervisor sent out details of the study via email to trans people registered on his UK based online lists – about 2500 people. Over 50 of these people requested and were given usernames and passwords. Six became regular contributors to the *Transstudy* site. Thus, the regular research population was small, as is the case in many qualitative analyses, making it difficult and inappropriate to generalise from information in the narratives elicited. However, instead of reliability, analysis of participants' narratives instead offered some measure of validity with regard to the presentation of gender in narrative.

For the purposes of this study, the Information Sheet,[1] offered to anyone agreeing to take part in the research, acted as a contract. It informed participants about: the purpose of the study; their decision on whether to take part; the advantages of taking part; ensuring their confidentiality; the use to which the research will be put; who was involved in the organisation of the research; and who reviewed the study. As recommended by Blaxter et al. (158), the contract referred to informed consent and the reporting and dissemination of the data.

### *Research authenticity – researcher/participant interactions*

Gaining reliable research data from participants in controlled scientific conditions has often worked to neglect consideration of sociological influences that shape the responses a participant might be disposed to elicit (Harding, 1991:143). Such sociological influences will have shaped the beings-in-process who populate any research forum, and this suggests that valid research findings on complex sociological issues cannot be striven for from participants until the researcher has at least some knowledge of participants' life-histories and the background of the social phenomena under investigation. A narrowing of the social distance, and lessening of the social boundary, between researcher and participant promises to engender more accurate narrative accounts as a relationship of trust emerges between the two parties.

Unstructured or open-ended topics and discussion formed the component parts of the *Transstudy*. Such topics may have engendered new perspectives and insights not gained from more structured interactions, and may have lead to a '... *re-examination of the assumption that more valid knowledge is produced when information is elicited in a format framed by the researcher's point of view*' (Cook and Fonow, 1990:76). The research was also designed to offer potential for empowerment through self-discovery by involving participants in the research process.

## Research authenticity – computer-mediated-communication

> The last 16 years have seen a major change in the trans community. The growth of home computer use in the 1990s, and the encouragement of many trans women at the forefront of information technology and internet development was to be crucial in the development of a new, geographically spread but no longer isolated, trans community.
>
> (Whittle et al., 2006: section 1.3)

From a practical perspective, computer-mediated-communication (CMC) offers advantages over face-to-face (FTF) interactions. Because CMC responses are written down, difficulties often experienced in recording and transcribing verbal interactions are overcome. Also, sociodemographic and demographic barriers to involvement in research can be surmounted to some extent because of the opportunity to communicate from a distance and not in the presence of a social group. Examples of such barriers are age, ethnicity, class, geographical location, culture and the presentation of sexual subjectivity itself, some of which were addressed by participant Kimana,

> As Sherman Alexi, a Spokane playwriter and poet said, "The internet almost makes up for the smallpos blankets." (Smallpox blankets, blankets used by US troops that died of smallpox and sent to the reservations in hopes that disease would kill us off, a known historical fact. ... I think he's right. I've been in touch with people from all over the world with it. It's a good way to teach others about our culture and the real history you don't find in books.It also allows us to learn, make new friends and even join in forums such as this, even way from way out on the prairie like Pine RIdge or the North Woods of Wisconsin or Alaska. Lalalala!
>
> (Kimana Jul 20th, 2006, in <Post-GRS people's sexuality>)

As noted by Prosser (1998:ch3), published autobiography inevitably involves attempts to impose logic and linearity on personal narratives of trans subjectivity. Therefore, the *Transstudy* site was designed to adopt a more accurate way to capture the essence of the development of subjectivity and self-image via the assessment of written 'conversation'. This more immediate form of communication may, through being more spontaneous, have engendered narratives less subject to conscious manipulation.

Some critics maintain that the natural behaviour or natural responses of CMC participants cannot be directly observed,

> The lack of non-verbal and social clues makes it more difficult for the researcher to monitor how interviewees are responding to questions about sensitive issues.
>
> (Blaxter et al., 2001:160)

However, detecting cues in FTF interaction requires extensive interaction. For instance, if an FTF interview is not part of an ongoing series of communication with the participant there is much less chance of attaining what Max Weber (1864–1920) called verstehen, or empathic understanding. Such understanding can be achieved in both FTF interaction and CMC if there are sufficient interactions between researcher and participant. When such an interactional relationship is established trust between researcher and participant evolves and consequently can lead to more open and detailed responses. Extensive communication of this kind also allows 'cross-examining' via comparison of a number of responses in order to check out the consistency of participant responses (Hammersley and Atkinson, 1994:154).

The immediate nature of FTF interactions can lead subjects to provide answers that they expect a certain interviewer to want, or to present the self in a certain modified way to evade judgment from a directly present researcher (Mann and Stewart, 2000:209). This can also occur in CMC, but probably not to such an extent because of physical distance between researcher and participant. Because of this kind of expectancy responding, and because participants will want to self-present in ways not necessarily conducive with their actual gender or gender-in-process, representations presented in CMC or FTF interactions may therefore be taken to refer to personas, rather than actual people, persona being the character that one presents to the world. Consequently, this research was intended to reveal narrative truths, rather than truths of actual subjectivity, where narratives of self inform narrative truths of self-representation, rather than of actual selves.

As Mann and Stewart discovered, extended narrative interaction usually leads to an accurate presentation of self-image via various narrative actions (2000). Studies have revealed that online self-presentation is usually rooted in a subject's real-life self-image (Wallace, 1999, in Mann and Stewart, 2000:208). Mann and Stewart remarked that '… *it is seen to be difficult to sustain a persona which is quite divorced from the "real" self*' (2000:210).

Feminist academic Stacey Gillis (2004:185) noted that, '*The Internet is thus vaunted [by third wave theorists] as the global consciousness-raising tool which the first and second waves lacked*', but argued that cyberfeminism, with regard to subverting gender, is actually failing to attain this lofty status. Gillis maintained that, according to Kira Hall, online interactions can intensify presentation and presence of real gender (189, 190), just as Mann and Stewart maintained but that this can mean such gender can be oppressive as it is in the non-online world. So, although CMC is not a way to evade the influence of gender, the *Transstudy* may have provided a forum of 'voice' for participants' gendered representations which may have had to be muted in the non-online or 'real' world.

### *Absence of a 'self-identified third wave feminists' primary study*

A similar data gathering process to the *Transstudy* in order to obtain narratives from self-identified third wave feminists proved too difficult to embark upon for the following reasons.

The author had access to an extensive list of subscribers to PFC and FTM online mailing lists for trans people, provided by the supervisor. The author decided to make use of this resource rather than having to find and approach self-identified third wave feminists with no such resource immediately available. Also, the *Transstudy* eventually took up so much time, and was of such a scale, that there was not enough time left to undertake primary research with third wave feminists.

The author predicted that he would have faced problems with undertaking personal research with natal non-gender-transitioned females, who probably form the majority of self-identified third wave feminists. This is because natal females may well have been more reluctant to communicate about personal issues with a natal male and the research ethos and subject matter required a considerable amount of personal input.

With hindsight, the author could have set up a more limited *Transstudy* to give time to investigate the potential for, and hopefully set up, a similar study for self-identified third wave feminists, after devising a well-thought-out strategy for researching with such people in a sensitive way.

## 5.2 Philosophical framework: queer inspired third wave feminism

It became evident that queer theory aligned closely with the research framework and the author's personally political philosophy, for instance in drawing from social constructionist theories of, for instance, Foucault and Butler. This alignment can also be highlighted by use of Stryker's metaphor of 'transgender rage', where a social space for those 'Othered' from gendered society can create a site for respect for their subjectivities as ongoing constructs (2006 [1994]). If the philosophical second wave was and/or is an equality seeking project it seems that the third wave seeks equity, meaning fairness and respect for difference rather than equivalence and assimilation. This move to gender inclusion was no doubt inspired by queer theory's ethos of gender equity, albeit with queer's more intensive focus on dismantling '... *stable categories*' (Fineman, 2009:5).

### *Introducing queer theory*

In the 1980s, queer theory challenged categorisations of gender by questioning the subject's necessary location on only one side of sexual dualisms and the very existence of such dualisms. Jay Prosser compared this challenge to the camp creation of a 'third space', a metaphor devised by Scott Long (1998:25). This space forms a gender variant standpoint position where the gender outsider can see gender dualism for what it is by virtue of seeing it as a whole (in a wider perspective), from without. Judith Butler seemed to write *Gender Trouble* (1990) from such a standpoint in order to argue that sexual categorisation is an effect of culture. Her theory therefore challenged the idea of gender as '... *primary and foundational*' (31). Queer theory has thus had a profound effect upon representations of sexual identities and subjectivities. Such representations have (in theory, if not in practice) often opposed medical, legal and binary coded definitions of gender/sexuality. Janet Halley linked queer theory to the project to support gender variance rather than definitively to explain it,

> I would now say that queer work will be more interested, descriptively and normatively, in practices than identities, in performativity than essences, and in mobility than stabilities.
>
> (2009:28)

Queer representations have also often involved a politically subversive side, which has been characterised as 'gender fuck' by Stephen Whittle (1996). This phrase indicates, in a rather direct manner, queer and transgender theory's implementation of theoretical, literary and activity-based means of challenge to the still ubiquitous gender heteronormativity of many societies.

The queer scene provided a theoretical and practical escape route from what is seen by some as the heteronormative tyranny of gender by theorising that men and women were not doomed to fulfil lives rutted in the (significantly often wrong) tracks of sexual subjectivity ascribed to them. However, trans people were ironically accused by some queer feminists of upholding the structures of heterogender by wishing to reassign as simply man or woman (Whittle, 2005:161). Conversely, Whittle (1996, 2002) argued that queer theory has sometimes privileged certain genderings (those involving same-sex desire), and therefore has failed to fully escape the economy of gender.

Although presenting gender in an entirely new way, queer theory has thus been steered by its roots, described by Whittle as '... *medico-legal discussions of sexual pathologies*' (1996:197). Queer's contemporary-modern manifestation is linked to modern sexual identities (rather than subjectivities) that share a genesis in the definitions of inverted identities offered by sexology and the reinterpretations of such identities as erroneous social development by the psychoanalytic movement, as addressed in Chapter 2. Despite this maintained link to certain genders and sexualities, Whittle perceived queer theory as '... *one of the greatest threats to the conceptual basis of modernist thought there has ever been*' (1996:200).

A failing of queer theory is that it does not tend to provide for those who need subjective labels with which to locate themselves socially and to provide a foundation for their subjectivity. It is of questionable use for those who wish for acknowledgment of what they perceive as oppressions deriving from the lived reality of their gender. More appealing theoretical movements for such people are offered by transgender studies and third wave feminism. Those championing trans theory/studies/practice found that Whittle's 'gender fuck' effect could often be transposed to their discipline, activity or subjectivity without a complete loss of subjective positioning. In transgender studies, 'gender fuck' has been expanded and revised in what Whittle calls, '... *not just deconstruction but also reconstruction' in order to allot more validity to those sexes/genders/sexualities that appear real to those who experience them'* (Whittle, 1996:204). Reconstruction can move on from deconstruction by involving political, critical and feminist aspects rather than being a purely philosophical exercise.

## *Discussing connections between queer theory and feminism*

Negative internecine conflations describing each other's factions have been manufactured by queer theory against feminism and vice versa, in a similar way to those arising between transgender and feminism, as described in Chapter 1, to the detriment of dialogic negotiations, '*For too long, feminism has been caricatured ... as being primarily a politics of anti-sex moralism, and queer theory has been conversely cast ... as being nothing but an uncritical celebration of sex*' (Romero, 2009:197).

As described in the next sub-section, Romero theorised that there have been more connections than disconnections between the two factions. Fineman (2009) suggested three major connections between much of feminism and queer theory: subversive elements, interdisciplinary perspectives and political ethos.

Philosophical third wave feminism seems particularly related to queer theory because of its socially constructive approach to gender, its radical element, its interdisciplinary ethos and intersectionality theory. Intersectionality theory maintains that individual and group subjectivities, and mainstream and/or alternative discourses interact to create a whole different subjectivity to its component parts. It seems to indicate the particularly inclusive overlap between third wave feminism and queer theory and seems to owe a large debt to those womanist philosophers who demonstrated that lived experience and social subjectivities combine to produce complex social standpoints.

In 'Toward a Queer Legal Theory', Stychin described how queer theory has highlighted categorical thinking in law and the 'in-process' nature of categories that otherwise seem non-time bound and cross-cultural, '*Queerness in part suggests an unwillingness to fix differences in any ultimate literality. Rather, queer favours a strategically articulated commonality forged from differently located subject positions*' (1995:141).

This bodes well for links between queer theory and the notions of genre and genealogy, and of postdifference. For Stychin, the law, from a queer perspective, is just as much in-process as human subjectivities,

> ... law as a locus of struggle can be dynamic, unstable, and unpredictable. I will suggest that law and legal reasoning can inadvertently contribute to the development of a 'queer' political stance and identity. In this regard, legal discourse often inscribes sexuality in a queer fashion and, in the process, legal reasoning itself becomes a queer phenomenon.
> 
> (1995:140)

Stychin considered that, rather than forming gender hierarchies and adopting the 'liberal assimilation' of subjectivity that marked what might be identified as the philosophical second wave of the lesbian and gay movement, queer theory developed a suspicion of definitions and lables (144). In this way queer tied in with the concept of formation of subjectivity through genre and genealogy, where subjectivities and their labels are taken to be 'in-process'. It seems that a genealogy of subjectivity is needed to allow gendered, ethnic and social 'Others' to connect with the oppressed factions of queer and feminism. Culbertson and Jackson view queer and feminism as complex and as built from a, 'multiplicity of differences' and that recognising this can point, '... *us to an exit from, and indictment of, this imagined queer-feminist divide*' (2009:138). Chapter 3 described how third wave feminism notably recognises such complexity and contradiction in subjectivities and movements. Culbertson and Jackson note how the law is characteristically slow to recognise these differences-in-process, and that this slowness has caused the 'Othering' of many gender variant people from social institutions and legal protection.

In the face of unnamed oppressions and oppressors, rather than losing subjectivity in liberal assimilation, queer theorists found that a strategic essentialism was required based upon personally political subjectivity. Stychin recognised the need for this by stating that, '*The strategy is to both assert categories as meaningful and strategically important, while avoiding closure in their definition*' (155). However, despite queer's attempts to dismantle essentialist categories and to avoid giving in to liberal assimilation, the bias towards lesbian and gay subjectivities in queer theory may have decreased inclusivity for all gender variant people. Stychin considered that,

> ... lesbian and gay politics has often seemed in practice less inclusive of difference than in stated theory. ... The focus on sexual categories thus slides easily into a one-dimensional view of 'otherness', which frequently has obliterated the complexity of the matrices of oppression in which subjects operate.
>
> (142)

This view of other gender variance as 'Other', led to the formation of hierarchies between gender variant subjectivities, seeming to mirror those to be found in heteronormativity, although Halberstam (1998) criticised easy readings of such hierarchies, as outlined in Chapter 3 on the subject of 'butch' and 'femme'. Culbertson and Jackson's description of, '... *the dense attraction and tragic conscription of radical critical movement to fixed and unitary identitarian politics and juridical liberal discourses*' (2009:136) also seems applicable to the philosophical second wave of feminism. Is has been argued that, in this way, queer and feminism have come to be associated with particular essentialised identities and that this has caused rifts between the two factions. Culbertson and Jackson described how dualisms within dualisms are formed when oppressed subjectivities essentialise themselves, with the effect of maintaining inside/outside binaries,

> Thus, getting the queer outside feminism – like getting the feminine outside partriarchy, or the homosexual outside heteronormativity – subtends even as it claims to subvert the inside/outside logic of fixed and unitary difference and differences, thereby excluding those racial, economic, national and other Others who are never really in or out of this inside/outside framework.
> (138)

In Chapter 1 it was argued that transgender and feminism have been blighted by exclusionary elements from within and without. It could be that transgender and feminism are sometimes biased towards their own hierarchically placed essentialised identities, for example 'transsexual' and 'woman'. This bias would be just as contradictory as the queer situation if transgender and feminism are supposed to be free from the fetters of essentialising gender. It seems that such contradiction must at least be contradiction-in-process and recognised contradiction if it is to potentially be inclusive for excluded and/or as yet unnamed subjectivities. Third wave feminism has focused upon the positive effects of identifying and accepting contradiction where no rational aeiological explanations are forthcoming or where such explanations may merely serve to cause divisions.

Halley theorised that queer theory's divergence from equality and rights based legal reform indicated an acceptance of the contradictory nature of sexual subjectivity,

> Why does that logic sound "queer"? I think it's because it is sex-positive, shame/abjection affirmative, irrationalist, and capable of seeing the paradoxical, fractured and/or "flipped" capacities in M, F, desire and power. Surely approaching questions of sexual politics or sexual regulation with that logic would lead us strongly away from the equality-is-freedom, victim's-truth model of legal reform that has become Catharine MacKinnon's ...
> (2009:25)

So, both third wave feminist and queer factions seem capable of recognising the possibility of contradiction in their own philosophical projects, as well as recognising contradiction in other social discourses. Halley provides an example of a potential contradiction that would need to be identified by inclusive social constructionist philosophies,

> [Queer work] ... will tend to affirm mobility over fixity, though this tendency always leads a queer theoretic project to contradict its anti-identitarian aspirations by turning mobility itself into a new, highly regulatory identity or a model for all fixities to envy.
> (2009:28)

Both queer theory and inclusive feminism have identified the kind of structural thinking identified by feminist legal academic Ann Scales, which, '... *tends to become second nature and as such thwarts evolution by discouraging human efforts to be and do better ...*' (2009:396). This type of thought includes the common-sense and essentialising discourses that curb creative thinking. Such discourses might manifest as religion, medicine (biological and psychological), the law, or even transgender, feminist and queer theory. They may work to cement people into identity by proffering what are taken to be universal aetiologies of human development.

### Third wave feminism: a focus on feminisation as positive

In Fineman's opinion, Culbertson and Jackson, '... *insist upon the impossibility of a simple choosing of sides in the alleged divide of "feminist versus queer"*' (2009:113). The author concurs with this belief but identifies particularly with the feminism that might be called the philosophical third wave because of its connection with feminine subjectivity and feminine ethical relations.

The author wished to investigate heteronormativity as a separatist discourse that may lie at the root of subordination of feminine or feminised subjectivity. According to feminist social construction theory, this kind of subjectivity forms by processes such as those identified in Chapter 2, i.e. silence and secrecy, infantilisation, and manipulations of reality. All gender variant subjectivities would seem to have incurred this kind of social emasculation, but, on a more positive note, feminisation may develop as a choice of lifestyle and subjectivity. Romero noted that, '*Much queer politics and queer theory is therefore suspicious of identity politics, which tend to categorise and simplify experience*' (2009:190–191). However, *subjectivity* politics is necessary for the personally political project of third wave feminism in order to reveal silent and secretly formed gender variant 'identities', and to reveal the preferred subjectivities of silenced gender variant people.

Gilligan concentrated upon negative feminisation in *In a Different Voice*. Although this may have seemed to be an essentialisation of women as the 'weaker sex', her ethics of care espoused investigation of individual subjectivities and circumstances, an ethical procedure key to queer practice. This procedure revealed that feminised gendering was in-process, or subject to gradual social evolution.

Mary Becker in 'Care and Feminists' described how Professor Katherine Franke perceived the emphasis on care in legal feminism as having built up an image of 'dependency and danger' pertaining to women's lives (2009:160). Franke considered that, because of this, women should not be culturally associated with care in the form of biological motherhood. However, Becker argued that special recognition need not essentialise those who are categorised, including those categorised as mothers. Feminist research has revealed the way that women have developed ethics of care through mothering type relations, and identifying those who have contributed in this way as 'women' or 'mothers' at least pays tribute to their special link to ethics of care.

### *Taking a break from non-feminism*

In 'Queer Theory by Men', Halley addressed the need she felt to 'take a break from feminism' (2009:15). This referred to the kinds of feminism perceived by her to be prevalent in the contemporary USA, rather than what Halley recognised as feminism herself. Halley identified three main types of feminism from which to be take a break: 'M/F feminism' (distinction between male and female), 'M>F feminism' (male as oppressively dominant of female) and 'carrying a brief for F feminism' (eulogising of the female) (5).

Halley described how, in her early theorising, Catherine MacKinnon promoted the concept of M/F feminism by concluding that the gendered separation inherent in the M/F dualism was brought about by institutionalised heteronormativity. For MacKinnon, the state and the law were both gendered male, '... *in the sense that they fully recapitulated male ontological and epistemological powers and were in a sense therefore fully dependent on female subordination to be what they were*' (Halley, 2009:12). However, by emphasising the existence of such overarching social hegemonies, Halley theorised that MacKinnon and many feminist and gay rights campaigners narrated themselves into victim status (14). According to Halley, cultural and radical feminism therefore inadvertently supported 'subordination-theory structuralism', where subordination of the female was embedded into the structure of society (20).

Halley considered that a queer perspective of law and subjectivities as in-process and not inescapably oppressive/oppressed was provided by queer theorists such as Duncan Kennedy. Kennedy, following on from Foucault's postmodern theory of sexuality, suggested the complexity of individual and structural subjectivities, a complexity which might allow, '... *the persistence of resistance, compromise and opportunism as strategies for negotiating the regime, rather than buying into it without reserve, so that the image of a fully rationalised, totalitarian gender system seems paranoid*' (Kennedy, 1993:157, quoted in Halley, 2009:21).

This kind of philosophical perspective would allow Halley to take a break from the prescriptive enclaves she perceived that feminism and gay rights had become in the US. However, it is perhaps the case that only some people have the choice to take a break from the kinds of feminism described by Halley, and that this does not include those with subjectivities not characteristically included into the kind of separatist feminisms that she describes.

It may happen that some of those with non-natal-female genders may, conversely, wish to take a break from non-feminism. This will sometimes be more of a 'staycation' than a break, if the person concerned has already actually held and espoused a feminist-inspired ethos already. Alternatively, it may involve a wish for immigration into feminism, rather than a temporary visit, if the chosen feminism is seen as different to the kind of separatist feminisms Halley described.

In assessing Halley's desire to take a break from feminism, Romero considered that,

> ... it is not necessary to take a break from feminism, as Halley argues, to be critical of or to work beyond feminist projects, as Halley desires. As I explain, the construction of Halley's point mistakenly presumes the existence of a readily identifiable body of consistent thought called "feminism" from which to take a break. Indeed, in order for Halley's articulation to work, she must ignore or label otherwise feminist efforts that have similar views about sexuality to her own.
>
> (2009:179)

Feminists and queer theorists always need to highlight the consequences of attempting to provide a set definition of the other faction. Romero asked whether it is, '... *dilutive of feminist and queer political mobilizations to suggest that we cannot substantively define feminism and queer theory*' (2009:197). However, it may be this very lack of definition that leads to commitment for some if they see their own or the other factions as a means of escaping suffocating social metanarratives provided by establishment discourse.

Romero provided an interpretation of feminist theoretical frameworks as open and evolving entities that seems to align with interpretations of third wave feminism, '... *many feminists embrace the idea that no one theory could ever provide a complete explanation; these feminists eschew totalising "grand theory" and instead opt for "middle-range theory" grounded in everyday experience ...*' (2009:185).

This kind of feminism involves theory-in-process that doesn't seek, for instance, to simply reverse power relationships formed by masculinism. It is not necessary to take a break from this kind of feminism, or to be barred from its shores, since it should be inherently self-critical and open to input from other inclusive philosophies.

We can just as readily conceive of taking a break from queer theory, as from feminism. This may be useful when considering that both are named discourses that acquire connotations from those names. However, Romero suggests we can critique those connotations without having to take time off from either faction if we recognise that, '... *a general or foundational differentiation between queer theory and feminism is neither possible nor desirable*' (190).

Romero considered that feminism and queer theory do have overlaps, '*I do not mean to posit ... that feminism and queer theory are distinct and segregated arenas of thought*' (180). This quote provides further support for a perspective of feminism and queer as genres with complex connections to each other. The desire for a break from either faction is best subject to philosophical examination, in order to add to the 'in-process' development of both. People should have the power to choose to identify with either faction, or both, without the other then having to be foregone or subsumed into the other.

## 5.3 Why narratives?

The philosophical framework of queer-inspired third wave feminism was considered of sufficient reflexive value to act as a guide to reading *Transstudy* narratives. Reflexivity involves consideration of inputs into meaning by both the person talking or writing and by the person listening or reading. The author considered that online narratives could yield such reflexivity. Below is an explanation of the reasons for choosing narratives as potential sources of gender variant and third wave feminist philosophy and discourse, starting with a consideration of how to begin the attempt to know those you research.

> Unless you immerse yourself in a lifestyle or people for MANY years you cant really learn much, you think you have but you simply cant. When I read Anthroplogical and Tibetology pepers I laugh my head of, and especially the translations of sacred texts…they get so much WRONG.
> (Leon Jul 23rd, 2006, in <How do you believe you will you age?>)

> You're right about fully understanding our Ways. They can't be more than touched on in a classroom, even with four year deggrees in "Indian Studies" or "Native American Culuture". I mean, give it a break. How can four years of classroom study make one fully understand the Ways of a People?
> (Kimana Aug 9th, 2006, in <Post-GRS people's sexuality>)

Carol Gilligan similarly argued that the only way to gain insight into women's lives was to listen to their own voices in order to gain a kind of 'view from within', *'Among the most pressing items on the agenda for research on adult development is the need to delineate in women's own terms the experience of their adult life'* (1982:173).

People's own narrative accounts allow them to fashion stories about their experiences and passions in order to, consciously or unconsciously, position their social subjectivity. It is these stories that are identified by sociological researchers as spoken or written narratives. As noted by narrative analyst Catherine Riessman, these stories are partly infused into the subject by the culture he or she is brought up in and manifest in the form of personal narratives, '… *culture "speaks itself" through an individual's story. Narratives speak in terms that seem natural, but we can analyse how culturally and historically contingent these terms are* …' (1993:5).

Cues or input from others shape the amount or type of information we elicit in a narrative, leading to a yet more distorted version of the original event or experience, as noted by Tracey Lee (2001) in her research investigating trans men's interactions with medical specialists. The narrative is then subject to the interpretation of the reader who will be similarly infused with cultural location. A distortion of the original event or experience is not necessarily a bad thing as it can lead to interesting insights about perceptions of the event and about the teller.

Feminist research has notably suggested a link between language and subjective formation, and most feminist researchers are likely to agree with the idea that 'you are what you speak'. This is the result of language forming and reproducing our societies, and consequently the individuals within, and then reflecting society when it is used. Identification of what Mary Talbot called 'language-as-mirror' (1998:14) allows those of us who need to, to subvert, if only slowly, the operation of oppressive language by applying a critical investigation of everyday language. This can be done by examining what is reflected in what is in actuality a distorted 'mirror', as a way to challenge its seeming inevitability or 'common sense'. Social construction theorists taking a critical look at language in discourse have portrayed sexual subjectivity as subject to constant Chinese-Whisper like creation of meaning, producing a distortion in the 'mirror' of language, and then a distortion in the social construction of the subject.

Critical discourse analysts such as Norman Fairclough (1989, 2003), Ruth Wodak and Ruth Wodak (2003), Teun A van Dijk (2008) and Mary Talbot (2003) have drawn from investigations of ideology and power relations by critical theorists such as Marx (1867), Gramsci (1971), Althusser (1970,1971), Foucault (1978) and Butler (1988). They have revealed that apparently self-evident or 'common sense' discourses, facilitated by written, spoken, bodily and image-based language, change over time depending upon who can influence the discourse in question.

Foucault theorised that challenges and changes to discourse depend upon, '... *a multiplicity of points of resistance*', that these points of resistance traverse, '... *social stratifications and individual unities*', and that changes could happen when silence and secrecy loosen the holds of power and provide for, '... *relatively obscure areas of tolerance*' (Foucault, 1998[1978]:95, 96, 101). These changes can eventually form a reconstructed discourse such as occurred with homosexuality in the nineteenth century, or such as happened during the 1980s AIDS pandemic. In both cases visibility of homosexuality led to increasing 'naming' where gay men re-appropriated their naming to reconstruct it in a positive or confident way, in order to escape imposed silent and secret narrative.

The idea of sexual subjectivity as in-process social construction enables a researcher to address what Mary Talbot, following on from work by Simone de Beauvoir (1949) and Monique Wittig (1992), identified as 'social essentialism'. This is the idea that subjectivity is restricted to certain categories and that everyone can accurately be allocated to some of these categories by others,

> In some writing on language and gender there is a tendency to treat the psycho-social categories of masculine and feminine as bi-polar. This is

particularly true of work on distinct interactional styles of men and women ... Such studies put essentialism out through the front door, only to let it in again at the back. That is to say, they do away with biological essentialism, just to replace it with a kind of social essentialism, which is just as bad.

(Talbot, 1998:13)

Social essentialism can be found in the dualistic operation of many narratives informed by dualistic discourse. We tend to use dualistic language (e.g. man/woman, white/black, sane/mad, straight/gay) all the time, leading us away from properly examining difference and coercing us into maintaining images of stereotypical 'Others'. Escape from dualistic representations might be facilitated by what Audre Lorde saw as cross-difference cooperation,

Within the interdependence of mutual (nondominant) differences lies that security which enables us to descend into the chaos of knowledge and return with true visions of our future, along with the concomitant power to effect those changes which can bring that future into being. Difference is that raw and powerful connection from which our personal power is forged.

(1984:112)

This is the inclusive approach to difference characteristic of philosophical third wave theory, contrasting with the exclusionary approach inherent to separatist masculinism and feminism.

Challenges to the essential categories of heteronormative gender have come from trans narratives, for instance in the autobiographies of Georgina Turtle, Roberta Cowell and Jan Morris, where the definition of who has real gendering with regard to naming such gendering came under scrutiny. More recently, Stephen Whittle described the confusion he endured when growing up as he wrought out self and social recognition for the sexual subjectivity that he seemed to have belonged to all along. Whittle described himself as originally a, '*male bisexual trapped inside a female body!*' (Self and Gamble, 2000:54). This is a good example of an individual's self-insight into the complexity of his own sexual subjectivity, encouraged by Will Self's narrative format, and was perhaps designed to be rather ironically complex in order to make a statement that trans people know about the complexity of gender. Trans subjectivities are nowadays generally much more socially acceptable and recognised than in the 1970s when Whittle transitioned, significantly because of trans people's access to self-expression.

Self-expression can lead to negative images of gender variance, and to negative consequences. For instance, it is debatable to what extent Nadia Almada's appearances in television reality show *Big Brother* were a positive forum for trans expression. Also, there is the phenomenon addressed by *Transstudy* participant Monica, where increased visibility leads to increased targeting by oppressors. Yet, refusing to self-express because of such incidents will lead back to gender variant people being subject to silent and secret representations by others.

A critic might ask what it is that narratives can tell us about the wider world when they are subject to the memories and prejudices of the narrator. The answer lies in the fact that narrative responses, when compared and contrasted with other narratives, can indicate how language moulds subjectivities and vice versa. Although personal narratives cannot be taken to be the truth, they still offer useful representations of people's perceptions.

It has been claimed that deliberately false subjectivity is generally difficult to maintain over extended narrative interaction (Mann and Stewart, 2000:212, 214). This is a disadvantage when searching for a forum free from the influence of gender, but is an advantage when providing a space for people's real selves to permeate narrative formats. In this way narratives tend to offer more of a whole picture of a participant's self-concept and beliefs than that offered by positivistic (factual and measurable) research. As the author noted in a personal contribution to *Transstudy*,

> Although providing identification for certain types of psychological suffering, information gained from the MMPI [Minnesota Multiphasic Personality Index] alone seems to fit people into previously designated personality categories, something that will always diminish the picture of the individual's whole subjective essence.
> (The Researcher May 3rd, 2006, in <What Causes Trans Subjectivity?>)

Narratives can also notably work to reveal instances of personal dissonance with society and culture, accounts of the occurrence of personal epiphanies, and the occasion of personal trauma. None of these may have surfaced in a positivistic approach to the same research. Catherine Riessman (1993) observed how women interviewed by Ginsberg (1989) narrated all three of these catalytic experiences when recounting the challenges of motherhood. Similarly, catalytic experiences are of particular relevance to study of the trans subject who is likely to encounter threats to their self, through contradiction of their self and self-presentation by others as well as through bodily dysphoria (the miss-matching of significant parts of the physical body to bodily/psychic subjectivity).

Dissonance, epiphanies and trauma have also traditionally been of pertinence to feminist investigations into the development of sexual subjectivity, initiated in consciousness-raising and coalesced into developmental accounts informed by psychoanalysis or social constructionism. Such investigations gave voice to the philosophical third wave in its project to transform hidden personal inequalities, oppression and victimhood into openly political agendas.

## Online debate – contemporary feminism and trans subjectivity

The advantages and disadvantages of debate via computer-mediated-communication (CMC) are introduced in this chapter, and commented upon alluding to Whittle's 'Trans-Cyberian Mail Way' in Chapter 1, but comment also needs to be made on how debate between feminists and trans people has developed using this media. Such debate can be posted up in the form of academic papers or can be in the form of online discussion forums. Responses in the latter will often be less crafted and more spontaneous, perhaps revealing insightful gut feelings and intuitions. The *Transstudy* itself was one such forum but similar trans forums include Trans Pulse Forums, Beginning Life forums, Susan's Place, and NuttycaTS. Reddit, sub-Reddits, 4chan forums deal with a wide range of feminist and trans issues but can be susceptible to gender variance phobia from internet 'trolls'. Feminist Facebook sites include The Network...Women Empowering Women! and regional Feminist Networks, providing an often more interactive experience because of the lack of anonymity.

Ealasaid Munro has identified a fourth wave of feminism that may have spawned from, and have as its essence, internet discussion forums but has been challenged by those who think that a new wave should have more of a defining substance than just its origin and location in the internet. Third wave feminists may see the fourth wave as an artificial upstart of a new wave, just as second wave feminists perceived the third. Criticising contemporary online feminist vs trans debate, Munro commented that, '*Whether or not internet campaigning actually enables change is a contested issue. There is concern that online discussion and activism is increasingly divorced from real-world conflicts*' (2013).

The issue of real-life gendered living versus textual debate covers many issues such as how Suzanne Moore and Julie Burchill used their powerful positions at the *New Statesman* and *The Guardian* to ridicule trans women, using exclusionary language that went against the spirit of inclusive feminism, and forming caricatures of trans women that bear no resemblance to real life. This caused a storm of discussion in a major social networking site, Twitter (Munro, 2013).

Paris Lees has also considered that social media spats do little to resemble real-life issues, '... *this isn't about rational debate any more, it's about an over-educated and time-rich bunch of narcissists on both sides who are completely and utterly addicted to a never-ending slanging match about absolutely nothing*' (20 August 2014).

Unfortunately, real-life interactions are also not guaranteed to elicit empathic understandings between the factions and have even descended into violence between trans and feminist people (Smith, 17 Sep 2017). At least online debate avoids this kind of interaction but can also avoid real-life activism because of its remove from real-life and tendency to promote a confusion of sound-bite discussion in a like-minded discussion 'bubble' with effecting real change. These bubbles may exclude those of a certain age, gender or feminist wave (Munro, 2013).

Nevertheless, online debate can and does affect the real-life world for good or bad, as noticed by Tina Vasquez with regard to the latter,

> In recent years, Brennan [Cathy, a 'radical feminist'] has become known for taking online arguments into real-world territory. She has contacted a trans woman's employer, posted the OK Cupid dating profiles of trans women, and contacted the mother of an outspoken supporter of transgender issues.
>
> (20 May 2016)

This kind of mis-representation and 'outing' of trans people can lead to textual, verbal and/or physical transphobic harassment. Vasquez promises a much more positive feminist approach to trans people, *'Our love, solidarity, and real-deal support as cisgender feminists is long overdue.'* She sees that 'radical' feminists target trans people for making out that, or being duped into thinking that, their gender is there from birth and is immutable. But, just like all feminists do not view gender as socially constructed, neither do all trans people view gender as biologically constructed.

Radical feminism, such as that associated with Brennan, has been blamed for the most vitriolic academic and online attacks on gender transition but the author argues that this really means 'separatist feminism' as, he argues, 'radical feminism' means radical (about various issues) and not necessarily separatist (from certain social groups). In online discussion, Paris Lees considers that, *'there is no such thing as "feminism that opposes transgenderism"'* (20 August 2014), so the attacks may rather be the result of a kind of 'female masculinism' if they resemble the aggression and lack of empathy traditionally associated with an overtly masculine approach.

As well as the separatist feminists such as Raymond, Jeffreys and Greer, Julie Bindel has added her name to the suspected separatists' list. Like Moore and Burchill, she has held a powerful position in the media and has argued that there would be little need for physical transition in a gender tolerant world, whether from gender variant people or from society in general. To save people from feeling compelled to join a heteronormativity that they may not identify with at all, Bindel suggested acceptance of other genderings as real, without requiring an accompanying kind of physicality (23 May 2007). Bindel retains this stance to date but denies it stands as a threat to trans people. She later apologised for the tone of a 2004 article on the subject of transition regrets.

In her article of 2007 (based upon the original in 2003) concerning the transition regrets of Claudia, Bindel includes the quote, *'I'll never have a relationship. Who's going to want me when they could get a real woman?'* from Claudia. This statement could be taken to imply that being a real woman requires a certain observable type of body. For trans people, they are real people because of *unobservable* features which may include inner biology and/or inner gendering.

*Third wave philosophy* 117

Bindel's articles have led to very heated chat room discussion with many trans people arguing that many a trans person would still wish to transition physically in a gender-accepting world and that they are really just men or women. Contrasting to this perspective, within the *Transstudy* site the author, Clarette and maybe Kimana seemed keen to propose the existence of a range of sexual subjectivities wider than the heteronormative and to self-describe as different to heteronormative.

It can be seen that, although online discussion doesn't necessarily reflect real-life subjectivity, it nonetheless can initiate interactive debate about gender variance and provide insights into perceptions of gendered subjectivity.

## 5.4 Semanalysis deriving from the semiotic

According to some feminists, our psychological development can affect the narratives that we provide. Such development, it is argued by post-Freudian analysts such as Kristeva, is not wholly determined by biological sex. In *Desire in Language: A Semiotic Approach to Literature and Art* (1969, translated 1980), Julia Kristeva merged semiotics (the study of languages as sign systems that produce meaning) and psychoanalysis (investigating conscious and unconscious elements in the mind), into 'semanalysis' or 'analytical semiology', adding a critical, political and reflexive endeavour[2] to both in order to draw social meanings from the signifying or communicative process, '*Semanalysis, as I tried to define it and put it to work in Σημειωτιχή, meets that requirement to describe the signifying phenomenon, or signifying phenomena, while analyzing, criticizing, and dissolving "phenomenon", "meaning," and "signifier"*' (Kristeva, 1980[1969:vii]).

Semanalysis therefore inspired the reading of narratives as sign systems linked to the personalities and social subjectivities of those who produce them, with the effect of revealing language as in-process or evolving,

> The intent of Julia Kristeva's semanalysis is to reveal the dynamics of the signifying process [signifiance]. The expression "engendering the formula" aptly illustrates the motile nature of the "signifier-emerging as text" ...
> (Prud'homme and Légaré, 2006)

> [Semanalysis involves] an insertion of subjectivity into matters of language and meaning ...
> (Kristeva, 1980[1969:viii])

Semanalysis introduced a critical dimension via its use of social theories to investigate language and employed reflexivity in order to investigate communication, '*Semanalysis, in order to avoid the necrophilia of other theories of language, must always question its own presuppositions and uncover, record, and deny its own ideological gestures*' (Oliver, 1998, referring to Sèméiotikè, 1969:78–79).

In this way Kristeva's analytical version of semiotics, or 'semiotic practice' was designed to manifest as an open and evolving narrative of its own,

> Semiotic practice breaks with the teleological vision of a science that is subordinated to a philosophical system and consequently even destined itself to become a system. Without becoming a system, the site of semiotics, where models and theories are developed, is a place of dispute and self-questioning, a 'circle' that remains open.
> (Kristeva, 1986:78)

Semanalysis expanded this critical function to explain how the speaking or writing subject, influenced by their semiotic mode of communication, can take part in a project of narrative subversion.[3] This mode of communication may have influenced those trans narrators and autobiographers who applied what might be called 'narrative messiness' in order to revise the concept of sexual subjectivity, which they saw having been constructed by a kind of 'lived messiness'.[4] When considering narratives from Clarette and Kimana, it seemed to me that their sometimes poetic and non-conformist language could be obscure but that it might derive from a different agenda-base than the 'verbally hygienic' language of medical reassignment, black letter law and elitist academia. The former types of narrative perhaps work to be inclusive of different readerships because of their grounding in real lives, passion and spirituality rather than institutional scripts and schemas. 'Narrative messiness' may thus particularly act as a conduit for the inclusion of gender varied voices into discourse. It may also, as in the words of Kristeva, work to, '... *demystify the idea that the community of language is a universal, all-inclusive, and equalizing tool*' (Kristeva, 1993:223).

Gender varied voices have to a large extent been silenced by exclusionary discourse such as gatekeeping imposed by professional discourses that control access to subjectivity, for instance via legal recognition or medical transition. Gatekeeping involves 'verbal hygiene' in order to control any deviance from the rules of language that gatekeepers deem to be right and proper. Kristeva visualised semanalysis as an escape from the closed system of much traditional science which presents its findings as self-contained and self-evident while relying on a 'common sense' schema (Kristeva, 1986:78, 79). This departure from closed systems of definition was similar to Foucault's idea of the dialogic (not self-contained) subversion of discourse or 'reciprocal elucidation' (Diamond and Quinby, 1988:xi), involving non-hierarchical reciprocity of dialogue in which differences are respected and the rights of individuals participating are taken to be central to discussion.[5]

The examination of narratives of science via critical/political/radical investigation would, according to Kristeva, produce a new model or 'structure', which comes with its own new meaning. This new structure may have been the kind of investigative model recommended by Imelda Whelehan when calling for an examination of the link between communication and subjectivity,

> ... what is needed is a more wide ranging study of language which links modes of speech as well as writing to women's multifarious and possibly conflicting social identities, in a much broader based interrogation of the means by which meaning is socially and culturally, as well as linguistically, embedded.
>
> (Whelehan, 1995:77)

Kristeva discussed how Marx portrayed the capitalist system as a historically and demographically contextual type of discourse that produced a particular kind of social relations. She expanded Marx's critical investigation of discourse by involving Freud's ideas of the influence that desire has upon language, a desire that precedes the articulation of signifiers (names and labels) and signified (named and labelled) in symbolic language. This is desire that, according to Kristeva, derives from the original bodily bond between mother and child. The desire, found in the realm of the semiotic, then bubbles away under the surface of the symbolic and manifests in communication as rhythmic articulation, tonal presentation and body language. Semiotic communication is superseded, but not replaced, by the symbolic when the child enters the world of spoken and written language, and manifests as a duality of language,

> [Kristeva] reveals a convergence with Lacan's linking of language to the unconscious. Lacan referred to the dual planes on which language operates ... that duality is such as to make it possible for semanalysis to be a critique of meaning ...
>
> (Roudiez, 1980[1969]:4)

Kristeva posited that the primary relation of child to maternal figure informs the child's semiotic/symbolic presentation of narrative in later life. She believed that semiotic communication, just like Carol Gilligan's ethics of care (Benhabib, 1992:191), can be developed, implemented and influenced by a person of any sexual subjectivity (Oliver, 1998). This association of parental function with gender has relevance to legal cases such as *X, Y and Z*, where the complexity of associating gender with parenting was revealed. The mantle of subjective moulding, initially provided by the primary body to body relationship, is taken up by relationships with significant others out in society, indicating for Kristeva that the subject is always one 'in-process', and not just formed by a pre-defined and finite early psycho-social process.

It appears that the semiotic cannot be accurately articulated because it is subject to the way that humans have developed their overt means of communication, i.e. the logocentric[6] constraints of spoken and written language known as the symbolic or speech and writing. Toril Moi called attempts to articulate the non-articulable, '... *the paradox of semiotics*' (1986b:75). However, Kristeva did not believe that the inaccessibility of the semiotic meant that all attempts to understand or assess its effects should be abandoned. She believed that attention to the semiotic can lead to 'intertextuality', her psychoanalytic term for the remodelling of an old discourse into something new via the merging of parts of old sign systems with new (Roudiez, 1980 [1969]:15). Kristeva believed that such a process ultimately forms human subjectivities, through the influence of narrative and discourse, rather than subjectivity being constructed from a psychoanalytically-defined process.

The spirit of semanalysis (as a critical, political, reflexive and dialogic procedure) was drawn upon by the author in order to form a tailor-made critical discourse analysis framework, and is applied throughout the chapters in order to take a critical and personally political perspective on discourses revealed by the *Transstudy* narratives. This perspective engenders a critique of apparently neutral or 'common sense' discourses such as gender heteronormativity and manifests in a recommendation of maternal relations as inter-wave philosophy and communicative technique, informed by gender variance as a whole experience of gender, and in the proposition of gender as a process.

## 5.5 Construction of the critical discourse analysis framework

The critical discourse analysis framework acts as an investigative template for the analysis in Chapters 6 to 8. The component parts of this framework are not, in reality, rigidly discrete but influence each other with the effect of moulding discourses and shaping subjectivity, if given the communicative space to do so, away from oppressive silence and secrecy. This may happen unintentionally or intentionally, and which of these it may be is very hard to discern from any record of communicative interaction or account of historical events. Nevertheless, identification of dialogic features, such as the four chosen for the framework, and indicating how they operate, seems to enhance our understanding of, and actual awareness of, discourses in society.

In line with Whittle's reading of critical discourse analysis (2002a:42), as outlined in Chapter 1, it was evident that only a tailor-made framework would be appropriate for an individual research project since only then will the framework address issues of relevance to a project's literature reviews and research. However, the author considered it acceptable to build up this particular framework by drawing from models of critical discourse analysis designed by theorists in this field. This is because these theorists discuss the kind of qualitative and people-centred investigations congruent with the author's political philosophy and aims as researcher. Below is a description of this critical discourse analysis framework, describing how each component may reveal discourses-in-process.

*Access*

Access to social structures, communities or events, for those with certain subjectivities, can operate in an exclusionary or inclusive manner, through the use of particular discourse. Access can rely on knowledge of means of communication, proximity to means of communication, social contacts, specialist knowledge and means of entry into subjectivity. Petra Wilson identified points of interaction that affect access to the law,

> ... one can begin to see the common threads found in the studies of access to law and unmet legal need: financial factors; knowledge and understanding of the institutions and organizations; personal, popular and idiosyncratic beliefs; and institutional factors.
>
> (1998:114)

Van Dijk (2001:303) described how exclusionary control of access (a form of social gatekeeping), by 'elite participants', such as the ability to belong to feminism discussed in Chapter 3, or access to narrative via 'verbal hygiene',[7] can act to negatively discriminate by preventing non-elite participants from shaping discourse.

In considering access for *Transstudy* participants, the author had to consider who might be 'Othered' or excluded from the *Transstudy* website. This may have occurred, for instance, as a result of language used within the site or in language used in the adverts placed for recruitment to the site. It is notable that there was a comparative lack of contributions from trans men, for reasons not indisputably apparent. On realising that some social groups, such as trans men, ethnicities and certain class groupings, may have been excluded from the site, the author decided to post up *Transstudy* topics entitled <Hidden Trans men?> and <Who might be the Others of the *Transstudy*?>, to at least initiate awareness and discussion of those possibly excluded.

A number of *Transstudy* participants were not actively involved with sociological gender studies and so were sometimes unfamiliar with sociological definitions of gender variance and the relation of these to areas of debate such as feminism and social constructionism. However, many participants had extensive experience of medical/legal/social/practical gender transition issues, engendering their access to transition/reassignment debate. At least six of the regular participants had professional occupations, perhaps further increasing their access to and willingness to participate in the *Transstudy* site, it being a written/computer-based exercise. Some participants complained that the author's *Transstudy* posts were sometimes obscurely socio-academic, a barrier to access that the author came to identify as 'sociobabble'.

### *Dialogic negotiation*

A process of mutual negotiation through various means of communication can lead to access to, or exclusion from, social structures and communities, depending upon who participates in the negotiation and their position in power relationships. This negotiation is a reciprocal, on-going and evolving feature of all human interaction,

> The relationships between the subject and the other, between the subject and itself, between the semiotic and the symbolic are all dialogic, in Kristevan theory.
>
> (Edelstein, 1993:200)

> It follows that in any interchange between people, there is a constant monitoring of the 'definition of the situation' that each participant is struggling to bring off.
>
> (Burr, 2003:114)

According to Bakhtin, 'dialogic' communication could occur in any written, visual, body or spoken language (Bakhtin and Emerson, 1984:42). Dialogic communication, a kind of two-way negotiation, may be cooperative through acquiescence or agreement, or non-cooperative through resistance. An individual's experience of social contexts, access and subjectivity will derive from and influence their use of certain features of negotiation with some features being unknown to them or inaccessible. Mutual negotiation can serve to maintain dominant discourses and hegemonic relationships by emphasising and repeating their features. However, it can also challenge such discourses or distort 'language-as-mirror' when people develop sufficient need to find an alternative to discourses that oppress them.[8] In this instance it resembles the 'dialogic model of ethics' championed by Seyla Benhabib as a to-ing and fro-ing tennis ball-like negotiation between two parties, ethical because of equal involvement in the negotiation.

As described earlier in the chapter, inclusive dialogic negotiation can be facilitated by a process identified by Foucault as 'reciprocal elucidation' (Diamond and Quinby, 1988:ix), '*In the serious play of questions and answers, in the work of reciprocal elucidation, the rights of each person are in some sense immanent in the discussion*' (Foucault, in interview with Paul Rabinow, May 1984).

Such negotiation seems to be a pivotal feature of the open and evolving discourse characteristic of a philosophical third wave, for instance in the critical engagement through 'solidarity' championed by bell hooks. It also links in with the mores of the ethics of care, valued by those interested in more traditionally feminine forms of communication where relationships are negotiated rather than asserted.

Iris Marion Young thought that 'symmetrical reciprocity' provided too much of an image of uncomplicated equal communication with others that overlooked rather than respected differences (Edwards and Mauthner, 2002:26). She suggested the term 'asymmetrical reciprocity' instead as a way to properly identify communication between individuals as it actually happens. Edwards and Mauthner seemed to follow this train of thought when they considered that, '... *conflict, disagreement and ambivalence' will occur in the research environment and [that] it is better to recognise these power imbalances than to try to deny them*' (2002:27). Asymmetrical reciprocity therefore depends upon the subjectivity, background, personality and social position of each person involved but can easily forgo the ethical balance inherent to Benhabib's dialogic model of ethics with too much of a dialogic power imbalance.

In assessing the silence of nature when dominated by industrial society, and providing an example of asymmetrical reciprocity, Jeff Bile recommends that dialogic negotiation involves communicating with those that appear silent rather than ignoring them because they are silent (2013:99). A masculinist purview has typically conflated the silent with nature and as something that is legitimately dominated by the might of masculinist culture. Nature has been conflated with most things non-white and non-imperialist in the past, including women, children, people of colour, non-human animals and so they are expected to be seen and not heard.

## *Resistance and acquiescence*

Power relations are always prevalent in negotiation and manifest as resistance or acquiescence, or combinations of both. Neither resistance or acquiescence are intrinsically positive or negative, they are ways of working with or against certain discourses. As described in the paragraphs above, dialogic interaction may serve to keep power relations intact, or may pose a challenge to such relations. A resulting discourse may manifest as an 'ideological force' (Parker, 2005:92). Ideologies connected to the ideas of resistance and acquiescence in discourse may broadly be referred to respectively as 'social conflict' and 'functionalism'. Social conflict ideologies see social relations as problematic in some way while functionalist ideologies see them as basically benign and designed to be in the interests of everyone. Social psychologist Vivien Burr theorised a greater prevalence of conflict than functionalism in the negotiation of subjectivity, '*The process of constructing and negotiating our own identities will therefore often be ridden by conflict, as we struggle to claim or resist the images available to us through discourse*' (Burr, 2003:110).

One way of investigating conflicting or functional social power relationships, formed and re-formed through resistance and acquiescence, is to look at the way that some groups, whether intentionally or not, control the action and cognition of others. This will often occur through consensual arrangements similar to what Louis Althusser identified as 'ideological state apparatuses', where elite agenda setting ensures that ideology is kept intact without overt coercion (1971). Such consensual relationships have been maintained by what Antonio Gramsci (1971) referred to as 'hegemony', a bond between individuals and groups of different social status in a mutually binding relationship of power. This usually manifests as 'acquiescence' to dominant discourses on the part of groups with lower social status. Subtle dominance, initiated by 'hailing' the subject into the discourse, is required to make the hegemonic relationship seem naturally given or as 'common sense'. Dominance in a hegemonic relationship cannot usually remain total, as Foucault theorised, and therefore can sometimes be contested in a process of active resistance that may lead to a modified, or even transformed, discourse.

### Schemata and scripts

Discourse can be revealed in the form of narrative schemata as noted by van Dijk,

> Let us give some well-known examples of discourse schemata. Stories, for instance, have a narrative schema ... Everyday conversations also have schemata. ... Scientific discourse, such as journal articles or lectures, may also have a conventional form, which often features an argumentative schema ... Language users learn such schemata during socialization, although for some schemata, such as those used in professional discourse, special training may be required.
>
> (1988:49)

Schemata and scripts are often confused with one another but a schema, in the psychological sense, is a broader framework of knowledge about a theme of personal relevance that is psychologically stored by the individual and is often shared by those in the subject's social community,

> Within cognitive psychology, a schema can be thought of as an abstract cognitive plan that serves as a guide for interpreting information and solving problems. Thus we may have a linguistic schema for understanding a sentence, or a cultural schema for interpreting a myth.
>
> (Young et al., 2003:7)

Scripts, on the other hand, are narrower plans for routine activities that consist of behaviours learnt to be appropriate for a certain situation, '*Schema-like memories for events (called scripts) influence how we remember events. A script for a restaurant might include information about food, waiters, paying the bill and so on*' (Train, 2007:176).

A script often works to support a schema. Sexologists John Gagnon and William Simon described human sexuality as a script; for them sexuality arose from the individual's interaction with social discourse rather than from biological essence or instinct, '*We created script theory in an attempt to have a device to describe how people go about doing sex socially, and to demonstrate the importance of social elements in the doing of the sexual*' (2005[1973]:312).

Schemata and scripts both save time that would be spent working out from scratch how to act in situations that resemble each other. Following schemata and scripts is not usually deliberate or conscious, but both can affect the content of an individual's account of events (narrative). Schemata and scripts are often so ingrained and rehearsed that individuals tend to perceive their own as 'natural' or 'common sense'.

*Subjectivity*

This critical discourse analysis component was designed to prompt consideration of what it is that identifies the narrator as a subject, how it is that the narrator chooses to identify him/her/hirself as a subject and how subjectivity is formed. The subjects of this research were, in a sense, 'narrative subjects' since they were known to the author through their written narratives. A subject is the conglomeration of the individual's self-presentation, experience and characteristics. These elements can work to inscribe background, ethnicity, class and gender into individual narratives in subtle ways. An individual may enact subjectivity by conforming to, resisting or subverting the identity schemata apparent in his/her/hir culture and society. Subjectivity may derive from social position and role, social contacts, specialist knowledge, dialogic power position and status (all as perceived by the self and by others).

According to Althusser (1971), it was possible to theorise how the individual was 'hailed' by certain ideologies, by a process he called 'interpellation'. Hailing is a key aspect in the attainment and maintaining of subjectivity:

> I shall then suggest that ideology 'acts' or 'functions' in such a way that it 'recruits' subjects among the individuals (it recruits them all), or 'transforms' the individuals into subjects (it transforms them all) by that very precise operation which I have called interpellation or hailing, and which can be imagined along the lines of the most commonplace everyday police (or other) hailing: 'Hey, you there!'
> 
> (1971:174–5)

Hailing involves a call to join an ideology and/or social subjectivity which the individual can accept or refuse, depending on their upbringing, personal beliefs and will power. For instance, media representations can 'hail' certain audiences by using keywords in the 'language' of the target audience.[9] Interpellation can be negative inclusion if it blinkers those being included to all those excluded and it can lock the subject within a certain type of discourse, '*If we accept or are unable to resist a particular subject position we are then locked into the system of rights, speaking rights and obligations that are carried with that position*' (Burr, 2003:111).

It is apparent that the opposite of hailing can occur for the alienated individual. Here the ideology calls out, "Hey, not you", to leave the alienated subject in no doubt of their excluded status but often in great doubt as to why they have been excluded. This line of thinking prompted the inclusion of the <Who might be the Others of the *Transstudy*?> and <Hey You!> topical *Transstudy* questions.

According to McAdams, individuals may gain subjectivity through agency, meaning their positioning in power relationships through experience of acceptance, achievement and access, and/or through communion, referring to relations of love and intimacy (McAdams, 2001). Both can derive from a positive 'hailing' experience. Agency is an emphasis of the individual and communion emphasises relations with others, bringing to mind comparisons of the ethic of justice (individual rights) with ethics of care (responsibility and communication with others), symbolic with semiotic language and paternal with maternal relations.

## *Agency*

Although discourses can seemingly lock people into subjectivity, Burr (2003) echoed Foucault by describing how people can gain enough agency to be able to remould those discourses through concerted actions. Individuals are therefore not, according to social constructionists, blank paper waiting passively to be written upon by discourse. A person may develop an irresistible compulsion to become other to their attributed identity and will look for the 'chink in the armour' or the Achilles heels of discourses, grand narratives or power structures, for instance to form a pocket of resistance to the mainstream 'silent and secret' and 'common sense' discourses that lock them into identity.

Challenging entrenched discourses has often transpired to be an arduous endeavour, but for some there seems little other choice if they are to adequately express their inner selves. Agency is essential to the notion that individuals can contribute to societal change through identifying and then reforming social discourses. The overall title of Chapters 6 to 8, 'Reconstructing Discourses', is based on this belief in individual and group action. This chapter is designed to reveal potential agency-forming discoursal tools.

Often, attempts will be made to dismantle an individual's agency, if it is evident that they are a threat to a dominant ideology. For instance, this has happened to feminists and trans people via the subtle technique of infantilisation,[10] in the way described in Chapter 2. Foucault made a point of criticising excessive or domineering agency, for instance by dismissing his own attributed roles as 'expert or prophet or truth teller' (Cooper and Blair, 2002: 519). It seems that he wished for people to acquire agency via dialogic negotiation, rather than through domineering or being dominated by others.

## *Communion*

McAdams describes communion as the individual's participation in an organism larger than itself, as a feeling of empathy with 'other organisms', and as 'noncontractual cooperation' or non-formal and non-hierarchical relations,

> Communion encompasses psychological and motivational ideas concerning love, friendship, intimacy, sharing, belonging, affiliation, merger, union, nurturance, and so on. At its heart, communion involves different people coming together in warm, close, caring, and communicative relationships.
> 
> (2001)

Communion is not necessarily more desirable for trans subjectivity and feminism than agency but is something that can temper the excesses of domineering agency. It characterises womanist communication and aligns closely with ethics of care. It can be relied upon to form open and evolving dialogic negotiation.

## *Discourse*

Discourses are formed from all the previous components of the framework and many others that are outside the scope of this book. Discourses encompass the whole system of social representation involving language (written, spoken and body), art, culture, narrative, appearance, behaviour and customs, and anything that can be discussed as 'text'. Discourse communities bind those who adhere wittingly or not to the mores of the discourse, and exclude those who do not. As well as possibly being an ideology, feminism can be a discourse, but for inclusive feminism it must be recognised and promoted as ideology-in-process or discourse-in-process otherwise it is bound to permanently exclude some gendered, ethnic or other social subjectivities.

Examples of discourses relevant to this book include those of transgender, feminism, law, ethics, medicine and politics. However, there will be other discourses, and discourses within discourses, maybe unidentified by anyone, affecting and combining known discourses. At any one time, a selection of discourses are at work producing what seem to be fixed biological and social identities, providing us with an image of which identities are real and which are not,

> For each of us, then, a multitude of discourses is constantly at work constructing and producing our identity. Our identity therefore originates not from inside the person, but from the social realm, a realm where people swim in a sea of language and other signs, a sea that is invisible to us because it is the very medium of our existence as social beings.
> (Burr, 2003:108–109)

Foucault (1998 [1978]) notably described how the discourse of homosexuality, partly because of its conscious formalisation and therefore visibility, was reversed to a large extent by gay-friendly people who transformed this discourse from silent and secret to articulated and open. Another example of discourse being revealed can be seen in Whittle's discussion of anti-trans feminism, particularly his analysis of Janice Raymond's *The Transsexual Empire*, where he revealed a discourse of radical separatism (Whittle, 2006b).[11] Raymond facilitated this discourse by stereotyping women and trans people into fixed social types. The discourse propounded that biology is destiny (because, she thought, it always led to the same social outcome) while eschewing any consideration that gender may be hidden by a bodily sex that conflicts with an inner gendering.

## 5.6 Creation of the reconstructing discourses

Third wave feminism's efforts to be guided by narratives rather than meta-narratives[12] might facilitate the formation of what Foucault proposed to be 'reverse discourses' (1998 [1978]:101). Like the gay-friendly people challenging the discourse of homosexuality in the mid-twentieth century, third wave theorists call for restructuring of narratives of gender in order to accommodate the complexity of sexual subjectivity. These are attempts to subvert the operation of discourses in order to replace them with 'discourses-in-process'. However, the term 'reverse discourses' suggests a mere reversal of the conventional which could transpire to be oppressive in its turn, so perhaps a more accurate label of this progressive subversion of discourse is needed, as suggested by Diamond and Quinby,

> We should also recall, however, that the power of a reverse discourse is precarious. As the eruption of the second wave of feminism in our period suggests, over the course of the century many tenets of nineteenth-century feminism have been appropriated into operations of disciplinary power – hence the need for a new wave.
>
> (Diamond and Quinby, 1988:xiii)

Second wave feminists' development of cooperative consciousness-raising ironically ensured that feminism did not sufficiently challenge oppressive discourses, including its own oppression of feminist 'Others'. This happened as a result of the consciousness-raising groups being mutually supporting and therefore less self-critical and inclusive than they could have been. The philosophical third wave offers potential to turn reverse discourses into empowering reconstructing discourses, discourses that are self-reflexively critical and subject to ongoing modification. It is important to identify what might be a reverse discourse and what might be a reconstructing one. For instance, many people still think that all of feminism is a reverse discourse where feminists simply want to reverse the positions of men and women so that women have dominance in social power.

Whittle suggested the reconstruction of postmodern research methodology into a personally political theoretical and activist movement. He recommended that this be, '... *not just deconstruction but also reconstruction*' (2002a:69). This idea of reconstruction emphasises the involvement of personal politics, passion for research and a consideration of society's 'Others'[13] and should heed Derrida's recommendation to re-interpret and iterate narratives in a caring fashion[14] via deconstruction. It also aligns with the personally political project of a *critical* or radically questioning discourse analysis (Whittle, 2006a:xii). This radical and/or caring aspect of reconstruction was hinted at by *Transstudy* participants, '*Regarding destucturing sentances and reconstructuring them , I do it all of the time, but not as a conscience effort. I've done it for years and find language outrageously funny*' (Kimana Dec 10th, 2005, in <Personalityism>).

Reconstructing themes elicited from the literature review and from readings of *Transstudy* narratives, became the main components (sections) of Chapters 6 to 8. These in turn were drawn upon to compose the three overarching reconstructing discourses of Chapter 9.

## 5.7 Conclusion

Section 1 of this chapter described how the research process involved an informal format, a narrative basis, and forming of connections between the research participants in order to establish an ethics of care. Some consideration was given to how people of what might be called certain 'social ethnicities' might be 'Othered' from the *Transstudy*, by developing topics, and providing analysis, on likely instances of exclusion. The small research population yielded valid (or in-depth), rather than reliable (or widely generalisable), information about the presentation of gender in narrative. Authenticity of research data deriving from researcher/participant interactions was striven for by implementing 'strong objectivity'[15] (objectivity that realises the influence of subjectivity) in order to narrow the social distance between researcher and participants. The *Transstudy* may also have avoided some problems of researcher/participant influence because of its use of open-ended questions, topics and discussion, leading to answers with more depth and insight.

The second section explained similarities between third wave feminism and queer theory, and the reasons for choosing a third wave feminism framework as a priority. As well as challenging notions of gender as primary and foundational, queer theory involves subversion of gendered language and representations in order to challenge heteronormativity. However, queer theory does not seem to have sufficiently addressed subjectivity politics and the lived reality of gender for some gender variant people. Appreciation of such lived realities can prompt efforts to achieve the reconstruction of real-life sexual subjectivity. The section noted more connections than disconnections between queer and philosophical third wave feminism despite negative internecine conflict between queer theory and feminism in general.

Queer theory champions the idea of subjectivity as genealogically formed while still allowing strategic essentialism (political standpoints from the perspectives of certain subjectivities). However, Stychin noted that queer's alignment with lesbian and gay subjectivities was hard to escape, just as transgender and feminism have sometimes been allied to certain essentialised identities. Halley theoretically lessened queer theory's tie to essential identities by construing queer as contradiction aware with regard to the complexity of gender, just as is notable of theorised third wave feminism.

The author wished to identify in particular with third wave feminism, rather than stand in opposition to queer theory. Feminism has particularly addressed social emasculation and third wave feminism particularly uses subjectivity politics, as opposed to identity politics, to challenge identities imposed upon the gender oppressed. Ethics of care, as espoused by philosophical third wave feminist Carol Gilligan, expose negative feminisation. Like Gilligan, other third wavers wish to pay particular respect to the history of womanist-type relations, such as those formed by ethics of care. Those not included into separatist feminism may wish to take a break from, or to emigrate from, not queer theory but from separatist or non-feminism.

Section three of this chapter, asking 'why narratives?', opened by suggesting that, 'you are what you speak', or that language forms our ideas of identity which, for social constructionists, is rather an on-going construct formed by interactive communication known as subjectivity. Acceptance of subjectivity as socially constructed can open the way for gender variant individuals to be involved with the defining of sexual subjectivity. In the latter half of the twentieth century, life narratives from gender variant people have tended to feature catalytic experiences that have allowed the narrator to transcend clinical or stereotyping definitions of sexual subjectivity by introducing the narrator as a real person with a real voice when the epiphany experience engendered an intense moment of self-insight.

Online debate has revolutionised the sharing of such experiences, for better and for worse, between feminists and trans people. It runs the danger of being divorced from the real world and being subject to the power of those who wield most power in the online world. It can quickly 'out' someone's subjectivity to many others without their permission. However, it can give voice to those with no other means of communicating about their gender and can challenge entrenched opinions.

In section four there is a description of how Kristeva's idea of 'semanalysis' as analytic technique promised the chance of an epistemological break from closed systems of gender definition. Overly clinical, complex, or 'verbally hygienic', language may derive from a predominance of symbolic language. A feeling for alternative modes of communication, when the more feminine form of the semiotic seeps through cracks in the symbolic mantle, can encourage understanding of subjectivity and subjective development via ethics of care, characteristic of the kind of maternal relations described in Chapters 3 and 8.

Section five described how the critical discourse analysis framework was designed as a background template for the analysis in Chapters 6 to 8. Critical discourse analysis theorists' guidance, combined with attention to themes in the literature reviews and *Transstudy* narratives, was used to develop a research framework for the *Transstudy*, in an attempt to reveal power structures in gender discourse. Discourses, which otherwise may remain unrecognised, can be revealed through critical research, to unearth unheard voices shrouded by oppressive discourses. Personal politics, passion for research communities and a consideration of real lives turn reconstruction into something more than theoretical deconstruction or the reversal of discourse that oppresses one set of people into one that oppresses another. Section 6 describes how the 'reconstructing discourses' of Chapter 9 were formed in an interactively informing process between literature reviews, primary research narratives and analysis chapter themes.

*Third wave philosophy* 131

In Chapter 6, the first part of the analysis of the *Transstudy* narratives and third wave feminism, themes concerned with the possibility and value of replacing essentialised identity with 'identity-in-process', or subjectivity, are introduced and assessed.

**Notes**

1. A copy of this is in the appendix.
2. As noted by Toril Moi in Kristeva (1986:74).
3. Kristeva explained how this was particularly evident in the work of Céline, Artaud and Joyce (Humm, 1992:212). Wright uses the words 'meaning deforming', 'subvert' (1992:194), 'undermine', 'destabilise', 'disruptive' (195) and 'ruptures' (196) to describe how Kristeva theorised that the subject can transform language in *Revolution in Poetic Language*. Toril Moi remarked how, '*semanalysis nevertheless ceaselessly subverts and transforms the meaning of the terms it appropriates*' (1986b:74).
4. Kate Bornstein applied this kind of textual subversion by involving her own life into her text in Chapters 13 and 14 of *Gender Outlaw* (1994), by suggesting how truth is channelled in different communicative forums and formats (157), by perceiving trans subjectivity as genre (144–145), and by addressing the lives of gender outsiders (159). In *Stone Butch Blues* (1993) Leslie Feinberg narrates the application of a 'messy' life to the production of a whole new perspective on gender.
5. For instance, the rejection of '*forms of identity to which we are tied*', as noted by O'Leary (2002:15).
6. A Western cultural way of understanding that privileges language over alternative means of communication.
7. A term administered by Ian Parker and described in chapter 7 s. 2 (2005:101).
8. Designated as the initiation of 'reverse discourses' by Foucault (1998 [1978]:95–99), see Chapter 1.
9. As described by Watson and Whittle (2005:191).
10. For instance, see Whittle (2006:195) for comments on Janice Raymond's infantilisation of the transsexual.
11. Other instances of trans-unfriendly feminist separatism are addressed in Chapter 2 in regard to Raymond and Jeffreys, Chapter 3 (Greer, Hausman, Millot and Raymond), Chapter 6 (Greer and Raymond).
12. Third wave feminist theory has been a kind of anti-theory, opposed to attempts to produce monolithic and self-sufficient ideas or general principles. third wave feminists have presented such attempts as 'grand narratives' or 'metanarratives' and have tried to avoid the solidification of feminism into its own metanarrative (Edelstein, 1993:198, 199). Third wave feminism is associated with the attempt to establish intellectual, political and relationship ethics rather than intellectual, political and relationship control.
13. Caputo saw Derrida's deconstruction as, '*Preparing for the incoming of the other, which is what constitutes a radical democracy – that is what deconstruction is*' (1997:44).
14. Caputo described how, '... *deconstruction is respect, respect for the other, a respectful, responsible affirmation of the other, a way if not to efface at least to delimit the narcissism of the self (which is, quite literally, a tautology) and to make some space to let the other be*' (1997:44).
15. Strong objectivity is Sandra Harding's term for scientific investigation that is self-critical (1991). It does not seek to present a 'view from nowhere' in a demonstration of 'verbal cleanliness' that denies the complexities of 'lived messiness'.

# 6 Identity essentialism to subjectivity-in-process
## The whole trans person

**Introduction**

One dilemma familiar to feminists, and one that affects most people's lives, is the deliberate or inadvertent human proclivity to construct dualisms and then to side with one part of a dualism be it radical/conservative, mind/body, white/black, justice/care or other socially ingrained pairings. Dualisms are apparent in the titles of Chapters 6 to 8 and are critically examined in each corresponding chapter in order to highlight the social conflict that they produce.

Lara Karaian addressed the essentialism/constructionism dualism by recommending that essentialism be investigated rather than vilified,

> [Diana] Fuss argues that Western feminism has fostered, "a certain paranoia around the perceived threat of essentialism" and that this has created an essence/constructionist binarism which feminist and queer theorists have argued is an equally simplistic framework. ... According to Fuss, "the radicality or conservatism of essentialism depends, to a significant degree, on who is utilizing it, how it is deployed, and where its effects are concentrated".
>
> (Karaian, 2006:184)

Identity essentialism has been strategically useful in its time, for instance when early feminism used the label 'woman' to highlight the particular social position of women in order to gain advances towards economic and political parity, with reliance on the law to back these advances up. It has also been useful for those trans people who had to, and still have to, manifest recognisably gendered behaviour and presentation in order to be accepted for reassignment treatment.

However, essentialism became evident as a problem area for feminists in the chronological second wave when having to confront what Gordene Mackenzie termed the, '... *horizontal hostilities directed against one another, instead of the real oppressors*' (1999:211), where women with oppressed subjectivities struggled to inhabit the plateau of 'woman' inhabited by white middle-class feminists. Many second wave feminists came to the conclusion that they would not want to be equal if it meant becoming equally oppressive as masculinists by doing down their black/lesbian/disabled/financially poor sisters. Philosophical third wavers looked to post-structural views of sexual subjectivity as a way to initiate the move away from fixed identity to fluid subjectivity that would allow connection with different womanly subjectivities. An example of this kind of reinterpretation can be seen in Alison Stone's reconstruction of 'woman' as a genealogy, rather than as an identity.

Sometimes people are essentialised into identity allocated to them by others. For instance, Chapter 4 addressed Cressida Heyes' argument that Carol Gilligan was essentialised as philosophically second wave and gender essentialist by some feminist reviewers. In a similar essentialising move, participant Monica defined feminists as political fanatics who only wished to respond to their opponents in reactionary fashion, '*Feminists always, always, always, always have a political agenda. They will deliberately misrepresent anything or make any allegation or portrayal if by doing so they will boost their cause. ... All they do is criticise*' (Mar 18th, 2005, in <Are there just feminie and masculine people now>).

Kimana presented a challenge to this kind of metonymic ascription, or essentialising of subjectivities into group identity, by suggesting that trans subjectivity is not the whole of what a person who transitions actually is,

> These are a few of the facets in my life, each showing a different part of the person that I am. I guess what I'm saying is that all people are like a finely cut diamond having several facets to it and each facet wonderful in it's own beauty, but they are only a part of the whole gem.
> (Kimana Jun 8th, 2006, in <Your Narrative Self>)

Clarette narrated the exclusion that can emanate from the cul-de-sac of fixed identity essentialism,

> It seems to me that any assertion of status ... the more essentialist especially ... tends to promote division. One reason why I prefer not to "do" status, I suppose. Gender status in particular is not a good basis for allocating power.
> (Clarette Feb 7th, 2006, in <Are there just feminie and masculine people now>)

In light of the above comments, this chapter title became, 'Identity Essentialism to Subjectivity-in-Process' to mark the required move away from identity essentialism by those holding a particularly third wave philosophy. 'Subjectivity essentialism' may be a positive kind of strategic essentialism used when certain discrimination of certain subjectivities needs to be revealed.

As well as addressing identity essentialism, third wave feminists need to be careful that they do not essentialise the third wave into its own philosophical box, or metanarrative ideology. The philosophical third wave is by definition

134  *Identity essentialism*

in-process and, at least theoretically, does not form islands of identity and ideology. This is why attempts to define the third wave might deprive it of its 'essential' subjective un-definability. The author respects readers' critical readings of third wave feminism as their 'choice' to define this wave in their own way, after all, he argues that the third wave is by definition indefinable because it is 'in-process' unlike defined metanarratives. No one should 'own' third wave feminism because of their attributed gendered or chronological identity.

## 6.1 Which gender variant subjectivities are real?

Professor of Philosophy Carlos Prado explained that, according to Michel Foucault, '*The subject's "conscious or self-knowledge" is an imposed one, but the individual experiences it as what he or she is …*' (Prado, 2000:61–62).

This experience of self-knowledge comes into play when both trans people and feminists have to battle with criticisms of their respective subjectivities.[1] As described earlier, within trans and feminist factions suspicion is sometimes targeted by those of one faction towards those of another. For instance, Monica enquired as to the realness of the Lakota Wioptula, in Kimana's community, as a trans subjectivity in <Are we all transvestites now?>,[2] '*I would only regard them as trans if they wanted to aquire male physical characteristics and dispose of their female ones*' (Feb 2nd, 2007).

Similarly, it has been seen that separatist feminist theorists have questioned the authenticity of transitioned gender and the ability of trans people to be genuine feminists. Monica expressed a concern that this suspicion is often held by those involved in women's groups, curbing trans women's access to these social forums,

> The fact is that women who join women's groups are seeking fellowship from other women. This is because other women will share the same life pressures most of which are caused by relationships with men. The last thing they want at a women's group is a man; and to these women trans women are just men dressed up.
> (Monica Mar 18th, 2005, in <Trans-friendly social groups?>)

In the <Some thoughts on non-trans gender-changers> topic thread Raelene took pains to suggest a difference between transsexuals and transgendered people, mentioning that, '*Transgendered is a life-style choice. Transsexual is a psychological compulsion*' (Jan 19th, 2007). She focused attention on '*muddying the waters*', in regard to legal and medical transition issues, that can occur when transsexuals are associated with the apparently more nebulous and indefinable 'transgender',

> Legal rights for transsexuals are a substantive issue in countries where they are lumped together with those who claim to be transgendered.
> (Jan 19th, 2007, in <Some thoughts on non-trans gender-changers>)

Here, difference is portrayed as an obstacle to trans rights rather than as a strength. Raelene also expressed a resentment of those she perceived as temporary visitors to, or perhaps like hooks' notion of tourists of the Otherness of, trans subjectivity, '*There is far too much pain in being transsexual to want to be associated with those who just want to pretend*' (Raelene Oct 22nd, 2005, in <Transgender Movement?>).

Muddying the waters for trans people by those classed as transgender was also addressed by Leon, '*Its a bit better now, but you have to really look and be your gender, those you "play" at it or transgender people confuse peoples image of a transsexual medical problem*' (Nov 29th, 2006, in <Some thoughts on Trans Acceptance and Freedom>).

Leon also expressed the view that transgender is too wide an umbrella term to do justice to the particular sexual subjectivity of the trans person previously known as transsexual (May 31st, 2006, in <Title of the *Transstudy*>). He further suggested that feminists and 'transgenderists' wish to remain in a state of anonymous and queer-like gender indefinability, '*Modern feminists and transgenderists diont want to be defined...transfolks do as the gender they actually ARE....thats with SRS or not depending how bad the dender dysphoria is between there bodies and minds*' (Leon Jun 26th, 2006, in <Trans and Feminist Theories>).

Subjectivity that falls foul of the requirements of heteronormativity, as transgender does for Raelene and Leon, will often be seen as unreal. This was also found to be the case with separatist feminist perceptions of trans subjectivity. We can see how heteronormativity is a kind of über-discourse that pervades both socially inclusive and socially exclusive discourses.

Some people in the wider community will openly ridicule those whose gender or gendered behaviour appears unreal, as occurred in a *TransEquality* case dealing with harassment of someone labelled by neighbours as 'transvestite'. The respondent was identified as such by rumours based upon flimsy evidence. Harassment (unwarranted words or actions that tend to upset, distress or insult another person) and victimisation (being targeted for complaining about harassment) resulted and were covertly supported by the reluctance of public authorities to intervene. This type of abuse can carry on for years with the targets being alienated by both community and state.

In the <Too womanly to be a woman?> topic thread participants discussed whether it is necessary for an individual to have a female body in order to be a real woman. Participant Alyssa expressed the idea that one could live in a certain gender without bodily reassignment into the sex associated with that gender (Aug 14th, 2006). However, Monica saw womanly gender and the female body as linked together in the minds of most trans women (Aug 10th, 2006). Later in the topic, the author pointed out that potential reassigning people have to live in their preferred gender for a significant period if the Real Life Experience (RLE) is required and that this backs up the idea that preferred gender precedes bodily reassignment because of the commitment involved to undertake this experience (The Researcher Aug 15th, 2006).

136  *Identity essentialism*

Like autobiographer Dhillon Khosla in Chapter 2, participant Shannon had to negotiate definitional hurdles with regard to being accepted as a real man, '... *amongst FTMs a frequent question is "What is a man anyway?". A lot of us have come up against the attitude, even from professionals, that in the absence of a genuine penis we can never be "real" men*' (Shannon Apr 7th, 2005, in <Male=man, female=woman?>).

Chapter 4 addressed such questions attending to the reality of trans subjectivities within the legal establishment, showing how these questions have extended to the status of trans people as parents and marriage partners. For instance, Stephen Whittle discovered that reality as a parent was only legally realised in a gendered way in *X, Y & Z*. Whittle's exclusion from fatherhood was later mirrored in the case of the 'pregnant man', Thomas Beatie (Czyzselska, Sunday July 6, 2008). In both cases motherhood and fatherhood still depended upon being defined as belonging to the biologically corresponding half of the heteronormative duality. Trans people, and people with trans-like personalities, often experience both gender roles and this may serve to make them more, not less, functional in important social roles such as partnering and parenting, allowing them to create a 'whole' family experience.

In a similar way to Whittle, Beresford, Fineman and Flynn (see Chapter 4), Kimana addressed the notion of the reality of the family unit by questioning its seemingly inevitable relation to biological relationship,

> Fortunately for me, and others, I searched out my Lakota family and the Tiospia[3] is spread throughout other Nations into a fair sized Tiospia. Now, I have more brothers, sisters, aunties, uncles, nieces and nephews than I dreamt possible. I have three adult children, grandchildren, one great-granddaughter and even a Kokum (Cree for grandmother). I'm closer to them than my biological family.
> 
> (The Author, quoting Kimana, Oct 25th, 2006, in
> <Trans Partners>)

For Kimana, the reality of subjectivity derives largely from the spirit world, which seems to provide her with much needed relief from the physical world. Although her version of subjective reality challenges that held by many in the industrial West, there is no one who can say conclusively that such a spiritual world does not exist. A more earthy version of this world is perhaps provided by the context of computer-mediated-communication (CMC), which has opened up opportunities for trans people to represent themselves, subject to what boundaries might be imposed by social influence, psychological development and bodily sex, as they would most wish to be recognised, rather than how they have been labelled by society, '*The virtual self, the point of communication in cyberspace, has created a space in which an actual self, the trans person with a trans identity, is to be recognised*' (Whittle, 2002a:82).

Many trans people have first-hand experience of living as virtually gendered, by others, in face-to-face communication, when trying their best to fit in with heteronormativity. Their real gendering lies below the gendered schema, with which they often feel compelled to fall in line until such time as the need to transition is all-consuming and practically possible. Trans people therefore often relate to the need to role play their preferred gender in a safe environment, for instance online, since they are much more aware of sexual subjectivity, or at least its representation, as a social construction that requires practice to achieve. If this awareness could be extended to portray trans and feminist subjectivities as, at least to some extent, socially constructed, then trans and feminist factions may be more open to understanding that differences can be found within each group subjectivity, '*Passing beyond metanarratives of identity and of gender allows for embracing of difference and a proliferation of possible subject-positions and gender performances*' (Edelstein, 1993:198).

## 6.2 Political subjectivity?

> ... it's generally easy to distance yourself from a dominant grouping, but not easy from a dominated grouping.
> (Clarette Apr 11th, 2006, in <Black Trans>)

It seems that Clarette is right when consideration is given to some groups' propensity to repel subjectivities that do not comply with a strict identity definition and to keep subjectivities corralled into identity stereotypes. If subjectivities are going to be rejected or dominated, those with such subjectivities will need to articulate their difference in order to reveal the domination at work. This articulation is a political expression of subjectivity.

*Transstudy* participants often baulked at the idea of sexual subjectivity deriving from or even being used as a base from which to express personal politics. For instance, Monica wished to blend into womanhood in an unremarkable way and did not see her sexual subjectivity as deriving from a personal political stance. Similarly, but in another gendered direction, Leon stated that, '*I dont want to be visible and OUT I want intergration as a man and be allowed to live as such*' (Aug 24th, 2006, in <Too womanly to be a woman?>).

For many trans people gendered utopia would involve full acceptance into their preferred gender, with no need to be labelled as trans anything. They would simply be men or women who had been involved in the process of transition, not passing as their preferred gender but being real members of that gender.

Some participants expressed discomfort with the author's stated identification with political subjectivity and portrayed it as a kind of luxury subjectivity in comparison with what they perceived to be the innate and compulsively driving force of trans subjectivity requiring physical reassignment. Similarly, and aligning with views noted in section 1 above, some *Transstudy* narratives suggested that trans subjectivities not requiring physical reassignment are a kind of 'trans by stealth' that can be frivolous and deceitful,

> I have a label..yes Transsexual due to the GIC proceedures, its on my medical notes ! but I want to be allowed to live as who I am NOW without fuss or banner waving or doing anything outrageous etc...transgenderists who miss behave amake life very difficult for us all.
>
> (Leon Aug 26th, 2006, in <Too womanly to be a woman?>)

Cowan noted that the legal case of Goodwin, '*recommends that transsexual people be recognised by UK law in their post-operative sex, that is, as men or women, not simply as a discrete rights claiming group*' (2004: 88). From statements such as the preceding quotes it can be seen that many trans people do not wish to belong to a category distinct from men or women. For those that may, they would like to be consulted about the construction and application of such a category. If the self-representations of any of these rights claiming groups is not recognised, whether they wish to be defined as heteronormative or not, then gender variant people will always be defined by the 'silent and secret' majority discourse.

Are gender variant people and 'transgenderists' fakes and troublemakers? Can such subjectivities, if they are sexual subjectivities in their own right, be reconceived as oppressed subjectivities that may contribute to the transgender movement if given social recognition? Perhaps this is only possible if people with these subjectivities reveal something about their gendered experience, presenting a 'view from somewhere' in the spirit of dialogic negotiation.[4] This would make the subjectivity personally political to some extent and therefore potentially recognisable in society and in law. However, 'out and proud' political transgendering is quite a different thing in theory, or in an online discussion site, compared to living this subjectivity in real day-to-day life. For instance, Monica, in <How do you believe you will you age?> commented that,

> Sorry. I know it is unfashionable to say this, (in this day and age of being 'out and proud') but there is just no substitute for stealth. I know I can't have my total stealth back again, but at least I can have surgery that will enable me to have a reduced radar signature.
>
> (Monica Jun 16th, 2006)

This radar signature can attract any type of discriminatory abuse. However, within the *Transstudy*, it might be that participants inadvertently manifested a narrative radar signature via a kind of philosophical and social 'voice coaching', similar to the process of gender socialization described by Carol Gilligan (1982) in *In a Different Voice*. Gilligan theorised that men and women's 'different voices', meaning personal communication emanating from differently gendered standpoints, are produced by this kind of coaching, rather than having the voices originally instilled into them by their different biological status (Heyes, Summer 1997:147). So, the radar signature emanating from voice coaching works in a personally political way even though the individual emitting it may not wish to be overtly political.

Trans people, mainly male-to-female reassigning people, often undertake literal voice coaching to develop a voice that matches a reassigned body. But, just like all men and women, trans people will go through a process of social voice coaching reflecting a lifetime of gendered conditioning from self and others. When the trans person transitions, social voice coaching is re-learnt to a significant extent and consequently the trans person has an awareness of 'voice' as a social construct. Voice coaching manifests in trans people's narratives in the form of insights into both heteronormative gendered experiences, engendering the kind of 'whole' experience of gender theorised in section 3 below.[5]

The aetiology of men's and women's ethics, philosophies and feelings is not proven but it seems that trans people, often veterans of both types of voice coaching, can provide lucid perceptions of gender differences and this is a manifestation of their personally political subjectivity. One of Sally Hines' research subjects referred to this kind of cross-gender intuition, '*William contrasts reflexive understandings of gender amongst trans people with a perceived lack of gendered awareness in nontrans people*' (2005:68). Autobiographer Max Wolf Valerio also provided such perceptions/understandings with aplomb, for instance in his autobiography, which includes a passage that comes across as a trans man's insight into what he perceived as emotionally driven women's communication, Valerio writes,

> Women's arguments now often appear to me to be informed more by emotion than by logic (or at least by as much emotion as logic). One transman, Rocky, summed it up like this: Men think about their feelings and women feel their thoughts. ... On oestrogen every object had an emotional weight. A specific emotional substance, a gravity that pulled feeling into it. The world had an infusion of feeling – tender, sentimental, subtle and deep.
>
> (2006:309)

Such perceptions seem to relate to the trans person's mythical status as 'trickster' or person who can mirror gender from both sides of the heteronormative gender divide (Valerio, 2006:326).[6] Such a notion of 'trickster' is described by Kimana as the proper and controlled use of 'coyote medicine',

> Coyote is the Trickster, so it causes all kinds of situations that make you reactive, not proactive in your thoughts words, and actions. I know a lot of people carrying Coyote medicine, not all Native or Traditional. ... There are two ways to deal with having Coyote Medicine. One is to allow it to take over and your life is chaotic, uncontrolled even if you think it's controlled, but makes things VERY interesting for you and those around you. The other is to use it, not let it use you. Coyote Medicine can be used for the humor and to lessen tensions in awkward situations or just to make people think.
>
> (Kimana Dec 28th, 2005, in <Abilities and aptitudes>)

Voice coaching, and controlled 'Coyote Medicine', can build up a personally political gendering, but is it the case that people in the industrial West are now living in a 'post-out'[7] society, where nobody needs to join a subjectivity based movement of their own? 'Post-out' means that no one should face the prospect of having to 'out' their sexual subjectivity because all sexual subjectivities are safely 'out' already. It is a concept suggested by the author's Master's dissertation supervisor, Claudia Castañeda. However, there are gender variant people who are still the target of very real oppression based on how others perceive their 'identity', as the author discovered when working for Press for Change's TransEquality project.

In support of the utopian notion of a 'post-out' society, Stychin called for a type of out-in-process, as a challenge to the demand for instant passing, '... *coming out evokes the idea of bounded space and it implies that the self is engaged in a simple "one off" movement from a constrained sphere into a broader public realm*' (1995:143). This brings to mind the kind of 'passing' required by the Real Life Test, perhaps less so since it became known as the Real Life Experience, and the accounts of almost magical gender transformations identified by Sandy Stone.

Heteronormative people are assumed to be 'out' all their lives but it is still usually much easier for most people to be out as heteronormative than out as gender variant. Epiphanies of the sort described in Chapter 8, where the subject might be described as coming out to themselves, should be joyous and open to sharing with others, not to be accompanied by fear of exposing oneself as alien. Coming out should also be a choice, not a compulsion set by friendly or unfriendly sources.

'Post-out' might enable a societal 'erotics of unnaming' as outlined in Chapter 2 where people with certain sexual subjectivities are not picked up by the heteronormative 'radar'. Monica provided narrative support for the value of 'unnaming' in ensuring a quiet life,

> Years ago, post-op gender reassignees would have nothing to do with pre-op gender reassignees and neither would have anything to do with transvestites or any other transgender grouping. ... However, a raprochment took place between all these categories so that they could join forces to fight for civil rights. The civil rights have been largely achieved, but to me this has been a pyrrhic victory. These lovely new civil rights have been obtained at the cost of something I valued much more, namely my invisibility and anonymity.
> (Aug 26th, 2006, in <Too womanly to be a woman?>)

However, Clarette, in <The Paper> *Transstudy* topic, suggested that even though unnamed, subjectivity still exerts a political influence through use of language,

> Politics exists whether or not the terms of debate are defined. Politics exists in the form of appearance, manners and actions, even without

language.... We have to be wary of how words are used if we are to successfully exist in a linguistic culture, and when these are words used in a specifically political context, it is even more necessary to be wary of them. Those who forget the past are condemned to repeat its mistakes.

(Jun 17th, 2006)

Although the non-articulation of gender in 'erotics of unnaming' can ensure a quiet life, free from the threat of harassment and discrimination, perhaps it is also a way of deferring to the discourse of heteronormativity by blending in, and is therefore definitely 'in' and not 'out'. A denial of the past through 'passing' is involved in this process, which can strike the inclusive mind as being an unnatural way to live one's life. Communicative bonding with similarly different others will be foregone in the life of the person gone stealth, with an accompanying neglect of their very valuable life experience that could be passed on to other gender oppressed people.

To conform or not to conform to heteronormativity perhaps depends on the perception of likelihood of reward. For a trans person there might be the reward of fitting in and accruing the social benefits that adhere to heteronormativity, just as women have benefited from some aspects of patriarchy. Conversely, others will have mustered a portfolio of life experience that informs them that they will never fit in, or that they do not wish to, so there are no further reasons or personal ethics motivating them to join the status quo.[8] Participant Alyssa narrated an alignment with the value of fitting in with heteronormative hegemony,

> Society is governed by it's 'mores' and to make it out there you really need to conmform to the requirements of chosen gender whether or not it is a particularly desireable nuiance. ... If you do conform to them [the mores], you are basically living in peace with the world, your not fighting and people are content with you.
> (Jul 26th, 2005, in <Gender Identity, question on transforming personality>)

Alyssa seemed to feel that the interpolative call of 'Hey, you there', hailing people into heteronormativity, could be successfully directed towards transitioning people. Such narratives reveal that the politically gendered need to understand that there are reasons for some trans people's needs to assimilate into heteronormativity. Stephen Whittle's wife, Sarah Rutherford, remarked that, *'To those who do not know the truth of our situation, we present ourselves as boringly conventional. We are white, heterosexual and middle class. Not only are Stephen and I conformist by nature, we've been together 18 years'* (Rutherford, 23 April 1997).

However, even if the Whittles are, at least outwardly, conformist it does not mean that they have not, and have not wanted to, take part in political gendering. One instance among many included their personally political

142  *Identity essentialism*

stance in a legal battle to form a family whose father had a different type of gendered history to heteronormative.

Others can perceive a person's gendering as political or not depending upon which presentation and behaviour is classed as political, and which is not. For instance, Currah (2006) highlighted how the US First Amendment does not protect the right to free expressive activity if that activity involves cross-gendered dress and presentation. Gender expression is not classed as political expression so it does not come under the veil of legal protection in the US. The reality is that we are all politically gendered to some extent, depending on who is representing our gender, how we represent it, and what position they and we have in the balance of representational power.

## 6.3 The whole trans person

> So we get hung up on whether or not the size of the bed nucleus of the stria terminalis under the influence of hormones is the defining point of gender identity, and other such issues. Which I suspect is reductionist. It is easy to forget the whole being in the process of analytical division. But did we know what the whole being was in the first place? Or is there such a thing? ... "Pre-modern" cultures of course do/did not always think that shape was necessarily representative of being either, so there are stories of shapeshifters ... wolves in sheeps' clothing and so on.
> 
> (Clarette Feb 18, 06, in <some cultural aspects of shapeshifting>)

Shapeshifting, in the sense portrayed by Clarette, might be interpreted to involve challenging ascribed identity with feelings of inner subjectivity in order to mould one's behaviour or even subjectivity into something more personally acceptable. This may be a familiar desire to those feminists and gender variant people who have felt the need to review their given sexual identity. Can shapeshifting as a concept tie in with the acceptance of trans subjectivities, or subjectivities realised through transition, as genuine and 'whole' subjectivities? One of the *Transstudy* topics was entitled <The Whole Trans person>, in response to Germaine Greer's invective against trans women, and to some extent trans men, in her 1999 book, *The Whole Woman*. Greer's dismissal of trans subjectivities came across as a very similar project to what she identified as masculinist annulment of 'woman' as a healthy and self-sufficient subjectivity. The author asked participants to consider whether trans subjectivities are 'whole' identities of their own, and not counterfeit versions of conventional gender, as portrayed by Greer.[9] The author wished to see what interpretations of 'whole' participants might venture.

After reviewing literature and *Transstudy* narratives, the author speculated that trans subjectivities are in fact more whole, in one perspective, than heteronormative sexual subjectivities since they often seem to derive from experience of the whole spectrum of human gender (Apr 9th, 2006, in <The Whole Trans person>); trans people have been 'voice coached' in the language of both genders. Trans people rarely see themselves as actually having been both heteronormative genders, but will often allude to experiences deriving from others' perceptions of them when they were pre-transition. As Jamison Green remarked,

> When I come out now it is to note that my experience is different from that of other men because I spent forty years in a female body; not that I used to be a woman, but that I have a bit more knowledge about what a woman experiences than do other men.
>
> (2004:43)

Whittle also claimed that trans subjectivities can manifest more of a whole experience of gendered subjectivity because of their basis in lives spent on both sides of the gender role divide. He pointed out that, '... *after all we are simply men and women of a trans history, and we have a particular expertise in spotting the difference between men's and women's lives*' (8 July 2007). Kimana in the *Transstudy* site narratively supported this kind of 'view from somewhere',

> Being a trans person has afforded us to experience things in ways others can only speculate about. We've been given the wonderful gift of understanding both the male and female aspects. I feel that it allows us to have twice as much experience as those that aren't trans.
> (Kimana Nov 19th, 2005, in <What we are = what we do?>)

This experience of gender is suggested to be a quality of lesbian and gay existence according to Stychin. Often having a history involving the theoretical and experiential analysis of the nature of gender, lesbians and gays are particularly open to the idea of negotiating the parameters and composition of gender variance, '*The boundaries of lesbian and gay sexuality thus are contested and continually crossed. ... for lesbians and gay men, it is perhaps relatively easy to recognise that categories have no natural or essential character*' (1995:143–144).

In 'Foucault's Monsters' (2007), Sharpe described how Foucault identified the confusion in law, from the Middle Ages to modern times, when presented with abnormal bodies of any description,

> ... human/animal creatures, conjoined twins and hermaphrodites can be viewed as problematizing a variety of legal questions concerning baptism, marriage and inheritance, as well as challenging core legal distinctions between man and animal, male and female, and the idea of the proper legal subject as a single embodied mind.
>
> (Sharpe, 2007:387)

Gender variant people may well still be perceived as having something like two minds, because of their gendered experiences, but this may be an advantage if viewed in an inclusive rather than separatist way.

A different interpretation of 'whole' was provided by participant Sadie who suggested that it is the realisation, or the psychological and social achievement, of gender that makes one feel whole,

> I don't think that simply being transgnedered makes you more human, but can confirm that being comfortable with your gender and all that it entails is one of the most humanising things of all, really. ... That may suggest that being caught in the mire of gender confusion makes you less human; I think there is some truth in that.
> (Sadie Jun 28th, 2005, in <Extremely open question>)

Some people need transition in order to achieve this feeling of gendered 'wholeness'. However, according to Greer, '*The transsexual is identified as such solely on his/her own script*' (2000:74). She suggested that this was a personal fancy rather than something born of desperate need. On the road to gender realisation, Clarette speculated that trans people have to build up a conscious script (maybe more accurately 'schema') of gender subjectivity not because of personal whim but because, as noted in section 2, industrial Western society has not provided this for them,

> In a culture in which trans people generally are not acknowledged as a legitimate part of the community ... which as many of us are aware is not unusual ;-) ... there is no socially legitimised "script" available. Thus inevitably, when we find that we are what we are, not what someone else decided we were, we are automatically identifying ourselves on our own script. And where the process of transition from socially assigned gender to personally perceived gender is not accepted as legitimate, again, inevitably, people are working with their own script. So in a sense, GG was not wrong, only describing the way things were. ... In many places, of course, she was out of date. Publicly available "scripts" have emerged, with varying degrees of acceptance, for both transitioning and non-transitioning trans identities, in many cultures where none existed before.
> (Clarette Apr 10th, in <The Whole Trans person>)

Perhaps new schemata/scripts for gender variant subjectivities will also emerge, or have existed in an unnamed way already. In 'The Transgender Rights Imaginary' Currah suggested that the state does not associate non-transitioning transgender or gender variant people's gender with any available gender schema, '... *transgender people are much less likely to have their gender acknowledged by the state and affirmed by the ideological apparatuses that reproduce hegemonic gender arrangements*' (2009:253).

Both Greer and Janice Raymond overlooked or dismissed the social constructionist idea that it is all people who are scripted into gendering. It seems that there is no social space left for gender variant people when they are castigated by some for emulating heteronormative schemata (notably separatist feminists) and castigated by others (notably reassigning trans people) when they do not. Many trans people are willing 'immigrants' to heteronormativity but are often vilified for being so just as they are vilified by others for not belonging to heteronormativity before or after transition. Such dilemma of rejection was put into stark relief in a murder case where trans woman Kellie Telesford was criticised by a Ms Greenberg for not following the masculine script by fighting back her attacker like a man,

> While we are referring to her as a female out of courtesy because that is how she wanted to be known. She was nevertheless a male with a man's strength and you would have thought that she, as a victim, would have fought her attacker but there was no signs.
> (Quoted by Dean, 8 July 2008)

Clarette's narrative in <The Whole Trans person> manifests a suspicion of equating any subjectivity with Greer's sense of 'wholeness', meaning whole heteronormativity, with Clarette preferring to describe hir own subjectivity as 'hole'. This seemed to mean a subjectivity open to and formed by ideas of diversity, for instance via communication, subjectivity-in-process and spirituality. Sie presented wholeness as the danger of cementing subjectivity into a certain schema; the danger of identity becoming, if unaware, obsession as it has for much of industrial society. This perception of wholeness (not 'holeness') brings to mind 'wholesome' portrayals of man and woman in the nuclear family, prevalent in 1950s USA and notably criticised by Betty Friedan in *The Feminine Mystique* (1963). Kimana (Apr 22nd, 2006) contributed to the whole/hole debate by describing the Native American concept of the spiritual person as 'hollow bones' where spirituality has a free flow through the person open to such communication.

As well as trans as spiritual 'hole', the notion of trans as 'whole' in its experience of the span of gender is narratively supported by Kimana who considered that her experience of man and womanhood stood her in good stead when partaking in men's and women's ceremonies, when counselling, and when generally interacting with men and women. At one military reunion for Vietnam veterans, Kimana described how, '*It was fun going from a genteel woman to "Wild Bill" the Pathfinder to a flirty woman and back to being genteel within a minute*', portraying the 'view from somewhere' common to many a trans subject in a light-hearted way (Apr 24th, 2006). This view was narratively portrayed as intuition and as a 'scourge', perhaps not only for herself but also of heteronormativity, in *The Well of Loneliness* by Radclyffe Hall,

> The eye of youth is very observant. Youth has its moments of keen intuition, even normal youth – but the intuition of those who stand mid-way between the sexes, is so ruthless, so poignant, so accurate, so deadly, as to be in the nature of an added scourge ...
> (Hall, 2005[1928]:81)

Kimana warned of the danger of presenting the worst aspects of gender to be found at the poles of heteronormative gendering (Apr 30th, 2006, in <The Whole Trans person>). The author also did so by using the expression 'oppressive femininity' to identify women's (and sometimes even men's) use of femininely polarised behaviour. Presentation of such behaviour as deriving from an essential essence does, it seems, pigeon-hole people into gendering and really moulds them into 'half a person' to paraphrase the title of a song addressing gender ostracism by indie rock group The Smiths. The author's interpretation of the lyrics, guided by the kind of character that seems to inhabit all The Smiths' songs, is that the lead singer Morrissey's character felt estranged from establishment discourses such as manhood and so wanted to rebel against them by having fantasies such as checking into a YWCA. He felt like half a person (not wholly manly, and therefore seen as a sub-man) when people with heteronormative genders may actually often be the real half genders. British law has characteristically supported such scripting into 'half-ness' by allowing people to choose, 'any gendering they want, as long as it is heteronormative'.

After being victim of oppressive heteronormativity, autobiographer Mark Rees (1996) described how, as he increasingly found himself through transition, his and other people's spotlights were taken off his own gendering and he found that he could invest more time in discovering others through deeper relationships. He used the metaphor of evolution from a shadow to a full person to describe his feeling of becoming real (123), mirroring comments, quoted in Chapter 2, on the experience of ghostly unreality by Jan Morris (1974). Rees commented that, '*Wholeness, I decided, was unobtainable if one was not being true to oneself*' (1996:179).

It became clear from participants' responses and from reviews of *The Whole Woman* that texts such as Greer's marginalise trans subjectivity. Greer donned the role of protector of 'women' as marginalised identity. This stance, and her polemic against trans people, seem ironic when trans men are often classed, by trans-unfriendly people, as natal women and when trans women strive in so many ways to live life as a full woman. Her stance also seems ironic when many a time gender variant people are considered as inferiorly gendered and are therefore 'Othered' from social life, just as women have generally been in the past. Gilligan explained how gendering into womanhood has traditionally meant becoming someone with a less than whole social experience,

> Girl's initiation into womanhood has often meant an initiation into a kind of selflessness, which is associated with care and connection but also with a loss of psychological vitality and courage. To become selfless means to lose relationship or to lose one's voice in relationships. This loss of relationship leads to a muting of voice, leaving inner feelings of sadness and isolation.
>
> (1995:124)

Kristeva questioned even the word 'woman' as being sufficient to encompass the complexity or whole spectrum of womanhood,

> Kristeva's works have prompted widespread criticism from feminists. She has been accused of anti-feminism because of her refusal of the category of woman, which involves, she believes, an essentialism and singularity that belie the subject's complex constitution.
>
> (Wright, 1992:199)

Imelda Whelehan highlighted the way that women have traditionally only been implanted into inclusion as whole gendered beings when they became a component of a nuclear family, *'The women's role is most often theoretically obliterated beneath considerations of status and husband's occupation, even though it could be powerfully argued that it is the woman's role which guarantees the existence of the familial form'* (1995:17).

Whelehan portrayed an image of woman like a queen on the chess board, very powerful and crucial to social institutions, but only allowed to move in a certain way and within a certain area of the social arena. Women are still often seen as less than whole if not connected to a family and have to be prepared to sacrifice themselves for the good of the 'king'.

Contrasting with texts such as Greer's, many *Transstudy* narratives and contributions to trans autobiographies and anthologies seem to tie in with philosophical third wave thinking's general move towards embracing 'Otherness' in general through visualising subjectivity in a similar way to Clarette's idea of the 'hole' (with a 'h') and Kimana's 'hollow bones' that allow a conduit for the flow of empathic communication. Perhaps this is the reality of people's wholeness; the threads of connection that they make with others and the fluidity of their subjectivity.

## 6.4 Identity as a process: subjectivity

Raymond vigorously criticised the idea that certain subjectivities could be created without a certain initial type of biological aetiology that she saw as transparently identifiable,

> One should be able to make choices about who one wants to be. But should one be able to make any choice? Should a white person attempt to become black, for example? The question is a moral one, which asks about the rightness of the choice, not the possibility of it. Should persons be able to make the choices that disguise certain facets of our existence from others who have a right to know ...
>
> (1979:116)

She did not conceive of anyone from other biological aetiologies having the moral right to become women, contradicting Foucault who maintained that the idea of permanently identifiable identity is a mirage that leads people to an oasis of deceptive essentialism (Diamond and Quinby, 1988). Foucault focused on the concept of the soul to argue that the self is not a singularity and the sole source of deliberate action, wishing to show that the self is a construct (Prado, 2000). He theorised that images of gender normativity were, if non-deliberately, created and that they exponentially increased in production in the Western world through introduction of mass social regulation from the seventeenth century onwards.

Prado pointed out how, in *Discipline and Punish*, Foucault theorised the production of the image of a normal person as a result of examining numerous reforms to the treatment of prisoners, with the resulting penal programme of rehabilitation from deviant to normal (2000:60). He found that, in some ways, images of normality proved functional but in others they worked to exclude certain people from subjectivity. Images of normality would set into concrete 'common sense' images of gender.

The *Transstudy* seemed to become a hotbed of discussion on the subject of identity versus subjectivity (subjectivity being more akin to Foucault's multiple and developing self). Most participants were keen to self-define, and consequently be socially defined, as originally man or woman rather than as trans or as having a subjectivity-in-process,

> I am a woman, I don't need to work at being so anymore, I've completed my journey – Now I just be.
> (Alyssa Aug 12th, 2007, in <Moving on and the losses that accrue>)

> I dont say I am trans, dont need to as I am not "trans" as a thing I am a man.
> (Leon Jun 28th, 2006, in <WHo do you feel after the SRS?>)

Few participants interpreted transitioning gender as involving any kind of difference to heteronormativity. However, exceptions are found in narratives ventured by Kimana and Clarette,

> I try not to think of myself as anything in particular, and find it unnecessary.
> (Clarette Oct 21st, 2005, in <NHS safeguards>)

> Although I am a woman in my mind ... most of the time, I still have enough masculinity to do things I need to on rare occasions. ... It's that Balance that allows me to attend and partake in Women's Ceremonies, yet do the same for Male Ceremoies without being disputed. Having Balance also allows me the ability to counsel couples or individuals in personal relationships. After all, I know both sides and can explain how a man feels to a woman and do the same for a man regarding women.
> (Kimana Apr 24th, 2006, in <The Whole Transperson>)

Some social constructionist trans theorists have suggested that gender subjectivity is an ongoing process of nurture rather than natally given or reassigned nature. For instance, a variant of gender nurture identified by US Air Force Psychiatrist George Brown seems to involve some pre-transition trans women's *'flight into hyper-masculinity'* (Brown, 2006[1988]) and the flight out of it into the quest for womanly gendering. Such gendered reversals were dramatically related by Monica, Kimana and Raelene, when writing about their own lives. It is not known whether there was a need felt to dramatically repress femininity in their earlier lives, or whether masculinity was overdone in early years and needed to be compensated, or whether there is another explanation. However, an essentialist and non-developmental interpretation would have designated these three participants as overtly masculine when looking at their early lives.

Essentialist fixing of identity can also happen after transition, for instance in the application of labels of transitioned subjectivity. Terms such as 'correct'[10] and 'inner'[11] suggest identity while 'acquired',[12] 'preferred'[13] and 'realignment'[14] suggest subjectivity. Whittle's use of the term 'preferred' might indicate an idea of gender as chosen, at least as a choice of achieving or presenting the gender. No one knows for sure whether gender is essential or in-process, as was highlighted in the review of gender cases and legislation in Chapter 4, so none of these labels can be classed as definitive. The absence of this certainty is part of the reason that the author aligns with those who argue for acceptance of gender variant 'in-process' subjectivities rather than a focus on the quest for their aetiology. This call for acceptance has been put forward by some trans narrators and was also, according to Timothy O'Leary, recommended as the most useful way to conceive the self by Foucault,

> What does matter for Foucault is that we should change our modes of relation to the self. This relation should not be conceived, in Sartrean terms, as either authentic or inauthentic: rather, it should be conceived as a 'creative activity' (OGE, 351). The self is not a foundation, a source or a starting point: it is an end, a task, a work which, although constantly worked, is never completed.
>
> (O'Leary, 2002:5)

Participant Leon suggested that often, and noticeably in the past, the existence of trans subjectivity has only become apparent to the trans person when they enter adulthood. Drafting of the EA 2010 involved trans lobbyists attempting to facilitate some representation of trans subjectivity in childhood without prematurely applying the label, of 'gender reassignment'.[15] The lobbyists' suggested term, 'gender variant', would allow young people to find their gendered selves while providing some recognition of variance in their daily (including school) lives. Younger people could be then introduced to the concept of gender variant and trans subjectivities without immediately having their identification as trans associated with illness and the need for physical reassignment. It seems that a similar kind of transition assessment for minors already occurs in Lakota culture but with an added spiritual element, as related by Kimana in <Different cultural aspects of being trans> Jan 8th, 2006,

> Throughout their cildhood and adolesence, children are encouraged to ask questions and experience a lot of diferent things on their own, providing it hurts no one. Should a boy wish to dress in a dress or blouse and skirt, maybe try on make-up, this isn't discouraged. Should a boy of ten or soask to be addressed in the feminine and wish to express as a girl in attire or light make-up for over a month, s/he is brought to a Winkte or Medicineman to be counseled. ... Often, the Winkte will arrange for an Inipi (Sweat Lodge sweatlodge), if they don't have their own altar. This is where the child and Elder ask the Spirits for a sign from the Spirit World to show if this child is Winkte. If so, training for the role is pursued. If not, then the child can just be accepted as going through an experimental phase of gender exploration.

Alyssa represented the idea of transition as a process of revealing rather than one of creation, '... *I would probably make the point that I'm not more feminine, just more able to express it*' (Nov 24th, 2005, in <How are we perceived?>). This seems similar to Raelene's narrated view of transition as a process that reveals the inner subjectivity of 'woman',

> I see transitioning as very much a temporary thing. It's a process of moving from one state to another. And having completed the process, one is no longer transitioning nor for that matter is one still transsexual. ... [Raelene preferred] Trans as an adjective that seeks to indicate a different history to other women. Thus a short woman, a tall woman, a married woman, a single woman, a trans woman. But most definitely a woman.
> (Raelene Dec 31st, 2006, in <Some thoughts on Trans Acceptance and Freedom>)

A postconventional ethical perspective would recognise this realised subjectivity by providing named recognition of the subjectivity, via an ethic of justice, but also recognition of how the subjectivity has been achieved by the individual, via ethics of care.

If it is accepted that the reality of subjectivity involves an on-going process, the implications of such a process in real life, and in the discourses of transgender, feminism and the law, require consideration. Kimana suggested that life is by definition a process and that an inclusive approach to change can ensure the survival of a community,

> I'll give you another think to tought about. Everything that doesn't change/grow will eventually die. ... Humans are like this. If they refuse to

*Identity essentialism* 151

allow new ideas or changes, they too become stagnent and begin to decay. ... if they don't evolve with changes around them, they die off and become extinct.

(Kimana Nov 29th, 2005–1:24 AM, in <What we are = what we do?>)

## 6.5 Conclusion

The essence of 'real subjectivity' was addressed in section one of this chapter. Feminist and transgender (as opposed to transitioning) subjectivities have been portrayed as 'muddying the waters' of gender by some transitioning people including some *Transstudy* participants, whether from the type of gender theory espoused by those belonging to these subjectivities or by the apparent nature of the subjectivities involved.[16] Muddying the waters can lead to the danger that all trans subjectivities are perceived as unreal, for instance by legal or medical establishments. Trans people involved with legal lobbying have picked up on the fact that the clear water of gender definition equals protection when, for instance, Press for Change contributed to the drafting of the EA 2010 and the EHRC Codes of Practice. Definition equals reality in conventional culture but, as has been the case for trans subjectivity in its involvement with the law, third wavers realise that defining subjectivity precisely is an almost impossible and potentially misleading endeavour. Third wave thinkers believe it is a more fruitful use of time to support and learn from gender variance than it is to try and define it precisely.[17]

Section two outlined how participants displayed a general antipathy to the notion of 'political subjectivity' ventured by the author since it struck them as luxury, unreal or troublesome compared to an all-pervading need to transition.[18] However, Clarette thought that political subjectivity was inevitable[19] and this subjectivity is arguably often revealed in narratives such as the autobiographies reviewed for Chapter 2, and in those to be found in the *Transstudy*.[20] Often, the gendered 'voice coaching' of the trans individual will reveal a personally political 'view from somewhere'. Being politically out and proud is not easy because of the stigma attached to oppressed gender, and an 'erotics of unnaming' can lead to a quiet life. Nevertheless, this may involve a life of hiding and subjective stagnation and there will come a time when oppressors apply political subjectivity to the gender variant individual whether they are 'out' or not, if they perceive that individual as different in some way.

As with section one, section three dealt with trans subjectivities as something other than counterfeit versions of heteronormative subjectivities. Trans people's experience of both sides of heteronormative gender suggests that they actually acquire more of a 'whole' perspective on gendered experience. Trans people's experience of the span of human gender is respected in Kimana's culture as 'hollow bones' or as a conduit for gendered insight. Germaine Greer's construction of the natal 'whole woman' assists to produce societal

'Others', many of whom are in actuality keen to follow scripts of heteronormative gendering, if only given the choice to do so. All people are scripted into gendering but trans people often, as noted by participant Clarette, have to derive their own scripts for gendered living because they are ostracised from conventional society.[21] Trans people's 'whole gendered experience' is not a superior kind of gender but can yield useful insights into the operation and development of gender.

Section four identified how, if most participants accepted 'subjectivity' (identity-in-process) as a concept, it was perceived as a temporary state on the road to the end state of being man or woman. Such views align with the traditional discourse of gender transition in Western industrial society. This discourse acts as a progress narrative of transformation from one heteronormative gender to another, verified by medicine and the law. It is a developmentalist discourse that is not developmental itself. Kimana provided an exception to this discourse by narrating gender as more of an on-going process, for example with reference to Lakota child development. Clarette suggested challenges to the static discourse of heteronormativity by considering that one may not wish to view oneself as gendered at all and that some people could exist as themselves within either female or male bodies.

Labels applied to the concept of gender transition can reveal perceptions of gender as either essential or 'in-process'. 'In-process' labelling such as 'gender variant'[22] can act as recognition of trans subjectivity while not labelling the individual as ill or as presently in need of medical intervention. The as yet futile, and possibly choice-denying quest for gender aetiology can give way to the promotion of gender acceptance if labels applied to gender transition suggest subjectivity as a process that nevertheless produces recognisable subjectivities. Also, recognition of subjectivity formed from a self-chosen social or physical process can indicate a dedication to that very subjectivity.

The first three sections of Chapter 7 introduce themes that address how gender variant people have been essentialised into 'Otherness', and yet they are still expected to blend into an essential heteronormativity. The final section discusses how gender variant people can challenge these two types of essentialism by forming a cohesive, but not dictatorial, gender 'movement of movement' where the movement itself is subject to reflexive criticism to ensure that it remains 'in-process'.

## Notes

1 For instance, Jan Morris, April Ashley and Mark Rees (Chapter 2), third wave feminists and women of colour (Chapter 3), April Ashley, Herculine Barbin, TransEquality clients, Goodwin and 'I', Stephen Whittle ('X'), P of *P v S & CCC*, Elizabeth Bellinger and Wilkinson and Kitzinger (Chapter 4).

2 The Wioptula is a woman warrior who lives as a man within the Native American Lakota community, which is part of a confederation of seven related Sioux tribes.

3 Tiospia is defined by Kimana as, '*an extended family of aunts, uncles, cousins and adopted family members) their community and Nation, when needed, without having*

*a need for title or status. They are chosen by the people, unless it's a hereditary thing, as in some tribes or Nations'* (Kimana Jan 2nd, 2006, in <Different cultural aspects of being trans>)

4   This articulation and openness of transgender subjectivity can form a response to Ahmed's criticism of the transvestite's mimicry of heteronormativity, outlined in Chapter 3.
5   For instance in accounts by Jamison Green (2004:43), Whittle (8 July 2007), and Kimana (Nov 19th, 2005, in <What we are = what we do?>).
6   This mythology is notably prevalent in Kimana's native culture and is a trait narratively displayed by Kimana in a number of her narratives.
7   A term suggested to the author by his Master's Supervisor, Claudia Castañeda, in 2000.
8   Such people have probably not been 'hailed' into conventional discourse, a process discussed in Chapter 5.
9   See Greer (2000: 'Pantomime Dames').
10  Sadie (Apr 27th, 2005, in <How long to be 'out' as pre-op?>).
11  The Researcher (Dec 31st, 2006, in <Some thoughts on Trans Acceptance and Freedom>).
12  Whittle and Turner (2007b:77).
13  Whittle, et al. (2007:2, 10, 12) and Alyssa (May 16th, 2005, in <How long to be 'out' as pre-op?>).
14  Alyssa (Oct 4th, 2005, in <NHS safeguards>).
15  For instance in the Public Bill Committee second Meeting, Afternoon 02/06/2009, Question 73.
16  For instance, in criticism ventured by Raelene (Jan 19th, 2007, in <Some thoughts on non-trans gender-changers>) and Leon (Nov 29th, 2006, in <Some thoughts on Trans Acceptance and Freedom>).
17  For instance see Morris, 1975 [1974]:153, Sadie Mar 21st, 2005, in <Is it helpful to pathologise transgendered subjectivity?> and *'I'* (2002) Para 70, all in Chapter 4 and Whittle, (2002:86,121) in Chapter 8.
18  As suggested by Leon (Aug 26th, 2006, in <Too womanly to be a woman?>) and Alyssa (Jul 26th, 2005, in <Gender Identity, question on transforming personality>).
19  Clarette (Jun 17th, 2006, in <The Paper>).
20  For instance, Mark Rees when outing his transitioned 'voice', Kate Bornstein (1994:158) and Leslie Feinberg (1996:ch10).
21  Chapters 2 and 7 examine how trans people have sometimes had to develop their own scripts for growing up.
22  As lobbied for in Question 73, Public Bill Committee second Meeting (Afternoon 02/06/2009).

# 7 Closed and static texts to open and evolving narratives
## Articulation and openness

**Introduction**

The narrative development evident in trans activist and author Leslie Feinberg's *Stone Butch Blues* works to reveal what seems to be a realistic account of the trans person's often rocky road to gendered self-realisation. Jay Prosser discussed how key themes in the book such as 'shame', bodily 'home', identity located in 'transition' and the novel as 'trans- or intergeneric space' reveal protagonist Jess Goldberg's finding of her own gendered self through processes of trial, error and negotiation with friends and foes (1998:179–191). In the <What we are = what we do?> topic thread the author suggested that the *Transstudy* may act as a similarly 'trans-generic space' by contributing to developing discourses of trans subjectivity through dialogic negotiation (Dec 14th, 2005).

Sue Stanley and Liz Wise criticised the distancing of ideological theorising from social life and experience, the latter of which they believed to be the only major influences on human interaction (1993:192). Investigating gendered life and experience, evident in true-to-life narratives like *Stone Butch Blues* or in real-life narrative, can be facilitated by working from the four reconstructing themes in this chapter. These themes promote discussion of how and whether sexual subjectivity and its related discourses are closed and static or open and evolving phenomena. This chapter also investigates how third wave texts, trans autobiographies and participants' narratives can challenge silence and secrecy in mainstream discourse.

## 7.1 Voice

> [Normi] Noel finds that one voice, speaking in a particular emotional register, can stop the emotional vibrations in a group of people so that the environment in the room becomes deadened or flat. When this happens, she observes, it looks like silence but in fact the feelings and thoughts – the psychological energy – often move into the place they can still live, and vibrate in silence, in the inner sense, until it becomes possible to bring them back into the world.
>
> (Gilligan, 1995:121)

Forums and formats need to be provided for the interpretations that individuals apply to their own sexual subjectivity. If not, people tend to be allocated to a particular type of gendering when their understanding of their own gender may be quite different. As noted in Chapter 2, there has been a general invisibility of trans narratives and philosophy until quite recent times. Self-presentations of sexual subjectivity by gender variant subjects were included in Krafft-Ebing's *Psychopathia Sexualis* (1893), Havelock Ellis's *Sexual Inversion* (1896), Magnus Hirschfeld's *Transvestites: The Erotic Drive to Cross-Dress* (1910), Sandy Stone's 'The Empire Strikes Back: A Posttranssexual Manifesto' (1991) and Leslie Feinberg's *Transgender Warriors* (1996). However, autobiographical trans narratives only came to prominence in the industrial West in the 1990s.

Voices conflicting with the traditional narrative schema of gender transition laid out between transition practitioner and trans client, especially before the advent of inclusive trans theory/writing, have often been, if inadvertently, silenced by the medical community. Lack of self-representations from trans people within establishment discourse can be linked to the oppression of silence and secrecy and/or to collusion involved in passing for reassignment, as notably theorised by Sandy Stone (1991:95). In the medical setting, the consultant/patient relationship still often seems to manifest as an unspoken 'expert/layperson' hierarchical dualism. For instance, some consultants will only recommend reassignment surgery for those promising post-operative heterosexuality, revealing a conflation of gender with sexuality.[1] However, the voice of medical specialists and legal representatives empathic with the trans community can also be muted as can be seen to apply to dissenting medical specialists and judges from the *Corbett v Corbett* case to the more recent case of Dr Russell Reid.

In law, silencing of self-representations operates when the trans person has to align with gender-universalising legislation, an alignment overlooking the observation that, in the opinion of Catharine MacKinnon, '... *articulation of the voice of the victim is crucial because laws about victimisation are typically made by people with power* ...' (quoted in Benhabib, 1992:195). Nevertheless, as described in Chapter 4, trans voices excluded by the law have been emphasised and developed by pressure groups formed by trans people for trans people.

A closer look at trans people's self-representations of gendered subjectivity, engendered by listening to trans people and trans-friendly theorists, reveals that not all trans people speak in exactly the same 'voice'. For instance, as can be seen in the <Hidden Trans men> topic, Dhillon Khosla's experiences of men's groups (2006:8), and in Tracey Lee's research, trans men have different gendered perspectives and experiences to other trans men, as well as people with other genders. Lee found that her research participants accounted for their sexual subjectivity in differing ways so that a metanarrative describing trans men's aetiology could not be formed. One of Lee's participants, Eric, decided to negotiate his transition through reconstructing the usual script for female-to-male transition and included what Lee identifies as a classic trans sub-plot of non-conformity in his transition narrative (2001:118, 121). These narratives challenge the essentialising of trans existence, notably carried out by separatist feminists, where they paint a picture of transitioning conformity.

In commenting on the lack of trans men's input into some trans discussion forums, it could be that trans men are used to feminine communication or informal organic discussion, perhaps deriving from their female-gendered upbringing. They are generally not in favour of having to give responses to set questions. This may be an example of communication 'in a different voice', to adopt Gilligan's expression. Writing with assertive opinions and stand-alone statements is perhaps still more of a mode of communication instilled into those brought up as male. However, even though working from set questions, it might be said that the *Transsstudy* subverted this mode of communication to some extent by encouraging free discussion and branching off from the topic being addressed.

Seyla Benhabib pointed out that Gilligan called her original work on ethics of care, 'In a Different Voice', rather than 'In a Woman's Voice' (1992:191). This is significant for third wave and/or transgender theory because both rely on the promotion of 'different voices', such as those of trans men, in order to achieve strength through diversity and in order to support voices traditionally silenced by masculinist discourse. In Chapter 4 it was argued that Gilligan's work on moral judgment and ethics identified differences in gender socialisation rather than deriving from immutable differences in sex. Benhabib reminded us that postmodernist feminists have disputed the strict divide between sex and gender where sex is seen as primary and given and gender is perceived as secondary and socialised (192). Both aspects of sexual subjectivity emerge as separately identifiable phenomena but both can be constructed from social interaction even if this is a process spanning many generations. With this approach to subjective difference, 'different voices' can be learnt by people with different sexual subjectivities meaning that they are not forever separated from each other by immutable difference.

### *Hailing/interpellation*

Acquiring social agency via the gaining of 'voice' may emerge from the kind of entry into subjectivity theorised by Louis Althusser as 'hailing' or 'interpellation' (1971). However, subjectivity gained through joining the 'club' of a particular social group is often gained at the expense of lost other subjectivity/ies. For instance, entry into patriarchy will entail a loss of connection with maternal relations and, as noted by Alecia Youngblood Jackson, entry into womanhood will often entail a loss of connection to manhood (2004:677).[2] Taking up the mantle of 'academic researcher' as a subjectivity can mean alienation from 'research participant' as a subjectivity. These are differentiations that form an unbalanced power relationship between subject (the other) and object (the 'Other'). Ignorance of the unfairness of unbalanced power relationships is bliss until knowledge arrives and when this happens, the power relationship will be subject to challenges from those unsettled by the status quo (Foucault, 1998[1978]).³ In the case of gender discrimination, such challenges have been made by trans people taking recourse to the law to challenge power relationships that define trans subjectivity, as described in Chapter 4.

Sara Ahmed theorised that hailing may, 'miss its mark', when those not hailed think that they have been and when those hailed believe that they have not (Summer 1995:24). The process of hailing may also include reverse hailing as outlined in Chapter 5. An instance of reverse hailing or a call of, 'Hey, not you', was narrated by Raelene In the <Hey You!> topic thread, when relating her rejection by a lesbian group for not, in their interpretation, being a woman-born-woman,

> I have definitely had a "Hey not you" from an older lesbian group. There is a group called Older Dykes who have monthly Sunday lunches. I e-mailed them as to whether trans women were welcome. The reply was "no way". ... "Women born women" groups cause a fair bit of grief to the trans community down here.
>
> (Nov 1st, 2006)

It is possible to relate Kimana's preferred mode of communication, outlined by her in <Abilities and aptitudes>, as face-to-face and with knowledge of those involved in the communication, to the philosophical third wave's alleged propensity to include different voices and communication methods into feminist debate. Kimana narrated an alignment with the third wave endeavour to get to know the individual that one wishes to 'hail', rather than basing choice of who to hail on who seems to display which social, ethnic or biological essential features.

### *Standpoint epistemology/ view from somewhere*

Reverse hailing can eventually endow the subject with a standpoint epistemology or insightful social viewpoint formed from their exclusion, as suggested by Foucault of those rejected from mainstream discourse (1998 [1978]:100,101). Many of those holding an oppressed epistemology, or theory of knowledge, are not blind to a discourse of oppression, as are many of those protected by the discourse, since the dominant discourse is a threat to their existence. The alienated subject develops a 'view from somewhere', as opposed to the kind of 'view from nowhere' that can seem to emanate from those identifying with a 'common sense' or apparently 'natural' discourse. However, Neil Thompson highlighted how 'marginalisation', 'invisiblisation' and 'infantilisation' all operate to silence a 'view from somewhere' by attempting to eliminate it from the 'common sense' discourse (1998:81–83).

According to Foucault, power imbalances between subjects, such as between those with a 'view from somewhere' and those with a 'view from nowhere', could be remedied by non-judgmental interaction in communication (Cooper and Blair, 2002). Although it is important to approach such communication with an open mind, a researcher attempting such interaction should remember that they can never really be a 'Modest Witness' with a 'view from nowhere'. Donna Haraway (1997:23) introduced the concept of the Modest Witness in discussing the supposedly distant and objective approach taken to research by modernist European male scientists.[4] Such 'witnesses' portrayed a professional position outside ideology and relationships while in fact being heavily imbued in their own privileged ideological and social positioning.

If, as Jackson (2004:676) theorised, a person recognises their social location instead of denying it, then that person can use the focused knowledge or admittedly 'partial perspective' emanating from this social positioning to provide special insights, just as suggested in Chapter 6 with regard to gender variant people's special insights into gender. Stephen Whittle noticed this kind of self-aware perspective as prevalent amongst trans people, and recommended its recognition and articulation by the trans person themselves, '... *the trans person's history and knowledge of the world is so different from that of "men born men" or "women born women". Yet the responsibility to recognise and articulate that position is no one else's but the self's*' (2006a:xiv).

Antonio Gramsci thought that revolutionary intellectuals, those who give voice to their communities, should originate from within, rather than from outside, the working class, if they were to build an ideology sympathetic to working class interests (Bocock, 1986:36–37). As noted by Robert Bocock, Gramsci suggested that only when intellectual leaders form a bond of, '... *"organic cohesion in which feeling-passion becomes understanding and thence knowledge (not mechanically but in a way that is alive)", that, "then and only then is the relationship one of representation"*' (Gramsci, 1971:418).

In the trans community, such a 'view from somewhere' leading to intellectual leadership and deriving from the working class has been personified by Leslie Feinberg. Belief in such empathic intellectual relations could be reapplied in order to recommend that researchers make concerted efforts to identify or empathise with their chosen research community. However, a researcher must no more look for unadulterated perspectives in participants' narratives than s/he should look for such in his/her/hir own. This is because all those involved with producing narratives operate with what can be classed as a 'view from somewhere' and there is, as Catherine Riessman contends, really no such thing as the 'view from nowhere', only a non-self-aware or denied 'view from somewhere' (1993:15).

## *Refusal to grow up*

One of the most pernicious threats to articulation of any view from anywhere faced by gender variant people comes in the form of infantilisation, as discussed in Chapter 2. Some, for instance those working from medical or media perspectives, would prefer that such people are seen (for the spectacle) but not heard since, once gaining a voice, they tend to upset the heteronormative applecart which demands certain schemata and scripts of behaviour from adult men and women. Infantilisation has even emanated from apparently trans-friendly sources, for instance when Harry Benjamin belittled trans people by theorising that,

> The often infantile and completely self-centered attitude of many transvestites and transsexuals is occasionally and strikingly illustrated, together with a deeply disturbed, unrealistic, frustrated frame of mind which is the more outspoken, the more the writer inclines toward transsexualism.
> (Benjamin, 1966:38)

This kind of personality stereotyping brings to mind that allocated to women in Victorian times,[5]

> As an 'angel in the house', woman has been credited with natural goodness, an innate allegiance to 'a law of kindness'. But this same description extols her as 'infantile, weak, mindless creature' in constant need of male supervision and protection ... the alleged angel was an image that all Victorian women were supposed to internalize.
> (Noddings, 1989:59, cited in Ussher, 1991:86)

> In a society [Victorian] that not only perceived women as childlike, irrational, and sexually unstable but also rendered them legally powerless and economically marginal, it is not surprising that they should have formed the greater part of the residual categories of deviance from which doctors drew a lucrative practice and the asylums much of their population.
> (Showalter, 1985[1987]:73)

In <How do you believe you will you age?> Monica, Leon and Kimana hinted at how trans people are likely to live longer and happier lives if they transition since only then are they fully self-realised, and can 'find themselves' sufficiently to be able to grow up. This is similar to the way in which Gilligan found that women could find themselves through ethics of care when relinquishing their ties to a kind of Victorian-like 'selflessness' in the name of womanhood,

> ... Jenny, another student in the college study ... articulates a morality of selflessness and self-sacrificing behavior, exemplified by her mother who represents her ideal.
> (1982:136)

160  *Open and evolving narratives*

> This relational ethic [ethics of care] transcends the age-old opposition between selfishness and selflessness, which have been the staples of moral discourse.
>
> (1982:xix)

As noted in Chapter 2, autobiographer Mark Rees noted that he remained 'boyish' when unable to realise his physical sex as a male adolescent (1996). For Judith/Jack Halberstam there was no point in growing up into an unsuitable kind of masculinity so s/he adopted tomboyism as a resistance technique to the imposition of masculinity (1998). These accounts of hindrance to development resemble a narrative description provided by Raelene,

> For me, as an male-to-female transsexual non of my female emotional needs were ever met prior to my acceptance of their legitimacy. And my emotional growth and maturity were severely stunted leading to what could be described as long-term emotional abuse.
>
> (Raelene Oct 22nd, 2005, in <What we are = what we do?>)

Sandy Stone helped to recuperate trans people into maturity, and to consequent social voice, by describing them as 'socially mature' (Whittle, 2005:163) and Monica looked forward to a healthy developmental outcome for trans girls when a proper means of gender attribution was established society-wide (Feb 21st, 2006, in <Transpregnancy>). The application of the label 'gender variant' to children showing trans characteristics would allow these children to articulate their gendering without being straitjacketed into a gender that can only cause them developmental confusion.

In Chapter 2 we saw how some members of one oppressed faction, feminists, have sometimes infantilised another, trans people, in order to act as gatekeepers to subjectivity, for instance when Raymond called trans people 'sick and immature' (1979) and when Greer conflated trans women with pantomime dames (2000). This direction of internecine[6] hostility has sometimes been reversed when trans people infantilised feminist narrative, '*I think terms like "Women born women" are divisive and bigoted. Also factually incorrect – surely they mean women born girl? And people using the term "womyn" – grow up. Get a life*' (Sadie Jun 4th, 2005, in <Camp Trans 2005>).

Sometimes trans people have even infantilised other trans people by portraying trans subjectivity as an immature outcome. Georgina Turtle did so in *Over the Sex Border* when equating the gender inappropriate behaviour of 'O-sexuals' with immaturity mentioning that, '*... immaturity is a word to be found exclusively in psychiatrists' reports*' (1963:96), while actually conflating male-to-female transvestism with transsexualism. However, sometimes immature presentation and behaviour is a simple practical mistake made by trans people trying to learn a new gender schema. For instance, as noted by Monica in <Too womanly to be a woman?>, the new male-to-female reassignee can come across as immaturely feminine by overzealous use of feminine paraphernalia (Jul 27th, 2006).

Feminists have also been subject to association with immaturity by other feminists[7] and this has stunted their access to voice in discourse. For instance, Rebecca Munford (2004) identified how contemporary 'Girlie' culture has been represented as infantile by second wave theorists such as Margaret Marshment in *Introducing Women's Studies* and Germaine Greer in *The Whole Woman*. Munford claimed that Girlie culture was, in fact, a philosophical third wave move designed to challenge heteronormativity, rather than adulthood, when adult women value elements of their childhood that freed them from expected gendering (148).

As we have seen, Gilligan realised that women had traditionally abdicated responsibility for moral decision-making in order to comply with the image of woman as caring, and to avoid hurting others through having to pass judgement (1982:74). However, this prevented them from being able to 'grow up' into the world of mature responsibility. A similar abdication of responsibility from involvement was expected of trans people presenting for medical reassignment until trans people began to gain a social voice in order to have some input into the negotiation of their transition.

Like Gilligan, Becker identified the dilemmas that can arise when people take up the mantle of responsibility when rejecting their gilded cage of dependency, '... *there are no solutions without down sides. Nor are there solutions which are guaranteed to work without any risk of unexpected consequences or of backfiring to harm those who were supposed to be helped*' (2009:170).

These dilemmas were also recognised by Halley who lent support to the argument that an ethics of care involves responsibility and that responsibility has to be accompanied by the knowledge that any decision will have positive and negative consequences,

> We might have to decide without knowing that our understanding of the situation is right, without knowing how our decision will play out, and even convinced that, in a system in which any decision will transfer some social goods from, say, women to men or men to women, there is no decision that we could possibly make that will not hurt vast numbers of real, actual people ...
>
> (2009:26)

The gaining of social voice will be accompanied by such dilemmas but the alternative is to be always infantilised and consequently silenced. Experience of 'hailing', a 'view from somewhere' and 'refusal to grow up' can all increase or decrease the trans person's societal access to voice. The trans person will therefore, like women excluded from feminism in the chronological second wave, often seek avenues other than the conventional in which to articulate their experiences.

### Critiquing the voice/silence binary

In *Silence, Feminism, Power*, Sheena Malhotra and Aimee Rowe note that, '*The articulation between silence and powerlessness is almost common sense within Western culture*' (2013:4) in their introduction to a feminist anthology that presents several challenges to this assumption. These editors note that women's voices, and notably those of feminists of colour, have been expressed through different media than just the written and spoken word and the author argues that one of these takes the form of actual and metaphorical quilting, described as a channel of womanist expression in Chapter 3. Malhotra and Rowe note how Native American people have communicated in ways that wouldn't register as communication in much industrialised culture, and how they have consequently become silenced in the noise of the industrial world. To re-establish their modes of communication will require others in their community and society to play suit. These communicative ways seem more reminiscent of 'communion' than 'agency', in the sense of these words introduced in Chapter 4, and to 'access' to discourse as discussed in Chapter 5.

Drawing from Adrienne Rich, Malhotra and Rowe argue that silence can be both oppressive and liberating because of its complex and contradictory nature (11). However, it has perhaps been notably oppressive for radical feminists of colour who the editors recognise as writing '*about the importance of coming to voice, of overcoming their silences, in order to liberate themselves and others*' (12). Other authors in the anthology present varied takes on the empowering potential for silence. Ann Russo admits that she had many opportunities to speak in feminist enclaves because of her privileged subjective position (2013: 34). Despite this, she sees the importance of dialogical negotiation rather than dialogical domination, '*stepping back from speaking and stepping up to active listening*' (36), and calls for a more mature type of communication where the aim is not just to reveal oneself as knowledgeable. As with Russo, the apparent contradiction of being in a position to speak about silence is not lost on Sarah de la Garza in the anthology (111). Thought must be given to whether a contradiction harms anyone else and, if so, one must take active steps to reveal and ameliorate the contradiction.

Quoting M Jacqui Alexander, Russo describes how admitting one doesn't know is a more useful contribution to knowledge than portraying oneself as someone who always knows in the manner of a patriarch, authoritarian or dogmatist. Silence of ethnicity in the case of whiteness (which, consciously or not, has been relied on as an unstated position of knowing things) can be addressed by negotiating its nature with others and one can be out about whiteness or can own it as a chosen, rather than natural, ethnicity. This requires loss of privileges associated with this 'invisible' subjectivity. In this way whiteness can join the band of 'postdifferent' subjectivities, many subtly classed as 'outsider', in being, '*grounded in differential belonging with a commitment to coalition building*' (41) rather than remaining an 'insider' identity. There is a need to acknowledge unequal divides, such as between ethnicities, and to turn them into equitable alliances rather than equal oppressions.

In the same anthology, Julia Johnson notes that, *'bourgeois liberals often demonstrated how not speaking and acting against racism reinforced white, middle-class, heterosexual privilege'* (58) but would those who do be accused of speaking for an ethnicity? This damned if you do or damned if you don't stand-off needs to be addressed if there is to be a break in the silence about whether those from a certain social ethnicity can own or participate in a certain area of subjective debate. In defence of non-oppressive silence, she claims that, *'The rhetoric of silence is qwe're because it speaks beyond a logocentric model and also disrupts a logocentric flow'* (61). This 'beyond' may emanate from the semiotic seeping through symbolic discourse.

A linguistic perspective by Robin Clair, citing the work of Debarah Tannen and Muriel Saville-Troike, might describe how the symbolic actually relies on the semiotic in order to exist as communication when, *'the bits of silence between consonants and vowels [that] allow language to be shaped and take form'* (2013:86). She points out that silence, just like non-silent language, can be oppressive or empowering or both at once. She focuses on the Warramunga ethnic group who believe that women and men return in the next life as the other gender and therefore experience whatever silence accompanies each gender. They may be said to have a 'whole' experience of gendered silence resulting from their collective series of lives. Perhaps such experience could be replicated to some extent by people role-playing different genders in their current lives.

Perhaps there is no real silence anywhere or none that we can imagine, just like scientists have found it impossible so far to display real nothingness or to articulate the nature of real nothingness. Silence may really be sound that is not detected by a certain individual, group or community. It is therefore probably a mistake to assume that just because someone is silent that they are not thinking or that they have nothing to say. Alexandra Fidyk, in the anthology, argues that, *'silence is not an absence, not a lack. Generative silence is ripe, full, fertile; it is always already becoming'* (117). Unless one attends to the silence of another, there is no opportunity to combine with the other, or the Othered, to form a communicative 'wholeness'. Such wholeness can challenge the voice/silence binary by asking whether it is a valid duality after all. Cherl Lossie asks us to, *'...revisit the way we look at, and live with, these dualities. And instead of seeing them as either/or, better/worse, higher/lower scenarios, to embrace them as both/and, equal/mutual...'* (134).

Fidyk claims that, *'when one acquires the skill of deep attendance, one in a sense forgets oneself and yet becomes something more than previously imagined'* (119). This may resemble the losing of oneself in the moment of 'jouissance', in the sense theorised by Kristeva, where, *'... the ego gives up its image in order to contemplate itself in the Other'* (1982:9). However, it may also work to establish a finding of the self, in the way conceived of as 'plaisir' by Roland Barthes, *'... a pleasure (plaisir) linked to cultural enjoyment of identity, to cultural enjoyment and identity, to the cultural enjoyment of identity, to a homogenizing movement of the ego ...'* (Heath, 1977:9).

Richard Middleton, referring to Barthes, contrasts jouissance to plaisir, where jouissance is an explosion of feeling where the subject transcends and/ or descends from the self,

> In this erotic process, the subject is deconstructed ('lost'), overwhelmed by the pleasures of jouissance. ... Plaisir results, then, from the operation of the structures of signification through which the subject knows himself or herself; jouissance fractures these structures.
> 
> (Middleton, 1990:261)

The communicative experience of finding self and others resembles plaisir as an establishment of self and the construction of subjectivity and is facilitated by communicating with others. Fidyk argues that, counter-intuitively, silence can work in this way to establish the self, *'partaking in practices of silence can lead to a sense of self that is always in relation with others, woven as a dynamic web of interconnectedness'* (2013:120). She states that, *'Seeing and "insight" indicate a readiness for otherness – a kind of welcoming the not-yet-known'* (121), which can be contrasted to the position of someone so blinkered by their own discourse paradigm that they cannot see or hear communication coming from alternative discourse. Overcoming this discourse blindness leads to dialogic negotiation, *'They participate in a dance, negotiating concepts, terms, and paradigms, to put forth his and her thinking and yet are receptive to the other's as well'* (121–122). Escaping an oppressive thought paradigm can in this way lead to a situation, *'When one is no longer externally directed (valuing power, control and predictable outcomes) and attunes to a deeper, inner resonance, the ego grows quiet and there arises an energy greater than itself'* (126).

## 7.2 Passing

> Initially, I thought the way to achieve status was to blend into society and cover our tracks. But one spends one's life waiting for the truth to emerge.
> 
> (Rutherford, 23 April 1997)

> Still, transsexuals know that silence can be an extremely high price to pay for acceptance.
> 
> (Stone, 1991:299)

Although a proliferation of different voices and 'silences' is commendable for gender inclusiveness, it is understandable that many trans people should seek to 'pass' into heteronormative gendering. Maintaining or presenting non-heteronormative subjectivity means developing a whole new gender schema, will almost certainly open the individual to ridicule and abuse, and will make it difficult to be accepted for specialist transition and reassignment help should this be required. Indeed, undermining the heteronormative gender schema is such a formidable prospect that it would be the stuff of nightmares for most people. Chapter 4 highlighted how the law has often expected transitioning people to pass as heteronormative in every way, including physically.[8] Legal and social penalties for not passing into gender schemata have been severe and have led to trans people being marginalised within heteronormative or even trans communities (Whittle, 2002a). Even for those trans people keen to pass as heteronormative, transition to the preferred gender can be an uphill struggle when societal approval is largely based upon perception and not substance,

> Whilst we fix the world, however, there's no denying that a trans woman who passes well will have a very different life experience from one who doesn't.
>
> (Burns, 20 June 2007)

> People form opinions about others within a couple of seconds and visual appearance plays an inordinately large part in how you are percieved. (If it looks like a duck and it quacks like a duck, then its a duck)! Every tiny hint of masculinity moves you nearer to the 'one man drag show' category.
>
> (Monica Jun 15th, 2006, in <How do you believe you will you age?>)

Stychin noted that Eve Kosofsky Sedgwick's idea of putting queer into practice was for the individual to declare themselves as queer, thereby refusing to pass as heteronormative (1995:146). This kind of self-representation is positive for choice but quite risky in many social scenarios and Stychin recognised that categorisations will still be imposed by others in the community, '... *categories continue to be invested with social meaning and, as a result of categorisation, different subjects experience a different material reality*' (147). Trans people and feminists have been the direct recipients of the effects of perception and often, quite understandably, wish to pass into heteronormativity.

This desire to pass can derive from the fact that many people are still brought up to accept that man and woman are the only conceivable genders and that one does not choose which of these to belong. *Transstudy* participants tended to indicate the power of such a heteronormative gender schema by regularly relating a desire on behalf of themselves or other trans people to pass,

> most people I know are "stealth" and would never tell anyone they were trans unlesss they were intimate with them ... although maybe thats more a trasnman thing..?
>
> (Leon Aug 4th, 2006, in <Being Trans: A blessing or a curse>)

> ... clothes are there to keep the weather off, first and foremost. Right? ... The identities we present may be there to keep social weather off, first and foremost...
>
> (Clarette Jun 4th, 2006, in <Your Narrative Self>)

Participant Ariel suggested that the requirement for a trans person to pass seamlessly into the heteronormative gender schema is being challenged within medical communities after many years of demanding very scripted presentations of gender,

> The old paradigm is dying, Dr (Eli) Coleman said. The notion of two sexes, the clear distinctions between cross dressers, transvestites, transsexuals. And, most interestingly, the need to be assured that individual will complete the sex reassignment process, the importance of "passing", and, believe it or not, the encouraging 'unnecessary' voice lessons and surgery.
>
> (Ariel Oct 25th, 2005, in <Who might be the 'Others' of the *Transstudy*?>)

However, Whittle criticised those managing trans people's RLE for continuing to what might be called 'heteronormalise' the transitioning experience more than necessary,

> However, I believe the RLT, or as I (and the WPATH SoC) would prefer it was called, the RLE (experience), is still fundamentally flawed in many clinical practices. It's practice often focus's the patient's mind on PASSING the test, whether by; 'passing', or, more likely, by persuading themselves that they are passing, or by pretending they are passing – or as the French psychoanalyst Collete Chiland might say for the majority; by deluding themselves or by an illusion of themselves. ... it should involve discussing whether the patient felt fully informed, whether genital surgery was appropriate for them at this stage, and of course such time as when the patient thought it was appropriate for them. It would not be about whether the practitioner, nor when the practitioner, thought it was appropriate for the patient.
>
> (Whittle, 10 September 2008)

Here, Whittle argued for active involvement of trans people in the negotiation of access to transition or to reassignment treatments. This would engender a deeper understanding of the person on the inside rather than the gender presentation that shows on the outside. Consideration must also be given to the fact that some pass more easily than others. Transition seems to have allowed Raelene to pass as herself rather than as her gender ascribed at birth,

> I am extremely contented just being me these days. For the vast bulk of my life there has been two opposing forces at work – 1) to meet

*Open and evolving narratives* 167

societies expectations of me and 2) to fulfill my own needs. Now they are as one.
(Raelene Sep 30th, 2006, in <Being Trans: A blessing or a curse>)

Post-op, psychologically it has been unbelievable. Before there was always a sense of having something to hide, now no-way. ... now I am ME in capital letters. Now I go out in shorts and a tee shirt, or a ballgown. There is no sense of unease, I smile a lot more.
(Raelene Dec 6th, 2006, in <Post-Op experiences>)

As discussed in section 1 of this chapter, when the trans person openly manifests their enhanced insight into the human condition from having inhabited both traditional gender roles, it helps us all, through drawing upon their narrated experience, to find ourselves more fully through knowledge of gender,

In essence, using the analogy given in Dr John Gray's book "Men are from Mars, Women are from Venus" a trans person learns to speak both martian and venusian at they end of their journey. :)
(Alyssa Aug 15th, 2006, in <Being Trans: A blessing or a curse>)

This narrated experience can mould our subjectivities in the way suggested by Sandy Stone, in an eloquent suggestion for an alternative to passing,

In the transsexual as text we may find the potential to map the refigured body onto conventional gender discourse and thereby disrupt it, to take advantage of the dissonances created by such a juxtaposition to fragment and reconstitute the elements of gender in new and unexpected geometries.
(Stone, 1991:296)

## 7.3 Choice

In "A Vindication of the Rights of Women," [Mary Wollstonecraft in 1792] argues that liberty, rather than leading to licence, is "the mother of virtue," ...
(Gilligan, 1982:129)

The essence of moral decision is the exercise of choice and the willingness to accept responsibility for that choice.
(Gilligan, 1982:67)

I believe that gender (self-) identification – both for transgendered and non-transgendered individuals – should not be categorized and should be a voluntary decision for everyone.
(Pershai, 2006:51)

In 'Undiagnosing Gender' Judith Butler described how a politics of naming leads gender variant people to having to be named as 'Other' to heteronormativity before any recognition of their suffering can occur, and before they can be shepherded into normality. Physical reassignment treatments are necessary for some gender variant people in order to realise their autonomy and maintain their power of choice in terms of which gender to live. However, the diagnosis that leads to these treatments is still largely heteronormative based and, as noticed by Butler, still often acts as a subtle diagnosis of homosexuality (2006:277). To increase autonomy of choice, Butler called for diagnosis of 'gender dysphoria' to be replaced by something like Jacob Hale's and Stephen Whittle's recommendations to treat the transitioning person as a client rather than as a pathological patient (281).

Reassignment treatments do not guarantee a state of 'passing', partly because the transitioner has still been pathologised by diagnosis and, whenever this is revealed, it can lead to discrimination or harassment. Butler argued that heteronormativity begets the need for exact diagnosis of gender function or dysfunction which in turn begets the need for gender variant people to pass as heteronormative,

> The only way to secure the means by which to start this transformation is by learning how to present yourself in a discourse that is not yours, a discourse that effaces you in the act of representing you, a discourse that denies the language you might want to use to describe who you are ...
> (288)

The possibility of dysphoria being a feature of society rather than of the individual, is not perceived to be possible in the heteronormative diagnostic reassignment schema so it is taken that it is gender variance that has to be cleansed from society, rather than gender normativity that has to be examined,

> ... the [DSM] diagnosis does not ask whether there is a problem with the gender norms that it takes as fixed and intransigent, whether these norms produce distress and discomfort, whether they impede one's ability to function ...
> (291)

> ... it seems that the only unhappiness is one created by an internal desire, not by the fact that there is no social support for such [gender variant] children, that the adults to whom they express their unhappiness are diagnosing and pathologizing them, that the norm of gender frames the conversation in which the expression of unhappiness takes place.
> (294)

A 'Judith Butler Real Life Experience', leading to any kind of diagnosis, would be much more open to variation of gender presentation and expression,

*Open and evolving narratives* 169

judging by her interpretation of gendered behaviour, for instance that found in children's doll play,

> ... the DSM assumes that the doll you play with is the one you want to be. But maybe you want to be her friend, her rival, her lover. Maybe you want all this at once. Maybe you do some switching with her.
>
> (2006:293)

Butler concluded that many children play as if they perceive that gender can be created or improvised (294).

In addressing the issue of imposed definitions of sexual subjectivity, Currah noticed how, in the 2000s US, the legal community would deploy the term 'transgender' to indicate a type of identity rather than gender expression with the effect that, '... *identity-based claims remain more juridically intelligible in the way they link identities to bodies, and so often produce better results*' (2006:13).

This legal operation based on the convenience of labelling gender came to effect in the US 2001 case of Nikki Youngblood, who lost her case through not being classed as 'transgender',

> ... Youngblood's advocates were not able to describe her long history of gender nonconformity as a medical condition or even as an identity, as Doe's attorneys had done, respectively, with their reliance on Doe's GID diagnosis and her "transgender status."
>
> (10)

Such instances explain why, with regard to choosing whether to base a claim on identity or on conduct,

> ... in cases that could be articulated either way, transgender rights advocates often rely on more seemingly fixed categories such as transgender or gender identity than on concepts apparently less anchored to identity categories, such as gender expression.
>
> (13)

Currah noted how, in the US and UK, this eventually meant that basing equality claims on what one chooses to do, or how one behaves, rather than how one is defined, became non-existent (14). Choice based subjectivity was seen as unreal compared to essence based subjectivity. According to Flynn, this essentialised definition of gendered being actually conflicted with the US constitution, which focuses upon individual freedom of choice,

> The determination of legal sex should be considered within the context of our constitutional values – values that reflect a deep suspicion of governmental intrusion on individual rights. ... the right to self-determination of

sexual identity. ... would attempt not only to reclaim a rights-protecting view of the Constitution but also envisions a world free of our current investment in policing a boundary between (or among) the sexes.

(2006:34)

Contradicting the resort to identity-based claims in courts of the 2000s US, in supporting the potential for choice in representation of sexual subjectivity in courtroom situations, Flynn argued that acceptance of gender representations to indicate legal sex would be simpler than the court having to determine the legal sex of a person (Flynn, 2006:35).[9] Such representations come from the people who actually experience different types of gender variance.

In addressing self-representations and self-empowerment, Gloria Steinem considered that, *'The greatest gift we can give one another is the power to make a choice. The power to choose is even more important than the choices we make'* (1995:xxvi). However, as noted previously, Gilligan theorised that women had become used to an abdication of choice deriving from their upbringing which told them not to rock the social boat by venturing opinions of their own, *'The strategies of withholding and denial that women have employed in the politics of sexual relations appear similar to their evasion or withholding of judgment in the moral realm'* (Gilligan, 1982:68).

Many trans people displayed a similar kind of deference to masculine authority when presenting for reassignment treatment in the 1950s to 80s, as argued by Sandy Stone (1991). Gilligan discovered that her female research participants could only make a move towards maturity when realizing they could choose to care for themselves as well as for others, and that this choice would often actually increase their ability to care for others,

... in order to care for another, one must first be able to care responsibly for oneself.

(Gilligan, 1982:76)

Care then becomes a universal injunction, a self-chosen ethic which, freed from its conventional interpretation, leads to a recasting of the dilemma in a way that allows the assumption of responsibility for choice.

(90)

Choice seemed to be absent as a significant aspect of early life for Rebecca Walker, after the advent of chronological second wave feminism. Walker narrated growing up with a code of feminist living that stifled the life out of any feminist spontaneity and critical self-insight (1995:xxix–xxx). She described how second wave feminists' collaboration in building up a prescriptive model of feminism led to the image of a formidable ideal that was impossible to live up to in reality. Feminists of Walker's generation came to feel anxious about living up to this model and Walker didn't want to 'pass' as an identikit feminist.

Similar to Walker, at college, Kristina Sheryl Wong (2003) felt constricted by the demands of a seemingly prescriptive feminist lifestyle. This led Wong to conclude that support for genuine self-expression should be a central tenet of third wave feminism. In *Catching a Wave* she remarked that, '*Third wave feminism is about embracing individual experience and making personal stories political*' (2003:295). She noted that prescriptive feminism was particularly severe for women from social groupings other than the white middle class because the philosophical second wave had the power to define feminist agendas in much of the late twentieth century.

Kimana from the *Transstudy* related a similar feeling of social suffocation to Walker and Wong when trying to satisfy the societal values that pertained to her post-reassignment gender role, '*One of the most difficult aspects of my transition has truuly been the dominant society's "moral values" that they try so hard to force on others*' (Jan 11th, 2007, in <What was the most difficult aspect of your transition?>).

Astrid Henry hinted at the importance of choice in becoming feminist (2004:7). Like Walker and Wong, she considered that if feminism is seen as the birth right of modern women, something inherited from their feminist 'mothers', feminism then becomes an essential and inevitable feature,[10] rather than a passionate choice. Yet, those whose subjectivities have 'Othered' them from feminism have often made it a passionate choice. This was true for those women of colour who carried out feminist activities while not feeling included in named feminism. Nikki Sullivan pointed out that '*... the political potential of a practice that is not seemingly self-consciously undertaken for transgressive purposes*' (2006:556) can still have political potential, as it did for those women of colour. The conscious choice of such a practice, rather than its association with certain subjectivities, seems to have potential that is more political since it is driven by passionate intent. A passionate feminist subjectivity would derive from choice of feminism as a genre and from a genre of subjectivity, rather than from feminism as a metanarrative and as linked to biological sex.

The choice to self-define was defended by participant Alyssa, for instance in <How are we perceived?>, Dec 16th, 2005, '*... I do mind being classed as "trans" but such is inevitable at this stage in my transition, I much prefer and always will prefer to be known as a Woman and not trans.*' This choice was also supported by Sadie in <Male=man, female=woman?>,

> I will normally go by how someone presents themselves: if they present as distinctly one gender, I would treat them as such. ... If someone tells me that they are not the same sex as they appear then I would also accept that at face value.
>
> (Mar 21st, 2005)

Kimana presented her alternatively cultured perspective on gender to suggest that society can still function when choice can mean choice of which gender to actually possess, involving a process of finding oneself through gender, and when this gender is not perceived as inferior to gender as natal-given or essential,

> Another historical/cultural lesson ... maybe two. Prior to the White people coming to the Americas, with their notions of male and female roles, we had no defined gender roles as such. Granted there were Winkte and Wioptula, but they were accept as personal preferences of the individuals involved.
> (Kimana Nov 25th, 2005, in <Omnisexual, bisexual, trisexual>)

Whittle and Turner pointed out that,

> ... the Gender Recognition Act offers those transsexual people who do identify as men or women, the right to be legally recognised as such even if one is a woman with a penis or a man with a vagina.
> (2007:8.8)

This meant that the individual could be liberated from the link of sexual subjectivity to biology, if they so desired. The gender of transition would be still have to be man or woman, but biology could be ambiguous and sexuality could be hetero or homosexual for any transitioning individual. In this way, the GRA 2004 provided some measure of legal protection from the effects of attributed gender labelling that stigmatise signs of gender variance. In addressing stigmatisation caused by labelling, Vivien Burr considered that,

> Such a recognition [of stigmatization] can be beneficial in itself, by relocating problems away from an intra-psychic domain and into a societal one. For example, 'depression' is a term which locates problems within the internal psychology of the individual. ... But in re-casting the problem at a social level rather than at the level of the individual a different analysis emerges. Such an analysis may suggest that the woman sees herself as oppressed rather than depressed.
> (2003:122)

Assessing people's personal interpretations in this way will make their choices in self-representation much easier to understand and will make it possible to understand that society can be dysphoric (having dysphoria), in imposing gender upon people, rather than it always being the transitioning individual who is classed as dysphoric.

Participant Raelene noted that the British NHS may be starting to offer services more conducive with a vision of the patient as an individual capable of making valid choices rather than as a pathology,

> The Department of Health has today published the following Press Release:

## Open and evolving narratives 173

> People with mental health problems will have more choice over their treatment under new guidance published by the Department of Health today.
>
> More choice in mental health will give people:
>
> Power to choose their own path through services and keep control over their lives; Preferences to choose how, when, where and what treatments they receive; Personalised services organised around their lifestyles.
> (Raelene Nov 6th, 2006, in <What should a modern Real Life Experience involve?>)

Choices in the management of their own gender transition for trans people are hypothetically part of this new choice panoply, but with very few Gender Identity Clinics, and, in the UK, the major clinic operating alongside the centre of gender reassignment surgeries in London, this is currently unlikely in practice.

### 7.4 'A movement of their own'?

> Both [Lib Dem MP Lynne Featherstone and Equality Minister Maria Eagle] felt that the trans community have a hard time, coming in for more discrimination than other minorities. Ms Eagle commented that the "learning disabled and trans individuals tend to suffer more overt prejudice from the rest of society than other groups at present". ... Both, in slightly different ways, put this down to the fact that the trans community were less well organised, less coherent in their demands than other minority groups.
> (Fae, 16 April 2010)

Within the trans community and amongst contemporary feminists, there has been discussion addressing the value of, and the existence of, movements that are specific to each faction, and the right to choose whether to belong to such movements. Challenges to the exact nature or existence of such movements have been made within each faction. For instance, *Transstudy* participant Sadie suggested that there was a trans *community* rather than a trans *movement*,

> I'd agree with Clarette and the [Monica] one here – yes there is a transgender community, in the same way as there is a community of foreign people in most cities. We all have a vaguely common background and so sometimes talk to each other because of it. There are some movements within the community but there is no 'transgender movement' in it's own right ...
> (Jul 12th, 2005, in <Transgender Movement?>)

Feminism has engendered heated debate over the existence of a possible third wave feminist movement. For example, Gillis and Munford seem to conflate third wave feminism with postfeminism when speculating that the third wave as a movement is a '... *competitive generational model [that] does not allow for a collective memory of female-based thought, empowerment and activism*' (2004:176). They also question the application of the wave metaphor to the first and second waves, as well as to the third, challenging the view of them as movements. They suggested that naming waves is a label too far and that 'feminism' itself is label enough to define what 'feminists' are all about and are trying to do. They also argued that, '*Feminism* – ... – *needs to be multiple, various and polyphonous* ...' (4). Polly Toynbee challenged the idea that there had been any second feminist wave or movement at all (6 June 2002), again challenging the enclosure of feminism into time-bound chunks.

However, the wave metaphor may be useful as a way to describe feminists of certain generations as formed both from their own chronological wave but from possibly differing philosophical waves, waves that may differ from each other in fundamental ways. As Henry described, waves as metaphorical sea waves emphasise both continuity and discontinuity (2004:24); although waves are significantly formed from what preceded, each new wave will make progress beyond those previous waves and so will change the nature of the feminist 'shore line'.

In a similar way to Toynbee, Henry highlighted the fact that we cannot really identify discreet feminist waves by affixing them with chronological start and finish time slots since feminism carried on before, between and after the temporal time slots allocated to these waves (20). Although not chronologically definable, a newly identified and inclusive philosophical wave could assist feminists and trans people to position themselves as having a freshly formed standpoint epistemology, needing to be identified as both originating from but different to other philosophical waves. The new wave could simply be entitled, 'third wave', as well as 'third wave feminist', in order to encompass other inclusive social philosophies and to create a movement of open membership.

Some feminists argue that 'third wave' should indicate a whole new variety of feminism if it is worthy of a new name but could it not just as validly indicate a new feminist impetus? Perhaps the existence of a third wave may be justified if it can simply act as a motivational device, which it may well do in contrast to just being called feminism. Helen Charles thinks that, '*To invent or adopt terminology to suit a proposed development is to trigger a development per se*' (1997:291) but that the constant changing of terms can hinder the motivation to develop a consistent movement.

Walker and Wong seemed to thirst for such motivation, as described in section 3 above. Literary historian Jane Spencer seemed to realise the value of such a jump start to feminist philosophy, '... *talking and writing about third wave feminism is wholly beneficial, fostering a recovering sense of feminist urgency*' (2004:12). While discussing Cathryn Bailey's addressing of the problem of feminist inter-wave conflict, Jacqueline Zita found support for the christening of a new wave in order to combat silencing from conservative discourse,

While Bailey is critical of this historical representation and finds it difficult to justify, by the criteria of age, decade, or content, the existence of a qualitively new 3$^{rd}$ wave, she nonetheless favours the pragmatic need to articulate 3$^{rd}$ wave feminisms against neo-conservative attempts to extinguish feminist consciousness and disassemble all traces of its former collectives.
(Summer 1997:2)

Ednie Kaeh Garrison saw value in the naming of third wave feminism as a way to distinguish it from postfeminism, '*While the "third wave" may not be a "wave" of feminism in the sense assumed by social movement scholars, the strategic invocation of the name as "political resistance" to the vocabulary of postfeminism is significant*' (Garrison, 2005:249).

Addressing the compartmentalisation of feminism, Gillis and Munford hypothesised that, '*The wave paradigm not only ensures that each generation must "reinvent the wheel" but also lends power to backlash politics and rhetoric*' (2004:177). For instance, Gloria Steinem complained that some third wave philosophising makes her, '*... feel like a sitting dog being told to sit* (1995: xxii)', pointing out that she and several other second wavers have been living out what are now classed as third wave feminist lifestyles and ethics for years. However, perhaps it is better to reinvent the wheel to some extent than to be left with no wheels at all in an era of waning feminist philosophy and activism. Successful feminism risks being confused with the pyrrhic victory of women's inclusion into masculinist capitalism. By reconstructing the wheel, third wave feminism seems to have generated enough heated debate to jump start feminists into considering what feminism was, is, what it could be, and where it is going.

Baumgardner and Richards detected a comparison of the third wave to the rebelling daughters of Grrrl and Girlie cultures (Gillis and Munford, 2004:176). However, rehabilitating the image of the mother from negative to positive, and the daughter from infantile to mature, has been part of the project of philosophical third wave feminists involved with 'maternal relations'. Henry stated that, '*Handed to us at birth, feminism no longer requires the active identification that it once did*' (2004:40), suggesting, similarly to Walker and Wong, that contemporary women and feminists have feminism handed to them on a plate. However, many of those who wish to identify with feminism may still be 'Othered' from this movement, just like women of colour were 'Othered' from the second feminist wave. These 'Othered' people, including many trans people, may wish to take a break from non-feminism by join an inclusive feminism and/or third wave because of their experiences of exclusion, rather than having to create a feminism/wave/movement of their own.

If included into the third wave feminist fold, trans people may, in fact, have a movement of their own to share in return, despite what some *Transstudy* participants have thought. Trans man Alex Whinnom described how, '*It wasn't until 1992, when Press for Change was founded, that the climate seemed right for collective political activism*',[11] seeming to remark on a movement whose time had come. Whittle referred to a blossoming 'trans community' in *Respect and Equality* and expanded this to explain how trans people have become their own theoretical community (2002a:51, 52, 71). It would seem that this new community, which because of its passion, activism and support would seem to indicate a movement, formed a philosophical alliance of people oppressed too much by universalising metanarratives, for instance of law, medicine and separatist feminism, to wish to form its own dictatorial narrative. It was also an alliance wishing to distance itself from membership requiring biological or social status to one based upon relations of inclusive difference.

Arguments for and against naming trans and feminist movements have addressed the exclusionary practice that a named movement can evoke,

> Some third-wave feminists prefer not to call themselves feminists, as the word feminist can be misinterpreted as insensitive to the fluid notion of gender and the potential oppressions inherent in all gender roles, or perhaps misconstrued as exclusive or elitist by critics. Others have kept and redefined the term to include these ideas.[12]

Similarly, Currah found indications, in the work of fellow trans theorists, of how internecine conflict might build up between gendered minorities if they coalesced into movements. For instance, Patrick Califa theorised that second wave type separation could come to blight the 'transgender movement' if it sought to focus on identity issues, and Rikki Wichins warned that a transgender movement that didn't '... *interrogate the fact of its own existence*' would repeat the normalising effects of other initially well-meaning social movements (Currah, 2006:5). Currah warned that consolidation into a movement could engender either, '... *a strategic and pragmatic point of reference or an erasure of the very different ways gender crossing is lived and experienced* ...' (5). For Currah, the transgender movement is dissoluble and can therefore engender the potential for escape from imposed gender 'Othering',

> ... the ultimate goal of transgender rights does not seem to be to contain gender nonconforming identities and practices within slightly expanded yet still-normative gender constructions and arrangements. ... The transgender rights movement might be described as an identity politics movement that seeks the dissolution of the very category under which it is organised.
>
> (2006:24)

Nevertheless, some gender variant people may wish to retain the hard-won naming of gendered or philosophical categories that they have carefully built up. If movements are based upon choice, then such people should feel comfortable to express or not to express their gendering while still belonging to a named gender variant movement.

Another argument against joining a category based movement included one suggested by *Transstudy* participants expressing the dangers of becoming associated with a social movement. They suggested that this can mark the individual out as a 'tall poppy', recalling the risks of political subjectivity outlined in Chapter 6, '*I guess that Alison's introduction to this topic thread indicates the dangers of deliberately or casually choosing to be a 'tall poppy' or to stick one's head above the parapet in a battle*' (The Author Nov 21st, 2006, in < Some thoughts on Trans Acceptance and Freedom >).

While acknowledging the dangers of publicising one's trans subjectivity, Clarette addressed a potential need for transgender to 'come out' as a movement in order to give a name and a voice to trans people's experiences via the exchange of verbal and written narrative,

> I've seen various arguments against publicity in various places. But if societies can become aware, then somewhere someone (or more than one) might be able to grow knowing that they are not alone in wondering what's wrong with them, and might be able to work out (even in the face of opposition) sooner that maybe it's not wrong at all. That, in my opinion, is the primary reason to have a transgender movement in the first place.
>
> (Clarette Nov 7th, 2005, in <What advice to a Newbie>)

This mirrors the argument put forward in Chapter 6 where a 'politics of naming' engenders out and proud subjectivity, where epiphanies of self-realisation are assisted by shared narratives. Sometimes, the need for a movement is a burning desire initiated by unbearable conditions. Tara Godvin ventured that the death of Brandon Teena initiated a trans based movement,

> Ten years ago, a handsome, brown-haired 21-year-old named Brandon Teena was raped and later murdered by two men after they discovered he wasn't born a man. ... The New Year's Eve tragedy in rural southeastern Nebraska inspired the award-winning 1999 film, "Boys Don't Cry". It also touched off a movement in the transgendered community. ... In the days after Teena was killed, a new generation of activists banded together to demand greater civil rights protections. Ten years later, 65 municipalities and states have hate crime laws that specifically include transgendered people, according to the Transgender Law Policy Institute.
>
> (Monday 29 December 2003)

## 7.5 Conclusion

Section one, on the subject of 'voice', suggested that the rise of the trans narrative has challenged the silent and secret hegemony between medical or legal specialist and client, a hegemony previously weighted in favour of the specialist's voice. However, both varieties of specialist still tend to work within the parameters of gender dualising discourse. This discourse derived from the time when April Ashley's lack of voice led to her, and subsequently other trans people, being treated as women have in much of industrial Western history: as passive and mute objects of patriarchs' determinations.

Entry into a certain type of gendered identity, for instance that required for admittance to gender reassignment, can often only occur for those people identifying with, and being identified with, the 'language' of the in-group, for instance, medical, legal, academic or gendered vernacular. Louis Althusser labelled this as a summoning process he called interpellation or hailing (1971). Those excluded from hailing hear the clarion call of, 'hey, not you' directed their way. This reverse hailing can paradoxically lead to the excluded forming 'different' social voices and 'views from somewhere', that can help them surface from silent and secret exclusion.

Although those excluded from hailing can find themselves apparently silenced, Malhotra and Rowe have, in their anthology, presented several takes on the idea of silence as empowering. Silenced voices may be heard via the channels of different media, by recognising and negotiating one's position in communication, by modesty in communication and via attempts to gender-swap in communication.

As discussed in section two on the subject of 'passing', transitioning people have to construct gender appearance and roles that so easily become 'Other' to heteronormative in the eye of the perceiver. People whose appearance falls outside of the heteronormative schema will incur suspicion from people in general and from regulatory discourses such as medicine and the law. Heteronormative discourse dictates that women and men must look uniformly different to each other and society will sanction those who fall outside of heteronormative parameters. During the course of passing as heteronormative, people who transition can find that they 'lose themselves' and their wealth of gendered experience through denial of their pre-transition history.

Section three, on 'choice', began by describing how Butler theorised that a negative 'politics of naming' labels gender variant people as 'Other' before consideration of their needs for physical and social adjustment. She suggested that treating the transitioning person as a client who can choose their subjectivity would reduce pathologisation for both transitioning and non-transitioning gender variant people. Diagnosis based in pathology engenders a requirement for transitioning people to pass into a gendered schema in order to be recuperated into heteronormativity. Individually diagnosed pathology means that it is always the individual, rather than society, who is viewed as pathological.

Currah explained how lack of official diagnosis left some legal subjects without legal protection based on definitional standing. Basing claims on what one chooses to do or be became inadmissible in legal procedure. However, philosophical third wave feminists suggested that the power to choose to represent as a gendering is more important, and can provide a more accurate result, than having an imposed definition of gender.[13]

*Transsstudy* participants supported the right to self-define, to choose to present a gender or not, but generally did not support the idea that the gender one has can be chosen. Presenting gender as a feature that can be chosen would deny what some participants saw as the inherent nature of their gendered identity and would lead to difficulty in persuading medical and legal practitioners that their gender is genuine and permanent. Nevertheless, a reliance on an individual's self-insight into their own gendering would seem invaluable when a true aetiology of gendered essence is still in fact unavailable, and perhaps not really desirable if it would work to eliminate choice, choice that could actually affect any discovered aetiology, if over a long period of time.

'Movement' was the key theme in section four where it was suggested that the wave metaphor can be adopted to show how feminism can be recycled in order to draw from the best parts of previous feminisms in order to constitute a new evolved form. It would not just be an exercise in differentiating a new wave from old waves for originality's sake. The 'movement of movement' key feature of 'waves' is very akin to the concept of subjectivity because these movements are not seen as superior to others and are not taken to be the end word in social development. The third wave should be socially constructed through dialogic negotiation with a constituency of membership through choice. Narratives from Clarette aligned with such representations of the third wave by providing an interpretation of feminism as organic in essence, in the sense of an evolving and living body. Hir vision also involved an inclusive idea of who could be feminism's constituents.

*Transsstudy* participants tended not to perceive the existence of any trans movement, or to wish for the existence of one. Being in such a movement would for them mark them as tall poppies when they wished to 'pass' into conventional society. However, political subjectivity or membership of a movement would seem to provide the best long-term option for all gender variant people by providing them with a name and a voice that will allow them and their experiences to emerge from silence and secrecy.

The first two sections of Chapter 8 discuss how closed and static views of gender variance lead to social exclusion. The second two sections discuss how to dismantle these views.

## Notes

1 Anne Bolin found that psychiatric consultants had an expectation that clients seeking reassignment treatments would promise (post-operative) heterosexuality (Namaste, 1996:193). Using an analysis of historical contexts, Bolin discovered that, just like people not seeking reassignment, these subjects actually possessed a range of personal sexualities. Gender was also conflated with heterosexuality in the legal case of the New Zealand case of Attorney-General v Otahuhu Family Court as explained by Sharpe (2006).
2 Not so much for trans people 'voice coached' into both dualised genderings.
3 Noted in reference to the reversed discourse of homosexuality by Foucault (1998 [1978]:101).

4 The Modest Witness resembles the expert applying weak objectivity, as described by Harding (1991).
5 According to Jane Ussher, to be a woman is to be classed as the psychic inferior of men, *'"Madness" acts as a signifier which positions women as ill, as outside, as pathological, as somehow second rate – the second sex'* (Ussher, 1991:11).
6 In this case within the community of the gender oppressed.
7 See Astrid Henry (2004:50).
8 For instance, in this section it was noted that the dualism of sex was upheld as necessary to marriage in John AC Forbes-Sempill v The Hon. Ewan Forbes-Sempill, and was definable by biological evidence.
9 There have been many examples of court confusion when determining sex for the purposes of establishing sexual subjectivity, as discussed in Chapter 4 and in this section and the next.
10 In Chapter 2 it was seen how Janice Raymond conflated the possession of XX chromosomes with feminist subjectivity (1979:135).
11 From http://www.pfc.org.uk/node/30.
12 From http://en.wikipedia.org/wiki/Third-wave_feminism.
13 For instance, Baumgardner and Richards (2000:24) and Gloria Steinem (1995:xxvi).

# 8 Exclusion to inclusion
## Postdifference for 'Others'

**Introduction**

Section themes in the previous two chapters have pointed to the need for compatible trans and feminist factions to be inclusive of subjective difference. Could it be that third wave thinkers, such as some feminists and some trans people are characteristically open to social inclusion for diverse social subjectivities? [B]ell hooks warned of the danger of movements based on single identity-type membership in movements or factions, and considered that the, '... *feminist movement, like other radical movements in our society, suffers when individual concerns and priorities are the only reason for participation*' (1984:62).

This was also an issue addressed by Audre Lorde who recommended that hierarchies and dualisms be challenged by looking at how social subjectivities intersect and can support or oppress each other (1984:48). Irene Diamond and Lee Quinby also aligned with an inclusive feminist ethos when considering that, '*For [Jana] Sawicki,* [1] *difference is a resource that helps us multiply sources of resistance*' (1988:xix), suggesting that inclusive feminism nurtures strength through diversity. Perhaps the third wave could be a multi-subjectivity and multi-issue based feminist/trans wave, while critically examining different subjectivities and theories that apply for inclusion into the feminist/trans landscape.

A wish for connection with real lives rather than with stereotyped identities matches with the tenets of 'solidarity', recommended by hooks as a postmodern concept of philosophical kindred. Solidarity connects to the way that viewing subjectivity as genre and genealogy can liberate the characteristically stifling mores of identity (rather than subjectivity) politics. A passage of text by participant Clarette suggested that tolerance of others lessens rather than increases the challenge to our personal subjectivities, '*More importantly still, individuality has become widespread. What someone else does is no longer such a challenge to our personal identities. Also known as tolerance ... though not yet universal*' (Clarette Jun 10th, 2005, in <gender presentation then and now>).

This chapter examines issues affecting the acceptance of subjective difference and how such difference can work to the benefit of third wave feminist and transgender factions.

## 8.1 Social cleansing

Leslie Feinberg's account of socially sanctioned purges of trans identity and expression in *Transgender Warriors* highlighted a kind of social cleansing, to paraphrase the expression 'ethnic cleansing', that persistently features in historical accounts of trans people in society (1996:37). At various stages in human history, heteronormativity initiated the attempt to eliminate certain trans subjectivities en masse, once what it is to be a man and a woman had been socially defined.[2] This was not usually murder, but involved the eradication of gender variant people of varying kinds, identified by those in advantageous positions in social power relations, from social life.

Exclusion and intimidation of gender variance, in some culture or another, is probably as old as human society and often appears in narrative form, for instance in the account of beleaguered King Sardanapalus of mythical Ancient Greece. Sardanapalus' enemies hounded him for a period of years for cross-dressing (even though, or perhaps because, it was carried out within the confines of his palace) (Bullough and Bullough, 1993).

In the eighteenth and nineteenth century Western world, such persecution has been carried out subtly via the requirements, by medical and legal gatekeepers, for the trans individual to fall in line with heteronormative expression, by undergoing transition with an expectation of bodily reassignment. This expectation has included the demand for a set period of Real Life Experience to demonstrate compliance with schemata of heteronormative gender. There has, so far, been no RLE or official recognition for non-heteronormative gender variance. The GRA 2004 and EA 2010 recognise transition as more of a social process than previous legislation,[3] but only as a process towards heteronormativity.

Social groups will often implement social cleansing to police any subjective variance in their midst, by using ridicule, violence or by subtly denying access to social environments such as community, family, work and leisure. Such processes occur when, according to sociologist Stanley Cohen, society identifies what it sees as a deviant or 'folk devil',

> An initial act of deviance, or normative diversity, (for example, in dress) is defined as being worthy of attention and is responded to punitively. The deviant or group of deviants is segregated or isolated and this operates to alienate them from conventional society.
>
> (2011[1972]:11)

The way that societal reaction, and the mass media particularly, segregate the deviant and bipolarize folk devils from the rest of the community, is a stronger basis [than perceptions based upon age difference] for attitude formation.

(74)

Participant Lysandra, when describing her experiences at work, narratively recounted such a process,

> My transgender experience is not respected in my workplace. It has been clearly communciated to me that I'll be tolerated professionally, but not respected. I am often excluded from work related social activities due to my transgendered status. There are no business lunches or after work invitations to the pub.
> (Lysandra Mar 7th, 2005, in <respected in your workplace>)

Whether Lysandra was transgendered, trans or transitioned, colleagues perceived her as different from heteronormative and therefore worthy of exclusion. The trans person ousted from society becomes like many immigrants or refugees; unable to find a social home and is seen as a dark and sinister foreigner, or social 'monster', who just serves to satisfy people's stereotypes. A sense of not belonging accompanies an expectation that life will have to change dramatically every so often in order to escape from alienation and oppression.[4]

Monica narrated an incident of a trans person being forcibly cleansed out of the work situation,

> A friend of mine ... was a mental nurse caring for children with severe disabilitites and behaviour problems. She expected her employers, the [...] Hospital, would be at least understanding. In fact, her all female colleagues were very supportive, but her employer virtually put her under house arrest in her tied flat. ... Finally, she was hounded out of her job and never practiced in nursing ever again, despite having skills that were to say the least special. But that was the seventies.
> (Monica Aug 27th, 2006, in <What should a modern Real Life Experience involve?>)

A similar situation reached the court environment, which at least meant that the victim gained visibility and voice as someone oppressed, something that would seem not to happen in most instances of trans oppression.[5] 'X' was a teacher in Brighton who suddenly found the flow of job offers from employment agencies drying up with no explanation.[6] Together with a former co-ordinator of Brighton's LGBT Community Safety Forum, she found that a reference revealing her trans history from a Brighton Council Manager had been supplied to her regular employment agency. Details of this reference had in turn been distributed to other agencies. Council and Employment Agency workers consequently obeyed hints from those in influential positions to disregard X's applications for work. It was direct discrimination of a surreptitious kind orchestrated by a self-purportedly LGBT-friendly Council.

Sometimes, and nearly always at some point in each trans person's life, the trans person will contribute to the policing of their own trans subjectivity by purging or hiding any trace of their own gender variance,

> I was married for twenty plus years, now with a 26 yr old daughter, yet in all that time my "ex" never knew anything about my predilection for dressing as a woman. I went to considerable lengths to hide everything. At one point in time I was the CEO of a quite sizable IT company, yet there I was busy hiding my activities like some disobedient child afraid of getting caught.
> 
> (Raelene Nov 8th, 2005, in <What advice to a Newbie>)

Whittle wondered why ostracisation is still on-going for trans people, often really for those *perceived* to be trans (Whittle, 2002a:38–39).[7] A lack of a cohesive and large-scale trans movement may be partly to blame. Oppression may be easy to get away with since establishing that a victim is trans is not as straightforward as it is for many social subjectivities. Identifying who is and is not trans has been a burden for trans people and, to be fair, the law from before *Corbett* to the EA 2010, but is still necessary for the recognition of trans people as a protected category. Identification of who is and is not gender variant has yet to be fully addressed, significantly because self-representations of gender variance are still largely held in suspicion by mainstream, and even trans and feminist, society.

As Christine Burns described, exclusion resulting from transition, especially if a newly transitioning person begins to appear in their preferred gender, can be very sudden for the trans person and the physical reassignment they rely upon to provide them with a hetero-congruent gendered appearance can take years,

> For me the shock was to loose almost every shred of my security all those years ago when I let people know my transsexual background and took the steps to do something about it. I lost practically every shred of security overnight and learned what it feels like to be an outsider.
> 
> (Reported by Dean, 2 June 2007)

It is not surprising that many trans and gender variant people seek to 'pass' into heteronormativity when faced with this kind of social alienation. This predicament has been ameliorated to some extent in the UK with the introduction of the EA 2010, which provides legal protection against direct discrimination for trans people, particularly important for those lacking immediate access to means of transition and for those who find it particularly difficult to pass as heteronormative.[8] However, this protection almost always comes after the horses of discrimination or harassment have bolted out of the social stable.

## 8.2 Immigrants and refugees

In the <Immigrants and Refugees?> and <Trans people and their cultural 'home'> *Transstudy* topic threads, a series of metaphors including 'immigrants', 'refugees', 'colonisers', 'emancipated slaves' and 'expatriates' were discussed by participants as to their suitability in describing the social situation of trans people. Monica coined the term, 'political defector' to describe her own 'defection' to a preferred gendered subjectivity. In <Types of Trans person> it can be seen that she would wish this subjectivity to eventually change into acceptance as a naturalised citizen in the gendered 'land' of her choice. Sadie provided yet another metaphor for trans subjectivity, '*Ex-pat syndrome: constantly wondering who of your friends is going to break next and go home – you maybe? Well, it would explain the likes of Charles Kane I guess*'[9] (Sadie Apr 13th, 2005, in <Types of Trans person>).

Kimana might be interpreted as being a 'refugee' in her own 'country', both because of her ethnicity and because of her trans subjectivity. Her narratives bring to mind the persecution portrayed by Leslie Feinberg in *Stone Butch Blues* in her protagonist's attempts to find a spiritual and physical 'home' away from her tormentors (Prosser, 1998). All *Transstudy* participants seem to have engaged in a search for a gendered 'home' that would give them full status as citizens in the gendered community.

Judith Halberstam (1998) pointed out that even though trans men cannot (as yet) achieve a fully reassigned body, it doesn't mean that they cannot or should not find a legitimate 'home' in their preferred gender.[10] Halberstam suggested that all people strive to seek a gendered 'home'. In this way s/he introduced a consideration of the usefulness of metaphors of travel and border crossings, notably also applied by Gloria Anzaldúa in *Borderlands/La Frontera* (1987[1999]), as a way to identify gender variance and transition. Here, the transitioning person, just like all other gendered people, does not change totally and suddenly but rather embarks on a journey of self-discovery. Halberstam noted that,

> In Chicano/a studies and postcolonial studies in particular, the politics of migration have been fiercely debated, and what has emerged is a careful refusal of the dialectic of home and border.
>
> (1998:170)

This seems to mean refusal of the notion of home as identifiable as being on one side of a border or another. Those in advantageous power positions often assign definitions of what is gendered 'home' and what is gendered 'border'. We could also ask who it is who has the power to migrate, travel, to set up a new gendered 'home' and to keep it running, and we can wonder, '... *who ... can afford to stay home*' (173).

Monica further developed the metaphor of trans people as 'immigrants' in the <Can feminism include input from and inclusion for born males?> topic thread,

> I beleive trans women experience a similar kind of treatment from feminists as that received by immigrants to Britain from the host population. ... To some British people the immigrant is one of his country's more enterprising individuals who may have valuable skills or qualifications and who wishes to throw in his lot with us, sink or swim, and is therefore one of our fellows. ... Other British people don't even want to hear what he has to offer: he is just another sponging foreigner, who is here to exploit our society and who should be sent home on the next plane. ... As an extreme example, read Germaine Greer's 'The Whole Woman', in particular the chapter called 'Pantomime Dames'.
>
> (Monica Mar 17th, 2005)

Monica aptly describes how trans people as immigrants offer a valuable 'view from somewhere' that benefits the host population, despite the fiercely parochial views of separatists like Greer. Even though trans people may do all they can to become naturalised citizens of their chosen gendered 'land', they may (still) retain the tag of outsider because of their different appearance and history of difference.

Sympathetic legislation will greatly facilitate access to the position of 'naturalised citizen'. However, in commenting upon The Sex Discrimination (Amendment of Legislation) Regulations 2008, Angela Clayton mentioned that,

> Press for Change believe that the Government has missed an opportunity to level up the protections afforded for trans people. Instead, once again, they have chosen to do the minimum required by European Law and making the most restrictive interpretation of what they can do within the enabling legislation.
>
> (Clayton, 8 December 2007)

Doing the minimum required by European Law has been a consistent feature of British law's approach to trans subjectivity, marking out its trans policy as one of maintaining subjective 'border check points'. This has also been the case even in the EA 2010 where trans people remain linked to the notion of 'gender reassignment' and their association with medical pathology is upheld, as is the expectation that they be rehabilitated into heteronormativity. The GRA 2004 has also featured 'doing the minimum required', in which, as Whittle commented, '*It appears to still be lawful to indirectly discriminate against transsexual people (even with a Gender Recognition Certificate) who are not, "intending to undergo, undergoing or have undergone gender reassignment"*' (Whittle et al., 20 December 2006:79).

This may be ameliorated to some extent by the new access to gender recognition proposals, set out by Women and Equalities Minister Justine Greening (Savage, 2017). People will not have to gain a doctor's report to officially transition and amend their birth certificates. A consultation on the

GRA 2004 is to be produced in late 2017 which will examine the possibility of removing the requirement for a medical diagnosis of gender dysphoria before a transitioning person can apply for gender recognition. There will also be an attempt to speed up the official legal and medical transition process. An earlier *Guardian* article stated that a key recommendation from a 2016 parliamentary committee report, 'was to shift the gender registration process away from "medicalised" questions to "self-declaration"' (Press Association, 2016), marking a move towards acknowledging the reality of trans people's self-representations.

The distinction between the 'real' transitioning person and the 'unreal' gender variant person marks the refuge taken by those who want to operate just within the confines of the law, but no further, when not wishing to treat gender variant people as fully included gendered citizens. An ethics of care approach to trans inclusion would target this kind of discrimination by focusing on individual circumstances. Recognising that there can be 'social dysphoria', as well as gender dysphoria would act as a narrative reversal of pointing the finger of blame.[11] If it is society that is ill, or deviant, then it should be recognised as such. Adherents to this idea must bear in mind that being trans often does involve mental distress but it seems that this distress may well initially derive not from disease but from unaccepted subjective difference. This perspective on gender dysphoria is supported in the World Professional Association for Transgender Health (WPATH) Standards of Care (7th Version, 2011:23), where it is recommended that, '*Mental health professionals assess clients' gender dysphoria in the context of an evaluation of their psychosocial adjustment …*', rather than purely searching for the identification of individual pathology.

As many have noted, from the work of Thomas Szaz in the 1960s[12] to Lawrence Stevens,[13] difference is conflated with pathology in a separatist heteronormative society. As a way of addressing this, the international *Stop Trans Psychopathologisation Campaign* lobbies for removal of the categories 'gender dysphoria' and 'gender identity disorders' from the DSM and ICD mental diagnosis manuals, as well as providing more general information, networking and lobbying activities. The campaign's motto is, '*Trans identities are not a disease*' (ILGA, 2012).

Monica claimed, as do many other trans people, that her type of difference was present at birth rather than being an acquired disease or being a result of social construction, stating,

> Quote: Kate Bornstein has described trans as 'gender euphoria' to lessen its association with illness.
>
> This is a ridiculous, not to say a stupid assertion. The experience of being transsexual is not 'euphoric'. On the contrary it is ABSOLUTE TORMENT. One is indeed ill, by reason of being in severe mental distress, but as the result of some congenital cause rather than the result of any actual disease process.
>
> (Jun 2nd, 2006, in <Title of the Transstudy>)

188  *Exclusion to inclusion*

Monica's description might support the adopting of the term, 'body dysphoria', rather than 'gender dysphoria' or 'social dysphoria', in order to describe the suffering that transitioning trans people undergo.[14] Social dysphoria stemming from dysfunctional society undoubtedly poses problems for those who transition.[15] Just as immigrants and refugees are often lumped together in one 'dangerous outsider' category, so is often the case for gender variant people. This process even happens in the courts where primitive ideas about what gender variant subjectivity involves often prevail,

> Hurst ... says that "courts often confuse sex, gender, and sexual orientation, and confuse them in a way that results in denying the rights not only of gays and lesbians, but also of those who do not present themselves or act in a manner traditionally expected of their sex.
> (Hurst, 2007:141, as quoted on Wikipedia by Aconway (see Assorted Authors, 18/02/2008)

From the discussion in this section it seems possible to argue that trans and all gender variant people should be seen as citizens of their gendered 'country' and should not have to apply for special entry to subjectivity via gender transition, unless, perhaps, there are psychological and physical health risks involved and/or unrealistic costs to the general population. Many do need assistance to transition and reassign but should not consequently be treated as alien immigrants.

## 8.3 Maternal relations

Some feminist and womanist commentators have identified maternal relations as an attribute of a utopian third wave feminism.[16] Kristeva's interpretation of the semiotic mode of communication and Gilligan's ethics of care seem to align with this inclusive philosophy. However, this idealistic vision is not realised in many real-life inter-feminist generational relations as lamented by bell hooks who warned that, *'Despite current focus on eliminating racism in feminist movement, there has been little change in the direction of theory and praxis'* (1984:53). [H]ooks saw the remedy for this in 'womanist' communication where the clique of academic conformity is replaced by a community of diversity, which respects the communicative idiosyncrasies of others, rather than producing its own variety of metanarrative and excluding language (1984:56).

Such a community might draw inspiration from, *'... the strength and vitality of women's essential role in neighbourhood and community politics'* noted by Diamond and Quinby as characteristic of the approach to local issues by feminist activists (1988:xvii). Ednie Kaeh Garrison also suggested the importance of local issues or micro-politics but wished for feminists to realise the global effect of such apparently localised matters, *'The perception that suffrage constitutes a national or universal issue, whereas anti-lynching is too specific and localized, speaks directly to the ease with which dominant feminists adopt dominant cultural values ...'* (2005:243).

Micro-political approaches can be distinguished from focus on single functional issues, as criticised in Chapter 4, because micro-political activism is often set within a broader framework or mind-set of challenging the roots of social problems. Maternal relations bode well for multi-issue theory and activism in their connection with breaking down stereotypes, introducing the 'view from somewhere' of the gender variant voice, and in applying womanist modes of communication.

Something like womanist communication is suggested as a feature of woman's conversation by autobiographer Max Wolf Valerio, who acquired special insights into what he saw as the downsides and upsides of this communication. He contrasted the bonding and jocular type of banter that comes as mandatory in some masculine circles (2006:205) with the, '*... verbal articulation of nuances and undercurrents of feeling, being able to analyse and talk freely about my emotions, thoughts, and life situations ...*' (206), characteristic of his time spent growing up as a girl. He speculated that speaking comes more naturally for those brought up as female (208),[17] bringing to mind a comment by Whittle suggesting that trans men may be used to informal organic discussion. This may reveal how those brought up in the female gender role (or who identify with such a role) tend to align more with semiotic communication in the sense of Kristeva's psychological perspective.

Ideas of who can and cannot articulate, and be involved in, maternal relations are complicated when trans subjectivities are taken into account. The author would argue that trans men can adopt them from experience of having grown up in the female gender role and trans women may take them on by adopting the female gender role. For instance, Monica narrated her process of gaining insight into the care burdens put upon women in <Hidden Trans men?> (May 18th, 2006) and Kimana revealed the often-prevalent need for the trans person to build their own 'extended family' of new friends and family, something known as 'Tiospia' in her native community,

> Luckily, I've had a strong support system throughout it [her transition] from my Native community, They have been there when I was ready to rip off heads and use them for bowling balls. ... Heck, my Tiospia has grown by leaps and bounds since those early days.
> (Kimana Aug 9th, 2006, in <Stephen says, 'Help'>)

Trans people often cannot depend upon established and hierarchically organised relations of nuclear or kin-based family so they develop and rely on a relational mode of trans community set up by committed individuals,

> We found that trans people experience many problems at home and in their neighbourhood, with some losing their family support network, their home and friendship circles. Some 45% of respondents reported

family breakdown which was due to their cross gender identity. 37% are excluded from family events and have family members who no longer speak to them because they have transitioned to their acquired gender, and 20% of respondents felt informally excluded from their local community and neighbourhood since their transition.

(Whittle et al., 20 December 2006:s. 2.10)

Issues of inter-generational communication, such as those addressed by semanalysis, ethics of care and womanist writers, also arose in the *Transstudy* threads. For instance, in <Hormone Regimes> Raelene seemed to take up a maternal (caring) approach when advising Alyssa even though this sometimes veered into the paternal (controlling). Narrative exchanges such as those between Raelene and Alyssa bring to mind those developed in debates between feminists from different chronological waves where misunderstandings occur but where knowledge disinherited by masculinist culture is nevertheless passed on via alternative communicative networks and patterns.[18] Participant Ariel suggested that generations of trans women have much to offer each other, '... *I also see first hand how much the older people could teach the youinger ones, and how much the younger ones could learn, if only they listened. And yes, the same applies the other way around*' (Ariel Nov 5th, 2005, in <Trans people and their cultural 'home'>).

This knowledge grapevine, similar to relations within the Tiospia in Kimana's community, can ensure that isolation does not separate trans and feminist people from their social or spiritual community.

## *Semanalysis linked with ethics of care*

The main way of breaking down gendered stereotypes is to interact with people to learn about their individuality, and this can be done via the dialogic methods of semanalysis and ethics of care. Kristeva's ethical outlook and investigative technique of semanalysis (1980[1969]) can be allied with Carol Gilligan's ethics of care (1982) because both interrogate the types of 'common sense' discourses that produce gendered stereotypes,

> Rather than being an abstract set of moral principles, ethics is, for Kristeva, a relational, dialogic practice in which one acknowledges both the otherness of the other and the otherness of the self to itself.
>
> (Edelstein, 1993:196)

> For her [Kristeva], ethics has more to do with the shattering than the maintenance of codes, more to do with free play than coercion, more to do with love than law.
>
> (200)

When one begins with the study of women and derives developmental constructs from their lives, the outline of a moral conception different

*Exclusion to inclusion* 191

from that described by Freud, Piaget, or Kohlberg begins to emerge and informs a different description of development.

(Gilligan, 1982:19)

Semanalysis interrogates discourse by applying a critical analysis of oppression and opens up the borders of narrative by critically examining symbolic language to reveal it as language-in-process rather than fixed meaning. Sandy Stone seems to suggest that the trans person can draw from their own bodily difference to infiltrate and reconstruct the operation of symbolic language,

> To attempt to occupy a place as a speaking subject within the traditional gender frame is to become complicit in the discourse which one wishes to deconstruct. Rather, we can seize upon the textual violence inscribed in the transsexual body and turn it into a reconstructive force.
>
> (Stone, 1991:295)

Gilligan articulated the claim that relations-based moral reasoning (ethics of care), more (but not exclusively) evident in girls' and women's communication, had been overlooked as a legitimate and worthwhile form of moral development. She claimed that this occurred because of the preponderance of males carrying out research into moral reasoning and of males being the subjects of research (1982:18).

Semanalysis and ethics of care investigate subjectivity-based oppression by taking into account the whole subjective experience of corporeal (bodily), psychological (gendered) and social (structural) features, not by essentialising the influence of one of these features, as has been the case in separatist, psychological and even social constructionist accounts.

To supplement semanalysis, Kristeva developed a 'herethics', influenced by '... *maternity and the pre-oedipal mother-child relation*' and by '... *libidinal excesses*' (Wright, 1992:197, 199). In 'Women's Time' she considered that the third feminist phase heralded the time for a new ethics influenced by women's experiences, '... *do women not participate in the upheaval that our society is experiencing on several levels (war, drugs, artificial insemination), an upheaval that will require a new ethics?*' (1993:224).

Gilligan suggested the possible source of this new ethics,

> The elusive mystery of women's development lies in its recognition of the continuing importance of attachment in the human life cycle. Woman's place in man's life cycle is to protect this recognition while the developmental litany intones the celebration of separation, autonomy, individuation, and natural rights.
>
> (1982:23)

She described how women in her Abortion Study eventually combined something like maternal relations and an ethic of justice to form a relationship of responsibility and rights with others and self. She explains that the women gained,

> ... a new understanding of the connection between self and others which is articulated by the concept of responsibility. The elaboration of this concept of responsibility and its fusion with a maternal morality that seeks to ensure care for the dependent and unequal characterises the second perspective [in a sequence of perspective development]. ... The third perspective focuses on the dynamics of relationships and dissipates the tension between selfishness and responsibility through a new understanding of the interconnection between other and self.
>
> (74)

### *Erotics of unnaming vs politics of naming*

In addressing the effects of stereotyping, rather than investigating, the other, Currah describes how Kimberlé Crenshaw argued that oppression manifests from reactions to perceptions of identities, rather than in reaction to known identity,

> That race, gender and even sex are categories that turn out not to be firmly grounded in biology or in science does not mean that they do not have powerful social and legal effects, effects that are both enabling and disempowering.
>
> (2009:252)

Oppression resulting from imposed perceptions leads to 'Othering' of those placed in a stigmatised grouping, a negative instance of political naming. A third wave narrative addressing connections through feelings of 'Otherness' was provided by Greg Tate who identified the socialising of the same-sex female community in his native New York, '... *obviously there is a lot more acceptance of lesbian sexuality among young working-class black women than anybody's talking about*' (1995:201). Although profoundly 'Othered' from mainstream society, these young women did not seem to automatically exclude people with other sexual subjectivities from their own social circles.

Participant Raelene also seemed to encounter a similarly inclusive approach from lesbians from younger generations, '*I must admit that in all my dealings with the lesbian community I have had total acceptance by the younger ones – below forty, and been considerably disliked by the older dykes*' (Raelene Nov 4th, 2006, in <Hey You!>).

It is not known whether this (narrated) difference in acceptance is an effect of age, generation or society. However, lesbian communities from all feminist generations may have to hide their sexual subjectivity for reasons of safety and personal security, just as is the case with many a gender variant or transitioning person. These communities may therefore attempt to operate an 'erotics of unnaming' identified by Harriette Andreadis of sixteenth and seventeenth-century women involved in same-sex relations (1999:125). As discussed in Chapter 2, it seems that those involved in female same-sex relations in that period 'unnamed' their sexuality before it was named in the first place in an effort to evade drawing attention to their gendered subjectivity (1999:131).

In a similar 'unnamed' operation, in twentieth-century women's sexual subjectivity and feminist politics, the women involved often undertook '... *antipatriarchal acts*' of which no-one was aware (Tate, 1995:204). This seemed to resemble a plain-clothes wartime resistance movement, subverting the enemy under their nose. It also parallels Kate Bornstein's recommendation for subversive action for trans people in the face of stifling heteronormativity (1994); a very different operation to Raymond's portrayal of trans women as patriarchal conspirators (1979:104).

Tate points out that many black women still view organised feminism through less than rose-tinted glasses, so they may well wish to be feminist in their own, less conspicuous, ways. This indicates a kind of personally political unnaming and seems to have been undertaken by Gina Dent, also writing in *To Be Real*, when she noted that, '*Black feminism, or "womanism," includes me and my grandmother, since it has never based itself on a self-conscious description of particular movements or strategies*' (1995:62).

Gloria Anzaldúa (1999[1987]) also identified this issue of personal/political unnaming versus naming, with respect to Chicano/a people who could pass as white. She interpreted this ability as more of a curse than a blessing since such people had to deal with the moral dilemma of whether to pass as someone from the more privileged ethnicity. To eliminate such dilemmas, society needs to develop a difference inclusive community where people can 'pass' as themselves rather than as identity stereotypes.

Is there any alternative to either 'erotics of unnaming' (invisible inclusion in an 'Othered' group) or 'politics of naming' (visible inclusion in this group or into a privileged group) to lessen the exclusionary effects that may result from both? The first can exclude people from subjectivity politics and the latter can exclude people without an acceptable subjectivity. An answer may be offered by the kind of 'politically postmodern identity' theorised and supported by several third wave theorists. This subjectivity (identity-in-process) would not act to exclude others based upon assumptions of inherent identity.

Inclusion into subjectivities based upon the desire to belong (via genre and genealogy), rather than what is taken to be essential identity, may allow hidden sympathisers to surface, as Tate observed,

> When I presented my conundrum to Lisa Jones she said, "well I can't write about that scene [the black lesbian scene] because I'm too much of an outsider". And like, I'm not? To which she replied, "you're an insider by virtue of your desire to be inside of it".
>
> (Tate, 1995:206)

The conundrum mentioned by Tate was his narrated dilemma of wishing to theorise black lesbian feminism and yet realising that black lesbian feminists may take exception to his engagement with their community as a male. Yet it appears that philosophical third wave feminists are (at least theoretically) keen to provide narrative access for men and trans people, as positively different others (small 'o'), to support feminism, as suggested by texts in third wave anthologies such as *To Be Real* (1995) and *Catching a Wave* (2003).

The acceptance of desire for subjectivity, such as Tate's, rather than the call for proof of identity, is supported to some extent, if only for people transitioning between heteronormative genders, by the explanatory notes to section 7 of the EA 2010, which address gender reassignment. In paragraph 43, it is stated that, '*This section replaces similar provisions in the Sex Discrimination Act 1975 but changes the definition by no longer requiring a person to be under medical supervision to come within it*'.

This chapter proposes that, in a fully inclusive society, neither trans people, lesbians, gay men, womanists, gender variant people or feminists from 'Othered' chronological waves should be expected to hide or 'unname' their subjectivity and history, even though their choice to do so must be respected. Maternal relations are based upon personal articulation of inner subjectivity and so are the prime vehicle for naming-in-process for those otherwise defined into oppression by silent and secret discourse.

## *Ethics of care to postconventional ethics*

Within the *Transstudy* discussion site, participants considered the way that trans people could be named or recognised in order that society can accommodate their issues in an ethical manner. Some participants called for recognition of essential identity whereas a smaller number called for recognition of gender as socially constructed. For some, genre and genealogy, both being based upon subjective definitions, would not provide a concrete enough definition for protection in law and treatment in medicine. In discussing the defining of subjectivity by categorisation and the relation of this to ethics, Clarette suggested that,

> The ethics of this seem to me to be about determining whether a social limitation is a good or bad one, or putting this in a different way, determining whether our perceived need for space is valid or delusion. It is not obvious to me that the world has to adapt itself to my shape; I merely request that I should have an equitable degree of elbow room. A society which commits itself to creating justice for all on equal terms would not insist on double-standards – morality is not different because your gender is different. And it's not different again because your gender is not polarised.
> (Clarette, Oct 31st, 2005, in <Omnisexual, bisexual, trisexual, or just plain straight, lesbian or gay?>)

Unlike some participants' calls for recognition of identity, Clarette's narrative calls for an ethics more focused upon individual subjectivities than on essentialised group identities. 'Value judgments' will affect both the ethic of justice and ethics of care although those applying ethics of care with 'strong objectivity'[19] would be likely to at least realise this effect. The interpretation of what Clarette calls a 'single standard of moral conduct for all' is debatable, does sie mean universal judgment or perhaps ethics of care if it is a flexible standard that can focus on the individual or case in question? The answer to this might be found in hir call for 'mindfulness' of the needs of others without the application of '... *preconceptions of what people need ...*' (Nov 5th, 2005, in <Omnisexual, bisexual, trisexual, or just plain straight, lesbian or gay?>), suggesting a narrative identification with semiotic communication and ethics of care.

In <What advice to a Newbie>, Raelene's narrative aligned with the ethical operation called for by Clarette when arguing that people should be treated as individuals with rights to individual choice and that this should apply to trans people wishing to modify their bodies. She stated that,

> I disagree with almost every aspect of the Harry Benjamin Standards of Care for trans people. And even more so with the people involved who seemingly would like to act as "control freaks" over the lives of others. ... Each and every one of us is a unique individual, and should be treated as such. There is no one size that fits all.
>
> (Nov 11th, 2005)

However, version 6 of these Standards of Care actually states that everybody should be treated as an individual, even when it comes down to gender reassignment surgeries, (2001:20, in 'XII: Genital Surgery'). Nevertheless, Raelene's quote aligns with trans critiques of the way the law has traditionally appointed itself as the arbiter of definitions, as described in Chapter 4. The attributing of sexual subjectivity by legal authority figures to trans respondents has been a feature of many legal cases from *Corbett* onwards and before.[20]

How might some participants' calls for recognition of essential identity and Clarette's call for recognition of subjectivity be reconciled in ethical procedure? Gilligan's interpretation of the concept of postconventional ethics might satisfy Raelene's call for individual attention but still retain recognisable guidelines to ward off the favouritism that can infiltrate a pure ethics of care (The Researcher Nov 13th, 2005, in <What advice to a Newbie>). The ethic of justice as part of postconventional ethics, informed by the on-going input from ethics of care, would provide a safety net for those with lack of access to the communicative means and ability necessary to be involved with ethics of care.

### Genre and genealogy

Postconventional ethics would need to identify those needing special social care. Instead of resorting to as yet unknown definition by aetiology, we could look to Sandy Stone's identification of trans person as 'genre' (1991:296) where trans subjectivity can be located in psychological or social domains, without defining its aetiology, whether biological, psychological or social. Also, we could consider Alison Stone's reinterpretation of 'woman' as genealogy (2004:85) and Foucault's description of genealogy as identity-in-process (1977:144, 1984:81).

Whittle quoted from Sandy Stone in Epstein and Straub to suggest how trans people have used their new self-definitional power to reclassify themselves as a 'genre' instead of 'a class or problematic third gender' (2002a:82). This meant a new self-definition as individual or group subjectivity-in-process but at the same time subjectivity with roots in material embodiment and psychological sexual subjectivity. Whittle maintained that there is a need for political and legal recognition of the exclusion that blights trans lives, rather than efforts to attempt the formidable task of identifying and defining trans people's biological or psychological difference to non-trans men and women (2002a:86, 121). Genre and genealogy could form an appropriate template for this endeavour, rather than relying on deterministic physical and psychological frameworks and current ideas of aetiology.

Significant changes in representing sexual subjectivity occurred in the period from early modern times to the present day, suggesting that aetiologies of sexual subjectivity have been in-progress, rather than having been definitive representations of the nature of sexual identities. An explosion in the number of defined sexual subjectivities followed the implementation of the scientific gaze directed at sexual subjectivity, as described by Foucault (1998[1978]) and mentioned in Chapter 2. For instance, when including vocal narratives from gender variant patients in his collection of case notes, e.g. from Case 99, Krafft-Ebing (1893) interpreted gender variance as a psychiatric abnormal pathology and Sigmund Freud introduced the idea of gender variance (in this case 'aberration' and 'inversion' meaning homosexuality) as a deviant or dysfunctional route[21] away from conventional gender (2000[1905]:2),

> [Freud's] first class of aberrations contains those sexual activities that are deviant in respect of the sexual object. The most important and largest population in this class consists of adults whose sexual object has been "inverted". These inverts, or homosexuals as they are ordinarily called, "vary greatly in their behaviour in several respects".
> (Marcus, 2000[1905]:xxxviii)

> We were thus led to regard any established aberration from normal sexuality as an instance of developmental inhibition and infantilism.
> (Freud, 2000[1905]:97)

Freud's perception of inversion seems reminiscent of the kind of 'progress narrative' identified and criticised by Marjorie Garber (1997[1992]), where gender variance is something dysfunctional and temporary. In contrast to such deterministic applications of theory, Havelock Ellis (1896) incorporated complete narratives from gender variant patients into his work and did not try to extrapolate from these accounts to form discreet medical types. Narratives inspired by Ellis's interpretation of gender variance provided enough information to suggest readings of gender variance as something other than homosexuality (Foster, 1985[1956]). These kinds of narratives engendered inter-trans negotiation where trans people put out feelers in order to articulate trans subjectivity into existence.

Currah proposed that the search for aetiology has been undertaken by both opponents of, and supporters of, gender variant rights, '... *the litigation strategies of transgender rights advocates are very much informed by the legacies of the civil rights movement, as are the strategies of those who oppose transgender rights, especially in the emphasis on immutability*' (2006:16).

The aetiological choice seemed to be that gender variant people were either made by medical means (supported by opponents of trans rights) or were made as their preferred heteronormative gender by God or nature at birth (as argued by supporters of these rights). Little truck was given to ideas of gender variant people choosing or developing gender, or being formed as gender variant at birth. However, later trans narrators began to express a desire to avoid the pursuit of aetiology altogether, seeing the quest to understand the effects of trans subjectivity as a more fruitful and productive endeavour. Whittle explained how this new perspective led to a third space beyond the quest for definition,

> It may be the case that transgender theorists may deny gender as cause and effect (Whittle, 1996a), but neither do they see it in terms of biological process. The new formulations are attempting to move beyond either definitional point, and to go into Bornstein's (1994) third space in which 'our own patchwork individual identities have come together to form a brilliant complex mosaic of theatre for our day' ...
> (Whittle, 1998:48)

In a similar vein, Romero ventured the opinion that, '*Sexual desire, for example, is too variable, too unpredictable, and too circumstantial to permit its full mapping and explanation*' (2009:184). The same seems to remain the case for sex and gender, despite scientific and legal attempts to attempt such mapping.

Currah considered that setting up gender aetiologies would set up new hegemonies that would inevitably contradict certain people's experience,

> The challenge for the movement as a whole, then, is not to identify the "right" theory of the relationship between sex and gender. Either disavowing the medical model ... or trying to establish that model as the only way for transgender people to proceed ... would entail the imposition of a new hegemonic norm, one that would not be true to many people's experience of gender.
> (Currah, 2009:255)

Currah suggested celebrating contradictions in sexual subjectivity, rather than trying to make sense of them,

> Rather than trying to make sense of all these contradictory accounts of sex, gender, and the relationship between them, rather than trying to develop the "one perfect theory" to unify them within the context of the larger transgender rights imaginary, we should, as a movement, be celebrating the incoherencies between them even as we continue to pursue rights claims by invoking particular constructions of gender definition.
> 
> (256)

Foucault portrayed the search for aetiologies as a fruitless endeavour, recommending that, '*The genealogist needs history to dispel the chimeras of the origin*' (1984:80) and he claimed that, '*… a genealogy of values, morality, asceticism, and knowledge will never confuse itself with a quest for their "origins", will never neglect as inaccessible the vicissitudes of history*' (1977:144).

He also raised the image of a subject-in-process, rather than one based upon a given aetiology, when theorising that, '*Where the soul pretends unification or the self fabricates a coherent identity, the genealogist sets out to study the beginning – numberless beginnings, whose faint traces and hints of colour are readily seen by a historical eye*' (1971:81).

Autobiographer Jan Morris suggested a transsexual aetiology but located this in the spirit, '*… I see it above all as a dilemma neither of the body nor of the brain, but of the spirit*' (1974:16), seeming to mean spiritual essence, just like Whittle has always thought of his trans subjectivity as part of the essence, if essence-in-process, that makes him Stephen. Jan eventually found it easier to view her transgender as, '*… sans cause, sans meaning …*' (153), echoing a sentiment by *Transstudy* participant Sadie,

> People who are hostile to us are still hostile whether being trans is a "lifestyle choice" or a "medical condition". … I am of the opinion that it isn't either, really. There may or may not be a medical cause: I don't care if there is as I am more concerned with living with it than the medical side. It's like a calling, really. I have to be this way, there is no other choice.
> 
> (Mar 21st, 2005, in <Is it helpful to pathologise transgendered subjectivity?>)

Here Jan and Sadie both displayed an alignment with a postmodern viewpoint where efforts to find out how the truth is produced and maintained are seen as more achievable than a genuine understanding of the truth. The perception of genders as 'genres and genealogies', rather than as definable essences, aligns with the notion of experiential formation of subjectivity, just as it aligns with maternal relations' quest for a deeper understanding of the individual rather than the production of umbrella aetiologies. Genre and genealogy address struggles for subjective definition that have moulded gender variant lives, such as those discussed in Chapters 2, 4 and 6 where people have had to narrate themselves into existence when there was no definitional space for them in mainstream discourses.

One such subjective definition was again provided by Jan Morris who narrated an experience of what might be called 'becoming real', by realising herself through reassignment, rather than becoming less real as separatist feminists have suggested is true of the reassigning experience, declaring that, '... *I no longer feel myself isolated and unreal*' (1974:145). Jan theorised that she became a woman by being treated as a woman, marking the influential effect that others have on gendering, and matching the experience of autobiographer Dhillon Khosla in the other transitioning direction. After bodily reassignment Jan felt that she had gained, '... *membership of a camp, a faction or at least a school of thought ...*' (1974:140), bringing to mind Alison Stone's concept of 'woman' as deriving from genealogy, and Stone's and Whittle's portrayals of 'trans person' as genre.

Perhaps it is also possible for gender variant people to enter the feminist 'camp', when implementing what Gayle Rubin identified as an 'action paradigm', if they were to empathise genuinely with a feminist ethos, '*In contrast to an identity paradigm, Rubin proposes an "action paradigm" in which feminist identity arises out of political commitment rather than female biology*' (Hines, 2005:75).

*Postdifference*

It can be said that trans people have a history of difference to both heteronormative genderings but, if subjectivity as genre and genealogy is an acceptable given, that does not logically mean that they should be excluded from heteronormative subjectivity. We gather from Astrid Henry (2004:78) and womanist writers that black women are different to both black men and white women. However, these writers have not suggested that a meeting of minds between these ethnic/gendered subjectivities can never occur. Separatist difference feminism has excluded not only women different to a certain image of ethnicity, class and body type, but also feminist-friendly men,

> ... [separatist feminists] are accused of failing to recognise that different men have differing degrees of access to power, and of denying the possibility that some men are sympathetic to feminist issues and do not consciously wield their potential power.
>
> (Whelehan, 1995:85)

> Kristeva has ... reserved her most severe criticisms for French radical feminism[22] or the kind of feminism which emphasizes women's intrinsic difference from men.
>
> (Moi, 1986a:10)

In the first and second chronological feminist waves, difference feminism contributed towards many gains for women by demonstrating that women nearly always have a different experience to men. However, feminism needed to evolve by recognising the evolution of the perception of the difference from essential to in-process, and the relevance to feminism of the experiences of those from different sexual and ethnic subjectivities. The philosophical third wave, as an ideal, is critical of fixed identity positioning and is differences-friendly in its openness to inclusion for subjectivities not previously thought of as associated with, or in need of assistance from, a feminist movement. Although supporting queer/postmodern critiques of essentialised identity and theory, it is also a faction critical of the loss of subjective positioning; maintaining that freedom from subjectivity politics is a luxury that only those in privileged positions in power hegemonies can afford. This wave therefore seeks to combine identity-in-process (subjectivity) with subjectivity politics.

Audre Lorde coalesced her feelings of 'outsiderness' to the second wave movement into a proposition that difference should be included and not excluded, '*We have no patterns for relating across our human differences as equals. As a result, those differences have been misnamed and misused in the service of separation and confusion*' (1984:115).

Lorde proposed that it was time to move on from the rigid essentialism of woman vs man, being a masculinist endeavour, in order to realise a genuinely feminist society. Experience was the key to explaining subjectivity for Lorde since experience could present a challenge to the dictates imposed upon subjectivity by the categories of body, sex, ethnicity, health and class. Rudolph Byrd (2009) used the phrases, 'lived experience' and 'life experience' several times when describing how Lorde involved her own experience in her writing. Echoing the moral code of ethics of care, Lorde recommended that difference should be sought out and celebrated, rather than treated with suspicion. She was considered 'Other' to the second wave by some of those 'within' but her 'Otherness' endeared her to excluded people. She suggested the need for cohesion with other 'Others' in order to form a coherent challenge to patriarchy, bringing to mind Anzaldúa's notion of the 'kindred' who do not fit and hooks's 'solidarity' (Lorde, 1984:112, Anzaldúa, 1983[1981]:209, hooks, 1984:63, 64). This cohesion has also been called for by philosophically third wave feminists and by trans people in search of a social and spiritual community, the successful resolution of which may form a 'postdifferent' (difference inclusive) coalition. It may be realised in the form 'genre' and lead to connection with sympathetic others via the concept of 'genealogy'.

Queer theory's concept of subjectivity as fluid or in-process theoretically allows those who have been 'Othered' to belong to the community of those who do not fit, '*The stance of queerness thus potentially provides a point of unity across differences of gender, sexual practices, and sexual orientation*' (Stychin, 1995:142). The queer ethos has thus been a refuge for those with no gendered place to go (144). This aligns closely with the ethos of 'post-difference', where difference is subject to celebration rather than ostracisation.

Some quotations relevant to Gilligan and Kristeva's work indicate their alignment with this concept of inclusive difference. For instance, a 27-year-old female participant in Gilligan's college student study narrated her feeling that she had developed a postdifferent-like perspective on life,

> On her own behalf, Hilary says somewhat apologetically that she has become, since college, more tolerant and more understanding, less ready to blame people whom formerly she would have condemned, more capable of seeing the integrity of different perspectives.
>
> (1982:136)

Another student, Kate, exemplified this perspective on postdifferent connection, resulting in a philosophy where, '*Responsibility now includes both self and other, viewed as different but connected rather than as separate and opposed*' (147).

Gilligan also noticed how Piaget's investigation into childhood moral development revealed a progression from requirements for similarity to a respect for fair treatment of difference, '*[Piaget] also notes how children's recognition of differences between others and themselves leads to a relativizing of equality in the direction of equity, signifying a fusion of justice and love*' (172).

Here the ethic of relationships is positioned by Gilligan as a mature development that supersedes an ethic of separation. An example of the valuing of subjective difference being put into practice is provided by Martin Moerings who described how the COC, a Dutch organisation for the integration of homosexuals, changed its concept of inclusion for homosexuals, in the period from the 1960s to the 1970s,

> The more moderate COC ... swapped integration for emancipation, changing the emphasis to the uniqueness of one's development and identity as a homosexual and one's specific position in society – in which, for example, marriage need not be copied as a way of giving shape to a relationship.
>
> (1998:126)

In this instance, the aim for being identical to heteronormativity changed to the aim to be equally valued, a state of equity, in order to allow for respect and toleration of difference. Postdifference, the state of trascending negative segregation by difference essentialisation, was here implemented into a real-life situation

## 8.4 Finding ourselves – epiphanies

> The starting point for a Foucauldian ethics is therefore the refusal of self, the rejection of those forms of identity to which we are tied – both by ourselves and by the institutions, values and practices of the societies we live in.
>
> (O'Leary, 2002:15)

Narratives of personal epiphanies, important for a postdifferent landscape, featured in a significant number of the autobiographies reviewed in Chapter 2, providing a challenge to difference essentialisation by introducing the real lives of gender variant people. For instance, Christine Jorgensen (1967) experienced finding herself through literature via the revelation of endocrinal knowledge and via an actual and metaphorical sea crossing, Mark Rees (1996) found a description of sexual subjectivity cohering with his own in the *Times* newspaper and Max Valerio (2006) experienced an initially disturbing but ultimately liberating epiphany of self-realisation when finding a book about female-to-male reassignment. Jorgensen (1967:22), the fictional Stephen Gordon in *The Well of Loneliness* (2005[1928]:ix, x, xiv, 186), and Stephen Whittle (Self & Gamble, 2000:52–53) all had intense moments in libraries when they realised they had found literature describing their gendered condition. Epiphanies will often be accounted for in retrospect by narrative means, as suggested by Jay Prosser (1998), and will therefore be subject to the caprices of memory, but all the same, they serve to demonstrate the feelings involved, the need for support and the interpretations of developing gender involved.

Narrative analyst Catherine Riessman theorised that, '*A primary way individuals make sense of experience is by casting it in narrative form … . This is especially true of difficult life transitions and trauma …*' (1993:4). Awareness of this narrative process can provide guidance for trans people's interactions with the law since it outlines the importance of 'finding' one's own gendered self in one's own time, rather than having it imposed by society. This marks a kind of dialogic negotiation of gender with oneself and with others in one's family and community, and is notably crucial for young people getting to grips with their own subjective being.[23] Gendered subjectivity is something that one is expected to live with for a lifetime so it is important that one is allowed to try and get it right.

Rather than the losing of oneself in the moment of 'jouissance', in the sense theorised by Kristeva (1982:9), the epiphany for the trans person seems to, at least eventually, involve a finding of the self, in the way conceived of as 'plaisir' by Roland Barthes (Heath, 1977:9). The narrative experience of finding self, though often terrifying at first, as related by many a trans person, eventually resembles plaisir as an establishment of self and the construction of subjectivity.

The suggestion that trans people are keen searchers of self is supported by instances in the autobiographies and *Transstudy* narratives, such as when Jan Morris suggested that the transvestite achieves a 'sexual *frisson* [her italics]' (1974:113) when cross-dressing, something which might seem narratively akin to jouissance. However, in contrast, she described the transitioning person as achieving something more substantial and on-going, like plaisir, in the realisation of the self. Less intimate friends almost expected a change in personality when Jan cross-dressed in early stages of transition but one couple found her to be, '*… surprisingly like the person they had always known …*' (115).

The epiphany is taken to be a valid part of human experience in Kimana's Lakota culture,

*Exclusion to inclusion* 203

> Basicaly, the Spirits will contact us in three ways. One is the actual vision where a Spirit comes and talks to you. This can be any living creature, even a snake or skunk. Then there is the dream that has a Spirit in it telling you something, often in a vague way that makes you have to anylize it and really think about it or have it inturpreted by someone. The last way is through a messege that comes to you, something like an epiphany. When you get the messeges, we often think, "Why didn't I think of that". It's so clear and obvious.
> (Mar 22nd, 2006, in <Dreams and Trans Subjectivity>)

The process of finding out who we really are is facilitated by social discourses inclusive of diversity and difference. Although people need to find themselves through association with others, we need to consider whether this is based upon the unnecessary exclusion of others if we are 'hailed' and they are not. Trans support groups such as Press for Change have endeavoured to broaden this scope for inclusive hailing by spreading knowledge of gender variance, but it has been an uphill battle for many years since heteronormativity is still the prevalent gender schema in Western industrial culture. Discourses of medicine, education and the law still have a long way to go before all gender variant people feel fully and appropriately 'hailed' and included. As Kimana mentioned,

> Now, I understood why I was meant to live. It gave me a purpose to not only live, but showed me that I really was sane. All I had to do was live the way I was meant to and everything would work out. I wasn't crazy after all, society just had no clue in how to deal with me. Sometimes, it still doesn't.
> (Kimana Jan 8th, 2006, in <School and trans-development>)

The epiphany, the personal moment of feeling hailed through personal choice, is an articulation of self-revelation for those denied a gender schema of their own.[24] It doesn't mark a magical, or necessary pleasurable, gender transformation, à la Jan Morris in the cocoon of the Burou clinic in Casablanca, but can later be seen as the moment of clarity shining through obscuring clouds of oppression.

## 8.5 Conclusion

In section one of this chapter, the way that gender variance has been purged or 'socially cleansed' from societies was addressed. People starting out on the road to transition are particularly ripe for oppression because they are perceived to be different from the norm. They may be conventionally gendered 'within' but this holds no water for the oppressors who require people to appear heteronormative. Social cleansing involves the subtle removal of 'undesirables' from what are taken to be important social situations and

204 *Exclusion to inclusion*

events, thereby denying these people the social engagement that can lead to social subjectivity.

Section two examined how trans people as 'immigrants or refugees' have to run the gauntlet of conservative social structures where people are expected to stay in their allocated subjective spaces. Anything different is a challenge to the hegemony of the status-quo and any variance from the norm is taken to be unacceptable deviance. Trans people's positioning as outside of gender by theorists espousing essentialist theory, has portrayed them as desperate immigrants wishing to enter the superior territory of heteronormativity, rather than as unacknowledged citizens. The law needs to recognise that trans people do not need to reassign into one or other side of the heteronormative divide in order to be responsible people with social, civil and human rights.

Section three suggested that the silent and secret undercurrent of second wave heteronormative feminism operated to exclude underprivileged women from its discourse of womanhood, and that silent and secret discourse 'Othered' gender variant people from heteronormativity. 'Maternal relations' has operated in the opposite, if far less privileged, direction as a characteristically inclusive discourse in allowing access to subjectivity by routes other than elitism or entry into the heteronormative hegemony.

In this section there is a description of how Kristeva's ethical mode involving the investigative method of semanalysis and Gilligan's formation of ethics of care both carry out the function of challenging 'common sense' gender stereotyping discourse by applying a critical analysis of oppression from a perspective informed by maternal relations. Both theorists suggest the need for a third phase of moral development to implement these relations.[25] This phase represents the mature outcome of such development.

Then it was suggested that a politics of naming draw from the rich social insights gained from erotics of unnaming so that the Otherness endured by gender oppressed people can be articulated into a view from somewhere. To enhance this social voice, it was claimed that the mindfulness inherent in ethics of care be combined with the ethic of justice to provide access to social forums, and protection provided by legal institutions, for excluded Others. Postconventional ethics, as theorised by Carol Gilligan, combines the two moral developments in order that one can police the operations of the other.

Genre and genealogy were suggested as ways to unite excluded others by recognition of their unifying experiences of difference. This involves a rejection of the search for aetiology in favour of identifying individuals by their associations, perceptions and life-long development. A positive approach to 'Otherness' and difference, namely 'postdifference' was introduced in this section in order to differentiate it from separatist difference exclusion. Postdifference draws from the font of difference to realise a genuinely inclusive feminist society based upon a coalition of 'Otherness'.

In section four it was proposed that, in the process of 'finding themselves', trans people often include instances of epiphany in their life story narratives. Provision can be made in law and medicine to respect the fact that trans people may have to endure these often frighteningly intense evaluations of their gendered selves but that these can be turned around into positive and enlightening processes of self-discovery, or 'plaisir', leading to a psychologically healthy person. Groups such as Press for Change have worked to engender trans people's understanding of their epiphanies of self-realisation so that they may be 'hailed' into their preferred gendering.

Now that, in some societies, trans people are not expected to collude totally with the discourse of heteronormativity by denying their pre-transition history, or to perceive their pre-transition selves as necessarily ill, they can read their epiphanies in a positive way in order to escape the machinations of silence and secrecy and to realise their gender in a more idiosyncratic way, '*Here, here, Raelene. ... your experience is uniquely interesting. "how come there are so many of you around nowadays?" Perhaps your answer should have been, "There is only one"*' (The Researcher Dec 6th, 2005, in <Is it helpful to pathologise transgendered subjectivity?>).

Chapter 9 reorganises themes discussed in Chapters 6 to 8 into three main areas of recommendation for future action, or three reconstructing discourses. These three areas form the ethos of a third wave philosophy that can be adopted by philosophically third wave feminist and/or gender variant people.

## Notes

1 Jana Sawicki is Professor of Philosophy and Women's Studies, Williams College, Massachusetts.
2 Such examples of social cleansing can be found in Feinberg (1996:62, 63) and in Bullough and Bullough (1993:ix, 23, 39–40).
3 (Government Equalities Office, 2011).
4 Leslie Feinberg's fictional account of a life of upheaval brought about by transphobic actions in *Stone Butch Blues* (1993) narratively illustrates the effects of social cleansing.
5 A conjecture based upon literature reviews, research and personal experience.
6 X v Brighton and Hove City Council [2006/7], as reported by Dean, Tracy (08 November 2008). Details taken from a report in the *Daily Mail* (17 December 2006).
7 The effects of discrimination and harassment on perception are to some extent addressed by the EA 2010.
8 An explanation of protection against perception that leads to direct discrimination can be found in the EA 2010 Explanatory Notes at Pt 2, chp 2, s.13, clarified in the third bullet point of explanatory note 63, and perception of protected characteristics also applies to 'Victimization' at Pt 2, chp 2, s.27.
9 Charles/Samantha Kane brought a case against Dr Russell Reid after complaining that he/she had been referred for reassignment surgery after only a month of living as a woman. The case had the effect of increasing gatekeeping checks at Gender Identity Clinics.
10 Bringing to mind the thoughts of Dhillon Khosla and participant Shannon, as recorded at the end of Chapter 2.
11 As suggested by Vivienne Burr in the case of depressed women (2003:122).
12 Szaz (1961) *The Myth of Mental Illness: Foundations of a Theory of Personal Conduct*.

13 See www.antipsychiatry.org/index.htm and the rest of the anti-psychiatry movement.
14 Bringing to mind Whittle's comparison of trans subjectivity to the sound emitting from a tree falling in the forest. If trans subjectivity was not witnessed by anyone else, like the sound from a tree being unheard, it would nevertheless still be there.
15 See Whittle et al. (20 December 2006:1.2, 2.2, 2.7–2.10).
16 For instance, Rebecca Dakin Quinn (Henry, 2004:2), Julia Kristeva (1993:206) and bell hooks (1984:44).
17 Scientific investigations have been carried out to support this assertion, for instance: Hunter, Gambell and Randhawa (2005), Colley and Todd (December 2002) and Janssen and Murachver (October 2004).
18 See the discussion centred around Astrid Henry's work in Chapters 3 and 7.
19 Sandra Harding's term for self-reflexive scientific research (1991).
20 Attribution of sexual subjectivity by determination of biological sex in Corbett was followed by determination of heterosexual functionality in the cases of X, Y & Z (1997) and Attorney-General v Otahuhu Family Court. However, in this section it was noted that Lord Winston bucked this trend, in House of Lords debates on the content of the GRA 2004, by pointing out what he saw as the infinite complexity of defining sex for the purposes of law (Whittle and Turner, 2007:8.2).
21 If not as degeneracy and not as exclusively innate nature or acquired trait (Freud, 2000[1905]).
22 Moi seems to mean 'separatist feminism' as radical feminism doesn't logically have to mean radical separatist feminism.
23 Finding oneself can be carefully facilitated by the application of the label 'gender variance' and pubertal deferral treatment to gender variant youngsters, as suggested in Chapter 6.
24 A feeling expressed by Clarette (Clarette refers to 'scripts' but this seems close to 'schemata' in meaning), as related in Chapter 6.
25 A development in the form of the third phase for Kristeva (1993:222), and in the form of postconventional ethics, after the ethic of justice and ethics of care, for Gilligan (1982:73).

# 9 Recommendations
## Ghosts in the machine

**Introduction**

Chapters 6 to 8 discussed threats to the empowerment of people oppressed by heteronormativity, and this chapter suggests ways that these threats may be overcome. As noted in Chapter 4, committed individuals have contributed to this empowerment by 're-engineering' the legal machine in order to facilitate gender oppressed people's inclusion into social discourses. For instance, April Ashley called for a challenge to what she narrated as the aloof and clinical discourse of the law (Fallowell and Ashley, 1982). Involvement with his own legal case[1] led Stephen Whittle to influence law from the inside rather than to be its object. His negotiations with trans people and the law initiated a paradigm change in trans people's self-awareness and self-acceptance, giving them the self-confidence to claim their own gender. Such inputs into legal discourse have moulded case law to introduce the gendered individual rather than the gendered stereotype as legal subject.

However, trans and gender variant voices still often manifest as metaphorical 'ghosts in the machine' of established discourses such as gender, medicine and the law, rather than as properly gendered citizens. Philosopher Gilbert Ryle used this term to critique René Descartes' mind–body dualism as an inaccurate separation of these dualised components, the mind being the 'ghost' in the body. However, this metaphor may aptly describe the social, rather than biological, phenomenon of many gender variant people's experience of disconnection within social discourses such as law, medicine, feminism, family, employment and leisure. This experience has included a feeling of invisible existence[2] or, at the other extreme, of being subject to reactions of fear or disbelief.

The machines of discourse are built up by reliance on the image of the Modest Witness[3] with a 'view from nowhere' imparting a perspective untainted by 'narrative messiness'. However, there are, in fact, no impartial discourses in human society. Personally political agendas pervade all strata of society but are shrouded by silence and secrecy masquerading under the guise of articulation and openness.

This chapter suggests how trans people, gender variant people and/or those with a third wave ethos can draw upon their particular kinds of narrative voice and experiences of difference in order to increase their visibility and voice in the discourse of the law, so that they become more than socially ethereal beings. The reconstructing themes have been reorganised into three recommended reconstructing discourses. These three discourses, '*Maternal Relations, Genre and Genealogy and Postdifference*' indicate how maternal relations can engender relations of genre and genealogy which can lead to a society based upon a 'postdifferent' or inclusive approach to difference.

## 9.1 Maternal relations

> As the years progressed and I read even more what other TS's wrote about themselves, I came to the realisation that for the forty odd years I had considered myself to be alone and unique, I hadn't been at all. We all have the same or very similar tales to tell.
> (Raelene Nov 7th, 2005, in <What advice to a Newbie>)

Uniqueness and commonality can both be revealed by implementation of maternal relations, via ethics of care, as discussed in Chapters 3 and 8. Within the research that led to the formation of this book, maternal relations emerged as the best potential means for amplifying the voice of those silenced by discourses of patriarchy and heteronormativity. Women and feminists of colour sowed the seeds for the reintroduction of feminists as a community, gaining inter-generational and inter-community knowledge from various media of expression. Some gender variant people have come to champion the value of community and movement to the trans and gender variant cause.

Gilligan and Kristeva theorised that communication deriving from maternal relations, rather than from an essential essence of womanhood, was an undiscovered fount of inspiration for ethical procedure. Gilligan uncovered the web of relational reasoning that girls and women characteristically use to establish moral viewpoints in hypothetical ethical situations.[4] Kristeva visualised the visceral semiotic current running under the veneer of the symbolic in the world of communication, like a discoursal[5] ghost in a machine, unable to be articulated in formal language but influential nonetheless. These related concepts of gendered articulation pertain closely to the communicative modes of philosophical third wave feminists and third wave gender variant people.

In Chapter 4, it was argued that Gilligan sought to present the connection between maternal reasoning and females as deriving from their upbringing rather than their birth-given nature. This theory ties in with Kristeva's belief that either men or women could fulfil the (psychological) maternal function to a significant extent, '*I think Kristeva, like other postmodernists, de-essentialises gender; she treats the maternal as metaphorically available to both men and women, but also considers maternity as a psychological experience shared by many women*' (Edelstein, 1993:201).

Maternal relations as a socially constructed, rather than a sexed feature, of gendered subjectivity can find support from accounts of trans people developing both gendered 'voices', before and after their gendered transition, as described in Chapters 6 and 7. Views based on stereotyped difference within difference have alienated trans people and feminists from each other and from their own, and have mimicked the paternal relations of hierarchical separation inherent in much modern-day society.

## *Voice*

Chapter 7 suggested that third wave theorists make efforts to seek out differently gendered voices obscured by identity essentialism[6] and by academic/medical/legal discourse. Certain forms of narrative schema/voice act as gatekeepers to discourse through presenting language as a barrier. A 'politics of naming' is one way of articulating voice in order to challenge the kind of isolation experienced by the gender oppressed. In drawing from the example of, '... *convicts of the 19th-century silence system* ...' (1974:43), Jan Morris described how isolation like hers could lead to the lack of ability to recognise oneself since in these circumstances there are no others with whom to use as measures of ourselves. To allay this kind of isolation, trans people and feminists working within their subjective communities can serve as living 'mirrors' of gender oppressed people's experiences. Trans people and third wave feminists can 'voice coach' one another in order that their experiences of gendering may articulate a challenge to silent and secret gender oppression.

Chapter 7 also developed the argument in Chapter 2 that infantilisation has been significantly deployed by the silent and secret authoritative voice in order to extinguish the social voice of gender variant people. This has backfired when those with infantilised subjectivities reject the terms of maturity laid down by those in privileged positions in the dominant social hegemony.[7] Trans people can re-appropriate the means of entry to adulthood by producing their own schema of growing up, derived from resourcefulness built up in the process of adopting a new schema of gendered presentation.[8] Trans people come to realise that maturity is in the eye of the beholder when trying to adapt to their chosen gendered schema and that what is mature for one gender is often classed as immature for the other.

## *Postconventional ethics*

Gilligan's concept of postconventional ethics combined ethics of care with the ethic of justice as two sides of an ethical 'Möbius Strip', apparently separate but running on from each other,

> For her [Gilligan] the ethic of justice (that everyone should be treated the same) should be added to the ethic of caring (that no one should be hurt) to produce a better outcome. Her conclusion is thus not to produce a separatist system of justice for women, nor to replace the ethic of justice with the ethic of caring.
> 
> (Smart, 1989:74)

The marriage of the ethics of care focus on responsibility and the ethic of justice's focus on rights might be said to resemble a union of philosophical first, second and third wave views. The more rights-focused first and second waves are complemented by the care-orientated third wave. The optimum strategy for a postconventional approach is not to essentialise subjectivity but also not to deny subjectivity-based oppression, as Scales points out, '*There is nothing to be gained by portraying any particular experience of oppression as inevitable or primary. At the same time, there is much to be lost from refusal to recognize the regularity of some kinds of injuries*' (2009:409).

A conflict of interest or dilemma between providing umbrella/universal protection[9] for all and a focus on individuals and/or identity groups has been identified by trans-friendly people involved with legal issues, as indicated by participant Clarette and by writer/trans woman Jane Fae,

> I am unsure whether I can prove the validity of a single standard of moral conduct for all ... I may have to appeal to value judgements.
> (Clarette Oct 31st, 2005, in <Omnisexual, bisexual, trisexual>)

> ... I [Fae] asked about whether the current approach to inequality – focusing on specific group needs – was the best solution, or part of the problem. Here some difference opened up, with [Labour MP] Ms Eagle arguing that government needed to target legal support and protection to those most in need of it – and [Lib Dem MP] Ms Featherstone being more concerned with advocating rights for all.
> (Fae, 16 April 2010)

This dilemma was also identified by Carol Smart, in a chapter section entitled 'Equality v Difference', as pertaining to women's battles for their gendered positions to be recognised in law,

> ... whether women should be given special treatment by the state and the law on the basis of their uniquely female capacities and supposed characteristics, or whether justice would be better served by treating women as equal to men, with equal rights and responsibilities.
> (1989:82)

Currah argued that the apparent umbrella versus special recognition dilemma, rights for all versus care-based focus on individual or group circumstances, need not be resolved by choosing one or the other, '... *I argue that the very different goals of working to dismantle gender as a coherent legal concept and working to expand gender to include trans people should not be seen as an either-or proposition*' (2009:245).

The implementation of the EA 2010 seemed to move some way towards combining these two apparently incompatible forms of moral procedure. This Act was designed to respect difference (in the form of equality strands) while incorporating the notion of equality under the banner of one Act. However, as mentioned in Chapters 4 and 8, reliance on 'gender reassignment' as the protected characteristic relevant to trans people meant that the interpretation of who is and who isn't trans was still restricted to those who transition between heteronormative genders, reducing the possibility of inclusion for all gender variant people.

The Yogyakarta Principles on the Application of International Human Rights Law demonstrate how universal ethics can be a positive affair when informed by those most closely affected by discrimination. Those most closely involved are the people who can provide a perspective informed by ethics of care. As previously suggested, particularly in Chapter 2, women and gender variant people have characteristically been excused from discourse based upon representations of their subjectivities as psychologically undeveloped and effusive; as immature. Despite all this, trans people and women have surfaced from discourse banishment to provide guidance into issues of human rights and moral relations, such as those addressed by the Yogyakarta Principles. These include citizens' rights to 'access', 'expression', 'participation' and 'recognition' (Whittle, 20 March 2007) and certainly work to inform an ethics of care.

### *'A movement of their own?'*

> As in so many other identity-based activist projects, one axis of identification is a luxury most people cannot afford. ... Identity politics must give way to some form of coalition if a political movement is to be successful.
>
> (Halberstam, 1998:159)

> ... why, when we can observe so many examples of successful political alliances, would we build a wall between other trans people and ourselves just because we are a little different (either in an imagined or a real sense)? Difference should be celebrated!
>
> (Hardie, 2006:128)

> I have urged others that as non-trans feminists we need to recognise that we have been trained in the prejudices that society purveys and that we need to learn how to offer respect and support to trans people.
>
> (Findlay, 2006:150)

> The "original feminist paradigm" is the concept of unity; the new paradigm is difference and coalition.
>
> (Garrison, 2005:250)

Previous chapters suggested that a coalition of third wave feminist and trans factions would be mutually beneficial, as suggested by Barbara Findlay above, and, in functional terms, when legal gains for feminists inform the legal claims of trans people and vice versa. This may occur when equal pay claims, lobbied for by women, can transfer to protect transitioned people or has occurred when umbrella protection from discrimination, as lobbied for by trans activists, was also afforded to women by the EA 2010. It also may derive from mutually reinforcing gains in the right to take time off work for physical needs, for pregnancy in women's case and reassignment surgeries for trans people. More broadly, this coalition would draw upon its knowledge of the complexity and contradictions of gender in order to challenge the requirement to blend into heteronormativity.

Consideration has to be given to whom a third wave coalition or movement might properly belong. It seems that a coalition can suffer if one faction is significantly more inflexibly ideological than another. If third wave feminists and the trans community are inherently inclusive of difference such ideological dominance should not happen. Both would properly belong to the gender varied and to those sympathetic to gender variance.

In Chapter 7 it was suggested that the evolution of feminism and/or transgender into a new wave or movement may serve as a motivational strategy, legitimising the use of a new feminist/transgender banner even if the new wave is not wholly differentiated from others. However, a reconstruction of feminism/transgender needs to be more than just an academic exercise that leaves real lives untouched and it must also free itself from ties to one (old or new) generation if it is not to alienate people on the grounds of age. This reconstruction could act as a specially formed feminist/transgender response to both micro-political and global issues spanning communities and regions, with one type of response informing the other.

## 9.2 Genre and genealogy

> I will propose that what women have in common is a relation and not a thing.
> (Zack, 2005:2)

Genre and genealogy are connected to third wave philosophy and ethics of care in that they promote understanding of the individual rather than the allocation of people into taxonomic groups that are very often derived from no more basis than cultural convention. Genre and genealogy allow for members of certain social subjectivities, such as 'third wave feminist' and 'trans', to be seen as different but compatible, members who offer strength in diversity and specialism. Some people understandably seek to escape connection with oppressed genre and genealogy because of the oppression involved. Therefore, greater awareness of the strength that can be gained through solidarity in genre and genealogy needs to be a feature of trans-feminist relations.

Parameters of group inclusion, when investigated by ideas of genre and genealogy, can be monitored and negotiated as advances are made in the understanding, rather than the precise definition, of the group subjectivity involved. In this way, subjective stereotypes can be subject to reconstruction.

Genre and genealogy identify subjectivities of choice and relations of passion, marking a quantum leap for social inclusion for the 'kindred' of those who do not fit.[10]

## Which trans and feminist subjectivities are real?

In Chapter 6 it was found that portrayals of non-transitioning trans subjectivity as whim, deviance, effusive or luxury mirrored accusations levelled at third wave feminism for being (variously) privileged, confused, immature, lethargic and aggressive. Both subjectivities have been perceived as infantile or unreal by others, including separatist feminists and what might be called separatist trans people. In the last century, oppressed women and then trans people eventually found themselves developing well-formed social and personal subjectivities partly because they had to struggle to gain a foothold in negotiation for the definitions of those subjectivities within social, medical, legal and academic discourses, and partly because of the standpoint epistemology (the 'view from somewhere') they gained from suffering oppression. Nevertheless, some people, and notably those influenced by a queer ethos, claim that the search for the realness of sexual subjectivity is a search for the pot of gold at the end of the rainbow,[11] '*In any event, labels do not define anything, we merely tie them on to remind ourselves, usually in very approximate terms, of the box's contents, so we can look in it for something we might need later...*' (Clarette Oct 27th, 2005, in <Omnisexual, bisexual, trisexual>).

Foucault's theory that relations are formed through genealogy, rather than deriving from the truth of identity,[12] could be recognised in law as the way to define subjectivities, including kin relationships, in the future. Wider interpretations of who can be a parent or partner are now given by the law, for instance by the GRA 2004 and the Civil Partnership Act 2004, although a father can still only be, even if post-transitionally, male and a mother female, and marriage partners must still be of opposite genders in most countries. This can lead to people assuming that genders are defined when in actuality they are not,

> The law only says that marriage is a union between a man and a woman ... but then it was assumed that the definition of those terms was so obvious and beyond question that there was no need to define them ... not even to the extent of suggesting that the social term "woman" was supposed to equate with any contemporary biomedical understanding of the term "female" (and vice versa).
> 
> (Burns, 1996)

Things have moved on for marriage in the UK where people with the same gender can marry but such a union is labelled as a 'same-sex marriage', meaning the institution of marriage itself is still segregated by gender.

People often wish for a biologically established relation with the group with which they wish to identify, for instance women who wish to be known as feminist in a separatist sense of difference, and trans women who wish to be known as biological women. However, when a biological aetiology is unavailable, relations of genre and genealogy can serve to unite people who are committed to 'trans' and 'feminist' as subjectivities rather than identities. Who is to say that these definitions are less real than those based upon supposed biological relations? Gaby Calleja of Malta Gay Rights Movement considered that,

> There are over 6 billion people in the world, and yet we assume there are only two genders. But contrary to popular perception, gender is a social construct; it is not fixed at conception as many people believe. There could be other genders apart from simply male and female.
> (Reported by Dean, 26 October 2008)

A shift towards interpreting trans subjectivity as deriving from a social process, rather than a physical one with medical supervision,[13] may be seen as a move towards a 'muddying of the waters' of trans subjectivity, as discussed in Chapter 6, if it becomes less clear who is and who is not trans. The drawback of a wide definition of trans subjectivity is that it makes it difficult to identify trans people for legal protection or medical intervention as a clearly defined group. Such definition can, for instance, more easily be derived in the classification of trans people as those, 'proposing to undergo, undergoing, or having undergone reassignment', as is the case in the EA 2010. However, as suggested in Chapter 2, restricting the definition of gender variance to this category can suffocate further investigation of gender variance.

Perhaps, as suggested by Cowan,

> The fundamental questions underpinning this discussion are should it ever be necessary to ask law to define sexual identity? The answer to this question may be no. Sex appears to be important in areas of criminal law, marriage law, and in the regulation of sports. However, this need not be the case – the UK could legislate for gender-neutral criminal offences, legalise same-sex marriage and could regulate sport on the basis of prohibiting athletes from taking hormones (including those required to maintain a change of gender) rather than interrogating what sex they are.
> (2005:90)

The author would not wish for transitioning athletes to be denied their reassignment hormones, but Cowan's general call for the lessening of gender dichotomies is a welcome one for inclusive relations. Parties interested in the quest to find an aetiological outcome, such as separatist feminists and heteronormative trans people, may spend their time hoping that the dice of aetiological outcome will come to rest in their favour, instead of just supporting that which they most desire or believe in.

### The whole trans person

> Foreignness is within us: we are our own foreigners, we are divided.
> (Kristeva, 1991:181)

> Thus the counterpoint of identity and intimacy that marks the time between childhood and adulthood is articulated through two different moralities whose complementarity is the discovery of maturity. ... The divergence in judgement between the sexes is resolved through the discovery by each of the other's perspective and of the relationship between integrity and care.
> (Gilligan, 1982:165)

'Voice coaching' can be drawn upon to examine how, when moving from passing as one gender to the realisation of their preferred gender, trans people have had to fashion their own schema of sexual subjectivity, even when their aim is to pass into heteronormativity.[14] These schemata will be different to heteronormative schemata because of the different routes to gender that trans people have to take. As a result, trans people can often draw upon aspects of gender from both heteronormative genders in order to reveal and develop unique aspects of gender. As suggested in Kimana's narratives of her native culture, this kind of mixed gendered personality can sometimes be seen as a repository for social insight in those cultures not automatically cleaved into two gendered halves.

The conclusion to Bellinger v Bellinger supported the notion of gender as developed, as what we might call genre and genealogy, by including legal consideration of, 'style of upbringing and living, and self-perception', as valid indicators of preferred sexual subjectivity. This replaced the as yet impossible attempt at defining aetiology through biological determination (Whittle, 2007:40), and uncritical reliance on the heteronormative gender schema.

The articulation of such new perspectives on gender might remedy the apocalyptic scenario visualised by transvestite autobiographer John Pepper where droves of people from each gender are vaguely fumbling in order to find the lost half of their true being. Pepper's vision seemed to aptly describe the marginalisation into oppressed or 'Other' gender that has blighted women's lives and has transformed trans people into heteronormativity's 'Others'. In assessing this vision, Annie Woodhouse noted that, '... *an ability to see gender as fluid, ranging from wholly masculine to wholly feminine would go a long way towards destroying such [gender] division ...*' (1989:420). The wholeness of a mature balance of gendered perspective is open to people of any gendering.

### Identity as a process: subjectivity

Kristeva replaced essentialist portrayals of the subject with ideas of the subject-in-process,[15] to indicate the shift from a second to a third phase of gender inclusive thinking (Oliver, 1998).[16] She maintained that the subject follows a process of psychoanalytically informed development, but saw more room for individual development, agency, and maternal influence within that process than Freud ever did,[17]

> The relationships between the subject and the other, between the subject and itself, between the semiotic and the symbolic are all dialogic, in Kristevan theory.
>
> (Edelstein, 1993:200)

> Kristeva argues that "we must maintain the autonomy of discourse with respect to the social level, because it is a level of autonomy that guarantees freedom. We can speak in a different manner than our familial and social determination".
>
> (203)

Kristeva's view of identity-in-process challenged portrayals of identity-in-stasis handed down by conservative society that precluded the possibility of gender variant or transitioning subjectivity. If trans subjectivity is presented as in-process some might take this to mean it is either unreal or that it is difficult to define. The medical community requires something to be defined before it can offer treatment and the legal community before it can offer special protection. Perhaps the only way to surmount the dilemma of whether to present gender as 'in-process' is to present gender as identifiable at any one point in time, but subject to a life-long process of fine tuning through dialogic negotiation informed by ethics of care.

It is important that all gendered subjectivities are seen as in-process, and not just gender variant ones, if the reality of gender construction is accepted. Carol Smart suggested that Catherine MacKinnon produced a unilateral account of subjectivity-in-process that portrayed women as being the only gender subject to this development, '... *it is problematic to posit that culture, history, language, ethnicity can construct female sexuality, whilst proposing that men are outside culture, merely being its makers*' (Smart, 1989:77).

Recognition of sexual subjectivity as a process, whether social, physical or spiritual, requires support from social structures such as family, community, education, law and medicine. Such support will be reciprocated when gender variant people (such as trans people and feminists) can contribute to society as fully included citizens.

### *Choice*

> In a just regime, one that celebrates individuals as authors of their own lives, one's gender identity should be the deciding factor in determining one's legal sex.
>
> (Currah, 2009:255)

Cowan noticed that Canadian law had opened up the possibility for self-perception of gender to affect legal determinations,

> ... legal and social acknowledgment of sexual identity in the UK remains rooted in the expert medical analysis of the state of the transsexed body/mind, while Canadian discussions of sexual identity in discrimination claims have been more open to the importance of self-perception in gender.
>
> (2005:85)

The choice to transition or not provides the individual with agency to define, or not to define, their sexual subjectivity, affording that individual some measure of control in the path that their life takes. Choice to self-define subjectivity can endow the individual with agency to escape the tyranny of assigned identity, identity that in many cases is entirely inappropriate. Choice in self-expression relies on the people often best placed to explain individual gender, the individuals themselves.

According to Cowan, choice may open up possibilities for new gendered expression and may lessen any social compulsion to transfer to the 'opposite' sexual subjectivity,

> I am not suggesting that individuals who wish to do so should not be allowed to define themselves as 'men' or 'women' in the traditional sense. But recognising the construction of binary sex involves recognising that there are many more possibilities than two, and therefore we should not try to fit disparate bodies/socially lived experiences into this artificial binary system. Surely this is a human rights issue.
>
> (2005:93)

> ... problems arise when someone who has changed sex and lives in their 'new' gender, changes their mind and wishes to change back again. Forcing subjects to live in a binary and dichotomous sex and gender system leads to a discourse of 'mistakes'.
>
> (93)

For these reasons, care has to be taken when advocating choice to transition for children and adolescents because their powers of informed choice are still often in early development. In negotiations of the draft Equality Bill, Press for Change considered that access to pubertal deferment treatment should be granted to those young people who evidence a strong desire to transition, in order that transition would be easier should they choose that route later in life.[18] Press for Change also argued that applying the label 'gender variant'[19] rather than 'gender reassignment' to such young people would help to eliminate any compulsion they might feel to label their own gender by marking them as not yet ready for full transition.

218  *Recommendations*

These innovations would have to be accompanied by an increase in trans awareness for school staff. Currah noted that, in the US of the 2000s, schools themselves were not acting as sites for gender reform,

> Forced [by her school] to choose between dressing in girls' clothing or having no picture in the [school] yearbook, [pupil] Youngblood chose the latter. When the yearbook was published, there was no picture of Youngblood in it. She had been cleansed from her school's official history – even her name did not appear.
>
> (2006:7)

> That schools are central to reproducing hegemonic cultural norms is made clear by the courts in the many decisions supporting gender-based dress codes in schools.
>
> (2006:7)

Viewing faulty attribution of gender at birth as eliminating choice, rather than later assuming pathology on the part of the gender variant individual, for instance in the school environment, aligns with the ethic of 'relocating problems away from an intra-psychic domain', as recommended by Vivien Burr.

Choice of subjectivity can also engender passion for that subjectivity rather than a feeling of compulsion to adhere to a given identity out of a sense of fear. This kind of choice can open up membership to the subjectivities 'feminist' and 'trans person' where 'feminist' is based primarily upon a personally political standpoint and where identifying as trans person or as someone seeking transition allows transition to be a positive and affirmative experience. In a minority of cases, it seems that choosing to transition gender, or to declare gender variance, may be a choice to be different to heteronormative. If heteronormativity rejects an individual should the individual not have the choice to find something different?

## 9.3 Postdifference

> And what happens when I begin to become that for which there is no place within the given regime of truth?
>
> (Butler, 2004:58)

> For men, the absolutes of truth and fairness, defined by the concepts of equality and reciprocity, are called into question by experiences that demonstrate the existence of differences between other and self.
>
> (Gilligan, 1982:166)

The reconstructing themes grouped into this discourse evidence ways in which gender variant subjectivities can flourish once maternal relations and genre/ genealogy provide the social space in which they can exist. Genre and genealogy engendered subjectivities formed from identification through choice rather than from assigned biological identity. Postdifference is genre and genealogy as positive and valued subjective difference, endowed with the agency granted by maternal relations to participate fully in society.

Postdifference involves recognition for all gender variance, helping to ensure that reassignment treatments are not erroneously sought in the individual's quest to realise their preferred gender. This recognition involves acceptance of difference, rather than the imposition of aetiology, in the identification of sexual subjectivity. Difference that openly challenges dualities such as man/woman and straight/gay can reveal sexual subjectivity as complex, for instance in the understanding that trans men and trans women are not simply the gendered opposites of each other and that people can possess gender different to the 'heteronorm'.

## Political subjectivity?

In the <The Paper> topic thread the author suggested the value of a kind of 'naming-in-process', rather than a politics depending upon fixed and dualised differences, concurring with the requirements of a move from second wave to third wave philosophical thinking (Jun 18th, 2006). This would be a way of articulating gendered experience without fixing it into essentialism, or by losing it from discourse as can be the case in an 'erotics of unnaming' or by diluting political subjectivity into uncritical postmodernist non-subjectivity. Third wavers have distanced their philosophy from the loss of subjectivity politics as discussed in Chapter 3. For instance, third wave theorist Ann Ferguson theorised that subjectivity is still often related to material and community influences but thought it possible that a subjectivity based politics could be based upon an inclusive third wave ethic (1997). This would differ to identity-based inclusion since, as according to Polly Toynbee, '*Women never will form one coherent mighty movement because gender is not enough as politics. But it is one way of thinking, one around which to build temporary coalitions on particular issues*' (6 June 2002).

## Passing

The continued debate about 'passing' into gender indicates that we are still not close to living in a 'post-out' society. Passing, usually meaning the endeavour to appear as one of the two heteronormative genders, operates to airbrush people out of history when the transitioning person is expected to deny their history of transition, or when all gender variant people feel they have to step in line with heteronormative discourse. However, it must be remembered that politicising a gender, or a refusal to pass unnoticed into heteronormativity, could affect all those who hold the political/non-passing gender since it 'outs' the gender in question. Nevertheless, a whole field of 'tall poppies' would be a formidable prospect for those inclined to single out and persecute the isolated (non-passing) 'tall poppy'.

Increased awareness of trans people since the 1970s has increased their visibility as targets for abuse, especially if they do not pass in public.[20] It could be that some trans people wish to evade transphobic harassment and discrimination, in seeking to assimilate into heteronormativity, '... *trans people do not seek secrecy, we are seeking privacy...*' (McNab, 15 June 2004). Such privacy was bolstered with the introduction of the GRA 2004 but privacy and passing will always be needed if oppressive gender hegemonies prevail. Passing as a requisite, rather than as a choice, seems to equate with the kind of forced lifestyles portrayed in *1984* by George Orwell. If medicine and the law encourage trans people to pass to the extent that history and subjectivity are denied this will forever situate trans subjectivities within, and subject them to, silent and secret discourse.

The GRA 2004 (and now the EA 2010) to some extent promote recognition rather than passing by not demanding bodily reassignment as a condition of achieving 'gender reassignment'. Trans people are not now legally required to pass physically as males and females but they are expected to pass as such in other measures of appearance such as dress, make-up and behaviour. The hegemony of heteronormative appearance prevails in practice and those trans people who fit into the heteronormative gender schema will still find it easier to gain medical, legal and social approbation of their claims to gender recognition.

### Social cleansing

Postdifference means inclusion for difference rather than difference exclusion in the way that transphobic people, separatist trans people and separatist feminists have sought to exclude gender variance. Trans oppression proceeds unnoticed if not defined, so a postdifferent paradigm would recognise gendered difference as evolving but identifiable, as the kind of 'politically postmodern identity' described in Chapters 3 and 6.

Highlighting the difference between difference separatism and difference inclusion, Gloria Steinem mentioned that, '*From Black Power to Gay Power, the goal is not to perpetuate difference, but to protest the invisibility, suppression, and political uses of difference*' (Steinem, 1995:xx).

As suggested in Chapter 7, oppressors rely on a mixed bag of oppressive devices to draw from in order to silence and exclude an oppressed subjectivity. They pick and mix from this bag to conjure up an armoury of oppressive devices that seem to reflect the natural order and 'common sense'. These devices include infantilisation, marginalisation, invisiblisation and scripts of inferiorisation such as those undermining the intelligence, mannerisms, appearance and customs of the target subjectivity in question. Forums for what Gilligan called 'voice', should be available for the 'different' to articulate their difference without imposing that difference upon the whole of society, as has heteronormativity when imposing its own difference as normality.

The law can prevent some of the worst excesses of these persecutions and misrepresentations by providing legal deterrents, but oppressors can still circumvent the law by excluding trans people in subtle ways. This might be done through indirect discrimination where the trans person is unable to participate because of a provision, criterion or practice that applies to everyone but in practice works to exclude the trans person. As a result of this denial of social access the excluded trans person effectively becomes an 'immigrant or refugee'; someone not treated as a full and conventional citizen.

## *Immigrants and refugees*

Social cleansing of difference has seen to it that feminists and trans people have been relegated to the margins of social discourses, and that some feminists and gender variant people have been relegated to the margins of these margins, like metaphorical immigrants and refugees. However, these people have applied their 'view from somewhere' to influence social discourses like ghosts in a machine who seep through chinks in the armour of social power relations.

Separatist exclusion, such as that experienced by the gender oppressed, is characteristically based upon difference perceived from a distance and was narratively addressed in the *Transstudy* by Clarette,

> ... it's generally easy to distance yourself from a dominant grouping, but not easy from a dominated grouping. That you don't get the choice not to be black, woman, moslem ... the dominant group will always see you that way and make you stay there. ... Political campaigns against domination and segregation have ... sought and accepted allies from any background, and of any identity. Our background still does not determine the validity of what we say.
> (Clarette Apr 11th, 2006, in <Black Trans>)

Clarette aligns with a postdifferent approach to political subjectivity by wishing to '... *accept allies from any background*' as a way to contest identity stereotyping. This approach combats the social dysphoria behind the demonisation of trans subjectivity that doesn't relocate or 'immigrate' into heteronormativity. By looking at individual trans lives, ethics of care can reveal that it is society that is regularly dysfunctional in its approach to trans issues rather than trans people being dysfunctional in their performance of gender.

Some *Transstudy* narratives[21] and third wave texts suggest that tolerance of others can lead to reinforcement and understanding of who we are rather than act as a challenge to our integrity. Postdifferent inclusion for difference leads to an understanding that the individuality of people often defines them more than their ascribed identification as social and biological types. Those we perceive as different to us may be more similar to us in philosophy and politics than those who share our gendered and ethnic features.

The concept of EU citizenship[22] holds the potential to transform the perception of trans people from alien immigrants into individual citizens. This concept was formally introduced in the Maastricht Treaty of 7 February 1992, via Article 17 (1) of the amended Treaties of Rome, was extended by the Treaty of Amsterdam, and has been developed by the European Court of Justice. EU Citizenship is intended as a way of integrating citizens into the whole Community and to provide them with a sense of belonging to that Community.[23] This Citizenship can act to protect those who are not protected by, or who have lost contact with, familial or close community ties, providing inclusion for those without conventional kin connections. It seems a shame that this concept of citizenship may be lost for most UK citizens in its departure from the European Union. It may be retained by naturalisation in, or becoming a citizen of, another EU country or by holding dual citizenship.

## 9.4 Practical applications of the recommendations

> Protections on paper are, of course, inadequate. The legal recognition of trans people is meaningful only when it is part of a larger social transformation.
> 
> (Currah et al., 2006:xxiii)

> Achieving equity will not be an end for trans people, but the start of a dramatic wielding of the cultural and social imagination.
> 
> (Currah et al., 2006:xxiv)

> One important lesson learned from the midcentury civil rights movement is that attention only to one single issue or identity results not in revolution, but in narrow and one-dimensional politics.
> 
> (Garrison, 2005:251)

> ... we have not addressed the social system that oppresses transgender, but merely have tried to upgrade it.
> 
> (Pershai, 2006:50)

> Feminist work which challenges the epistemological neutrality of the legal system ... is necessarily less attractive to those who equate politics with institutional forms of change. The production of ideas is seen as a very inadequate substitute – even when we know the old methods of law reform have been tried and failed.
> 
> (Smart, 1989:84)

In the fifth quotation above, Carol Smart highlights how philosophical recommendations can be seen as less tangible and practical than concrete single-issue legislative change. However, 'different voices', identified by Gilligan and Kristeva as revealed by ethics of care and protected by maternal relations, can reveal law as a certain kind of discourse that will dictate the content of single issues unless its basic structure, or social roots, are identified and modified. For Kristeva, maternal relations came in the form of a semiotic voice forming a ghostly presence in symbolic language which, if drawn upon, can challenge apparently common-sense and ethical discourse, '... *the psyche represents the bond between the speaking being and the other, a bond that endows it with a therapeutic and moral value*' (1993[1979]:206).

In order to address the social roots of gender oppression, largely driven by separatist perceptions of difference, the law needs to recognise that there is more to gender than heteronormativity, and more to gender oppression than the wording of certain legislation, '*Whilst there is a need for more rigorous enforcement of the law, that factor alone would be insufficient to achieve the changes in attitudes that trans people encounter daily at work ...*' (Whittle, 2002b:1).

In *Legal Queeries* Moran et al. (1998) called for legal enquiry that investigates the construction of discourses rather than making attempts to fit in with such discourses. This kind of enquiry will direct attention towards the roots of gender discrimination rather than follow a traditional reformist agenda. Several authors in the book investigate these constructions. Moerings revealed how the discrepancy between the content of the law in Dutch society and the practice of this law reveals that the law is not actually part of the social ethos in this society, '*Significantly he [Moerings] identifies a disparity between the well intentioned laws and the practical usage made of them and he suggests that political compromise in their enactment is one of the causes of this discrepancy*' (Moran et al., 1998:7).

In the same volume, legal theorist Elena Loizidou portrayed the law as stern isolated father figure with a lack of connection to the 'shop floor' of gender, noting that, '*The criminal law's denial of interdependence actually leads to various miscarriages of justice*' (Moran et al., 1998:8).

Currah et al. described how a focus on society rather than biological aetiology might improve gender variant lives rather than merely work to categorise them,

> ... the effectiveness with which the transgender movement addresses the diversity of its constituents will depend less on finding a satisfactory vocabulary and more on how actual strategies for social change are implemented.
>
> Whether we have psychological features in common or share a particular twist in our genetic codes is less important than the more pressing search for justice and equality.
>
> (2006:xiv)

There is a need for a cultural ethics of care, not just a professional ethic applied to legal cases. Ethics of care needs to be a social discourse, embedded into society, in order to implement the ability for society to address its own social roots. The following practical applications of the recommendations suggest how the roots of gender oppression can be challenged by addressing the construction of discourse.

## Maternal relations

*1. Implement a politics of naming*

Increased input into the naming of genders for gender variant people would allow them to form a concept of their own gendering which may not fit into heteronormative discourse. This would prevent them from living out a life of nameless isolation. Inclusivity features in the theory and communication of philosophical third wave thinkers, who need the legal sanction of a category of 'gender variance' in order to create and maintain a social space for gender variant people. Gender variance needs to be conceived of as a mature developmental outcome so that gender variant people are allowed access to social 'voice'.

*2. Make provision for case law tailored to individual circumstances*

Networks of relations aimed at improving the law for gender oppressed people have operated along the lines of what Seyla Benhabib identified as a dialogic model of ethics.[24] This has involved a focus on case law tailored to individual circumstances (via the ethics of care) with a view to creating foundational legislation that recognises particular circumstances of gender oppressed people (via an ethic of justice). In this way, legislators become aware of the special route to gendering experienced by trans people, and how they can cater for this route when drawing up legislation. As noted by Lara Karaian on the subject of this special route,

> Legal theorist Douglas Kropp, for example, takes the position that we need to break from our fixation on the "grounds" of discrimination such as sex, race, age and so on, and instead we must increase our focus on the lived experience of rights claimants.
> (Karaian, 2006:188)

Scales points out that gender inclusive lawyers have notably been involved in ethics of care like approaches to individual cases, *'The good lawyers I know were already epistemologically poststructuralist. They knew that they were re/presenting a text (which they called "cases" or "clients"), in a vortex of interpretational fluidity'* (2009:397). The progressive nature of these approaches to legal cases needs promoting as a feature of ethics of care based legal operations.

*3. Form a third wave/trans coalition to investigate how legal gains for feminists inform the legal claims of trans people and vice versa*

The Yogyakarta Principles encourage input from those most closely affected by particular kinds of discrimination so that oppressed people can mould the law from the inside rather than always being its object. A balanced unity of diversity between trans people and feminists will allow cross-subjective input into negotiations with the law in order to initiate a challenge to the silent and secret discourse that oppresses their gendered subjectivities. Karaian supported this kind of approach by considering that, '... *progressive legal activists would be more accountable to the communities they are representing if they were to incorporate greater complexity and diversity into their legal arguments*' (2006:182–3).

Lobbying power would be increased exponentially with a diversity union based upon politics of self-representation, rather than coercion into essentialised identity politics. Drawing from the notion of 'voice coaching', and as suggested in Chapter 6, gender oppressed people often have particular abilities to reveal the effect of gendering on people's lives by questioning and revealing the common sense operation of gender.

### Genre and genealogy

*4. Abandon a search for aetiology in favour of the provision for difference*

Genre and genealogy can highlight the realities of relational connection as a challenge to unproved biological essentialism, affording gender variant people the choice to have their gender fully recognised and accepted, for instance in modified Gender Recognition and Equality Acts. In this way genre and genealogy offer more inclusive definitions of gender than, for instance, those established in the rulings of *Corbett v Corbett* and *Bellinger v Bellinger*. The EA 2010 abandons a search for medical aetiology in favour of the provision for some measure of gendered difference, albeit difference that has to assimilate under the banner of heteornormativity. However, acceptance rather than aetiology will not happen in practice unless authorities are persuaded to promote gender equity (respect for self-representations rather than imposing assimilation) and to seek the prevention of all types of discrimination, to bring the spirit of the EA into the community.

Provision for difference would recognise the way that different socially formed genders can input differently into discourse, as mentioned in respect of women's ethical perspective in Chapter 4 and in respect of trans men's ability with speech in Chapter 8. These differences can be considered in the drawing up of policy documents. Robert Shapiro and Harpreet Mahajan (1986) found that women and men respond differently to differently worded policies and Paul Kellstedt et al. (2010) found that there were differences in responses by men and women to changes in governmental public policy. Policies constructed by differently gendered people would increase access to this forum of social 'voice'.

Scales criticised the liberal assimilationist agenda that might develop from being tied to governmental policy,

> Employing access to governmental power, however, is not automatically cool. Professor Ruthann Robson (1992, 2002) has been right in her original and prolific work, consistently illustrating the "domesticating" effects of voluntarily engaging with and seeking legitimation from the law.
> (2009:406)

However, the alternative to involvement is lack of access and voice and consequently acceptance based on knowledge. The roots of social change must be tended to wherever they may be found. What hooks, and then Scales (407), identified as radically critical, but non-competitive, engagement or 'solidarity', must be established with those working in influential discourses, such as government, in order for gender inclusion to occur.

*5. Reposition sexual subjectivity as a process*

A classification of 'gender variance' rather than 'gender reassignment' would position transition as a process rather than as change and the gender variant person could consequently 'find themselves' without pressure to conform to a certain biological and behavioural template. Consideration of, 'style of upbringing and living, and self-perception', as in the case of *Bellinger v Bellinger*, as valid indicators of gender should be included into wording of future Gender Recognition and Equality Acts. This can be done by challenging both Acts' requirements for a commitment to the process of reassignment,

> ... legal recognition for all purposes, can now be obtained without medical treatment, as such, and it will only be with such an extension of the legal principle beyond gender reassignment that we shall see the vast majority of the UK's trans people, who are not transsexual, obtain rights as individuals, which they can enforce.
>
> (Whittle et al., 2006:11)

*6. Make legal provision for choice of sexual subjectivity*

If the law classifies gender in a rigid way it can make a trans person's journey to gendered accomplishment a tough assignment. It can also shroud reasons behind discrimination targeted towards the trans person by not recognising that trans subjectivity is different to heteronormative subjectivity in that it involves transition or, for gender variant people, that it may entail different gendering. Application of the label 'gender variant'[25] rather than 'gender reassignment' to potentially transitioning adults as well as children, will provide a social space for them to be recognised for legal protection but not to feel compelled to choose one gender or another until they are ready to do so.

**Postdifference**

*7. Promote recognition rather than passing*

The EA 2010 has ensured that protection from discrimination is available for transitioning people regardless of whether or what reassignment treatment they have had, and therefore whether they pass as heteronormative or not. However, this protection usually means remedy after the discrimination has taken place. More pro-active recognition of all gender variance could transpire from inclusive initiatives. For instance, the Government could promote recognition by ensuring that public appointments boards have an obligation to positively encourage gender variant people to seek public appointments. Such initiatives would encourage recognition of hard fought for subjectivity formed by those with a gender variant history, and would include gender variant people into employment. Also, recognition of non-heteronormative-based 'Real Life Experience', for those who find it hard to 'pass' or do not wish to 'pass' into heteronormativity, would facilitate inclusion and recognition for people with a gender variant history.

As discussed when referring to the work of Butler in Chapter 7, medical diagnosis of gender variance is still largely seen as a diagnosis of dysfunction, not as an indication of something valuable (2006). Recognition of gender variance would lead to increased respect for, and understanding of, gender variant sexual subjectivities.

*8. Develop a legal category of 'gender variance' in order to challenge imposed perceptions of gender*

Defining every gender variation for the purposes of the law would be a formidable endeavour, so a general 'gender variant' category could serve to include those who are perceived to fall outside the parameters of heteronormativity. People would then not feel so compelled to choose one of the two heteronormative genders. 'Gender variance', as a legal category, would also protect the transitioning person, including the minor, who have to wait years for reassignment treatments that ensure heteronormative appearance, while not compelling the individual to be associated with the process of physical reassignment. Oppressors will often not wait this long for a fully heteronormative expression so protection against direct discrimination and/or harassment based upon perception, initiated by the EA 2010, is a particularly important component of trans legal protection. Difference, such as gender variance, that doesn't seek to eradicate other difference can then be included into society as healthy diversity.

*9. Transform the perception of gender variant people from 'gender immigrants' to individual citizens*

The EU concept of citizenship[26] recognises the right of everyone to citizenship without resorting to received notions of gender or ethnicity. Citizenship includes all subjects living in its community as full citizens and respects their social and demographic subjectivities, promoting recognition rather than assimilation. An application of this concept to gendered citizenship, in whichever country, would encourage an 'ethics of participation', in the sense described by Richard Bellamy and Alex Warleigh (1998), rather than purely an 'ethics of integration'. Promotion of participation should have the effect of preventing the subtle exclusion of gender variant people by indirect discrimination.

Gender variant people can then be respected by their acceptance into, rather than assimilation into, gendered society. This will mark them as citizens rather than objectified 'immigrants'. When this acceptance allows gender variant people to slowly but significantly enter into positions of articulation in public and private society, complexities of real life gendering, often revealed by gender variant people's experience of personal epiphanies, can be used to challenge the operation of 'common sense' gender schemata.

## Notes

1. X, Y & Z in Chapter 4 s. 4.
2. For instance, in the way described by Jan Morris (1974:14–15, 106–7).
3. Donna Haraway's concept of 'Modest Witness' (1997:23), explained in Chapter 2.
4. Gilligan's main investigation into this phenomenon was carried out in the abortion study (1982:71–105).
5. This term is used by critical discourse analyst Fairclough as an adjective of 'discourse' (2003).
6. This kind of essentialism and the responses it has engendered by trans people was discussed in Chapter 6.
7. As narratively undertaken by Mark Rees in *Dear Sir or Madam* (1996) and by Judith Halberstam in *Female Masculinity* (1998).
8. For instance, as narrated by Max Valerio (2006:328).
9. The author takes 'umbrella protection' to mean consideration of how to protect and respect a range of subjectivities by applying standard anti-discriminatory law.
10. A reference to the quote from Gloria Anzaldúa (1983 [1981]:209) in *This Bridge Called My Back*.
11. Such as Jan Morris (1975 [1974]:153), Sadie Mar 21st, 2005, in <Is it helpful to pathologise transgendered subjectivity?>, Sandy Stone (1991:296), Stephen Whittle (2002a:82), Dhillon Khosla (2006:8) and Shannon (Apr 7th, 2005, in <Male=man, female=woman?>).
12. Foucault theorised that the image of self that we take to be identity is built up by experience (Foucault 1984:87), and this interpretation is described by Prado (2000:53–84). Foucault's interpretation of the self as a subject-in-process is described by O'Leary (2002:5, 7, 9, 13, 14, 16) and by Prado (2000:57, 67, 72, 81) who refers to Foucault's image of the self as a 'soul'.
13. As described in the Explanatory Notes to the Equality Act 2010, see the Government Equalities Office (http://www.equalities.gov.uk/equality_act_2010.aspx).
14. As suggested in a quote from Clarette (Apr 10th, 2006, in <The Whole Trans person>) – see Chapter 6.
15. As described by Edelstein (1993:196, 200, 202). Kristeva also described feminism as in-process (1993:199). In *New Maladies of the Soul* she speaks of, '*the singularity of each woman, her complexities, her many languages*', when challenging the general use of the phrase 'woman' (1993:221).
16. In *New Maladies of the Soul* Kristeva associated the third phase with increasing interdependence (1993:201), with a call for recognition of subjectivity as 'free and flowing' (221) and with a perspective rather than a mass movement (222).
17. Gilligan also perceived the possibility of such idiosyncratic development (1982:7,24–25,39,98).
18. Press for Change (May 2009).

19 Discussed as Question 73 at the Public Bill Committee 2nd Meeting (Afternoon 02/06/2009).
20 As related by Whittle et al. (20 December 2006:56), and by Monica (Mar 11th, 2005, in <respected in your workplace> and Jun 15th, 2006, in <How do you believe you will you age?>).
21 For example, Clarette Jun 10th, 2005, in <gender presentation then and now>.
22 European Commission (updated: 09/03/2012).
23 See point 1.1.1 in Committee of the Regions (2000).
24 It seems that Benhabib resembled Mikhail Bakhtin in thinking that dialogic communication is evident in all human communication (Bakhtin and Emerson, 1984:42).
25 As lobbied for by PFC in draft negotioations of the Equality Bill, for instance in Question 73, Public Bill Committee 2nd Meeting (Afternoon 02/06/2009).
26 Provided by the European Commission (updated: 09/03/2012).

# Appendix

## List of *Transstudy* topics

Each topic is followed by the name of the participant who originated the topic. 'Ed' indicates the author.

(A) A few *Transstudy* statistics, Ed
(B) A Gender Spectrum – Collected Thoughts, Raelene
(C) A Third Way?, Ed
(D) Abilities and aptitudes, Monica
(E) Anankastic (obsessive/compulsive) personality, Monica
(F) Are there just feminine and masculine people now … ?, Ed
(G) Are There Male Rapunzels?, Ed
(H) Are we all transvestites now?, Ed
(I) Being Trans : A blessing or a curse, Leon
(J) Being Un-PC oops, Leon
(K) Belittling Britain?, Ed
(L) Black Trans, Ed
(M) 'Blanket' Theories of Sexual Development, Ed
(N) Camp Trans 2005-2, Ed
(O) Camp Trans 2005, Ed
(P) Can feminism include input from and inclusion for born males?, Ed
(Q) Changes to Your Self-Presentation?, Ed
(R) Christian Institute vs the GRB, Ed
(S) Cyber-Gendering, Ed
(T) Damage from unfavourable dramatic portayal of transgender, Monica
(U) Dane Bagger, Ed
(V) Different cultural aspects of being trans, Kimana
(W) Do you still feel slightly out of kilter even after transition and SRS ?, Leon
(X) Does one have to act to be a woman?, Ed
(Y) Does one's sexual subjectivity change in different circumstances and over time?, Ed
(Z) Dreams and Trans Subjectivity, Ed

Appendix  231

(AA) Dreams can come true – Contribute a dream ?, Raelene
(AB) Duelling Dualisms?: Speech vs Writing and Presence vs Absence, Ed
(AC) Escaping Gender?, Ed
(AD) Exploitation of transsexuality by broadcasters, Monica
(AE) Extremely open question, Alyssa
(AF) Film Portrayals of Trans, Ed
(AG) freedom of expression, Clarette
(AH) Gender Identity, question on transforming personality with regards to sexual subjectivity(Preferred, Alyssa
(AI) Gender norms, Alyssa
(AJ) gender presentation then and now ;-), Clarette
(AK) Grieving for what we never had?, Clarette
(AL) Hey You!, Ed
(AM) Hidden Transmen?, Ed
(AN) Hormone Regimes, Raelene
(AO) How are we perceived?, Monica
(AP) How do you believe you will you age?, Monica
(AQ) How do you define 'Sexuality'?, Ed
(AR) How do you wish to know your sexed self?, Ed
(AS) How long to be 'out' as pre-op?, Ed
(AT) Identity, Subjectivity and 'Gene Reassignment Surgery', Ed
(AU) Immigrants and Refugees?, Monica
(AV) Introduction, Patricia
(AW) Is it helpful to pathologise transgendered subjectivity?, Ed
(AX) Jouissance, Ed
(AY) Loved Ones and New GR Certificate, Monica
(AZ) Male=man, female=woman?, Ed
(BA) Min and Max Transition Ages?, Ed
(BB) more perceptions etc., Clarette
(BC) NHS safeguards, Alyssa
(BD) Omnisexual, bisexual, trisexual, or just plain straight, lesbian or gay?, Ariel
(BE) Open questions *please*, Imogen
(BF) Open Topic for discussion – approved by Ed, Alyssa
(BG) Personalityism, Ed
(BH) Post-GRS people's sexuality, Ed
(BI) Post-Op experiences, Alyssa
(BJ) Psychodemographic Questionnaire?, Ed
(BK) Purging, Ed
(BL) respected in your workplace, vocational environment or social settings?, Ed
(BM) Russell Reid vs Charles Kane & Charing Cross saga, Leon
(BN) School and trans-development, Ed
(BO) Self-Presentation within Relationships, Ed
(BP) some cultural aspects of shapeshifting?, Clarette

(BQ)  Some thoughts on non-trans gender-changers, Raelene
(BR)  Some thoughts on Trans Acceptance and Freedom., Raelene
(BS)  Spiritual or religious beliefs, Monica
(BT)  SR, SA, SA, SC, SR or ST?, Ed
(BU)  Stephen says, 'Help', Ed
(BV)  Tabloid manipulation of trans representations, Ed
(BW)  The effect of administration of oestrogens/androgens into old age., Monica
(BX)  The Paper, Ed
(BY)  The *Transstudy* is Dead, Long Live the *Transstudy*!, Ed
(BZ)  The Whole Transperson, Ed
(CA)  Title of the *Transstudy*, Ed
(CB)  Too womanly to be a woman?, Alyssa
(CC)  Trans and Feminist Theories, Ed
(CD)  Trans and Intersex, Ed
(CE)  Trans Marriage, Ed
(CF)  Trans Parenting, Ed
(CG)  Trans Partners, Ed
(CH)  Trans-friendly social groups?, Ed
(CI)  Transgender Movement?, Ed
(CJ)  Trans-Naming?, Ed
(CK)  Transpeople and their cultural 'home', Ed
(CL)  Transpregnancy, Monica
(CM)  'Transsexual' = an adjective?, Ed
(CN)  Transsexual sexuality, Alyssa
(CO)  Trans-sexuality?, Ed
(CP)  Types of Transperson, Ed for Sadie
(CQ)  What advice to a Newbie, Raelene
(CR)  What Causes Trans Subjectivity?, Ed
(CS)  What should a modern Real Life Experience involve?, Ed
(CT)  What was the most difficult aspect of your transition ?, Leon
(CU)  What we are = what we do?, Ed
(CV)  WHo do you feel after the SRS ?, Leon
(CW)  Who might be the 'Others' of the *Transstudy*?, Ed
(CX)  Your Narrative Self?, EdTopics last saved: 29 May 2007.
Total number of topics: 102.
Time period covered: From <respected in your workplace> Ed Feb 5, 2005–6:01 AM to <Moving on and the losses that accrue> Ed Aug 15th, 2007–11:09 AM.

**Table of cases**

- A v Chief Constable of West Yorkshire Police, (1999) IT Case No 2901131/98

- Attorney-General v Family Court at Otahuhu [1995] NZFC Otahuhu, Fam LR 57
- Bellinger v Bellinger [2001] EWCA, Civ 1140
- Bellinger v Bellinger [2003] UKHL 21, [2003] All ER (D) 178 (Apr)
- Chessington World of Adventures Ltd v Reed [1997] IRLR 556, EAT
- Chief Constable of West Yorkshire Police v A [2004] UKHL 21
- Corbett v Corbett [1970] CA, 2 All ER 33
- Goodwin v UK Government (1995) ECHR, Application No 28957/95
- I v UK Government, [1994] ECHR, Application No 25608/94
- L v Lithuania, (2007) ECHR, Application No 27527/03
- P v S and Cornwall County Council [1996], ECJ, Case C-13/94 IRLR 347
- Wilkinson v Kitzinger & Others [2006] HC, HRLR 36
- X v Brighton and Hove City Council [2006/7]
- X, Y and Z v UK (1997), ECHR, 24 EHRR 143

## Table of legislation

- Civil Partnership Act 2004
- Civil Union Act [SA]
- Equality Act 2006 (EA 2006)
- Equality Act 2010 (EA 2010)
- Equal Pay Act 1970
- Gender Recognition Act 2004 (GRA 2004)
- Human Rights Act 1998 (HRA 1998)
- Sex Discrimination Act 1975
- Sex Discrimination (Amendment of Legislation) Regulations 2008
- Sex Discrimination (Gender Reassignment) Regulations 1999

# Bibliography

Ahmed, Sara (Summer 1995) 'Theorising Sexual Identification: Exploring the Limits of Psycho-analytic and Postmodern Models', *Australian Feminist Studies*, vol 22: 9–30.
Ahmed, Sara. (1998) *Differences That Matter: Feminist theory and Postmodernism*, Cambridge: Cambridge University Press.
Alfonso, Rita and Jo Trigilio (Summer1997) 'Surfing the Third Wave: A Dialogue Between Two Third Wave Feminists', in Jacqueline N. Zita (ed) *'Third Wave Feminisms', Hypatia, Special Issue: A Journal of Feminist Philosophy*, vol 12, no. 3: 7–16.
Allen, Robert (1954) *But for the Grace: The True Story of a Dual Existence*, London: W H Allen.
Althusser, Louis (1971) 'Ideology and Ideological State Apparatuses', in *Lenin and Philosophy and other Essays*, trans. by Ben Brewster, New York: Monthly Review Press, pp. 121–176.
Althusser, Louis and E Balibar (1970) *Reading Capital*, London: New Left Books.
Andreadis, Harriette (1999) 'Theorising Early Modern Lesbianisms: Invisible Borders, Ambiguous Demarcations', in Mary Ann O'Farrell and Lynne Vallone (eds) *Virtual Gender: Fantasies of Sub-jectivities and Embodiment*, Michigan: University of Michigan Press, pp. 125–146.
Anzaldúa, Gloria (1981) 'La Prieta', in C Moraga and G Anzaldúa (eds) *This Bridge Called My Back: Writings by Radical Women of Colour*, New York: Kitchen Table (Edit. 1983), pp. 189–209.
Anzaldúa, Gloria (1987) *Borderlands: The New Mestiza = La Frontera*, 2nd edn, San Francisco: Aunt Lute (Edit. 1999).
Assorted Authors [includes Aconway] (2002) *Gender*, Wikipedia, acc. 05/11/2010, at www.wikigender.org/index.php/Gender, Last mod. 18/08/2010.
Atkins, Susan, and Brenda M Hogget (now Hale) (1984) *Women and the Law*, Oxford: Blackwell.
Austin, Paula (2002) 'Femme-Inism: Lessons from my Mother', in Daisy Hernandez and Bushra Rehman (eds) *Colonize This!: Young Women of Color on Today's Feminism*, Berkeley, CA: Seal Press, pp. 157–169.
Backer, Larry Cata (1998) Chapter 13: 'Queering Theory: An Essay on the Conceit of Revolution in Law', in Leslie J Moran, Daniel Monk and Sarah Beresford (eds) *Legal Queeries: Lesbian, Gay and Transgender Legal Studies*, London and New York: Cassell, pp. 185–203.
Bailey, Cathryn (Summer1997) 'Making Waves and Drawing Lines: The Politics of Defining the Vicissitudes of Feminism', in Jacqueline N Zita (ed) *'Third Wave*

*Feminisms'*, *Hypatia, Special Issue: A Journal of Feminist Philosophy*, vol 12, no. 3: 17–28.
Bakan, David (1966) *The Duality Of Human Existence: Isolation and Communion in Western Man*, Boston, MA: Beacon Press.
Bakhtin, Mikhail Mikhaïlovich and Caryl Emerson (ed) (1984) *Problems of Dostoevsky's Poetics: Volume 8 of Theory and History of Literature*, Minneapolis, MN: University of Minnesota Press.
Barbin, Herculine and Michel Foucault (1980) *Herculine Barbin: Being the Recently Discovered Memoirs of a Nineteenth-century French Hermaphrodite*, trans. by Richard McDougall, New York: Pantheon Books.
Barthes, Roland (1977) *Image, Music, Text*, essays selected and translated [from the French] by Stephen Heath, London: Fontana.
Bartlett, Frederic C (1932) *Remembering: A Study in Experimental and Social Psychology*, Cambridge: Cambridge University Press.
Baudrillard, Jean (1990) *The Transparency of Evil: Essays on Extreme Phenomena* London, New York: Verso (Edit. 1993).
Baumgardner, Jennifer and Amy Richards (2000) *Manifesta: Young Women, Feminism, and the Future*, New York: Farrar, Straus and Giroux.
BBC News (2002), 'Transsexual Rights', *Newsnight*, 12 July.
Becker, Mary (2009) Chapter 9: 'Care and Feminists', in Martha Albertson Fineman, Jack E Jackson and Adam P Romero (eds) *Feminist and Queer Legal Theory: Intimate Encounters, Uncomfortable Conversations*, Farnham and Burlington: Ashgate, pp. 159–177.
Bellamy, Richard, Alex Warleigh-Lack (1998) 'From an Ethics of Integration to an Ethics of Participation: Citizenship and the Future of the European Union', in *Millennium: A Journal of International Studies*, vol 27, no. 3: 447–470.
Belsey, Tina A C and Michael A Peters (2007) *Subjectivity and Truth: Foucault, Education, and the Culture of Self*, New York: Peter Lang.
Benhabib, Seyla (1992) Chapter 6: 'The Debate over Women and Moral Theory Revisited', in *Situating the Self: Gender, Community and Postmodernism in Contemporary Ethics*, Oxford: Blackwell, pp. 178–202.
Benhabib, Seyla (1995) Chapter 7: 'The Debate over Women and Moral Theory Revisited', in Joanna Meehan (ed.) *Feminists Read Habermas: Gendering the Subject of Discourse*, London and New York: Routledge, pp. 181–204.
Benjamin, Harry (1953) 'Lessons from Jelke Sex Trial: (As Seen by a Sexologist)', publisher not identified, 1953.
Benjamin, Harry (1966) *The Transsexual Phenomenon*, New York: Julian Press.
Beresford, Sarah (1998) Chapter 4: 'The Lesbian Mother: Questions of Gender and Sexual Identity', in Leslie J Moran, Daniel Monk and Sarah Beresford (eds) *Legal Queeries: Lesbian, Gay and Transgender Legal Studies*, London and New York: Cassell, pp. 57–67.
Bile, Jeff (2013) Chapter 7: 'Silence and Voice in More-than-Human World', in Sheena Malhotra and Aimee Carrillo Rowe (eds) *Silence, Feminism, Power: Reflections at the Edges of Sound*, Basingstoke: Palgrave, pp. 95–100.
Bindel, Julie (2007) 'Mistaken identity', in *The Guardian*, 23 May.
Blaxter, Loraine, Christine Hughes and Malcolm Tight (2001) (2nd edn) *How to Research*, Buckingham and Philadelphia: Open University Press, pp. 154–161.
Bocock, Robert (1986) *Hegemony*, Chichester: Ellis Harwood Limited, London: Tavistock.

Bornstein, Kate (1994) *Gender Outlaw: On Men, Women and the Rest of Us*, New York: Vintage.

Brown, George R (1988) Chapter 37: 'Transsexuals in the Military: Flight into Hypermasculinity', in Susan Stryker and Stephen Whittle (eds) (2006) *The Transgender Studies Reader*, New York and London: Routledge, pp. 537–544.

Bulbeck, Chilla (1998) *Re-Orienting Western Feminisms: Women's Diversity in a Post-Colonial World*, Cambridge: Cambridge University Press.

Bullough, Vern L and Bonnie Bullough (1993) *Cross Dressing, Sex, and Gender*, Philadelphia: University of Pennysylvania Press.

Burns, Christine (1996) 'Transsexuals and the False Hope of the Identity Card', at www.pfc.org.uk/node/562.

Burns, Christine (1997) Activist Profile, acc. 11/05/2007, at www.pfc.org.uk/node/27.

Burns, Christine (20 June 2007) 'UK: A Feast of Interviews and Comment', *PfC News* [Online], (no longer available online, acc. from researcher's private collection).

Burr, Vivien (1995) *Social Constructionism*, London and New York: Routledge.

Burr, Vivien (2003) (2nd edn) *Social Constructionism*, London and New York: Routledge.

Butler, Judith (Dec, 1988) 'Performative Acts and Gender Constitution: An Essay in Phenomenology and Feminist Theory', in *Theatre Journal*, The Johns Hopkins University Press, vol. 40, no. 4, 519–531, acc. 09/11/17 at www.jstor.org/stable/3207893.

Butler, Judith (1990) (10th Anniversary Edition) *Gender Trouble: Feminism and the Subversion of Identity*, New York and London: Routledge (Edit.1999).

Butler, Judith (2004) *Undoing Gender*, London and New York: Routledge.

Butler, Judith (2006) Chapter 14: 'Undiagnosing Gender', in, Paisley Currah, Richard M Juang and Shannon Price Minter (eds) *Transgender Rights*, London, Minneapolis: University of Minnesota Press, pp. 274–298.

Byrd, Rudolph P, Johnnetta B Cole, Beverly Guy-Sheftall (eds) (2009) *I Am Your Sister: Collected and Unpublished Writings of Audre Lorde*, Oxford: Oxford University Press, pp. 3–39.

Caputo, John D (1997) *Deconstruction in a Nutshell: A Conversation with Jacques Derrida*, New York: Fordham University Press.

Chakraborty, Mridula Nath (2004) Chapter 16: 'Wa(i)ing it All Away: Producing Subject and Knowledge in Feminisms of Colour', in Stacy Gillis, Gillian Howie and Rebecca Munford (eds) *Third Wave Feminism: A Critical Exploration*, Basingstoke: Palgrave, pp. 205–215.

Charles, Helen (1990) 'Womanism: Recognising Difference, One Direction for the Black Woman Activist', *University of Kent at Canterbury: Women's Studies Occasional Papers*, Paper No. 21.

Charles, Helen (1997) Chapter 23: 'The Language of Women: Re-Thinking Difference', in Heidi Safia Mirza (ed.) *Black British Feminism*, London and New York: Routledge.

Chesler, Phyllis (1972) *Women and Madness*, New York and London: Four Walls Eight Windows (Edit. 1997).

Clair, Robin (2013) Chapter 6: 'Imposed Silence and the Story of the Warramunga Woman: Alternative Interpretations and Possibilities', in Sheena Malhotra and Aimee Carrillo Rowe (eds) *Silence, Feminism, Power: Reflections at the Edges of Sound*, Basingstoke: Palgrave, pp. 85–94.

Clandinin, D Jean and F Michael Connelly (2000) *Narrative Enquiry: Experience and Story in Qualitative Research*, San Francisco: Jossey-Bass.

Clark Mane, Rebecca L (2012) 'Transmuting Grammars of Whiteness in Third-Wave Feminism: Interrogating Postrace Histories, Postmodern Abstraction, and the Proliferation of Difference in Third-Wave Texts', *Signs*, vol 38, no. 1: 71–98.

Clayton, Angela (8 December 2007) 'Goods, Facilities & Services – Protection in Law for Trans People', *PfC News* [Online], (no longer available online, acc. from researcher's private collection).

Cohen, Stanley (1972) *Folk Devils and Moral Panics*, Abingdon: Taylor and Francis (Edit. 2011).

Colley, Ann and Zazie Todd (December 2002) 'Gender-Linked Differences in the Style and Content of E-Mails to Friends', in *Journal of Language and Social Psychology*, vol 21, no. 4: 380–392.

Combahee River Collective (1986) *The Combahee River Collective Statement: Black Feminist Organizing in The Seventies and Eighties*, Kitchen Table: Women of Color Press.

Committee of the Regions (2000) 'C156/12: Opinion of the Committee of the Regions on "EU Citizenship"', in *Official Journal of the European Communities*, acc. 15/06/2008, at http://eur-lex.europa.eu/LexUriServ/LexUriServ.do?uri=OJ:C:2000:156:0012:0017:EN:PDF.

Conway, Lynn (2000–2003) 'What Causes Transsexualism?', acc. 12/09/2009 at http://ai.eecs.umich.edu/people/conway/TS/TScauses.html.

Cook, Judith A and Margaret Fonow (1990) 'Knowledge and Women's Interests: Issues of Epistemology and Methodology in Feminist Sociological Research', in Joyce McCarl Nielsen (ed.) *Feminist Research Methods: Exemplary Readings in the Social Sciences*, Boulder, San Francisco and London: Westview Press, pp. 69–93.

Coon, Dennis (2000) *Introduction to Psychology: Gateways to Mind and Behavior*, Independence: Wadsworth Publishing.

Cooper, Martha and Carole Blair (2002) 'Foucault's Ethics', in *Qualitative Enquiry*, vol 8, no. 4: 511–531.

Cowan, Sharon (2004) 'That Woman is a Woman: The Case of Bellinger v Bellinger and the Mysterious Disappearance of Sex', in *Feminist Legal Studies*, vol 12, no. 1: 79–92.

Cowan, Sharon (2005) 'Gender is no Substitute for Sex: A Comparative Human Rights Analysis of the Legal Regulation of Sexual Identity', in *Feminist Legal Studies* vol. 13, no. 1: 67–96.

Cox, Ana Marie, Freya Johnson, Annalee Newitz and Jillian Sandell (1997) 'Masculinity without Men, Women Reconciling Feminism and Male-Identification', in Leslie L Heywood and Jennifer Drake (eds) *Third Wave Agenda: Being Feminist, Doing Feminism*, Minneapolis, MN: University of Minnesota Press, pp. 178–205.

Culbertson, Tucker and Jack Jackson (2009) Chapter 7: 'Proper Objects, Different Subjects and Juridical Horizons in Radical Legal Critique', in Martha Albertson Fineman, Jack E Jackson and Adam P Romero (eds) *Feminist and Queer Legal Theory: Intimate Encounters, Uncomfortable Conversations*, Farnham and Burlington: Ashgate, pp. 135–152.

Currah, Paisley (2006) Chapter 1: 'Gender Pluralisms under the Transgender Umbrella', in Paisley Currah, Richard M Juang and Shannon Price Minter (eds) *Transgender Rights*, London, Minneapolis: University of Minnesota Press, pp. 3–31.

Currah, Paisley (2009) Chapter 13: 'The Transgender Rights Imaginary', in Martha Albertson Fineman, Jack E Jackson and Adam P Romero (eds) *Feminist and Queer Legal Theory: Intimate Encounters, Uncomfortable Conversations*, Farnham and Burlington: Ashgate, pp. 245–258.

Currah, Paisley, Richard M Juang and Shannon Price Minter (eds) (2006) 'Introduction', in *Transgender Rights*, London, Minneapolis: University of Minnesota Press, pp. xiii–xxiv.
Czyzselska, Jane (2008) 'Pregnant with Discrimination', at www.guardian.co.uk, 6 July.
David, Miriam E (2004) 'Feminist Sociology and Feminist Knowledges: Contributions to Higher Education Pedagogies and Professional Practices in The Knowledge Economy', in *International Studies in Sociology of Education*, vol 14, no. 2: 99–123.
Dean, Tracy (2 June 2007) 'UK: Christine Burns MBE is The New Chair of The NW Equality and Diversity Group [NWRA]', *PfC News* [Online], (no longer available online, acc. from researcher's private collection).
Dean, Tracy (19 June 2007) 'UK: A Framework for Fairness Consultation Events', *PfC News* [Online], (no longer available online, acc. from researcher's private collection).
Dean, Tracy (8 July 2008) 'UK: Petition Response [no. 10]', *PfC News* [Online], (no longer available online, acc. from researcher's private collection).
Dean, Tracy (8 November 2008) 'UK: Editorial, news & feature articles on council discrimination case [GScene]', *PfC News* [Online], (no longer available online, acc. from researcher's private collection).
Dean, Tracy (26 October 2008b) 'MT: Joanne to Go All the Way in Her Fight to Get Married [Malta Today]', *PfC News* [Online], (no longer available online, acc. from researcher's private collection).
De Beauvoir, Simone (1949) *The Second Sex*, London: Picador (Edit. 1988).
De la Garza, Sarah Amira (2013) Chapter 8: 'Inila: An Account of Opening to Sacred Knowing', in Sheena Malhotra and Aimee Carrillo Rowe (eds) *Silence, Feminism, Power: Reflections at the Edges of Sound*, Basingstoke: Palgrave, pp. 101–113.
Delombard, Jeannine (1995) 'Femmenism', in Rebecca Walker (ed.) *To Be Real: Telling the Truth and Changing the Face of Feminism*, New York: Anchor, pp. 21–33.
Dent, Gina (1995) 'Missionary Position', in Rebecca Walker (ed) *To Be Real: Telling the Truth and Changing the Face of Feminism*, New York: Anchor, pp. 61–75.
De Vos, Pierre (2007) 'Separate is Never Equal: The Same-Sex Marriage Debate in South Africa', in *Lesbian and Gay Psychology Review*, vol 8, no. 1: 45–51.
Diamond, Irene and Lee Quinby (eds) (1988) *Feminism and Foucault: Reflections on Resistance*, Boston: Northeastern University Press.
Dicker, Rory and Alison Piepmeier (eds) (2003) *Catching a Wave: Reclaiming Feminism for the 21st Century*, Boston, MA: Northeastern UP.
Dillon, Michael (1946) *Self: A Study in Ethics and Endocrinology*, London: William Heinemann.
Dyer, Clare (2004) 'The Guardian Profile: Lady Brenda Hale', in *The Guardian* (Online), at www.guardian.co.uk/uk/2004/jan/09/lords.women, 9 January.
Edelstein, Marilyn (1993) 'Toward a Feminist Postmodern Poléthique: Kristeva on Ethics and Politics', in Kelly Oliver (ed.) *Ethics, Politics and Difference in Julia Kristeva's Writing*, London and New York: Routledge, pp. 196–214.
Edwards, Rosalind and Melanie Mauthner (2002) Chapter 1: 'Ethics and Feminist Research: Theory and Practice', in Tina Miller, Melanie Mauthner, Maxine Birch and Julie Jessop (eds) *Ethics in Qualitative Research*, London: Sage, pp. 14–31.
Ekins, Richard and King, David (1996) *Blending Genders: Social Aspects of Cross-Dressing and Sex-Changing*, London and New York: Routledge.
Ekins, Richard (1997) *Male Femaling: A Grounded Theory Approach to Cross Dressing and Sex Changing*, London: Routledge.

Ellis, Havelock with John Addington Symonds (1896) *Sexual Inversion*, North Stratford: Ayer Company Publishers Inc.
Ellis, Havelock (1928) *Eonism and Other Supplementary Studies*, Philadelphia: F A Davis Company.
Equality Act 2010, Chapter 15, Explanatory Notes, Commentary on Sections, Part 2, Chapter 1, Section 7, at www.legislation.gov.uk/ukpga/2010/15/notes/division/3/2/1/4.
European Commission Justice (2012) 'EU Citizenship and Free Movement' (Updated: 09/03/2012) acc. 24/05/2012 at http://ec.europa.eu/justice/citizen/index_en.htm (obsolete), now available at http://ec.europa.eu/justice/citizen/index_en.htm.
Fae, Jane (2010) 'Analysis: Who's Courting the Trans Vote?', in *Pink News*, 16 April.
Fairclough, Norman (1989) *Language and Power*, London: Longman.
Fairclough, Norman L (2003) *Analysing Discourse: Textual Analysis for Social Research*, London: Routledge.
Fallowell, Duncan and April Ashley (1982) *April Ashley's Odyssey*, London: Jonathan Cape.
Feinberg, Leslie (1993) *Stone Butch Blues*, Milford: Firebrand Books.
Feinberg, Leslie (1996) *Transgender Warriors: Making History from Joan of Arc to Dennis Rodman*, Boston, MA: Beacon Press.
Felski, Rita (1994) Chapter 40: 'Fin de siecle, Fin du sexe: Transsexuality, Postmodernism, and the Death of History', in Susan Stryker and Stephen Whittle (eds) (2006) *The Transgender Studies Reader*, New York and London: Routledge, pp. 565–573.
Ferguson, Ann (1997) 'Moral Responsibility and Social Change: A New Theory of Self', in Jacqueline N Zita (ed) *'Third Wave Feminisms'*, Hypatia, Special Issue: A Journal of Feminist Philosophy, Summer, vol 12, no. 3: 116–141.
Fidyk, Alexandra (2013) Chapter 9: 'Attuned to Silence: A Pedagogy of Presence', in Sheena Malhotra and Aimee Carrillo Rowe (eds) *Silence, Feminism, Power: Reflections at the Edges of Sound*, Basingstoke: Palgrave, pp. 114–128.
Findlay, Barbara (2006) 'Acting Queerly: Lawyering for Trans People', in Krista Scott-Dixon (ed) *Trans/Forming Feminisms: Trans-Feminist Voices Speak Out*, Toronto: Sumach Press, pp. 145–153.
Findlen, Barbara (1995) *Listen Up: Voices from the Next Feminist Generation*, Seattle: Seal Press.
Fineman, Martha Albertson, Jack E Jackson, and Adam P Romero (eds) (2009) *Feminist and Queer Legal Theory: Intimate Encounters, Uncomfortable Conversations*, Farnham and Burlington: Ashgate.
Fineman, Martha Albertson (2009) 'Introduction: Feminist and Queer Legal Theory', in Martha Albertson Fineman, Jack E Jackson and Adam P Romero (eds) *Feminist and Queer Legal Theory: Intimate Encounters, Uncomfortable Conversations*, Farnham and Burlington: Ashgate, pp. 1–6.
Fiske, John (1987) *Television Culture*, New York: Methuen.
Flynn, Taylor (2006) Chapter 2: 'The Ties That (Don't) Bind: Transgender Family Law and the Unmaking of Families', in Paisley Currah, Richard M Juang and Shannon Price Minter (eds) *Transgender Rights*, London, Minneapolis: University of Minnesota Press, pp. 32–50.
Foster, Jeanette (1985) *Sex Variant Women in Literature*, Tallahassee: Naiad Press.
Foucault, Michel (1971) 'Nietzsche, Genealogy, History', in Paul Rabinow (ed), *The Foucault Reader*, London: Penguin (Edit. 1991), pp. 76–100.
Foucault, Michel (1975) *Discipline and Punish: The Birth of the Prison*, London: Vintage Books (Edit. 1995).

Foucault, Michel (1977) *Language, Counter-Memory, Practice: Selected Essays and Interviews*, New York: Cornell University Press.
Foucault, Michel (1978) *The Will to Knowledge. The History of Sexuality: Vol 1*, trans. by Robert Hurley, London: Penguin (Edit. 1998).
Foucault, Michel (1984) 'Polemics, Politics and Problematizations, interview with Paul Rabinow', in Paul Rabinow (ed) (1994) *Ethics, Volume 1 of Essential Works of Foucault 1954–1984*, trans. by Lydia Davis, London: Penguin, pp. 111–119 (Edit. 2000).
Foucault, Michel (1984) *The Use of Pleasure: The History of Sexuality: Vol 2*, Harmandsworth: Viking (Edit. 1986).
Freud, Sigmund (1905) *Three Essays on the Theory of Sexuality*, Jackson, TN: Perseus Books, Trans and ed. James Strachey (Edit. 2000).
Friedlin, J (26 May 2002) 'Second and Third Wave Feminists Clash Over the Future', at https://womensenews.org/2002/05/second-and-third-wave-feminists-clash-over-the-future/.
Frith, Gill (1993) 'Women, Writing and Language: Making the Silences Speak', in Diane Richardson and Victoria Robinson (eds) *Introducing Women's Studies*, Basingstoke: Macmillan, pp. 151–176.
Gagnon, John H and William Simon (1973) *Sexual Conduct: The Social Sources of Human Sexuality*, 2nd edn, New Jersey: Transaction Publishers (Edit. 2005).
Gamble, Sarah (ed.) (1998) *The Routledge Companion to Feminism and Postfeminism*, London and New York: Routledge (Edit. 2006).
Garber, Marjorie (1992) *Vested Interests: Cross-Dressing and Cultural Anxiety*, New York: Routledge (Edit. 1997).
Garrison, Ednie Kaeh (2005) Chapter 13: 'Are We On a Wavelength Yet?: On Feminist Ocean-ography, Radios, and Third Wave Feminism', in Jo Reger (ed.) *Different Wavelengths: Studies of the Contemporary Women's Movement*, New York and London: Routledge, pp. 237–256.
Gilligan, Carol (1982) *In a Different Voice*, Cambridge: Harvard University Press.
Gilligan, Carol (Spring 1995) 'Hearing the Difference: Theorizing Connection', in *Hypatia*, vol 10, no. 2: 120–127.
Gilligan, Carol (2011) *Joining the Resistance*, Cambridge: Polity Press.
Gillis, Stacy and Rebecca Munford (2004) 'Genealogies and Generations: The Politics and Praxis of Third Wave Feminism', in *Women's History Review*, vol 13, no. 2: 165–183.
Gillis, Stacy (2004) Chapter 15: 'Neither Cyborg Nor Goddess: The (Im)Possibilities of Cyber-feminism', in Stacy Gillis, Gillian Howie and Rebecca Munford (eds) *Third Wave Feminism: A Critical Exploration*, Basingstoke: Palgrave, pp. 185–196.
Gillis, Stacy, Gillian Howie and Rebecca Munford (eds) (2004) *Third Wave Feminism: A Critical Exploration*, Basingstoke: Palgrave.
Ginsberg, Faye D (1989) *Contested Lives: The Abortion Debate in American Community*, Berkeley, CA: University of California Press.
Glover, David and Kaplan, Cora (2000) *Genders*, London and New York: Routledge.
Green, Richard and John Money (1969) *Transsexualism and Sex Reassignment*, Baltimore, MD: The Johns Hopkins Press.
Godvin, Tara (Monday December 29, 2003) 'Transgendered Community Remembers Teena's Murder', acc. 16/03/2005 at www.planetout.com/news/article.html?2006/11/27/2 (obselete) now available at http://prince.org/msg/105/74207.
Golumbia, David (Summer 1997) 'Rethinking Philosophy in the Third Wave of Feminism', in Jacqueline N Zita (ed) *'Third Wave Feminisms'*, *Hypatia, Special Issue: A Journal of Feminist Philosophy*, vol 12, no. 3: 100–115.

Government Equalities Office (2011) Equality Act 2010, acc. 26/06/2011, at www.equalities.gov.uk/equality_act_2010.aspx.
Gramsci, Antonio (1971) *Selections from the Prison Notebooks*, London: Lawrence and Wishart.
Green, Jamison (2004) *Becoming a Visible Man*, Nashville, TN: Vanderbilt University Press.
Greer, Germaine (2000) *The Whole Woman*, London: Anchor.
Grice, Elizabeth (22 March 1997) 'Stephen Whittle, Law Lecturer', *Daily Telegraph*, at www.pfc.org.uk/news/1997/etgrice1.htm.
Halberstam, Judith (1998) *Female Masculinity*, Durham NC: Duke University Press.
Hale, C Jacob (1998) 'Consuming the Living, Dis(re)membering the Dead in the Butch/FTM Borderlands', in Susan Stryker (ed.) 'The Transgender Issue', in *GLQ: A Journal of Lesbian and Gay Studies*, vol. 4, no. 2: 311–348.
Hall, Radclyffe (1928) *The Well of Loneliness*, Ware: Wordsworth Editions (Edit. 2005).
Hall, Stuart (1992) 'The Question of Cultural Identity', in Stuart Hall, David Held and Tony McGrew (eds) *Modernity and its Futures*, Cambridge: Polity Press, pp. 274–316.
Halley, Janet (2009) Chapter 1: 'Queer Theory by Men', in Martha Albertson Fineman, Jack E Jackson and Adam P Romero (eds) *Feminist and Queer Legal Theory: Intimate Encounters, Uncomfortable Conversations*, Farnham and Burlington: Ashgate, pp. 9–28.
Hammersley, Martyn and Paul Atkinson (1994) *Ethnography: Principles in Practice*, London: Routledge.
Haraway, Donna (1985) 'A Manifesto for Cyborgs: Science, Technology, and Socialist Feminism in the 1980s', in *Socialist Review*, no. 80, 65–107.
Haraway, Donna (1997) *Modest_Witness@Second_Millenium. Female-Man©_Meets_OncoMouse$^{TM}$*, New York and London: Routledge.
Hardie, Alaina (2006) 'It's a Long Way to the Top: Hierarchies of Legitimacy in Trans Communities', in Krista Scott-Dixon (ed) *Trans/Forming Feminisms: Trans-Feminist Voices Speak Out*, Toronto: Sumach Press, pp. 122–130.
Harding, Jennifer (1998) *Sex Acts*, London, Thousand Oaks, New Delhi: Sage.
Harding, Rosie (2007) 'The Promise of Rights and the Reality of Law: Implications of the Decision in Wilkinson v Kitzinger', in *Lesbian and Gay Psychology Review*, vol 8, no. 1: 15–20.
Harding, Sandra G (1991) *Whose Science? Whose Knowledge?*, Milton Keynes: Open University Press.
Hauser, Richard (1962) *The Homosexual Society*, London: Bodley Head.
Hausman, Bernice L (1995) *Changing Sex: Transsexualism, Technology, and the Idea of Gender*, Durham and London: Duke University Press.
Hausman, Bernice L (1999) 'Virtual Sex, Real Gender: Body and Identity in Transgender Discourse', in Mary Ann O'Farrell and Lynne Vallone (eds) *Virtual Gender: Fantasies of Subjectivities and Embodiment*, Michigan: University of Michigan Press, pp. 190–216.
Hausman, Bernice L (2006) 'Body, Technology, and Gender in Transsexual Autobiographies', in Susan Stryker and Stephen Whittle (eds) (2006) *The Transgender Studies Reader*, New York: Routledge, pp. 335–361.
Heath, Stephen (1977) 'Translator's Note', in Roland Barthes, *Image, Music, Text*, London: Fontana, essays selected and translated [from the French] by Stephen Heath.

Hebert, Laura A (March 2007) 'Taking "Difference" Seriously: Feminisms and the "Man Question"', in *Journal of Gender Studies*, vol 16, no. 1: 31–45.

Henry, Astrid (2004) *Not My Mother's Sister: Generational Conflict and Third-Wave Feminism*, Bloomington and Indianapolis: Indiana University Press.

Hernandez, Daisy and Bushra Rehman (eds) (2002) *Colonize This!: Young Women of Color on Today's Feminism*, Berkeley, CA: Seal Press.

Hewitt, Nancy (2010) *No Permanent Waves: Recasting Histories of U.S. Feminism*, Chapel Hill, NC: Rutgers University Press.

Heyes, Cressida J (Summer 1997) 'Anti-Essentialism in Practice: Carol Gilligan and Feminist Philosophy', in Jacqueline N Zita (ed) *'Third Wave Feminisms', Hypatia, Special Issue: A Journal of Feminist Philosophy*, vol 12, no. 3: 142–161.

Heywood, Leslie L and Jennifer Drake (eds) (1997) *Third Wave Agenda: Being Feminist, Doing Feminism*, Minneapolis, MN: University of Minnesota Press.

Hines, Melissa (January 2004) 'Androgen and Psychosexual Development: Core Gender Identity, Sexual Orientation, and Recalled Childhood Gender Role Behaviour in Women and Men with Congenital Adrenal Hyperplasia (CAH)', in *Journal of Sex Research*, vol 41, no. 1: 75–81.

Hines, Sally (2005) Chapter 4: '"I Am a Feminist But...": Transgender Men and Women and Feminism', in Jo Reger (ed.) *Different Wavelengths: Studies of the Contemporary Women's Movement*, New York and London: Routledge, pp. 57–77.

Hirschfeld, Magnus D (1910) *Transvestites: The Erotic Drive To Cross-Dress* (Originally Published As Die Transvestiten in 1910), trans. by Michael A. Lombardi-Nash, Buffalo, New York: Prometheus Books (Edit. 1991).

Hirschfeld, Magnus D (1926) *Chirurgische Eingriffe bei Anomalien des Sexualleben in Therapie der Gegenwart*, no. 61, 451–455.

Holmes, Morgan (2006) Chapter 6: 'Deciding Fate or Protecting a Developing Autonomy? Intersex Children and the Colombian Constitutional Court', in Paisley Currah, Richard M Juang and Shannon Price Minter (eds) *Transgender Rights*, London, Minneapolis: University of Minnesota Press, pp. 102–121.

hooks, bell (1984) Chapter 4: 'Sisterhood: Political Solidarity between Women', in *Feminist Theory: From Margin to Centre*, Boston, MA: South End Press, pp. 43–65.

hooks, bell (1989) *Talking Back: Thinking Feminist Thinking Black*, London: Sheba Feminist Publishers.

hooks, bell (1992) Chapter 2, 'Eating the Other: Desire and Resistance', in *Black Looks: Race and Representation*, London: Turnaround, pp. 21–39.

hooks, bell (1997), 'Sisterhood: Political Solidarity Between Women', in Anne McClintock, Aamir Mufti and Ella Shohat (eds), *Dangerous Liaisons: Gender, Nation, and Postcolonial Perspectives*, Minnesota, MN: University of Minnesota Press, pp. 396–411.

Howie, Gillian and Ashley Tauchert (2004) 'Feminist Dissonance: The Logic of Late Feminism', in Stacy Gillis, Gillian Howie and Rebecca Munford (eds) *Third Wave Feminism: A Critical Exploration*, Basingstoke: Palgrave, pp. 37–48.

Hoyer, Niels (1933) *Man into Woman: An Authentic Record of a Change of Sex*, London: Jarrolds (Edit. 1937).

Huang, Jessica (22 October 2002) 'Julia Kristeva's The System and the Speaking Subject: An Outline', acc.: 03/07/2011, at www.eng.fju.edu.tw/Literary_Criticism/feminism/kristeva_1.htm.

Humm, Maggie (ed.) (1992) *Feminisms: A Reader*, London: Harvester Wheatsheaf.

Hunter, Darryl, Trevor Gambell & Bikkar Randhawa (2005) 'Gender Gaps in Group Listening and Speaking: Issues in Social Constructivist Approaches to Teaching and

Learning', in *Educational Review*, vol 57, issue 3: 329–355, acc. 19/08/2006, at www.tandfonline.com/doi/abs/10.1080/00131910500149416.

Hurdis, Rebecca (2002) 'Heartbroken: Women of Color Feminism and the Third Wave', in Daisy Hernandez and Bushra Rehman (eds) *Colonize This!: Young Women of Color on Today's Feminism*, Berkeley, CA: Seal Press, pp. 279–292.

Hurst, Charles E (2007) *Social Inequality: Forms, Causes, and Consequences*, 6th edn, Boston, MA: Pearson College Division.

International Lesbian, Gay, Bisexual, Trans and Intersex Association (ILGA) (2012) 'Stop Trans Pathologization Campaign 2012', acc.12/02/2012 at http://ilga.org/ilga/en/article/mBGt6bB1GM.

Irigaray, Luce (1985) Chapter 2: 'This Sex Which is Not One', in *This Sex Which is Not One*, Ithaca: Cornwell University Press, pp. 23–33.

Jackson, Alecia Youngblood (2004) 'Performativity Identified', in *Qualitative Enquiry*, vol 10, no. 5: 673–690.

Janssen, Anna and Tamar Murachver (October 2004) 'The Relationship between Gender and Topic in Gender-Preferential Language Use', in *Written Communication*, vol 21 no. 4: 344–367.

Jeffreys, Sheila (2004) 'Allowing Alex's Sex Change Shows Up a Gender-Biased Family Court', in *The Australian*, 19 July.

Jeffreys, Sheila (2005) *Beauty And Misogyny: Harmful Cultural Practices In The West*, Hove: Routledge.

Johnson, Julia R (2013) Chapter 4: 'Qwe're Performances in Silence', in Sheena Malhotra and Aimee Carrillo Rowe (eds) *Silence, Feminism, Power: Reflections at the Edges of Sound*, Basingstoke: Palgrave, pp. 50–66.

Jorgensen, Christine (1967) *Christine Jorgensen: A Personal Autobiography*, San Francisco, CA: Cleis Press.

Jouve, Nicole Ward (2004) 'Introduction: Challenges', in Stacy Gillis, Gillian Howie and Rebecca Munford (eds) *Third Wave Feminism: A Critical Exploration*, Basingstoke: Palgrave, pp. 199–204.

Karaian, Lara (2006) 'Strategic Essentialism on Trial: Legal Interventions and Social Change', in Krista Scott-Dixon (ed) *Trans/Forming Feminisms: Trans-Feminist Voices Speak Out*, Toronto: Sumach Press, pp. 182–191.

Kellstedt, Paul M, David A. M. Peterson and Mark D. Ramirez (2010) 'The Macro Politics of a Gender Gap', in *Public Opinion Quarterly*, vol 74, no. 3: 477–498.

Kennedy, Duncan (1993) *Sexy Dressing etc: Essays on the Power of Politics of Culture Identity*, Cambridge, MA: Harvard University Press.

Khosla, Dhillon (2006) *Both Sides Now: One Man's Journey through Womanhood*, London: Penguin.

Kornacki, Martin (1 Oct 2010) 'Equality Act Comes Under Criticism from All Sides', in *The Training Journal*, at www.trainingjournal.com/news/equality-act-comes-under-criticism-from-all-sides/ [Online], (no longer available online, acc. from researcher's private collection).

Krafft-Ebing, Richard Von (1893) *Psychopathia Sexualis*, trans. by Charles Gilbert Chaddock, Philadelphia and London: F A Davis.

Kristeva, Julia (1969) *Desire in Language: A Semiotic Approach to Literature and Art*, Oxford: Blackwell, edited by Leon S Roudiez and translated from the French, Séméiôtiké: Recherches pour une Sémanalyse, Paris: Edition du Seuil (Edit. 1980).

Kristeva, Julia (1982) *Powers of Horror: An Essay on Abjection*, New York: Columbia University Press.

Kristeva, Julia (1986) 'Semiotics: A Critical Science and/or a Critique of Science', in Toril Moi (ed) *The Kristeva Reader*, Oxford: Blackwell, pp. 74–88.

Kristeva, Julia (1991) *Strangers to Ourselves* (translated by L S Roudiez), New York: Columbia University Press.

Kristeva, Julia (1979) *New Maladies of the Soul*, New York: Columbia University Press (Edit. 1993).

Kristeva, Julia (1993) 'Women's Time', in *New Maladies of the Soul*, New York: Columbia University Press, pp. 201–224.

Koyama, Emi (2003) 'Transfeminist Manifesto', in Rory Dicker and Alison Piepmeier (eds) *Catching a Wave: Reclaiming Feminism for the 21st Century*, Boston: Northeastern UP, pp. 244–259.

Kuhn, Thomas (1962) *The Structure of Scientific Revolutions*, Chicago: University of Chicago Press.

Lee, Tracey (2001) *Female To Male Transsexuality: A Study of (Re)Embodiment and Identity Transformation*, PhD Thesis, University of Warwick, Centre for The Study of Women and Gender.

Lees, Paris (2014) 'The Trans vs. Radical Feminist Twitter War Is Making Me Sick', 20 August, *Vice* [Online].

Lorde, Audre (1984) *Sister Outsider*, Freedom, CA: The Crossing Press.

Lossie, Cheryl (2013) Chapter 10: 'Hear I Meet the Silence: The Wise Pedagogue', in Sheena Malhotra and Aimee Carrillo Rowe (eds) *Silence, Feminism, Power: Reflections at the Edges of Sound*, Basingstoke: Palgrave, pp. 129–138.

Mackenzie, Gordene O. (1999) Chapter 10: '50 Billion Galaxies of Gender: Transgendering the Millennium', in Kate More and Stephen Whittle (eds) (2006) *Reclaiming Genders: Transsexual Grammars at the Fin de Siècle*, New York: Routledge, pp. 193–218.

Malhotra, Sheena and Aimee Carrillo Rowe (eds) (2013) *Silence, Feminism, Power: Reflections at the Edges of Sound*, Basingstoke: Palgrave.

Mann, Chris and Fiona Stewart (2000) *Internet Communication and Qualitative Research: A Handbook for Researching Online*, London: Sage.

Marcus, Steven (2000) 'Introduction', in Sigmund Freud (1905) *Three Essays on the Theory of Sexuality*, Jackson, TN: Perseus Books, Trans. and ed. James Strachey (Edit. 2000).

Marshment, Margaret (1993) 'The Picture is Political: Representation of Women in Contemporary Popular Culture', in Diane Richardson and Victoria Robinson (eds) *Introducing Women's Studies*, Basingstoke: Macmillan, pp. 123–150.

Marx, Karl (1867) *Das Kapital: Kritik der Politischen Oekonomie*, Hamburg: Verlag von Otto Meisner.

Mattio, Sean (10/07/10) 'Dude Looks Like a Lady: Cross Dressing and the Progress Narrative', acc. 09/11/17 at http://teachmix.com/performlit/content/dude-looks-lady-cross-dressing-and-progress-narrative.

McAdams, Dan P (2001) 'Coding Autobiographical Episodes for Themes of Agency and Com-munion', Northwestern University, pdf document, acc. 11/12/2010 at www.sesp.northwestern.edu/docs/Agency_Communion01.pdf. (rev. April).

McKeon, Michael (1995) 'Historicizing Patriarchy: The Emergence of Gender Difference in England, 1660–1760', in *Eighteenth-Century Studies*, vol 28, no. 3: 300.

McNab, Claire (1997) Activist Profile, acc. 09/08. 2007, www.pfc.org.uk/node/29.

McNab, Claire (2004) 'PFC's Claire Mcnab Gives Evidence to the Select Committee on Home Affairs' Investigation into the Government's ID Card Scheme', at www.

publications.parliament.uk/pa/cm200304/cmselect/cmhaff/130/4061502.htm. (15 June).

Middleton, Richard (1990) *Studying Popular Music*, Milton Keynes, Philadelphia: Open University Press.

Moerings, Martin (1998) Chapter 9: 'The Netherlands: Front Runners in Anti-Discrimination Laws', in Leslie J Moran, Daniel Monk and Sarah Beresford (eds) *Legal Queeries: Lesbian, Gay and Transgender Legal Studies*, London and New York: Cassell, pp. 125–138.

Moi, Toril (1986a) 'Introduction', in Toril Moi (ed) *The Kristeva Reader*, Oxford: Blackwell, pp. 1–21.

Moi, Toril (1986b) 'Introduction to Semiotics: A Critical Science and/or a Critique of Science', in Toril Moi (ed) *The Kristeva Reader*, Oxford: Blackwell, pp. 74–75.

Moraga, Cherrie (1983) 'La Guera', in Cherrie Moraga and Gloria Anzaldúa (eds) *This Bridge Called My Back: Writings by Radical Women of Colour*, New York: Kitchen Table, pp. 27–34.

Moraga, Cherrie and Gloria Anzaldúa (eds) (1983) *This Bridge Called My Back: Writings by Radical Women of Colour*, New York: Kitchen Table (Edit. 1983).

Moran, Leslie J, Daniel Monk and Sarah Beresford (eds) (1998) 'Introduction', in *Legal Queeries: Lesbian, Gay and Transgender Legal Studies*, London and New York: Cassel, pp. 1–9.

More, Kate and Stephen Whittle (eds) (1999) *Reclaiming Genders: Transsexual Grammars At The Fin De Siecle*, London and New York: Cassell.

Morgan, Joan (1999) *When Chickenheads Come Home to Roost: My Life as a Hip-Hop Feminist*, New York: Simon & Schuster.

Morgan, Robin (ed.) (1970) *Sisterhood Is Powerful: An Anthology of Writings from the Women's Liberation Movement*, New York: Random House.

Morris, Jan (1974) *Conundrum*, London: Coronet (Edit. 1975).

Munford, Rebecca (2004) Chapter 11: 'Wake Up and Smell the Lipgloss: Gender, Generation and the (A)politics of Girl Power', in Gillis, Stacy, Gillian Howie and Rebecca Munford (eds) *Third Wave Feminism: A Critical Exploration*, Basingstoke: Palgrave, pp. 142–153.

Munro, Ealasaid (2013) 'Feminism: a Fourth Wave?', in *Political Insight* [Online], vol 4, no. 2.

Nagel, Thomas (1986) *The View from Nowhere*, Oxford: Oxford University Press.

Namaste, Viviane Ki. (1996) '"Tragic Misreadings": Queer Theory's Erasure of Transgender Sub-Jectivity', in Brett Beemyn and Mickey Eliason (eds) *Queer Studies: A Lesbian, Gay, Bisexual and Transgender Anthology*, New York and London: New York University Press, pp. 183–204.

Namaste, Viviane Ki. (2000) Chapter 3: 'Beyond Textualist and Objectivist Theory: Toward a Re-flexive Poststructuralist Sociology', in *Invisible Lives: The Erasure of Transsexual and Transgendered People*, Chicago and London: The University of Chicago Press, pp. 39–70.

National Geographic (2011) *Albania's Sworn Virgins*, video, acc. 22/09/2011, at http://video.nationalgeographic.com/video/player/places/culture-places/beliefs-and-traditions/albania_swornvirgins.html.

Nobus, Dany (1999) *Life and Death in the Glass – A New Look at the Mirror Stage*, in *Key Concepts of Lacanian Psychoanalysis*, New York: Other Press.

Norton, Rictor (1992) *Mother Clap's Molly House: The Gay Subculture in England 1700–1830*, London: GMP.

Oakley, Ann (1974) *Housewife*, London: Allen Lane.
Oakley, Anne and Juliet Mitchell (eds) (1998) *Who's Afraid of Feminism? Seeing Through the Backlash*, London: Penguin.
O'Farrell, Mary Ann and Lynne Vallone (1999) *Virtual Gender: Fantasies of Subjectivity and Embodiment*, Michigan: University of Michigan Press.
O'Leary, Timothy (2002) *Foucault and the Art of Ethics*, London and New York: Continuum.
Oliver, Kelly (1998) 'Summary of Major Themes: Julia Kristeva, "Kristeva and Feminism"' acc. 15/12/2010 at www.cddc.vt.edu/feminism/Kristeva.html.
Orr, Catherine (Summer 1997) 'Charting the Currents of the Third Wave', in Jacqueline N Zita (ed.) *'Third Wave Feminisms', Hypatia, Special Issue: A Journal of Feminist Philosophy*, vol 12, no. 3: 29–45.
Parker, Ian (2005) *Qualitative Psychology: Introducing Radical Research*, Maidenhead: OUP.
Patel, Pragna (1997) Chapter 21: 'Third Wave Feminism and Black Women's Activism', in Heidi Safia Mirza (ed.) *Black British Feminism*, London and New York: Routledge, pp. 255–268.
Pearce, David (1998) *Brave New World?: A Defence Of Paradise-Engineering*, BLTC Research.
Pershai, Alexander (2006) 'The Language Puzzle: Is Inclusive Language a Solution', in Krista Scott-Dixon (ed.) *Trans/Forming Feminisms: Trans-Feminist Voices Speak Out*, Toronto: Sumach Press, pp. 46–52.
Pozner, Jennifer L (2003) 'The Big Lie: False Feminist Death Syndrome, Profit, and the Media', in Rory Dicker and Alison Piepmeier (eds) *Catching a Wave: Reclaiming Feminism for the 21st Century*, Boston, MA: Northeastern UP, pp. 31–56.
Prado, Carlos G (2000) *Starting with Foucault: An Introduction to Genealogy*, 2nd edn, Oxford: Westview Press.
Press Association (2016) 'Government to Review 2004 Gender Recognition Act', *The Guardian* (Online), 7 July.
Press for Change (May 2009) 'Submission to the Parliamentary Committee on the Draft Equality Bill', email from Press for Change in researcher's collection.
Prosser, Jay (1998) *Second Skins: The Body Narratives of Transsexuality*, New York: Columbia University Press.
Prud'homme, Johanne and Lyne Légaré (2006) 'Semanalysis: The Generation of the Formula', acc. 21/07/2010 at www.signosemio.com.
Public Bill Committee 2nd Meeting (Afternoon 02/06/2009) Debates, proceedings and transcripts of evidence (session 2008–2009) – Equality Bill 2008–2009, at www.publications.parliament.uk/pa/cm200809/cmpublic/equality/090602/pm/90602s01.htm.
Raymond, Janice G (1979) *The Transsexual Empire: The Making of The She-Male*, Boston: Beacon Press.
Raymond, Janice G (1996) Chapter 15: 'The Politics of Transgenderism', in Richard Ekins and Dave King, *Blending Genders*, London and New York: Routledge, pp. 215–223.
Rees, Mark (1996) *Dear Sir or Madam*, London: Cassell.
Rees, Mark (1997) Activist Profile, acc. 30/05/2009at www.pfc.org.uk/node/1025.
Reger, Jo (ed.) (2005) *Different Wavelengths: Studies of the Contemporary Women's Movement*, New York and London: Routledge.
Ribbens, Jane and Rosalind Edwards (1997) Chapter 1: 'Living on the Edges: Public Knowledge, Private Lives, Personal Experience', in Jane Ribbens and Rosalind Edwards (eds) *Feminist Dilemmas in Qualitative Research*, London: Sage, pp. 1–23.

Richardson, Diane and Victoria Robinson (1993) *Introducing Women's Studies*, Basingstoke: Macmillan.

Riessman, Catherine Kohler (1993) *Narrative Analysis*, London: Sage.

Robson, Ruthann (2006) Chapter 15: 'Reinscribing Normality? The Law and Politics of Transgender Marriage', in Paisley Currah, Richard M Juang and Shannon Price Minter (eds) *Transgender Rights*, London, Minneapolis: University of Minnesota Press, pp. 299–309.

Romero, Adam P (2009) Chapter 10: 'Methodological Descriptions: "Feminist" and "Queer" Legal Theories', in Martha Albertson Fineman, Jack E Jackson and Adam P Romero (eds) *Feminist and Queer Legal Theory: Intimate Encounters, Uncomfortable Conversations*, Farnham and Burlington: Ashgate, pp. 179–198.

Roudiez, Leon S (1969) 'Introduction', in Julia Kristeva, *Desire in Language: A Semiotic Approach to Literature and Art*, Oxford: Blackwell, edited by Leon S Roudiez and translated from the French, Séméiôtiké: Recherches pour une Sémanalyse, Paris: Edition du Seuil (Edit. 1980).

Russo, Ann (2013) Chapter 3: 'Between Speech and Silence: Reflections on Accountability', in Sheena Malhotra and Aimee Carrillo Rowe (eds) *Silence, Feminism, Power: Reflections at the Edges of Sound*, Basingstoke: Palgrave, pp. 34–49.

Rutherford, Sarah (1997) 'The Wife's Story', in *The Guardian*, 23 April.

Savage, Michael (2017) 'Gender Reassignment Could Be Streamlined Under Proposal', *The Guardian* (Online), 27 July.

Scales, Ann (2009) Chapter 20: 'Poststructuralism on Trial', in Martha Albertson Fineman, Jack E Jackson and Adam P Romero (eds) *Feminist and Queer Legal Theory: Intimate Encounters, Uncomfortable Conversations*, Farnham and Burlington: Ashgate, pp. 395–410.

Schofield, Pieta (24 June 2009) 'Open University Requires Divorce Before it Will Respect Gender, Academics and Researchers in Transgender/Transsexual Studies', email from trans-academic@jiscmail.ac.uk, 24 June, (no longer available online, acc. from researcher's private collection).

Scott-Dixon, Krista (2006) *Trans/Forming Feminisms: Trans-Feminist Voices Speak Out*, Toronto: Sumach Press.

Self, Will and David Gamble (2000) *Perfidious Man*, London: Viking.

Shail, Andrew (2004) Chapter 8: 'You're Not One of Those Boring Masculinists, Are You? The Question of Male Embodied Feminism', in Stacy Gillis, Gillian Howie and Rebecca Munford (eds) (2004) *Third Wave Feminism: A Critical Exploration*, Basingstoke: Palgrave, pp. 97–109.

Shapiro, Robert Y and Harpreet Mahajan (1986) 'Gender Differences in Policy Preferences: A Summary of Trends from the 1960s to the 1980s', in *Public Opinion Quarterly* vol 50, no. 1: 42–61.

Sharpe, Andrew N (2006) 'From Functionality to Aesthetics: The Architecture of Transgender Ju-risprudence', in Susan Stryker and Stephen Whittle (eds) (2006) *The Transgender Studies Reader*, New York: Routledge, pp. 621–631.

Sharpe, Alex (2007) 'Foucault's Monsters, the Abnormal Individual and the Challenge of English Law', in *Journal of Historical Sociology*, vol. 20, no. 3: 384–403.

Showalter, Elaine (1987) *The Female Malady: Women, Madness, and English Culture, 1830–1980*, London: Virago (Edit. 1985).

Siegel, Carol (2000) *New Millennial Sexstyles*, Bloomington: Indiana University Press.

Smart, Carol (1989) *Feminism and the Power of Law*, London and New York: Routledge.

Smith, Adam (2017) 'Woman injured as feminists and transgender groups fight at Speakers' Corner', 17 September, *Metro* [Online].

Solange, Davin (2005) Chapter 1: 'Public Medicine: The Reception of a Medical Drama', in Martin King and Katherine Watson (eds) *Representing Health: Discourses of Health and Illness in the Media*, Basingstoke: Palgrave Macmillan, pp. 22–47.

Spencer, Jane (2004) 'Introduction: Genealogies', in Stacy Gillis, Gillian Howie and Rebecca Munford (eds) *Third Wave Feminism: A Critical Exploration*, Basingstoke: Palgrave, pp. 9–12.

Springer, Kimberley (2002) 'Third Wave Black Feminism?', in *Signs: Journal of Women in Culture and Society*, vol. 27, no. 4: 1059–1082.

Stanley, Liz and Sue Wise (1993) *Breaking Out Again: Feminist Ontology and Epistemology*, London and New York: Routledge.

Star, Hedy Jo (1963) *I Changed My Sex!*, Novel Books.

Steady, Filomina Chioma (ed.) (1985) *The Black Woman Cross-Culturally*, Rochester: Schenkman Books.

Steinem, Gloria (1995) 'Foreword', in Rebecca Walker (ed.) *To Be Real: Telling the Truth and Changing the Face of Feminism*, New York: Anchor, pp. xiii–xxviii.

Stone, Alison (2004) 'On the Genealogy of Women: A Defence of Anti-Essentialism', in Stacy Gillis, Gillian Howie and Rebecca Munford (eds) *Third Wave Feminism: A Critical Exploration*, Basingstoke: Palgrave, pp. 85–96.

Stone, Sandy (1991) Chapter 11: 'The Empire Strikes Back: A Posttranssexual Manifesto', in Julia Epstein and Kristina Straub (eds) *Body Guards: The Cultural Politics of Gender Ambiguity*, New York and London: Routledge, pp. 280–304.

Stryker, Susan (1994) 'My Words to Victor Frankenstein above the Village of Chamounix: Per-forming Transgender Rage', in Susan Stryker and Stephen Whittle (eds) (2006) *The Transgender Studies Reader*, New York: Routledge, pp. 244–256.

Stryker, Susan and Stephen Whittle (eds) (2006) *The Transgender Studies Reader*, New York: Routledge.

Stychin, Carl F (1995) Chapter 8: 'Towards a Queer Legal Theory', in *Law's Desire: Sexuality and The Limits of Justice*, Oxford, New York: Routledge.

Sullivan, Lou (2006) Chapter 12: 'A Transvestite Answers a Feminist', in Susan Stryker and Stephen Whittle (eds) *The Transgender Studies Reader*, New York: Routledge, pp. 159–164.

Sullivan, Nikki (2006) Chapter 39: 'Transmogrification: (Un)Becoming Others(s)', in Susan Stryker and Stephen Whittle (eds) (2006) *The Transgender Studies Reader*, New York: Routledge, pp. 552–564.

Szaz, Thomas (1961) *The Myth of Mental Illness: Foundations of a Theory of Personal Conduct*, New York: Harper Perennial.

Talbot, Mary (1998) *Language and Gender: An Introduction*, Cambridge: Polity Press.

Talbot, Mary, Karen Atkinson and David Atkinson (2003) *Language and Power in the Modern World*, Edinburgh: Edinburgh University Press.

Tate, Greg (1995) 'Born to Dyke', in Rebecca Walker (ed.) *To Be Real: Telling the Truth and Changing the Face of Feminism*, New York: Anchor, pp. 195–207.

*The Harry Benjamin International Gender Dysphoria Association's Standards of Care for Gender Identity Disorders, Sixth Version* (2001), XII: Genital Surgery, at www.wpath.org/Documents2/socv6.pdf

The Smiths (1987) *Half a Person*, B-side of 'Shoplifters of the World Unite, London: Rough Trade.

Thomas, Robert McG Jnr (1996) 'Dan Kiley, 54, Dies; Wrote 'Peter Pan Syndrome'', *New York Times* 27/02/1996, 15/05/2010, at www.nytimes.com/1996/02/27/us/dan-kiley-54-dies-wrote-peter-pan-syndrome.html?src=pm.
Thompson, Neil (1998) *Promoting Equality*, Basingstoke: Macmillan.
Toynbee, Polly (2002) 'The Myth of Women's Lib', in *The Guardian* 06/06/2002, acc. 16/05/2010, at www.guardian.co.uk/world/2002/jun/06/gender.pollytoynbee?INTCMP=SRCH.
Train, Belinda (2007) *Introduction to Psychology*, Cape Town: Pearson Education South Africa.
Turtle, Georgina (1963) *Over the Sex Border*, London: Victor Gollancz.
Ussher, Jane M (1991) *Women's Madness: Misogyny or Mental Illness?*, Hemel Hempstead: Harvester Wheatsheaf.
Valerio, Max Wolf (2006) *The Testosterone Files*, Emeryville, CA: Seal.
Van Dijk, Tuen A (1988) *News as Discourse*, Hillsdale, New Jersey: L Erlbaum Associates.
Van Dijk, Teun A (2001) 'Principles of Critical Discourse Analysis', in Margaret Wetherell, Stephanie Taylor and Simeon Yates (eds) *Discourse Theory and Practice: A Reader*, London: Sage Publications Ltd, pp. 307–315.
Van Dijk, Teun (2008) *Discourse and Power*, Basingstoke: Palgrave Macmillan.
Vasquez, Tina (2016) 'It's Time to End the Long History of Feminism Failing Transgender Women', 20 May, *Bitch Media* [Online].
Walby, Sylvia (1992) 'Post-Post-Modernism?: Theorising Social Complexity', in Michelle Barrett and Anne Phillips (eds) *Destabilising Theory: Contemporary Feminist Debates*, Cambridge: Polity Press, pp. 31–50.
Walker, Rebecca (ed.) (1995) 'An Introduction', in *To Be Real: Telling the Truth and Changing the Face of Feminism*, New York: Anchor, pp. xxviv–xl.
Walker, Alice (1983[1976]) *In Search of Our Mothers' Gardens: Womanist Prose*, London: Harcourt Brace Jovanovich.
Walters, William A W and Michael W Ross (1986) *Transsexualism and Sex Reassignment*, Oxford: Oxford University Press.
Watson, Catherine and Stephen Whittle (2005) 'Slicing through Healthy Bodies: Transsexuality and the Media Representation of Body Modification', in Martin King and Katherine Watson (eds) *Representing Health: Discourses of Health and Illness in the Media*, Basingstoke: Palgrave Macmillan, pp. 184–205.
Weiss, Gilbert and Ruth Wodak (2003) *Critical Discourse Analysis: Theory and Interdisciplinarity*, Basingstoke: Palgrave Macmillan.
Weisstein, Naomi (Winter 1997) 'Power, Resistance and Science', in *New Politics*, vol. 6, no. 2, acc. 14/05/2010at http://nova.wpunj.edu/newpolitics/issue22/weisst22.htm.
Wetherell, Margaret, Stephanie Taylor and Simeon Yates (eds) (2001) *Discourse Theory and Practice: A Reader*, London: Sage Publications Ltd.
Whelehan, Imelda (1995) *Modern Feminist Thought*, Edinburgh: Edinburgh University Press.
Whinnom, Alex (1997) Activist Profile, acc. 11/07/2009, www.pfc.org.uk/node/30 (obselete).
Whittle, Stephen (1996) Chapter 14: 'Gender Fucking or Fucking Gender?: Current Cultural Contributions to Theories of Gender Blending', in Richard Ekins and Dave King (eds) *Blending Genders*, London and New York: Routledge, pp. 196–214.
Whittle, Stephen (1997) Activist Profile, acc. 11/07/2009, at www.pfc.org.uk/node/31 (obselete).

Whittle, Stephen (1998a) 'The Trans-Cyberian Mail Way', in *Journal of Social and Legal Studies*, vol 7, no. 3: 389–408.

Whittle, Stephen (1998b) Chapter 3: 'Gemeinschaftsfremden – or How to Be Shafted by Your Friends: Sterilisation Requirements and Legal Status Recognition for the Transsexual', in Leslie J Moran, Daniel Monk and Sarah Beresford (eds) *Legal Queeries: Lesbian, Gay and Transgender Legal Studies*, London and New York: Cassell, pp. 42–56.

Whittle, Stephen (1999) 'Introduction 2', in Kate More and Stephen Whittle (eds) (1999) *Reclaiming Genders: Transsexual Grammars At The Fin De Siecle*, London: Cassell, pp. 6–11.

Whittle, Stephen (2002a) *Respect and Equality: Transsexual and Transgender Rights*, London: Cavendish Publishing.

Whittle, Stephen (2002b) 'Employment Discrimination and Transsexual People: A Study Comparing Pre- and Post P v S Experiences', Manchester Metropolitan University, at www.gires.org.uk/wp-content/uploads/2014/09/employment-dis-full-paper.pdf.

Whittle, Stephen (2005) 'Sustaining Values – Feminist Investments in the Transgender Body', in Yekani Haschemi and Beatrice Michaelis (eds) (2005) *Quer Durch die Geisteswissenschaften*, Berlin: Querverlag, pp. 157–167.

Whittle, Stephen (2006a) 'Foreword', in Susan Stryker and Stephen Whittle (eds) *The Transgender Studies Reader*, New York: Routledge, pp. xi–xvi.

Whittle, Stephen (2006b) Chapter 15: 'Where Did We Go Wrong? Feminism and Trans Theory – Two teams on the Same Side?', in Susan Stryker and Stephen Whittle (eds) *The Transgender Studies Reader*, New York: Routledge, pp. 194–202.

Whittle (2006c) 'Impossible People: Viewing the Self-portraits of Transsexual People', in A Rogers (ed.) *Parody, Pastiche and the Politics of Art: Materiality in a Post-material Paradigm*, Birmingham: Article Press.

Whittle, Stephen, Lewis Turner and Maryam Al-Alami (20 December 2006) *Engendered Penalties: Transgender and Transsexual People's Experiences of Inequality and Discrimination*, Commissioned by the Equalities Review, at www.ilga-europe.org/sites/default/files/trans_country_report_-_engenderedpenalties.pdf.

Whittle, Stephen (2007a) '"Respectively male and female": The Failures of the Gender Recognition Act (2005) and the Civil Partnership Act (2005)', in *Lesbian and Gay Psychology Review*, vol 8, no. 1: 36–44.

Whittle, Stephen and Lewis Turner (2007) '"Sex Changes"? Paradigm Shifts in 'Sex' and 'Gender' Following the Gender Recognition Act?', in *Sociological Research Online*, vol 12, issue 1, January, acc. not known, at www.socresonline.org.uk/12/1/whittle.html (Restricted access to full text).

Whittle, Stephen (20 March 2007) 'Launch of Yogyakarta Principles on Sexual Orientation & Gender Identity!', *PfC News* [Online], (no longer available online, acc. from researcher's private collection).

Whittle, Stephen (8 July 2007) 'Equal Opportunities Commission consultation on the future of gender equality', *PfC News* [Online], (no longer available online, acc. from researcher's private collection).

Whittle, Stephen (2008) 'Whittlings', acc. not known, at http://whittlings.blogspot.com, 10 September.

Wilson, Petra (1998) Chapter 8: 'What's in a Name: Naming Legal Needs in AIDS Service Organisations', in Leslie J Moran, Daniel Monk and Sarah Beresford (eds) *Legal Queeries: Lesbian, Gay and Transgender Legal Studies*, London and New York: Cassell, pp. 113–124.

Wittig, Monique (1992) *The Straight Mind and Other Essays*, Hemel Hempstead: Harvester Wheatsheaf.
Wong, Kristina Sheryl (2003) 'Pranks and Fake Porn: Doing Feminism My Way', in Rory Dicker and Alison Piepmeier (eds) *Catching a Wave: Reclaiming Feminism for the 21st Century*, Boston, MA: Northeastern UP, pp. 294–307.
Woodhouse, Annie. (1989) 'Breaking the Rules or Bending Them?: Transvestism, Femininity, and Feminism', in *Women's Studies International Forum*, vol 12, no. 4: 417–23.
World Professional Association for Transgender Health (2011) *Standards of Care for the Health of Transsexual, Transgender, and Gender Nonconforming People*, v7 at www.wpath.org/documents/Standards of Care_FullBook_1g-1.pdf.
Wright, Elizabeth (1992) *Feminism and Psychoanalysis: A Critical Dictionary*, Oxford: Blackwell.
Yep, Gust A. and Suan B. Shimanoff (2013) Chapter 11: 'The US Day of Silence: Sexualities, Silences, and the Will to Unsay in the Age of Empire', in Sheena Malhotra and Aimee Carrillo Rowe (eds) *Silence, Feminism, Power: Reflections at the Edges of Sound*, Basingstoke: Palgrave, pp. 139–156.
Young, Jeffrey E., Janet S. Klosko and Marjorie E. Weishaar (2003) *Schema Therapy: A Practitioner's Guide*, New York and London: Guilford Press.
Zack, Naomi (2005) *Inclusive Feminism: A Third Wave Theory of Women's Commonality*, Lanham: Rowman and Littlefield.
Zalewski, Marysia (2003) 'Is Women's Studies Dead?', in *Journal of International Women's Studies*, vol 4, no. 2: 117–133.
Zita, Jacqueline N (ed.) (Summer 1997) 'Introduction', in *'Third Wave Feminisms', Hypatia, Special Issue: A Journal of Feminist Philosophy*, vol 12, no. 3: 1–6.
Zucker, Kenneth J. and Susan J. Bradley (1996) *Gender Identity Disorder and Psychosexual Problems in Children and Adolescents*, New York: Guilford Press.

# Index

*A v West Yorkshire Police* 88
'aberration' 196
academic feminism 60–4, 65
academic reification 66n4
acceptance of gendered subjectivities 4–7, 15, 182
access in critical discourse analysis 120–1
acquiescence in critical discourse analysis 123–4
'action paradigm' 199
activism, women's 63
adolescence 33; choice to transition in 217
aetiology: abandoning search for 42, 65n1, 225–6; acceptance vs 4–7, 15; vs genre and genealogy 197–8; and personally political postmodern identity 43
agency 57, 81–7; in critical discourse analysis 126; subjectivity through 125–6
Ahmed, Sarah 10, 43–4, 157
AIDS pandemic, reconstructed discourse on 112
Albania, Sworn Virgins in 36
Albrecht, Lisa 54
Alexander, M Jacqui 162
Alexi, Sherman 101
Allen, Robert 20, 28, 33
Almada, Nadia 113
Althusser, Louis 22, 123, 125, 156, 178
analytic semiology 117–20
Andreadis, Harriette 23, 193
anthologies 61–2
antipatriarchal acts 193
anti-trans feminism 127, 131n11
Anzaldúa, Gloria: and gender immigrants 185; on 'kindred' 53, 200; and third wave as open and evolving

discourse 61–2; on unnaming vs naming 193; on womanism 54, 56, 59
*April Ashley's Odyssey* (Ashley) 20
Ashley, April 20, 71–3, 178, 207
assimilation, recognition vs 227–8
'asymmetrical reciprocity' 122–3
Atkins, Susan 69–70
attachment 191
*Attorney-General v Otahuhu Family Court* (New Zealand) 72, 85
Austin, Paula 61–2

Backer, Larry Cata 25–6, 63
Bailey, Cathryn 174–5
Bakan, David 57
Barbin, Herculine 71, 77–8, 81
Barrie, J M 27
Barthes, Roland 163–4, 202
Baudrillard, Jean 43
Beatie, Thomas 136
Beaumont Society 82
Becker, Mary 108, 161
Beginning Life forums 115
Bellamy, Richard 227
Bellinger, Elizabeth 85
*Bellinger v Bellinger* (2003) 73, 85–6, 95, 225, 226
Benhabib, Seyla: on dialogic negotiation 122, 123, 224; on ethical methodology 99, 224; on postconventional ethics 89, 90, 91–2; on third wave feminism 41; on voice 156
Benjamin, Harry: on coalition 13; on gender confirmation 71; on gender dysphoria 5; on infantilisation 27, 159; Standards of Care of 195
Beresford, Sarah 79–80
Bile, Jeff 123
Bindel, Julie 116–17

biological sex and sexual subjectivity 206n20
biologically defined stereotypes 13
bipolar gendering 23, 28, 35, 38
black feminists: and choice 171; and difference inclusiveness 199; importance of family to 83–4; lesbian 194; and personally political postmodern identity 44; and third wave as open and evolving discourse 61–2; and unnaming vs naming 193; and voice/silence binary 162; and womanism 53–60, 64–5, 66n5
'black letter law' 68
Blair, Caroline 13
body dysphoria 31, 114, 188
body searching, restrictions on 88
Bolin, Anne 179n1
'border check points' 186
border crossings 185
border subjectivities 59
'border zone' 31–2
*Borderlands/La Frontera* (Anzaldúa) 185
Bornstein, Kate: on 'gender euphoria' 187; on genre and genealogy 197; and quilt metaphor 58; on separatist discourse 9; textual subversion by 131n4; on unnaming vs naming 193
*Both Sides Now* (Khosla) 21
boundaries 48–9, 170
*Bowes v Hardwick* 76
the boy 24, 27, 29
boyishness 160
Bradley, Susan 40n3
*Breaking out Again* (Stanley and Wise) 99
Brennan, Cathy 116
Brent Asian Women's Refuge 66n8
Brown, George 30, 149
Bulbeck, Chilla 7
Burchill, Julie 115, 116
Burns, Christine 18n10, 183
Burou, Georges 71
Burr, Vivien 123, 126, 172, 218
*But for the Grace* (Allen) 20
butch/femme identities 48–9, 106
Butler, Judith: on choice 178; on coalition 10; and critical discourse analysis 112; on gendered behaviour 168–9; on infantilisation 33; on personally political postmodern identity 44, 45, 46; on politics of naming 168, 178; and queer theory 103–4; on quest for aetiology 4, 5, 6; on recognition vs passing 227

Buzzanell, Patrice 59
Byrd, Rudolph 200

Califa, Patrick 176
Calleja, Gaby 214
Canadian law 74
Canguilhem, Georges 76–7
capitalist system 119
'Care and Feminists' (Becker) 108
career feminism 61, 65
case(s), table of 232–3
case law tailored to individual circumstances 224
Castañeda, Claudia 140
catalytic experiences 114, 130
*Catching a Wave* (anthology) 61, 171, 194
categorisation: in narratives 112–13, 114; and passing 165; and postconventional ethics 194; and queer theory 103–4, 106; in third wave feminism 108
changeling 24
Charles, Helen 55, 59–60, 174
chat rooms 7, 115–17, 130
Chesler, Phyllis 51–2
Chicano/a people passing as white 193
Chiland, Collete 166
child development 84, 152
childhood: choice to transition in 217; moral development in 201; trans subjectivity in 149–50, 160
children's games 27–8, 169
choice 86, 167–73, 178–9; recommendations on 216–18
*Christine Jorgensen: A Personal Autobiography* (Jorgensen) 20
cisgender feminists 116
citizenship 222, 227–8
civil partnership(s) 75
Civil Partnership Act 2004 75, 213
civil union(s) 75
*Civil Union Act* (South Africa) 75
Clair, Robin 163
Clark Mane, Rebecca 53, 55, 59
Clayton, Angela 186
cloak of secrecy 22–3
CMC (computer-mediated communication) 7, 101–2, 115–17, 130, 136
coalition: assessing potential for 10–13; formation of 13–15; to investigate effects of legal gains 211–12, 224–5; potential for 1–13
'the code' 12
Cohen, Stanley 182

"coherent identities" 90
Coleman, Eli 166
collaborative process 59
collective process 59
collective subjectivities 15
Colombia 80–1
*Colonize This!* (Hernandez & Rehman) 61
coming out 140
Commission for Equality and Human Rights 93
'commodification of Otherness' 55–6
commonalities, fictitious 46
common-sense discourses 108, 190
communal activity 58
communication: computer-mediated 7, 101–2, 115–17, 130, 136; inclusive 47; and subjectivity 118–19; womanism and 60
communicative stance 13
communion 57–8, 65, 81–7, 126–7
community: of diversity 188; feminists as 208
community orientation 51, 53
community politics, women's essential role in 188–9
compartmentalisation of feminism 175
complexity, gendered 47–8, 50, 64
computer-mediated communication (CMC) 7, 101–2, 115–17, 130, 136
confessional media 21–2
confidentiality in *Transstudy* 100
connections: building of 13–15; investigation of 1–13
consciousness-raising groups 7, 128
constructionism, dualism of essentialism and 132
continuum 38
contradiction: in queer theory 107; in third wave feminism 47–50, 64
*Conundrum* (Morris) 20
Cook, David 44
Cooper, Martha 13
cooperation 126
Corbett, Arthur 20, 71
*Corbett v Corbett/Ashley* (1970): and agency and communion 85; annulment in 20; and heteronormative gender 71–3; and 'Othering' 76, 77, 81; and postconventional ethics 195, 206n20; and 'real' trans identities 35; and search for aetiology 225; and voice 155
Cowan, Sharon: on agency and communion 85, 86; on heteronormative gender 72–4; on political subjectivity 138; on sexual identity 214, 217
Cowell, Roberta 113
Cox, Anna Marie 10–11
coyote medicine 37–8, 139–40, 153n6
Crenshaw, Kimberlé 192
criminals, rehabilitation of 148
critical analysis, inclusive 61
critical discourse analysis: access in 120–1; agency in 81, 126; in building connections 14–15; communion in 81, 126–7; construction of framework for 120–7, 130; dialogic negotiation in 121–3; discourse in 127; resistance and acquiescence in 123–4; schemata and scripts in 124; subjectivity in 125–6; and use of narratives 112
cross-difference cooperation 113
cross-dressing 142, 202
cross-gender intuition 139
cross-generational relations 52
Culbertson, Tucker 75
Currah, Paisley: on choice 169, 218; on gender aetiologies 197–8, 223; on internecine conflict 176; on legal protection 178; on political subjectivity 142; on postconventional ethics 210; on schools 218; on stereotyping 192; on trans awareness in schools 218; on transgender movement 223; on umbrella protection vs special recognition 210; on whole trans person 144
cyberfeminism 102

Daly, Suzanne 84
Damasio, Antonio 28
Davis, Angela 44
de Beauvoir, Simone 8, 26, 76, 112
de facto parenthood 84–5
de la Garza, Sarah 162
de Vos, Pierre 75
*Dear Sir or Madam* (Rees) 20
'decolonial analysis' 55
deconstruction 128, 131nn13–14
deep attendance 163
'definitional incoherence' 76
Delombard, Jeannine 11, 48, 50, 51
Dent, Gina 193
Descartes, René 207
*Desire in Language: A Semiotic Approach to Literature and Art* (Kristeva) 117
detached objectivity 14
deviance 182–3

*Diagnostic and Statistical Manual of Mental Disorders V* (DSM V) 4, 18n2
dialogic model of ethics 90, 122, 123
dialogic negotiation: and connection between queer theory and feminism 105; in construction of critical discourse analysis framework 121–3; and epiphanies 202; and political subjectivity 138; and voice/silence binary 162, 164
dialogic subversion of discourse 118, 131n5
Diamond, Irene 63, 128, 181, 188
Dicker, Rory 47–8, 61
difference: as equality strands 210–11; inclusion vs exclusion for 220; provision for 225–6; unifying experiences of 204
difference exclusion 220
difference feminism 200
difference inclusiveness 41–2, 44–5, 46, 199–201, 220
difference separatism 220
*Different Wavelengths* (anthology) 62
Dillon, Michael 38
*Discipline and Punish* (Foucault) 148
discourse 22; in critical discourse analysis 127; feminism as 127; of homosexuality 127; reconstructing 2, 112, 128–9, 130, 131nn13–14; reversed 1–2, 128, 131n8, 179n3
discourse analysis, critical 14–15, 81, 112, 120–7
discourse communities 127
discourse-in-process 128
discrimination, protection from 226–7
dissonance, personal 114
diversity, community of 188
drag performativity 6
Drake, Jennifer 47, 51, 53, 59, 61
DSM V *(Diagnostic and Statistical Manual of Mental Disorders V)* 4, 18n2
dualisms 48, 81, 104, 132

EA 2006 (Equality Act 2006) 93
EA 2010 *See* Equality Act 2010 (EA 2010)
Eagle, Maria 173, 210
ECtHR (European Court of Human Rights) 20, 78–9, 83
Edelstein, Marilyn 67–8
EHRC (Equality and Human Rights Commission) 151

Elbe, Lili 20, 25, 37
Ellis, Havelock 155, 197
empathic understanding 102
empathy: and coalition 11, 14, 16; communion as 126; and personally political postmodern identity 44; and postconventional ethics 88
'The Empire Strikes Back: A Post-transsexual Manifesto' (Stone) 155
employment discrimination 82
Enlightenment era 23
epiphanies 114, 140, 201–3, 204–5
Equal Pay Act 1970 69
equal pay claims 212
equality: claims based on 169; vs equity 95, 103; and ethic of justice 92; masculinist perception of 69; in queer theory 103, 107
Equality Act 2006 (EA 2006) 93
Equality Act 2010 (EA 2010) 93–5, 96; and agency and communion 85; on gender reassignment 93–4, 96, 186, 194, 211, 214; and gender variance as legal category 227; and heteronormative gender 71; and identity as process 149, 151; and 'Othering' 77, 78; on protection from discrimination 226–7; on provision for difference 225; and social cleansing 182, 183; and trans people as immigrants 186; on umbrella protection vs special recognition 210–11, 212
Equality and Human Rights Commission (EHRC) 151
Equality Bill 217
Equality Bill Committee 16
Equality Directives 93
equality strands 210–11
equity: vs equality 95, 103; and post-difference inclusiveness 201
erotics of unnaming: and inclusion 192–4, 204; in lesbian communities 193; and political subjectivity 140, 141, 151; vs politics of naming 192–4; and silence and secrecy 23, 40n5; and third wave as open and evolving discourse 63; in womanism 53–4
essence-in-process 198
essential attribute, bodily sex as 70
essentialisation: of gender 72–3, 74; of group identity 63; of sexual and philosophical subjectivities 11, 16; of trans existence 156
essentialised differences 10

essentialised identities 44–5, 46, 106–7
essentialising discourses 108
essentialism: dualism of constructionism and 132; identity 132–53; as problem area for feminists 132–3; social 112–13; strategic 129
ethic of justice 67; and coalition 12; and Equality Act 93–5, 96; and 'hailing' 125; and heteronormative gender 72; and identity as process 150; and inclusiveness 204; postconventional ethics and 91–2, 209–10; and struggle for single functional issue legislation 69
ethic of relationships 201
ethic of separation 201
ethical approach to qualitative research in Transstudy 98–100
ethical framework for Transstudy 98–103
ethics: dialogic model of 90, 190–1; postconventional 67, 87–93, 95
ethics of care: and agency and communion 83; and coalition 10, 11–12, 13, 16; cultural 223; and Equality Act 93–5, 96; and 'hailing' 125; and heteronormative gender 72; and identity as process 150; and inclusion 187, 190–2, 204; and negative feminisation 108, 128–30; and nonviolence 92; and 'Othering' 79; parenthood and 119; postconventional ethics and 67, 83, 87–93, 194–5, 209–10; and post-difference inclusiveness 200; in research 99, 129; and responsibility 161; semanalysis and 190–2; as social discourse 223; and struggles for single functional issue legislation 69; and subjective development 130; and womanism 54, 65
'ethics of integration' 227
ethics of investigation 13–14
'ethics of participation' 227
ethics-in-process 98–9
ethnicity, silence of 162–3
ethos of inclusion 8
European Convention of Human Rights 83
European Court of Human Rights (ECtHR) 20, 78–9, 83
European Court of Justice 82, 222
European Law, minimum required by 186
European Union (EU) citizenship 222, 227–8
European Union (EU) Commission 93

exclusion 181–206; conclusions on 203–5; erotics of unnaming vs politics of naming for 192–4; from ethics of care to postconventional ethics for 194–5; and finding ourselves (epiphanies) 201–3; genre and genealogy for 195–9; and maternal relations 188–201; metaphor of immigrants and refugees for 185–8, 204; overview of 181–2; post-difference for 199–201; semanalysis and ethics of care for 190–2; by social cleansing 182–5, 203–4, 205n4, 221
'ex-pat syndrome' 185
expectancy responding 102
extended family of trans people 189–90
Eyre, Jane (fictional) 58

Facebook 115
face-to-face (FTF) interactions 101–2
factions 2, 15
Fae, Jane 210
Fairclough, Norman 112
family 83–4, 147
famous names 50n, 66n4
fatherhood 82–3, 97n12, 136
Featherstone, Lynne 173, 210
Feinberg, Leslie: on lived messiness 131n4; on personally political postmodern identity 44; and refugee metaphor 185; on silence and secrecy 24; on social cleansing 182, 205n4; on voice 154, 155, 158
Felski, Rita 43–4, 52
'female masculinism' 116
Female Masculinity (Halberstam) 31
The Feminine Mystique (Friedan) 145
femininely polarised behaviour 146
femininity, oppressive 146
feminisation: negative 108, 130; positive 108–9
feminism: anti-trans 127, 131n11; of colour 44, 53–60; compartmentalisation of 175; definition for 109; as discourse 127; first wave 41; fourth wave 115; and queer theory 104, 105–8, 129; re-radicalisation of 61, 62; separatist 3, 15, 27, 39, 116, 130, 199, 206n22, 213; taking a break from 109, 130; see also second wave feminism; third wave feminism
feminist(s): as community 208; infantilising by 160, 161; 'Othering' by 175; as political fanatics 133
feminist activists 188–9

feminist anthologies 61–2
feminist consciousness-raising groups 7
feminist essentialisation of womanly identity 11
feminist inter-wave conflict 174–5
feminist movements 176, 181
Feminist Networks 115
"feminist osmosis thesis" 46
feminist separatism 15; trans-unfriendly 127, 131n11
feminist subjectivities as real 213–14
feminist-inspired critical discourse analysis 14–15
Ferguson, Ann 219
'fictitious commonalities' 46
Fidyk, Alexandra 163, 164
figureheads 50n, 66n4
finding oneself 21, 24–5, 40n2; and inclusion 201–3, 204–5
Findlay, Barbara 211
Findlen, Barbara 61
Fineman, Martha 84, 108
First Amendment rights 142
first wave feminism, 'woman' identity in 41
first wave of gender legislation 68–70
'Flight into Masculinity' 30
'folk devil' 182–3
Forbes-Sempill, Ewan 70–1
foreignness 215
forums and voice 155
Foucault, Michel: on aetiology vs acceptance 15; on agency 126; on Herculine Barbin 71, 78; on coalition 10, 12, 13; and critical discourse analysis 112; on dialogic subversion of discourse 118, 131n5; on discourse of homosexuality 127; on ethics 88; on genealogy 45, 58, 198, 213; on hegemony 123–4; on identity as process 147–8, 149, 196; on 'monsters' 76–7, 143–4; and queer theory 103; on reciprocal elucidation 97n14, 118, 122, 131n5; on reverse hailing 157–8; on reversed discourse 1–2, 128, 131n8, 179n3; on self-knowledge 134; on sexual subjectivity 5; on silence and secrecy 21–2, 23, 39; on subject-in-process 228n12; on subjectivity 42–3, 87, 97n14; on 'truth' 49
'Foucault's Monsters, the Abnormal Individual and the Challenge of English Law' (Sharpe) 76–7
fourth wave feminism 115
Franke, Katherine 108
freedom 88, 89; of choice 169–70

Freud, Sigmund 25, 26–7, 119, 196
Friedan, Betty 145
Frith, Gill 58
FTF (face-to-face) interactions 101–2
functional parenthood 84–5
'functionalism' 123
'functionality' 72
Fuss, Diana 132

Gagnon, John 124
Garber, Marjorie: on infantilisation 27, 28, 29, 32, 33; on progress narrative 196; on 'real' trans identities 36–7, 38; on silence and secrecy 24; on transvestites 6, 10
Garfinkel, Harold 6
Garrison, Ednie Kaeh: on inter-wave philosophy 50, 51; on maternal relations 188–9; on personally political postmodern identity 46; on third wave feminism vs postfeminism 175; on womanism 54
gatekeeping 118, 121, 160, 182, 209
gay existence, experience of gender in 143
gay men, female spouses of 22–3
gay relations, and sodomy laws 76
gay subjectivities, queer's alignment with 129
'Gemeinschaftsfremden' (Whittle) 80
gender: automatic ascribing of 43–4; defined 17; legal definitions of 195, 206n20; as set of relations 5; as social construct 214
gender androgyny 44
gender borderlands 37
'gender confirmation treatment' 71
gender construction 10–11
gender discourses, age of 21
gender dualism 81, 178
gender dysphoria: in acceptance vs search for aetiology 4, 5; and choice 168, 172; and immigrants metaphor 187–8; and 'real' gender variant subjectivities 135
'gender euphoria' 187
gender expression vs identity 169
gender fluidity 215
gender formation, social constructionist accounts of 5, 194
'gender fuck' 104–5
gender identity disorders 4, 187
gender indefinability 135
gender legislation *see* legislation
gender negotiators 7

gender nonconformity and labelling 169
gender oppression 15, 16
*Gender Outlaw* (Bornstein) 131n4
gender performers 7
gender reassignment: defined 93; and Equality Act 2010 93–4, 96, 186, 194, 211, 214; and Equality Bill 16; and family cohesion 82–3, 97n12; vs gender variant 217, 220, 226; as protected category 85; in Sex Discrimination (Gender Reassignment) Regulations 70; and transition 17
Gender Reassignment Regulations 1999 69, 70, 88
gender reassignment surgery 9, 12–13, 20, 36, 37
Gender Recognition Act (GRA) 2004: and agency and communion 82, 85; and choice 172; and Equality Act 94; and heteronormative gender 71, 73–5; and 'Othering' 81; on parenting and marriage 213; on recognition vs passing 220; and social cleansing 182; and trans people as immigrants 186–7
Gender Recognition Bill 85
Gender Recognition Certificates 73, 186
Gender Recognition Panel 73, 74
gender signifiers 43
gender signs, stereotyped 10
gender socialization 138–9
gender subjectivities in process 216
gender transition: and parenthood 82–5; workplace discrimination due to 82
gender transition clinic 27
*Gender Trouble* (Butler) 103–4
The Gender Trust 82
gender variance: in childhood 149–50; defined 16; developing legal category of 224, 227; vs gender reassignment 217, 220, 226; vs homosexuality 197; as temporary 196; and transition as process 226
gender variant cause, value of community and movement to 208
gender variant people: as citizens vs immigrants 227–8; 'Othering' of 77; trans vs 187
gender variant subjectivity: narration of 19; as real 134–7, 149; third wave feminism and 41, 48
gender voice coaching *see* 'voice coaching'
gender-based rearing 9
gender-based socialisation 9

gendered behaviour 168–9
gendered complexity 47–8, 50, 64
gendered differences 18n6
gendered essence, choice of 86
gendered 'home' 185
gendered reversals 149
gendered scripts 6
gendered stereotypes, breaking down 190
gendered subjectivities, acceptance vs searching for aetiology of 4–7, 15
'Genealogies and Generations' (Gillis, Howie & Munford) 52
genealogy: and coalition 11, 16; and contradiction 48; and heteronormative gender 70; and inclusion 181, 193, 194, 195–9, 204; and inter-wave philosophy 52; and 'Othering' 77, 95; and personally political postmodern identity 45, 46, 64; and postconventional ethics 90; and postdifference inclusiveness 200; and queer theory 105, 106, 129; recommendations on 212–18, 225–6; solidarity in 212; 'woman' as 133; and womanism 58
'generational account of feminism' 52
generative silence 163
genetic determinism 38
genitalia as prime indicator of sexual subjectivity 35
genre: and contradiction 48; and heteronormative gender 70; and inclusion 181, 193, 194, 195–9, 204; and personally political postmodern identity 45, 46, 64; and postdifference inclusiveness 200; and queer theory 105; and 'real' trans identities 38, 40; recommendations on 212–18, 225–6; solidarity in 212
Gilligan, Carol: on acceptance vs search for aetiology 4; on choice 170; on coalition 10, 12, 14; on contradiction 49–50; on equality 69; essentialised identity of 133; on ethics of care 16, 190–2, 204, 222; on gender socialization 138; on infantilisation 27–8; on maternal relations 188, 208; on moral decision-making 161; on narratives 110; on negative feminisation 108, 130; on parenthood 119; on postconventional ethics 67, 87, 88–9, 90–1, 92, 195, 204, 209; and postdifference inclusiveness 201; on silence and secrecy 25; on 'voice' 156, 220; on womanism 57

Gillis, Stacy 48, 52, 102, 173-4, 175
'Girlie' culture 161, 175
Godvin, Tara 177
*Goodwin* case 78, 79, 85, 86, 138
Gordon, Stephen (fictional) 25, 35
Government Equalities Office 93
GRA *see* Gender Recognition Act (GRA) 2004
Gramsci, Antonio 123, 158
"grand theory" 109
Gray, John 167
Green, Jamison 143
Greening, Justine 186
Greer, Germaine: on contradiction 49; on divide between feminism and transgender 2, 116; on 'Girlie' culture 161; on personally political postmodern identity 46; on trans women 142, 144, 145, 146, 147, 151-2, 160, 186
group identity, essentialising of subjectivities into 133
Grrrl culture 175
'gynandry' 24

'hailing' 178; and epiphanies 203; and political subjectivity 153n8; and refusal to grow up 161; reverse 157-8, 178; and subjectivity 125-6; and voice 156-7
Halberstam, Judith/Jack: on connection between queer theory and feminism 106; on contradiction 48; on immigrants and refugees 185; on refusal to grow up 31, 32, 160; on separatist discourse 9
Hale, Brenda 69-70, 88
Hale, Jacob 9, 31-2, 168
'half-life' 20
Hall, Kira 102
Hall, Radclyffe 145
Hall, Stuart 6
Halley, Janet 104, 107, 109-10, 129, 161
harassment of transvestite 135
Haraway, Donna 37-8, 44, 158
Harding, Jennifer 4, 7
Harding, Sandra 14, 18n8, 30, 131n15
Harris, Evan 18n10
hate crimes 177
Hauser, Richard 22-3
Hausman, Bernice 9-10, 19, 35, 46, 48
Hebert, Laura 62-3
hegemony 76, 97n7, 123-4, 197
Henry, Astrid: on choice 171; on difference inclusiveness 199; on maternal relations 51, 175; on third wave as open and evolving discourse 61, 63-4; on wave metaphor 174; on womanism 53, 54, 57
'herethics' 191
hermaphrodite 77-8
Hernandez, Daisy 61
'heteronormalising' of transitioning experience 166
heteronormative appearance 178
heteronormative discourses 9, 33, 178
heteronormative gendering 95, 97n1, 182
heteronormative legislation 70-6
heteronormative promises, 'Othering' from 15
heteronormative reassignment 9, 12-13
heteronormative script 10, 15
heteronormativity 17; conforming to 141; mimicry of 153n4; recuperation into 77-8; rehabilitation into 186; as separatist discourse 108; by trans people 145-6, 148; and trans subjectivity 135
heterosexuality, promise of post-operative 155, 179n1
Heyes, Cressida J 89, 133
Heywood, Leslie L. 47, 51, 53, 59, 61
hierarchies vs networks 51
Hines, Sally 2, 3, 139
hip-hop feminism 62
'hir' 17
Hirschfeld, Magnus 27, 155
Holmes, Morgan 80-1
homophobia and law 72-3, 75
homosexuality: in 1950s 22-3; discourse of 127; Freud on 196-7; gender variance vs 197; Krafft-Ebing on 23-4; and postdifference inclusiveness 201; reconstructed discourse on 112; reversed discourse of 179n3; and transitioning 168
hooks, bell: on exclusion 181; on interwave philosophy 50, 52; on maternal relations 188; on Otherness 18n5, 135; on personally political postmodern identity 44; on separatist discourse 8, 15; on solidarity 122, 181, 226; on womanism 54, 55, 56
Howie, Gillian 51, 52, 60, 61
Hoyer, Niels 20
hypermasculinity, flight into 149

'I' case 78
identity 17; essentialised 44–5, 46, 106–7; vs gender expression 169; inverted 104; as process 147–51; social construction theory of 42–3; as subjectivity 45, 70, 148; after transition 149
identity essentialism 132–53; conclusions on 151–2; exclusion due to 133; and identity as process 147–51; overview of 132–4; and political subjectivity 137–42; and which gender variant subjectivities are real 134–7; and whole trans person 142–7
identity paradigm 199
identity politics 108, 176, 181, 211
identity stereotypes 137
identity-in-process 147–51, 152; and genre and genealogy 196; and personally political postmodern identity 42–4; and postdifference 200; recommendations on 215–16; and unnaming vs naming 193
'ideological force' 123
'ideological state apparatus' (ISA) 22, 40n4, 123
immaturity 26–34, 39, 158–61, 209
immigrant metaphor 185–8, 204; recommendations on 221–2, 227–8
impartiality 90, 207
*In a Different Voice* (anthology) 89, 90, 108, 156
*In Search of Our Mothers' Gardens* (Walker) 54
*Incidents in the Life of a Slave Girl* (Jacobs) 58
inclusion 181–206; conclusions on 203–5; erotics of unnaming vs politics of naming for 192–4; from ethics of care to postconventional ethics for 194–5; ethos of 8; and finding ourselves (epiphanies) 201–3; genre and genealogy for 195–9; and maternal relations 188–201; metaphor of immigrants and refugees for 185–8, 204; overview of 181–2; postdifference for 199–201, 220; semanalysis and ethics of care for 190–2; by social cleansing 182–5, 203–4, 205n4; of women of colour 55
inclusive communication 47
inclusive community 51
inclusive critical analysis 61
inclusive difference 18n6
inclusive feminism 61, 181
inclusive philosophies 13

inclusive theorists 10–11
Industrial West 35
infantilisation: and agency 126; and voice 158–61, 209; and womanism 66n5; and gender variant people 26, 28
in-group internecine exclusion 3–4
initiation 146
interdependence 228n16
inter-generational communication 190
International Bill of Gender Rights 84
internecine conflict 176
internecine exclusion 47; challenging of 1–4, 15; and queer theory 105
internecine hostility 160, 180n6
Internet 101, 102, 115–17, 130
'interpellation' 125–6, 156–7, 178
intersectionality theory 105
intersex 20, 29, 78, 80–1
intersex medicine 4
'intertextuality' 119–20
inter-trans negotiation 197
inter-wave conflict 174–5
inter-wave philosophy 50–3, 65
*Introducing Women's Studies* (Marshment) 161
intuition 145
'inversion' 196–7
inverted identities 104
invisibilisation of women of colour 53, 66n5
invisibility of trans narratives 155
invisible differences 77
Irigaray, Luce 49, 65n2
ISA ('ideological state apparatus') 22, 40n4, 123

Jackson, Alecia Youngblood 156, 158
Jackson, Jack 75
Jacobs, Harriet 58
Jeffreys, Sheila 2, 36, 46, 116
*John A C Forbes-Sempill v The Hon Ewan Forbes-Sempill* (1967) 70–1
Johnson, Julia 8, 163
Jones, Lisa 193
Jones, Lynn 18n10
Jorgensen, Christine 20, 25, 38, 72, 202
'jouissance' 163–4, 202
Jul, Kimana 101
justice, reconstruction of 92
'justice orientation' 91

Kane, Charles/Samantha 185, 205n9
*Kantaras* case 84
Karaian, Lara 132, 224

Kellstedt, Paul 225
Kennedy, Duncan 109
Khosla, Dhillon 21, 39, 136, 155, 199
Kiley, Dan 28
kin connections 7
'kindred' 53, 200
Kingston, Maxine Hong 54
Kohlberg, Lawrence 25
Koyama, Emi 11
Krafft-Ebing, Richard von 23–4, 155, 196
Kristeva, Julia: on acceptance vs search for aetiology 4; on coalition 10; on ethics 190–1; on 'jouissance' 163–4, 202; on maternal relations 51, 52, 64, 208, 222–3; on personally political postmodern identity 44; on postconventional ethics 88–9; on post-difference inclusiveness 199, 201; on self-images of trans people 67; on semanalysis 117–20, 130, 131n3, 188, 189, 190–2, 204; on subjectivity-in-process 215–16, 228n16; on third wave feminism as open and evolving discourse 61; on 'woman' 41, 147; on womanism 53, 57
Kroker, Arthur 44
Kropp, Douglas 224
Kuhn, Thomas 14

labelling 23; by feminists 160; and gender nonconformity 169; and Gender Recognition Act 172; of gender variant children 160; in identity essentialism 132; queer theory and 104, 106, 152
Lacan, Jacques 67, 119
Lakota culture: child development in 152; epiphanies in 202–3; extended family in 152–3nn2–3; and gender variant subjectivities 134, 136; and identity as process 150
language: and 'hailing' 178; political subjectivity through 140–1; and subjective formation 112, 130; symbolic 118, 121, 130, 131n7
'language-as-mirror' 112, 122, 131n8
law: interactions with 11; and queer theory 105; silencing of self-representation in 155
Lee, Tracey 5, 111, 155–6
Lees, Paris 115, 116
legal definitions of gender 195, 206n20
legal gains, investigating effects of 224–5

*Legal Queeries* (Moran) 223
legislation 67–97; agency and communion in 81–7; conclusion on 95–6; Equality Act 2006 as 93–5; first wave of 68–70, 95; heteronormative 70–6; 'Othering' in 76–81; overview of 67–8; postconventional ethics in 67, 87–93, 95; second wave of 68–70, 95; on single functional issues 68–70, 95; table of 233; third wave of 81–7, 96
lesbian communities, inclusive approach from 192–3
lesbian existence, experience of gender in 143
lesbian identity 79
lesbian mothers 79
'lesbian sex wars' 48
lesbian subjectivities, queer's alignment with 129
lesbianism: butch/femme identities in 48–9; in sixteenth and seventeenth centuries 23, 40n5; vanilla 48
Lever, Janet 27–8
'liberal assimilation' 106, 225
'life experience' 200
life-histories of research participants 100
linguistic perspective 163
*Listen Up* (Findlen) 61
listening, deep 163
'lived experience' 200
'lived messiness': and contradiction 47–8, 49, 64; and inter-wave philosophy 50; and semanalysis 118, 131n4
lobbying power 225
lobbyists, trans 149
local issues, women's essential role in 188–9
logocentric constraints 119, 131n6
Loizidou, Elena 223
London Gender Symposium (1969) 31
Long, Scott 103
'looking with' 13
Lorde, Audre 54, 113, 181, 200
Lossie, Cheryl 163
Lothstein, Leslie 28
Lotter, John 31
Love, Courtney 47

Maastricht Treaty 222
McAdams, Dan P 57, 87, 125, 126
Mackenzie, Gordene 9, 132
McKeon, Michael 23
MacKinnon, Catherine 68–9, 90, 107, 155, 216

Maclean, Mavis 88
Mahajan, Harpreet 225
Male Ceremonies 148
Malhotra, Sheena 162, 178
*Mamela v Vancouver Lesbian Connection* 74
*Man into Woman* (Hoyer) 20
marginalised identity, 'women' as 146
marriage: and agency and communion 86; duality and laws of 165, 180n8; and heteronormative gender 71, 73, 75, 97n5; and 'Othering' 81; same-sex 73, 75, 81, 86, 213; of trans people 136
Marriage (Same Sex Couples) Act 2013 [M(SSC) 2013] 73, 75, 81
Marshment, Margaret 161
Marx, Karl 119
masculinism: female 116; structural dominance of 69–70
masculinist perception of equality 69
masculinist standard 28
mass media 182–3
maternal relations: and feminism as positive 108–9; and inclusion 188–201; inter-wave philosophy and 50–3, 65; and naming-in-process 194; and postconventional ethics 89; recommendations on 208–12, 223, 224–5; rehabilitating image of mother in 175; and semiotic communication 119, 130; silence and secrecy and 204; as socially constructed 208–9; and womanism 57
Mattio, Sean 32–3
medical community, silencing of voices by 155
medical diagnosis 186–7
medical discourse 35
medical models 8, 9, 19
medical narrative 35–6
medical separatist discourse 10
medically defined stereotypes 13
"Men Are from Mars, Women Are from Venus" (Gray) 167
men's groups 155
mental health condition 4
messiness: lived 47–8, 49, 50, 64, 118, 131n4; narrative 118, 207
metanarratives: and contradiction 49, 64, 65n2; and creation of reconstructing discourses 128, 131n12; and subjectivity-in-process 133, 137; and taking a break from non-feminism 110; and third wave as open and evolving discourse 63; of trans men's aetiology 155–6
micro-issues 59–60
micro-political approaches 59–60, 189
micro-politics 59–60, 189
"middle-range theory" 109
Middleton, Richard 164
*A Midsummer Night's Dream* (Shakespeare) 24
migration 185
mind-body dualism 207
'mirror stage' 67
'missionary role' 56
mixed gendered personality 215
'Modest Witness' 158, 180n4, 207
Moerings, Martin 201, 223
Mohanty, Chandra 46
Moi, Toril 119, 131n3
Molly Houses 40n3
'monsters' 76–7, 86, 95, 143–4
Moore, Suzanne 115, 116
Moraga, Cherríe 54, 61–2
moral decision-making 161
moral development: and maternal relations 190–2, 204; and postconventional ethics 87, 90, 91–2; and postdifference 201
moral values of dominant society 171
morality: emanating from men vs women 87; of responsibility 50; of rights 69
More, Kate 62
'mores' 141
Morgan, Joan 57
Morgan, Robin 62
Morris, Jan: on epiphanies 202, 203; personal narrative of 20, 113; on postconventional ethics 198–9; on 'real' trans identities 37; on voice 209; on whole trans person 146
mother(s): definition of 79–80; lesbian 79; rehabilitating image of 175; and semiotic communication 119, 130; trans people as 136
mother figure 57
motherhood and feminisation as positive 108–9
'movement' 173–7, 179; recommendations on 211–12
[M(SSC)] Marriage (Same Sex Couples) Act [M(SSC)] 2013 73, 75, 81
multi-issue activism 63
multiplicity 47–8
Munford, Rebecca 48, 52, 161, 173–4, 175

Munro, Ealasaid 115
Murdock, George 83

Nagel, Thomas 14
Namaste, Ki 6, 11–12, 13
naming of movements 176
'naming-in-process' 219
narration of gender variant subjectivity 19
narrative(s) 154–80; choice in 167–73; conclusions on 177–9; critiquing binary of voice and silence in 162–4; of gender variance 5, 14; hailing/interpellation in 156–7; 'movement of their own' in 173–7; overview of 154; passing in 164–7; and refusal to grow up 158–61; as sign systems 117–20; standpoint epistemology/view from somewhere in 157–8; in *Transstudy* 111–17, 130; voice in 154–64
narrative interaction, extended 102
'narrative messiness' 118, 207
narrative subversion 118, 131n3
'narrative visibility' 7
natal birth 17
Native Americans: communication by 162; concept of spiritual person of 145; *see also* Lakota culture
'naturalised citizen' 186
nature, silence of 123
nature/nurture debate 42
NdegéOcello, Me'Shell 47
negative feminisation 108, 130
neighbourhood, women's essential role in 188–9
networks vs hierarchies 51
The Network...Women Empowering Women! 115
neutrality 90
*New Maladies of the Soul* (Kristeva) 41, 228n16
'Nietzsche, Genealogy, History' (Foucault) 58
Nissen, Marvin Thomas 31
*Nixon v Vancouver Rape Relief Society* 74
*No Permanent Waves* (anthology) 62
Noel, Normi 154
non-feminisms, taking a break from 109–11, 130, 175
nonviolence 92
*Not My Mother's Sister* (Henry) 51
'nuclear family' 83–4, 147
NuttycaTS 115

Oakley, Anne 50
'objective' research, feminist theory and philosophy vs 49–50
objectivity 30

'The Obligatory Transsexual File' (1991) 5, 8–9
O-boys 30
O-girls 30
O'Leary, Timothy 149
O-men 20, 30
online forums 7, 115–17, 130, 137
'onus of care' 95, 97n19
open-ended topics and discussion in research 100
'opposite' sex 35
oppressed Other 8
oppressed subjectivities: gender variant people as 138; women with 132–3
oppression: due to perceptions of identity 192; and postconventional ethics 210; shared experiences of 45–6; social cleansing and 192, 203, 220; stereotyping and 192; and 'view from somewhere' 213; from white culture 56
oppressive devices 220
oppressive femininity 146
oppressors, feminists as 47
Ormrod, Roger 35, 71, 86
O-sexuals 29, 160
ostracisation 182–5
'Other' 41; monstrous 76–7, 86, 95; oppression of feminist 128; other gender variance as 106
'Othering': and coalition 10, 11, 15; by feminists 175; in gender legislation 76–81, 95; of heteronormative transitioning people 76; and oppression 192; in politics of naming 168; in research 99; from *Transstudy* website 121, 129; of women 76
'Otherness': commodification of 55–6; embracing 147; and erotics of unnaming 204; and postdifference inclusiveness 200; rage and shared 45; tourists of 9, 18n5, 135
'out,' being 140
'outing' of trans people 116
out-in-process 140
*Over the Sex Border* (Turtle) 29–30, 160
O-women 20

*P v S and Cornwall County Council* (1996) 82, 95

pantomime dames 29, 160, 186
pantomime depiction of Peter Pan 29
paradox 47–8
parenthood: and agency and communion 82–5; association of gender with 119; and ethics of care 119; and 'Othering' 79–80, 81; and 'real' gender variant subjectivities 136, 213; in third wave of gender legislation 96; by trans people 136, 213
*Paris Is Burning* (film) 35
Parker, Ian 131n7
participation 227–8
passing 164–7, 178, 180n8; and coalition 12; and 'Othering' 78; and political subjectivity 140, 141; recognition vs 226–7; recommendations on 219–20, 226–7; and refusal to grow up 33; and silence and secrecy 24; and social cleansing 183; and voice 155; as white 193
passionate stance 14
Patel, Pragna 58, 66n7
pathologisation: vs acceptance of gendered subjectivities 4; and choice 168, 172–3, 178; and genre and genealogy 196; and immigrants and refugees 186–7; and silence and secrecy 23
patriarchal community or society 36
patriarchal conspirators, trans people as 193
patriarchal view 14
patriarchy of eighteenth and nineteenth centuries 23
Pepper, John 215
'perception' 78
performativity of gender 33, 46
persona(s) 102
personal dissonance 114
personal epiphanies 114
personal narratives 19–20
personal subjectivity 5
personal trauma 114
personally political postmodern identity 42–7, 64, 193, 198
personally political stance 14
Peter Pan 27, 29
Peter Pan Syndrome (PPS) 28–9
*The Peter Pan Syndrome* (Kiley) 28
philosophical framework *for Transstudy* 103–11
Piaget, Jean 25, 201
Piepmeier, Alison 47–8, 61
Pierce-Baker, Charlotte 58

'plaisir' 163–4, 202, 205
'plausible personal history' 5
Pliny the Elder 70
political activism, women's 63
'political defector' 185
political fanatics, feminists as 133
political postmodern identity 42–7, 64, 193, 198
political subjectivity 137–42, 151; recommendations on 219
politics of naming: and choice 168; erotics of unnaming vs 192–4; recommendations on 209, 224; and silence and secrecy 23, 24, 39, 204; and third wave feminism 41
positivistic research, feminist theory and philosophy vs 49–50
postconventional ethics 67, 87–93, 96; and Equality Act 93–5; ethics of care and 83, 87–93, 194–5, 204; and identity as process 150; and inclusion 194–5, 204; recommendations on 209–11
postdifference 199–201, 204; recommendations on 218–22, 226–8
postfeminism 44, 51, 174, 175
postmodern identity, personally political 42–7, 64, 193, 198
post-operative heterosexuality, promise of 155, 179n1
'post-out' society 140, 219
post-structural views of sexual subjectivity 133
poststructuralist deconstruction 63
'A Posttransexual Manifesto' (Stone) 9, 24, 37
Potter, Mark 97n5
power relations 22, 112, 123–4, 156–7, 158
powerlessness, silence and 162
Pozner, Jennifer L. 63
PPS (Peter Pan Syndrome) 28–9
Prado, Carlos 22, 134, 148
'preferred gender' 17
'pregnant man' 136
prescriptive feminist model 170–1
Press for Change: on agency and communion 82; on epiphanies 203, 205; on Equality Act 94, 151; on gender variant vs gender reassignment 16, 217; on heteronormative gender 71; on political subjectivity 140; on pubertal deferment treatment 217; on trans movement 175; and trans people as

immigrants 186; and 'TransEquality' legal cases 17
pre-symbolic language 53
Prince, Virginia 13
prisoners, rehabilitation of 148
privileged feminists 56
process, identity as 147–51
progress narrative 32–3
pronouns 17
property laws 70
Prosser, Jay: on computer-mediated communication 101; on epiphanies 202; on evolving narratives 154; on queer theory 103; on 'real' trans identities 38; on unnameable identity 19
prostitution 62
protected category: gender reassignment as 85; trans people as 183
protection: from discrimination 226–7; umbrella/universal 210–11, 212, 228n9
'pseudohermaphroditic' individuals 38
psychiatry 4, 21
psychoanalysis 39, 43, 67, 104, 117
*Psychopathia Sexualis* (Krafft-Ebing) 23–4, 155
psychosocial development 26–7
pubertal deferral treatment 206n23, 217
puberty 30, 31, 32
public appointments boards 227
Public Sector Gender Equality Duty 78, 93

qualitative research, ethical approach to 98–100
queer family structure 84
queer project 16
queer representations 104
queer theory 103–5, 129; connections between feminism and 105–8, 129; definition for 109; and postdifference inclusiveness 200–1; and subjectivity politics 129; taking a break from 109
'Queer Theory by Men' (Halley) 109
'Queering Theory' (Backer) 25–6
queer-inspired third wave feminism 103–11
queerness 8
quilting metaphor 58–9, 65, 162
Quinby, Lee 63, 128, 181, 188

racial feminist struggle 53
radical feminism 116
radical separatism 127, 131n11
rage, transgender 45, 103
rape 74
rationality 22

Raymond, Janice: on chromosomal sex 180n10; on contradiction 48; on failure to grow up 27; on identity as process 147; on internecine exclusion 2; on medical discourse 19; on personal political postmodern identity 46; on 'real' trans identities 35–6; on scripting into gendering 144; on separatist discourse 8, 9, 116, 127; on trans people 160, 193
'reading' 78
real: becoming 199; gender variant subjectivity as 134–7, 151
Real Life Experience (RLE): and heteronormative gender 73; and political subjectivity 140; and 'real' gender variant subjectivities 135; and recognition vs passing 166, 227; and social cleansing 182
Real Life Test 140
real subjectivities 213–14
'real' trans identities 34–9, 40
'realised gender' 17
'reassignment' 16, 17
'reassignment' surgery: and coalition 12–13; and passing 168; and 'real' trans identities 36, 37; and separatist discourse 9; and silence and secrecy 20
'reciprocal elucidation' 97n14, 118, 122, 131n5
*Reclaiming Genders* (More & Whittle) 62
recognition vs passing 220, 226–7
recommendations 207–29; on case law tailored to individual circumstances 224; on choice 216–18; on gender immigrants and refugees 221–2, 227–8; on genre and genealogy 212–18, 225–6; on identity as process 215–16; on investigating effects of legal gains 224–5; on legal category of 'gender variance' 227; on legal provision for choice of sexual subjectivity 226; on maternal relations 208–12, 224–5; on movements 211–12; overview of 207–8; on passing 219–20, 226–7; on political subjectivity 219; on politics of naming 224; on postconventional ethics 209–11; on postdifference 218–22, 226–8; practical applications of 222–8; on real trans and feminist subjectivities 213–14; on search for aetiology vs provision for differences 225–6; on sexual subjectivity as process 226; on social cleansing 220–1; on voice 209; on whole trans person 215

reconstructed themes 96
reconstructing discourse 2, 112, 128–9, 130, 131nn13–14
Rees, Mark: on agency and communion 82; on epiphanies 202; on explaining trans lives 20–1; on refusal to grow up 30–1, 32, 33, 160; on whole trans person 146
reflexive account 14
reflexivity 49, 65n3, 111
refugee metaphor 185–8, 204; recommendations on 221–2, 227–8
'refusal to grow up' 26–34, 39, 158–61
'refusing to engage' 31
rehabilitation into heteronormativity 186
Rehman, Bushra 61
Reid, Russell 155, 205n9
relational qualities 89
re-radicalisation of feminism 61, 62
research 98–131; absence of 'self-identified third wave feminists' primary study in 102–3; access in 120–1; agency in 126; authenticity of 100–2; communion in 126–7; computer-mediated communication in 101–2; conclusions on 129–31; connections between queer theory and feminism in 105–8; critical discourse analysis framework in 120–7, 130; dialogic negotiation in 105, 121–3; discourse in 127; ethical approach to qualitative 98–100; ethical framework in 98–103; feminisation as positive in 108–9; inclusive methodology for 99–100; narratives in 111–17, 130; online debate in 115–17, 130; 'Othering' in 99; philosophical framework in 103–11; queer theory in 103–5; queer-inspired third wave feminism in 103–11; reconstructing discourses in 128–9, 130, 131nn13–14; researcher/participant interactions in 100; resistance and acquiescence in 123–4; schemata and scripts in 124; semanalysis in 117–20, 130, 131n3; subjectivity in 125–6; taking a break from non-feminism in 109–11, 130
researcher/participant interactions 100
resistance in critical discourse analysis 123–4
*Respect and Equality* (Whittle) 80, 176
responsibility for moral decision-making 161, 192
'responsibility orientation' to morality 91
reverse discourses 1–2, 128, 131n8, 179n3

reverse hailing 157–8, 178
Rich, Adrienne 162
Riddell, Carol 9
Riessman, Catherine 111, 114, 158, 202
RLE *see* Real Life Experience (RLE)
Robson, Ruthann 225
Roiphe, Kate 64
Romero, Adam P 84, 108, 110–11, 197
Rose, Jacqueline 29
Roth, Martin 71
Rowe, Aimee 162, 178
Rowe, Aimee Carrillo 59
Rubin, Gayle 199
Russo, Ann 59, 162
Rutherford, Sarah 141
Ryle, Gilbert 207

same-sex marriage 73, 75, 81, 86, 213
Sandoval, Chela 54
Saville-Troike, Muriel 163
Sawicki, Jana 181
Scales, Ann 108, 209, 224, 225, 226
schemata: in critical discourse analysis 124; of transitioning subjectivity 144, 215
schools, trans awareness in 218
scientific discourse 22, 39
scientific paradigm, Western 35
Scott, Myka 82
Scott-Dixon, Krista 2, 62
scripts: in critical discourse analysis 124; of transitioning subjectivity 8–9, 144–5, 152
SDA (Sex Discrimination Act 1975) 69, 70, 94, 97n19, 194
second wave feminism 2; on essentialism 46, 132–3; prescriptive model built up by 170; and reconstructing discourse 128; social construction theory in 42–3; 'woman' identity in 41
second wave of gender legislation 68–9, 70–6
secrecy 21–6, 39, 155, 177, 204
Sedgwick, Eve Kosofsky 165
self 149
Self, Will 113
self-agency 91, 97n18
self-aware perspective 158
self-centredness 31
self-declaration 187
self-definition 86, 171–2, 179, 196
self-determination of sexual identity 169–70
self-discovery journey 185, 205

self-empowerment 170
self-expression 113–14, 171
self-images of trans people 67
self-knowledge 134
selflessness 146, 159–60
self-perception, gender and 73, 86–7
self-presentations of sexual subjectivity 155
self-reflexive standpoint epistemology 13
self-reflexively critical discourse 128
self-reflexively evolving phenomenon 14
self-representations 155–6, 170
self-revelation 203
semanalysis 117–20, 130, 131n3; and ethics of care 190–2; and inclusion 188, 190–2, 204
semiotic language 53, 117–20, 188, 189, 223
semiotic practice 118
separate and single sex services (SSEs) 94
'separate but equal' 75
separatism 8
separatist difference 18n6
separatist difference feminism 199
separatist discourse(s): heteronormativity as 108; revealing of 7–10, 15
separatist feminism: and infantilisation 27, 39; and internecine exclusion 3, 15; and online attacks 116; and post-difference 199, 206n22; and 'real' trans and feminist subjectivities 213; taking a break from 130
separatist trans people 213
Sevenhuijsen, Selma 92
sex: definition of individual's 72; determinants of 86–7
"sex change" 19
Sex Discrimination Act 1975 (SDA) 69, 70, 94, 97n19, 194
Sex Discrimination (Gender Reassignment) Regulations 1999 69, 70, 88, 186
sex reassignment surgery 9, 12–13, 20, 36, 37
sex work 62
sexology 39, 43, 104, 124
sexual discourses, age of 21
sexual identity: need for law to define 214; self-determination of 169–70
*Sexual Inversion* (Ellis) 155
sexual orientation, defined 17
sexual subjectivity: choice in representation of 170, 180n9; defined 17; genitalia as prime indicator of 35; in legal case 86; legal provision for choice of 226; medical and legal aetiologies of 15; post-structural views of 133; and power relationships 5; as process 216, 226; self-definition of 38; self-presentations of 155; social construction of 6; third wave feminism and 48; of trans people 215
sexuality, defined 17
Shail, Andrew 11
Shakespeare, William 24
shapeshifters 142
Shapiro, Robert 225
shared victimization 56
Sharpe, Andrew 72–3, 76, 85, 95, 143–4
Sheffield, Krystyna 82
Sherman, Robert 72
'shifting boundaries' 39
Siegal, Carol 57
signifiers 43
silence 21–6, 39; as both oppressive and liberating 162; critiquing binary of voice and 162–4, 177–8; of ethnicity 162–3; generative 163; and maternal relations 204; of nature 123; and voice 154–5
*Silence, Feminism, Power* (Malhotra & Rowe) 162
silencing of voices 155
Simon, William 124
single-issue legislative change 222
'sisterhood' 52, 56
*Sisterhood Is Powerful* (Morgan) 62
Smart, Carol 49–50, 68–9, 210, 216, 222
Smith, Alice 58
social cleansing 182–5, 203–4, 205n4; recommendations on 220–1
'social conflict' 123
social constructionism: on acceptance vs search for aetiology 5, 6, 7, 15; on agency 126; and feminisation as positive 108; on gender formation 5, 194; on gender subjectivity as ongoing process 149; on heteronormative gender 72; on language in discourse 112, 130; on personally political postmodern identity 42–3, 46, 64; and postconventional ethics 87, 89; and queer theory 103; on 'real' trans identities 38; on scripting into gendering 144–5
social customs 6
social discourse 2
social dysphoria 187, 188, 221
social emasculation 129

'social essentialism' 112–13
social factions 2, 15
social group, women as 46
social justice 88, 89
social media 7, 115–17, 130
social separatism 10
social roots, of gender oppression 222
social voice 161, 204
socially inclusive philosophy 13
sociological influences on research participants 100
sodomy laws and gay relations 76
'solidarity': and dialogic negotiation 122; and genre and genealogy 212, 226; and inclusion 181; and separatist discourse 8, 15, 18n4
South Africa 75
Southall Black Sisters 18n4, 66n8
special treatment 210–11
Spencer, Jane 174
Spivak, Gayatri 60
Springer, Kimberley 58
SSEs (separate and single sex services) 94
Standards of Care for trans people 195
standpoint epistemology 157–8, 174, 213
Stanley, Sue 154
Star, Hedy Jo 37
Steady, Filomina 55
Steinem, Gloria 170, 175, 220
stereotyped gender signs 10
stereotyping: and oppression 192; of transvestites and transsexuals 159; of women in Victorian Era 159, 180n5
sterilisation, compulsory pre-operative 80
Stevens, Lawrence 187
Stone, Alison: on coalition 11; on heteronormative gender 70; on personally political postmodern identity 44, 46; on postconventional ethics 90; on third wave feminism 41; on 'woman' as genealogy 133, 196, 199
*Stone Butch Blues* (Feinberg) 131n4, 154, 185, 205n4
Stone, Sandy: on acceptance vs search for aetiology 4, 5; on choice 170; on explaining trans lives 19; on genre 196; on passing 167; on personally political postmodern identity 45–6; on political subjectivity 140; on 'real' trans identities 37, 38, 40; on separatist discourses 8–9; on silence and secrecy 24, 26; on social maturity 160; on symbolic language 191; on voice 155

*Stop Trans Psychopathologisation Campaign* 187
stranger fetishism from white culture 56
strategic essentialism 129, 133
'strong objectivity' 129, 131n15
Stryker, Susan: on acceptance vs search for aetiology 4; on personally political postmodern identity 44, 45; and queer theory 103; on separatist discourse 9; on third wave as open and evolving discourse 62
Stychin, Carl: on 'Othering' 76; on passing 165; on personally political postmodern identity 45; on political subjectivity 140; on queer theory and feminism 105–6, 129; on whole trans person 143
sub-factions 3
subject-in-process 43, 198, 215–16, 228n12
subjective development 33, 67–8; and ethics of care 130
subjective formation, language and 112, 130
subjectivity(ies): border 59; communication and 118–19; in critical discourse analysis 125–6; defined 3, 17; differences in 41; essentialised into group identity 133; gendered 4–7, 15; identity as 45, 70, 148; and identity as process 147–51; personal and cultural constructions of 7; political 137–42; recommendations on 215–16; social construction theory of 42–3, 64, 89; in third wave feminism 43–4, 48; women with oppressed 132–3
subjectivity essentialism 133
subjectivity politics 7, 64, 129, 200
subjectivity-in-process: and agency and communion 86; conclusions on 151–2; and heteronormative gender 72; and identity as process 147–51; identity essentialism to 132–53; overview of 132–4; and personally political postmodern identity 45; and political subjectivity 137–42; and postdifference inclusiveness 200–1; recommendations on 215–16, 228n16; and which gender variant subjectivities are real 134–7; and whole trans person 142–7
subordination-theory structuralism 109
subversive action 193
Sullivan, Andrew 75
Sullivan, Nikki 171

sumptuary laws 40n3
Susan's Place 115
Sworn Virgins (Albania) 36
symbolic language 118, 121, 130, 131n7
'symmetrical reciprocity' 122
Szaz, Thomas 187

Talbot, Mary 112
'tall poppy' 177, 179, 219
Tannen, Deborah 163
Tate, Greg 11, 192, 193–4
Tauchert, Ashley 51, 60, 61
Teena, Brandon 31, 177
Telesford, Kellie 145
*The Testosterone Files* (Valerio) 21
textual subversion 131n4
'That Woman Is a Woman' (Cowan) 73, 75, 85
Thatcher, Margaret 36
'The Combahee River Collective Statement' 61
'Theorising Early Modern Lesbianisms' (Andreadis) 23
theory-in-process 109
'third space' 103, 197
*Third Wave Agenda* (Heywood & Drake) 61
third wave feminism 41–66; conclusions on 65–6; contradiction in 47–50, 64; difference inclusive 41–2, 44–5, 46; essentialising of 133–4; inter-wave philosophy and maternal relations in 50–3, 57, 65; open and evolving discourse of 60–5; overview of 41–2; personally political postmodern identity in 42–7, 64, 193, 198; vs postfeminism 44, 174, 175; post-structural views of sexual subjectivity of 133; and queer theory 104, 105–8, 129; queer-inspired 103–11; self-description as 42; womanism as 53–60, 65, 66n7; women of colour in 44, 53–60, 61–2, 64–5, 66n5
*Third Wave Feminism* (anthology) 62
third wave feminist movement 173–4
*The Third Wave: Feminist Perspectives on Racism* (anthology) 54
third wave philosophy 98–131; conclusions on 129–31; critical discourse analysis framework in 120–7; ethical framework in 98–103; narratives in 111–17; philosophical framework in 103–11; reconstructing discourses in 128–9; semanalysis in 117–20, 130, 131n3
third wave/trans coalition *see* coalition
*This Bridge Called My Back* (Moraga & Anzaldúa) 61–2
Thompson, Neil 66n5, 157
Tiospia 136, 152–3n3, 189
Tipton, Billy 32, 33
*To Be Real* (anthology) 48, 60, 61, 193, 194
tolerance 181
tomboyism 32, 33, 160
'Tourist of Otherness' 9, 18n5, 135
'Toward a Queer Legal Theory' (Stychin) 105
Toynbee, Polly 174, 219
'trans' 16
trans anthologies 62
'trans by stealth' 137, 138, 165–6
trans community 173, 176, 189–90
trans existence, essentialising of 156
trans forums 115
trans identities: 'real' 34–9, 40; and sex reassignment surgery 37
trans lives: explanation of 19–40; infantilisation and 'refusal to grow up' in 26–34; real identities in 34–9; silence and secrecy in 21–6
trans lobbyists 149
'trans man' 16, 18n10
trans movement 173, 175–7, 179, 183; recommendations on 208, 223
trans narratives, invisibility of 155
trans people: ethics of care to postconventional ethics for 194–5; extended family of 189–90; gender variant vs 187; heteronormativity by 145–6, 148; as immigrants and refugees 185–8, 204; increased visibility of 220; infantilising by 160–1; labelling of 160; living as virtually gendered 136–7; muddying the waters for 135, 151, 214; 'Othering' of 76, 77; 'outing' of 116; as parents and marriage partners 136; as patriarchal conspirators 193; as protected category 183; self-images of 67; self-representations of 155–6; as separate category 138; separatist 213; sexual subjectivity of 215; social cleansing of 182–5, 203–4, 205n4; Standards of Care for 195; as trickster 139–40, 153n6; use of term 18n10; 'voice' of 155–6; whole 142–7, 151–2,

215; workplace discrimination against 82
Trans Pulse Forums 115
trans subjectivity(ies): in childhood 149–50, 160; and coalition 12, 14, 16; and Equality Act 93; and genealogy 198; heteronormativity and 72, 135; and identity as process 149; in Lakota 134, 152–3nn2–3; muddying the waters of 135, 151, 214; and narratives 113; non-transitioning 213; and 'Othering' 78–9; and personally political postmodern identity 45; as political 137–42; in process 147–51, 215–16; as real 36–7, 134–7, 213–14; schemata of 144, 215; scripts of 8–9; and separatist discourse 9–10; and silence and secrecy 26; as whole identities 142–7; and whole person 133; witnessing of 206n14
trans women 16, 18n10; as patriarchal infiltrators of women's spaces 36
'Trans-Cyberian Mail Way' (Whittle) 115
TransEquality project 17, 93, 135, 140
transfeminism 2
*Trans/Forming Feminisms* (Scott-Dixon) 62
transgender: authenticity of 134–7; defined 16; as identity vs gender expression 169; vs transsexual 134–5
transgender rage 45, 103
'The Transgender Rights Imaginary (Currah)' 144
transgender studies 104–5
*The Transgender Studies Reader* (Stryker & Whittle) 62
*Transgender Warriors* (Feinberg) 155, 182
transgenderism 17, 44
transgenderists 4
'trans-generic space' 154
transition: defined 17; essentialist fixing of identity after 149; as social process 182, 226
transition regrets 116
transitioning as temporary phenomenon 150, 152
transitioning experience, 'heteronormalising' of 166
transphobic harassment 116
transsexual(s) and transsexualism: and acceptance vs search for aetiology 4; defined 16, 70; and Equality Act 94; and heteronormative gender 72, 74; infantile attitude of 159; and personally political postmodern identity 43; and 'real' trans identities 36; script of 144; vs transgender 134–5
*The Transsexual Empire* (Raymond) 35–6, 127
'transsexual men' 16
'transsexual' surgery as patriarchal control of deviant identity 36
'transsexual women' 16
*Transstudy* 98–131; and absence of 'self-identified third wave feminists' primary study 102–3; access in 120–1; agency in 126; coalition in 14; communion in 126–7; computer-mediated communication in 101–2; conclusions on 129–31; connections between queer theory and feminism in 105–8; critical discourse analysis framework for 120–7, 130; dialogic negotiation in 105, 121–3; discourse in 127; ethical approach to qualitative research in 98–100; ethical framework for 98–103; feminisation as positive in 108–9; format of quotes from 17; internecine exclusion in 2–3; list of topics in 230–2; narratives in 111–17, 130; online debate in 115–17, 130; philosophical framework for 103–11; queer theory in 103–5; queer-inspired third wave feminism in 103–11; reconstructing discourses in 128–9, 130, 131nn13–14; recruitment to 100; research authenticity of 100–2; researcher/participant interactions in 100; resistance and acquiescence in 123–4; schemata and scripts in 124; semanalysis in 117–20, 130, 131n3; subjectivity in 125–6; taking a break from non-feminism in 109–11, 130
transvestites and transvestism: and acceptance vs search for aetiology 6; boys as 24, 27; changeling and 24; Garber on 36–7; and gender signifiers 43; harassment of 135; infantile attitude of 159; mimicry of heteronormativity by 153n4; and separatist discourse 10; as sexually immature 29; as state of infancy 27; as temporary 32
*Transvestites: The Erotic Drive to Cross-Dress* (Hirschfeld) 155
'trapped in the wrong body' 24, 35
trauma, personal 114
Treaties of Rome 222

Treaty of Amsterdam 222
trickster, trans person as 139–40, 153n6
Trojan Woman 36
truth 30, 49
Turtle, Georgina 20, 29–30, 113, 160
Twitter 115

Ulrich, Karl Heinrich 35
umbrella protection 210–11, 212, 228n9
'Undiagnosing Gender' (Butler) 168
universal protection 210–11, 212, 228n9
unreal gendered beings 35
US constitution, freedom of choice in 169–70
Ussher, Jane 180n5

Valerio, Max Wolf 21, 33, 139, 189, 202
Valverde, Marianne 81
van Dijk, Teun A 112, 121, 124
Vancouver Rape Relief Society (VRRS) 74
vanilla lesbianism 48
Vasquez, Tina 3
'verbal hygiene' 118, 121, 130, 131n7
verstehen 102
*Vested Interests* (Garber) 33
Vey, Sandor 24
victim status 109
victimization: laws about 155; shared 56; of transvestite 135
Victorian Era 21, 39, 159, 180n5
'view from nowhere' 14, 66n6, 157, 158, 207
'view from somewhere': empathy and 16; and erotics of unnaming 204; and legal discourse 67, 96; and 'lived messiness' 64; and maternal relations 189; oppression and 213; and political subjectivity 138; and postconventional ethics 88; and 'real' subjectivity 40; refusal to grow up and 28, 161; and standpoint epistemology 157–8; of trans people as immigrants 186, 221; and 'voice coaching' 151; and whole trans person 143, 145
'view from within' 111
"A Vindication of the Rights of Women" (Wollstonecraft) 167
visibility and targeting by oppressors 113–14
'voice' 154–64, 177–8; communication in different 156; critiquing binary of silence and 162–4, 177–8; and hailing/interpellation 156–7; and personally political postmodern identity 44; recommendations on 209; and refusal to grow up 27, 28, 158–61; silencing of 155; and social cleansing 220; and standpoint epistemology/view from somewhere 157–8; of trans people 155–6
'voice coaching' 138–9, 140, 142–3, 151, 179n2; recommendations on 209, 215, 225
'voice' from nowhere 14
'voices from somewhere' 61
VRRS (Vancouver Rape Relief Society) 74

*W v W* 86
WAF (Women Against Fundamentalism) 58
Walker, Alice 54, 55, 57, 58, 66n7
Walker, Rebecca: on choice 170; on third wave as open and evolving discourse 61; on third wave feminism 41, 42, 174; on womanism 57
Warleigh, Alex 227
Warramunga ethnic group 163
wave metaphor 50, 174, 179; as chronological 50, 51, 73; as philosophical 40, 51
Weber, Max 102
Wegener, Einar Mogens 20
*The Well of Loneliness* (Gordon) 35, 145, 202
*The Wendy Dilemma* (Kiley) 28–9
Westerns scientific paradigm 35
Whelehan, Imelda 83–4, 118–19, 147
Whinnom, Alex 175–6
white discourse 53
Whittle, Stephen: and acceptance vs search for aetiology 4, 7; on anti-trans feminism 127, 131n11; on coalition 12, 14–15; on computer-mediated communication 115; on epiphanies 202; and FTM Network 82; on 'gender confirmation treatment' 71; on Gender Recognition Act 73, 172; on 'heteronormalising' of transitioning experience 70, 166; on identity as subjectivity 44, 45, 149; on infantilisation and refusal to grow up 27, 31; on maternal relations 189; on negotiation of access to transition or reassignment treatments 166–7; on parenthood 79–80, 82–3, 84, 136; on pathologising 168; on political

subjectivity 141; on postconventional ethics 89–90; on queer theory 104–5; on reconstructing discourses 128; on self-aware perspective 158; on self-definition 196; on separatist discourse 9; on sexual subjectivity 113; on shared experiences of oppression 45–6; on silence and secrecy 25; on social cleansing 183; on third space 197; on third wave feminism as open and evolving discourse 62; on trans community 176; on trans people and law 207; on trans people as immigrants 186; on trans subjectivity 198, 206n14; on 'transgender' 16, 18n10; on whole trans person 143
whole trans person 142–7, 151–2, 215
*The Whole Woman* (Greer) 142, 146, 161, 186
Wichins, Rikki 176
*Wilkinson v Kitsinger* 76, 97n5
*The Will to Knowledge* (Foucault) 21
Wilson, Petra 121
Winkte 150, 172
Wioptula 134, 152n2, 172
Wise, Liz 154
Wodak, Ruth 112
Wollstonecraft, Mary 167
woman(en): category of 147; female body and real 135; as genealogy 133; as marginalised identity 146; 'Othering' of 76; self-identity of 79; as social vs biological group 46; in Victorian Era 159, 180n5
'woman' identity 41, 79
womanism 53–60, 65, 66n7; and difference inclusiveness 199; and erotics of unnaming 193; and maternal relations 188–9; and postconventional ethics 89; and third wave philosophy 130
Women Against Fundamentalism (WAF) 58

*Women and the Law* (Atkins & Hale) 69–70
"women born women" groups 157
women of colour: and choice 171; and difference inclusiveness 199; importance of family to 83–4; lesbian 194; and personally political postmodern identity 44; and third wave as open and evolving discourse 61–2; and unnaming vs naming 193; and voice/silence binary 162; and womanism 53–60, 64–5, 66n5
women's activism 63
Women's Ceremonies 148
women's groups 134
"women's issues" 46
Women's Studies 61, 62
*Women's Time* (Kristeva) 88–9, 191
Wong, Kristina Sheryl 60, 171, 174
Woodhouse, Annie 10, 215
work related social activities 183
work situation, social cleansing in 183–4
workplace discrimination 82
World Professional Association for Transgender Health (WPATH) Standards of Care 187

*X, Y and Z v UK* (1997) 79–80, 82–3, 119, 136
Xtravaganza, Venus 35

Yogyakarta Principles on the Application of International Human Rights 211, 224–5
Young, Iris Marion 122
Youngblood, Nikki 169, 218

'ze' 17
Zita, Jacqueline 88, 174–5
Zucker, Ken 40n3

Made in the USA
Monee, IL
18 September 2023

42904375R00155